Identity Research and Communication

Identity Research and Communication

Intercultural Reflections and Future Directions

Edited by Nilanjana Bardhan and Mark P. Orbe

LEXINGTON BOOKS
Lanham • Boulder • New York • Toronto • Plymouth, UK

Published by Lexington Books
A wholly owned subsidary of Rowman & Littlefield
4501 Forbes Boulevard, Suite 200, Lanham, Maryland 20706
www.rowman.com

10 Thornbury Road, Plymouth PL6 7PP, United Kingdom

British Library Cataloguing in Publication Information Available

Library of Congress Cataloging-in-Publication Data

The hardback edition of this book was previously cataloged by the Library of Congress as
follows:

Identity research and communication: intercultural reflections and future directions /
edited by Nilanjana Bardhan and Mark P. Orbe.
  p. cm.
Includes bibliographical references and index.
1. Ethnicity. 2. Group identity. 3. Intercultural communication. I. Bardhan, Nilanjana. II.
Orbe, Mark P.
GN495.6.I346 2012
305.8—dc23

                                                                2012003635

ISBN 978-0-7391-7304-6 (cloth : alk. paper)
ISBN 978-0-7391-9073-9 (pbk. : alk. paper)
ISBN 978-0-7391-7305-3 (electronic)

Printed in the United States of America

This book is dedicated to John T. Warren. You and your work live on—through us.

Contents

Acknowledgments

This book is the result of a process that began in Fall 2010. The Department of Speech Communication at Southern Illinois University-Carbondale, USA, began the work of organizing a mini-working conference of intercultural communication scholars whose works focus on pressing theoretical, methodological, pedagogical and praxiological issues pertaining to the subject of identity. Identity remains a central topic within the discipline, as we hope the rest of this book demonstrates. The essays that emerged from this conference, which was held in Carbondale, Illinois, in April 2011, along with some invited essays from colleagues whose work is invaluable to the topic at hand, fill the pages of this book.

We wish to thank the SIUC Department of Speech Communication, the SIUC College of Liberal Arts, and the SIUC Office of the Provost for supporting and funding the conference that made this book possible. We also wish to thank Lenore Lautigar and Johnnie Simpson at Lexington Books for recognizing the value of this project, and for being immensely supportive throughout the editing and production process. Special thanks go to Brenda J. Allen for writing the foreword to the book, to Tabatha Roberts, Thurgood Marshall Fellow in the School of Communication at Western Michigan University (WMU), and Krystin Searle, a senior in the WMU School of Communication, for their assistance with preparing the index. And finally, this book would not have been possible without the rigorous intellectual work that has been put forth by all our contributors. We thank you sincerely. John Warren's energy was with us in person part of the way. We all picked up where he left off, and carried on to make this project a success. Thank you, John.

Foreword

Brenda J. Allen

Identity has become a principal topic in numerous disciplines as scholars seek to theorize and study how humans construct and enact notions of themselves and/as others, and it seems to be gaining momentum. Increased interest in identity results from persistent pressing problems such as conflict between various identity groups, as well as related—but relatively newer—concerns about globalization. As Judith Martin and Thomas Nakayama (2003) explain, "We live in a rapidly changing world in which intercultural contact will continue to increase, creating a heightened potential for both conflict and cooperation" (p. xviii). Within the burgeoning body of scholarship about identity, various areas of communication studies figure prominently, as theorists and researchers illuminate and analyze the central role that communication plays in per/re/forming identity. Intercultural communication scholarship promises to provide particularly pivotal insight and information about identity because it focuses on various, specific aspects of social and cultural identity.

Identity Research and Communication: Intercultural Reflections and Future Directions helps to fulfill that promise by presenting an exciting, fresh collection of essays on identity research in the field of intercultural communication. The authors include established and emerging scholars whose work centers around identity research. Many of them infuse provocative personal narratives which enliven their research and help them to develop or critique theoretical perspectives. However, they do not focus on theory just for theory's sake. Rather, they also demonstrate the importance of theory for research and practice. Moreover, their work spans diverse transnational theoretical perspectives. Thus, this volume responds positively to critiques that intercultural studies tend to focus too much on the United States.

In addition, the authors concentrate primarily on concepts that have surfaced or become foregrounded in the twenty-first century, and that have tremendous potential for effecting social change. These include: power, privilege, intersectionality, critical selfhood, hybridity, diaspora, cosmopolitanism, queer theory, globalization, and transnationalism, immigration, gendered and sexual politics, self-reflexivity in research, positionality, and agency. As they explore such topics, the authors are careful to connect them to related, traditional perspectives in intercultural communication, including enduring debates about theories and methods.

Additional strengths of this volume rest in the wide variety of mainly qualitative methods (e.g., autoethnography, focus groups, ethnography, and case studies) that the authors employed, as well as the expansive range of sites and identity categories on which they focused. These include a political activist community, the English-speaking Caribbean, refugees in India's Partition, Chinese college students, the U.S. Southwest, Chinese American diasporic authors, and biracial/multiracial identity in the United States. Many of the authors describe and analyze identity politics in higher education such as advocating performative pedagogy, being a gay intercultural scholar, or enacting cross-racial queer coalitions.

Based on these and other positive attributes, *Identity Research and Communication* makes numerous notable contributions to the study of communication and identity in general, and specifically to intercultural communication studies of identity. First, by including scholarship from veteran *and* budding scholars, editors Nilanjana Bardhan and Mark Orbe provide a platform for an array of original, *avant-garde* projects and ideas while also bridging generations of academicians. In addition to advancing scholarship, this may also encourage and validate newer or aspiring members of the professoriate, and reinvigorate senior scholars. Second, their conscientious emphasis on transnational perspectives not only highlights important issues, but it also justifies the need for them. Third, because they incorporated many newer concepts related to identity, the volume offers up-to-date information and insights. In addition, including a variety of qualitative methods demonstrates their utility while also providing exemplars for future researchers. Equally as important, the projects yielded a wealth of significant implications for additional study.

Basically, this cutting-edge collection far exceeds the editors' goal of producing a comprehensive volume that tracks the state of identity research in intercultural communication studies. It signals and substantiates the continued evolution of intercultural communication scholarship, and I believe that it will become a beacon and a basis for future research. I applaud the editors and the authors for creating a viable, valuable resource for novice and expert researchers, educators, and practitioners.

Brenda J. Allen
University of Colorado Denver
October 2011

Introduction

Identity Research in Intercultural Communication

Nilanjana Bardhan and Mark P. Orbe

THE IMPORTANCE OF IDENTITY RESEARCH IN INTERCULTURAL COMMUNICATION

Who needs "identity"? —Hall, 1996, p. 1

Stuart Hall asks the above question with the intent of underscoring the pressing need to continue the study of cultural identity in current times, times in which blurring boundaries have produced the simultaneous effects of identity essentialism/protectionism and hybridity in intercultural communication. Such effects have led to increased connections as well as conflict across difference. Within intercultural communication, the study of identity occupies a key place because intercultural communication, put another way, involves the study of identities in communicative interaction in various contexts. In a transnational world marked by "complex connectivity" (Tomlinson, 1999, p. 2) as well as enduring differences and power inequities, it is necessary to understand how we perceive the self in relation to the culture other. Such understandings play a central role in how we communicatively negotiate relationships, build alliances, address conflict, promote peace, and strive for social justice across cultural differences. Identity issues permeate across various levels of intercultural communication—from the micro to the macro, and from human to mediated communication. Therefore, it is clear that identity remains a central topic within intercultural communication. In this volume, our collective effort is to evaluate extant research and chart out directions for future research.

Identity has been a topic of great interest within the social sciences, especially social psychology and communication, since the early twentieth century (Y. Y. Kim, 2007). Within intercultural communication specifically, identity research has experienced growth since the late 1980s. According to Cupach and Imahori (1993), identity is "self conception—one's theory of oneself" (p. 113). Yep (2002) defines cultural identity as "politi-

cal, fluid, and nonsummative" (p. 61). Within cultural studies and intercultural communication research, two views of identity are prominent.
The first view, as Hall (1990) describes, is that of the one true self or core
that hides under many layers; the second view is that identity is a process, more of a verb than a noun, and is "a matter of 'becoming' as well as
of 'being'" (p. 225). Research coalescing around the first view tends to
strive for positive knowledge claims about true cultural identity while
research following the second view tends to take a more dynamic and
postmodern view of cultural identity.

In the next section of this introductory chapter, we briefly trace the
key theories, concepts, and models of identity that have emerged through
the various trajectories of identity research in intercultural communication with the goals of acknowledging accomplishments and identifying
patterns and gaps. Next, we describe the significance of this volume and
what it contributes to our ongoing quest of theorizing the communicative
complexities of self-other intercultural relations. Finally, we explain the
thematic logic of how this volume is organized and provide brief sum-
maries of the chapters.

TRACING TRENDS IN IDENTITY RESEARCH

Researching identity in intercultural communication is complex since the
very concept of identity, and the ways it is experienced in various cultures, tend to differ philosophically. For instance, as Allen (1997) writes,
the modern Western Cartesian notion of the atomistic, highly individualistic and rational self (I think, therefore I am), a product of Enlightenment
thinking, assumes a clear distinction between self and other. In contrast,
the concept of the self (or even "non-self") in Eastern philosophies, such
as those influenced by Buddhism and Hinduism, is assumed to be more
holistic and, in a cosmic sense, inseparable from others and from nature.
According to Hecht, Warren, Jung and Krieger (2005), in African cultures,
the self is perceived as harmonious and coalesced with others; in Asian
cultures rooted in Confucianism, the individual self in downplayed for
the sake of collective harmony and tradition; and in cultures influenced
by Greek philosophy, identity is conceptualized in individualistic and
oppositional terms (I am this because I am not that). Since most of the
identity research in intercultural communication has emerged from U.S./
Western contexts so far, the more individualistic approaches to identity
have been prevalent in theory.

Key Accomplishments

Key theories and models of identity that have emerged in our field
include Identity Negotiation Theory (Ting-Toomey, 1993), Cultural Iden-

tity Theory (Collier, 1988), Identity Management Theory (Cupach and Imahori, 1993), Communication Theory of Identity (Hecht, 1993), and Y. Y. Kim's (2008) Intercultural Personhood model. In addition, Cultural Contracts Theory (Jackson, 2002a) and Co-Cultural Theory (Orbe, 1998) provide significant insight into how identities are negotiated during intercultural interaction.

Ting-Toomey's Identity Negotiation Theory (INT) is a group-oriented theory that sees ethnic and cultural identities as relational and impacted by context. The core assumption of the theory is "that human beings in all cultures desire both positive group-based and positive person-based identities in any type of communicative situation" (Ting-Toomey, 2005, p. 217). The focus of INT is the development of individual skills for competent identity negotiation across cultural and ethnic groups. Of note, this theory emphasizes the importance of acknowledging cultural and ethnic identity salience as opposed to cultural and ethnic identity (Ting-Toomey, 2009). Collier's (1988) Cultural Identity Theory (CIT) also assumes that cultural (group) identities are relational, that identities have multiple dimensions, and that these dimensions are influenced by context. Identities are enduring as well as changing, they "emerge in everyday discourse and in social practices," and are transmitted to new members (Collier 1998, p. 131). Collier's theory is both interpretive and critical in nature (Ting-Toomey, 2009) and does not focus as much on intercultural competency and skills building as INT. Cupach and Imahori's (1993) Identity Management Theory (IMT) draws from both INT and CIT and focuses on effective identity negotiation skills building through appropriate intercultural facework. According to them, a basic premise of the theory is that intercultural interlocutors go through three interdependent and cyclical phases—trial, enmeshment and renegotiation—in their relationship, and manage facework differently in each phase. According to Imahori and Cupach (2005), IMT "is still in its infancy and needs a lot of maturing" (p. 207); however, the potential of providing insight into intercultural communication identities is evident.

Hecht (1993) and his colleagues have worked over the years to develop the Communication Theory of Identity (CTI), which is a theory of identity that puts communication before ethnicity/culture rather than the other way around. In other words, according to CTI, communication constructs identity and is not simply a vehicle for expressing cultural identities. The theory posits that four interrelated layers of identity—personal, enactment, relational and communal—span the personal to societal levels of identity construction, thereby encompassing individualistic as well as collectivist approaches to identity (Hecht et al., 2005). CTI, as an identity theoretical framework, has been used to explore identity among diverse U.S. populations including Arab women (Witteborn, 2004), people of color (Drummond and Orbe, 2009), international students (Jung, Hecht, and Wadsworth, 2007), and U.S. immigrants (Urban and Orbe, 2010). More recently Y. Y. Kim (2008), based on her ongoing research on the adaptation process for migrants, has offered the Intercultural Personhood model, which transcends the U.S. context and addresses transnational identity dynamics. According to Y. Y. Kim, the model emerges from "the experiences of acculturation, deculturation, and the stress-adaptation-growth dynamic" and an intercultural identity is an "open-ended, adaptive, and transformative self-other orientation" (2008, p. 364). Of particular relevance to the focus of this edited volume are the ways in which the theory addresses issues of identity inclusivity and identity security (Y. Y. Kim, 2005a).

In addition to the above theories and models, Jackson's (2002a) Cultural Contracts Theory and Orbe's (1998) Co-Cultural Theory provide insight into identities in intercultural interaction. Emerging from the study of interactions between African Americans and European Americans, Cultural Contracts Theory describes three kinds of cultural contracts — ready-to-sign (non-negotiable), quasi-completed (somewhat negotiable) and cocreated (very negotiable) — that play out in intercultural identity relations. Communication scholars have utilized this theoretical frame to gain insight into how individuals negotiate their identities within the context of race, culture, and power in the United States (Drummond and Orbe, 2010; Jackson and Crawley, 2003). Orbe's (1998) Co-Cultural Theory focuses on the strategic ways in which traditionally underrepresented group members negotiate their "cultural differentness" in their interactions with others (see also Orbe and Spellers, 2005). As such, co-cultural studies have provided insight into how identities are enacted through different communicative practices, both from the perspective of diverse U.S. populations (Cohen and Avanzino, 2010; Kirby, 2007) and co-cultural groups within global contexts (Bashir, 2009; MacLennan, 2011; Matsunaga and Torigoe, 2008)

Certain models of cultural identity development are also part of the literature, and have focused on the identity development of non-dominant and dominant groups in the United States. These models are usually linearly (albeit interrelatedly) conceptualized, and show that non-dominant cultural identities tend to develop faster than majority group cultural identities because of higher awareness of difference on the part of the former (Martin and Nakayama, 2010). Some examples include the identity development model for African Americans developed by Cross (1991), for Asian Americans developed by Sodowsky, Kwan, and Pannu (1995), for Latina/o Americans developed by Ruiz (1990) (cited in Ting-Toomey, 2005), and for biracial and multiracial persons (Poston, 1990). Majority group identity development models have also been developed (e.g., Hardiman, 2003; Rowe, Bennett, and Atkinson, 1994). Regarding the development of migrant identities, social psychologist Berry's (1992) work on adaptation has influenced much work in intercultural communication (e.g., Y. Y. Kim 2001; Lysgaard, 1955).

A recent key contribution to identity literature was made by John Warren, to whose memory this volume is dedicated. Warren (2008) shifts the focus from identity to the notion of difference. Drawing upon the works of Judith Butler and Gilles Deleuze, he advocates for more sophisticated theorizing of difference in intercultural communication since the ways in which difference is enacted is intricately linked to identity. According to Warren, if we can understand the performative/repetitive nature of difference, we can interrupt negative performances and create possibilities for change and social justice (also see Warren and Toyosaki in this volume). Also along critical lines, and in advocating for more dynamic theories of identity, Mendoza, Halualani, and Drzewiecka (2002) conceptualize cultural identity as non-unitary, historically produced, performative, double-sided, resignifiable, unforeclosed, and as dynamic translation. More recent works involving diaspora and hybridity theory (e.g., Bardhan, 2011; Halualani and Drzewiecka, 2002; Hegde, 2002; Moreman, 2011; also see chapters by Bardhan, Chawla, Cheng, Hao, Sobré-Denton and Sun in this volume) are currently taking identity theorizing in intercultural communication in more postcolonial, postmodern and transnational directions.

Patterns and Gaps

In reviewing identity literature in intercultural communication, Y. Y. Kim (2007), Martin and Nakayama (2010), Shin and Jackson (2003) and Yep (2004) have noted certain epistemological and ontological assumptions and paradigmatic trends. The functional and interpretive perspectives have been prominent, followed by the relatively more recent advent of the critical perspective (Shin and Jackson, 2003). The functional trend tends to be positivist assuming a subject-object divide in research while the interpretivist approach tends to assume that identities are intersubjectively co-constructed through communicative interaction. The critical perspective also assumes the social constructionist nature of identities, but focuses primarily on issues of power, hegemony, context and intercultural oppression (Martin and Nakayama, 2010). Postcolonial, postmodern and performative perspectives, often infused with critical thought, are very recent and have yet to gain critical mass in the identity research repertoire.

Particularly in functional and interpretive research, identity has been conceptualized mainly at the cultural group level (e.g., race, ethnicity, nationality), and a dialectic is presented between the individual and th group/culture (Y. Y. Kim, 2007; Shin and Jackson, 2003). Across ' digms, identity is mostly assumed to be flexible, adapti except perhaps in some critical research (Y. Y. Kim, 2 and Nakayama (1999, 2010) and Yep (2004) argue tha have something useful to offer and that we should consi butions to identity research dialectically, a view with which we are in agreement, given recent research that has demonstrated the great potential of such an epistemological approach (Hopson and Orbe, 2007).

So, where do we go from here? Hall (1996) notes that while unitary Cartesian notions and positive knowledge about identity have been subjected to the critical lens of deconstructionism, the work is not done yet. We are simply at a point in our study of identity which, borrowing from Derrida, Hall calls "thinking at the limit" (p. 1), a point where positive and deconstructionist forms of knowledge are jostling with each other in search of newer paradigms that will engender new ways of thinking about the subject. It is obvious that there are some gaps in the extant identity research in our field. First, the focus has mainly been on the U.S./Western context and there is a need for more transnational theories of identity in the context of globalization (Y. Y. Kim's Intercultural Personhood model is a good start in this direction). Second, there are some "usual suspects" when it comes to picking markers of difference (or, identity categories) when it comes to research, i.e., race, ethnicity, and nationality. As Warren (2008) has noted, difference is key in the study of identity, and difference plays out in many ways in this world. For example, one much neglected marker of difference in identity research within our field is sexuality (see chapters by Berry, and Pattisapu and Calafell in this volume). Such identity differences await further exploration in our field.

Third, the notion of intersectionality (Crenshaw, 1991), or how identity is a complex and simultaneous interplay of various markers of cultural difference, has yet to be developed into a theory of identity in our field. Linked to intersectionality is the matter of alliance building across cultural differences (see Chávez's chapter in this volume). Once we can theoretically grapple with more than one difference at a time, we may be able to better figure out strategies for forming alliances for social justice across seemingly unbridgeable cultural differences. As Bakhtin (cited in Conquergood, 1991) has pointed out, "The most intense and productive life of culture takes place on the boundaries. . . . " (p. 2). This boundary perspective is crucial for identity research since boundaries are not simply divisions but also "membranes and bridges" (Rosaldo, 1989. p. 217) and spaces of invention. And finally, speaking of borders, there is a need for more identity research in our field from postcolonial, performative and feminist perspectives that are well equipped to address the "in-between" spaces and dynamic processes of identity in intercultural communication. As Conquergood (1991) eloquently notes:

> All that confidence in continuous traditions and innocent encounters with pristine cultures has been shattered in our post-colonial epoch. Borders bleed as much as they contain. Instead of dividing lines to be patrolled or transgressed, boundaries are now understood as criss-

crossing sites inside the post-modern subject. . . . From the boundary perspective, identity is more like a performance in process than a postulate, premise, or originary principle. (pp. 184, 185)

Our identity theorizing needs to account for such complexities, and much exciting work remains to be done.

SIGNIFICANCE OF THIS VOLUME

In April 2011, the intercultural communication faculty at the Department of Speech Communication at Southern Illinois University-Carbondale and scholars doing notable work on identity and culture came together for a working style mini-conference at the Touch of Nature Environmental Center in southern Illinois. Our goal was to "landscape" identity research. Two days of intense paper presentations, dialogue, and discussion led to the eventual production of this volume. While John Warren— our colleague, friend and phenomenal scholar of communication, culture and critical communication pedagogy—could not be with us due to his sudden and sad passing earlier that month, his spirit and scholarship infused our work over those two days. Much of that is evident within this volume as well, which we dedicate to him.

In the previous section, we traced some of the gaps in extant identity literature and noted some of the growth areas of scholarship. This volume addresses those gaps and presents some of the cutting-edge identity work currently being done by U.S.-based scholars. The chapters are theoretical pieces, some of which are supported by empirical data from ongoing studies. The main strength of this volume is its primary focus on the more recent concepts related to identity scholarship that have emerged over the last decade or so. These concepts include power, privilege, intersectionality, hybridity, diaspora, cosmopolitanism, alliance building, difference, queer theory, globalization and transnationalism, (im)migration, gendered and sexual politics, critical selfhood, self-reflexivity in research, positionality, agency, ethics, dialogue and dialectics, to name a few. We believe that the interpretive, critical, postcolonial, performative, pedagogical and transnational flavors of these chapters mark this volume as a significant contribution to identity research in intercultural communication.

ORGANIZATION OF THE BOOK

This edited volume contains sixteen chapters organized into five different sections: (1) Identity, pedagogy, and praxis; (2) Identity and home/spaces; (3) Identity and the global-local dialectic; (4) Identity and the liminal; and

(5) Theorizing "doing" identity. In order to assist the reader in following the organizational framework of the anthology, the contents of each section are previewed here.

Part I: Identity, Pedagogy, and Praxis

The first section, *Identity, Pedagogy, and Praxis,* offers the reader an introduction to the essence of the core values of the book including the inextricable ways in which intercultural communication identity research intersects with both pedagogy and praxis in various communities. The first chapter, "Performative Pedagogy as a Pedagogy of Interruption: Difference and Hope," is coauthored by John T. Warren and Satoshi Toyosaki. Initially submitted in draft form by Warren, Toyosaki worked courageously to complete the chapter by weaving his voice with Warren's in order to conceptualize performative pedagogy as interruption. This chapter explores how difference is theorized in teaching and learning cultures, explicates a performative theory of difference.

In the second chapter, Karma R. Chávez engages the concept of intersectionality. Her chapters, "Doing Intersectionality: Power, Privilege, and Identities in Political Activist Communities," works to theorize intersectionality—the interlocking nature of identity and power—within the context of intercultural communication and identity scholarship. More specifically, Chávez argues that intersectionality can be a useful tool for critical intercultural and activist scholars as they work to understand operations of culture, identity and power. Through a brief case study of political activism, she demonstrates both the possibilities and difficulties for intercultural dialogue and relating in localized contexts.

"Understanding Identity Through Dialogue: Paulo Freire and Intercultural Communication Pedagogy," authored by Sandra L. Pensoneau-Conway, is the next chapter in part I. This chapter is based on the premise that reengaging Freire's elements of dialogue can lead to a keener understanding of theoretical implications and practical applications of dialogue. Within her chapter, Pensoneau-Conway rearticulates Freire's notion of dialogue and explores how it can highlight, complicate, and extend contemporary discussions of identity and intercultural communication pedagogy. Within this framework, she explores a number of questions: How can teacher-scholars understand classroom participants' cultural identities through engaging in Freirean dialogue?, How can dialogue inform our understanding of cultural identity?, and finally, How can each of these concepts work synergistically to inform intercultural communication pedagogy?

The final chapter in this section is coauthored by Krishna Pattisapu and Bernadette Marie Calafell. Their chapter, "(Academic) Families of Choice: Queer Relationality, Mentoring, and Critical Communication Pedagogy," charts their shared pedagogical and academic experiences as queer women of color. Through reflections of their relationships with John T. Warren, their chapter promotes a consideration of the importance of coalitions within and across race and sexuality in intercultural communication and identity research. Throughout the chapter, they argue that through dialogue, critical intercultural communication scholars can establish powerful coalitions with academic families of choice whom can assist in the navigation of academic contexts that attempt to silence and erase select voices. Ultimately, Pattisapu and Calafell's chapter demonstrates how scholarship that privileges personal experiences both methodologically and theoretically can work to build a body of literature that is more inclusive, potentially transformative, and pedagogically liberating.

Part II: Identity and Home/Spaces

The second section of the edited volume features two chapters that highlight how home reflects a productive site for scholars interested in exploring intersections of intercultural communication and identity. The fifth chapter is authored by Richie Neil Hao who reflects on a three-week stay in his birthplace, the Philippines, to critically engage current literature on cultural reentry. In "Cultural Reentry: A Critical Review of Intercultural Communication Research," Hao critiques existing literature that fails to resonate with his own transcultural experiences. Throughout the chapter, he works to problematize conceptualizations of cultural reentry that ignore alternative interpretations, and in doing so, fail to address those individuals who maintain multiple home spaces through increased technology, migration, and multiple cultural associations. Within this context, Hao discusses the implications of his experiences in terms of the theoretical, methodological, pedagogical and praxiological issues inherent in identity related scholarship in intercultural communication.

The next chapter follows Hao's lead and explores the intersections of identity and home in the oral histories of refugees in India's Partition of 1947. More specifically, Devika Chawla uses "Performing Home/Storying Selves: Home And/As Identity in Oral Histories of Refugees in India's Partition" to demonstrate the value of a flexible narrative approach to explore identity, something that she defines as the story that we tell about ourselves. Her chapter regards home as a spatial, discursive, poetic, and contradictory imaginary that features multiple narrations of individual and family identity. Within this conceptualization, Chawla leads readers through multidimensional explorations of several questions including: What is home? Is it about connection to origins, a sense of belonging, or ongoing negotiations of becoming and unbecoming? Is home a poetic space that unleashes the imagination? Do home/s—as places or states— represent constructs that are necessary and indispensable? and finally, What is the relationship between physical and emotional homes and the selves that we perform? In short, Chawla's chapter is a storied contemplation on the nexus of home, travel, dwelling, and identity, something that offers an innovative critical analysis of intercultural communication identity research.

Part III: Identity and the Global-Local Dialectic

Three chapters focusing on identity and the global-local dialectic comprise the third section of the book. In her chapter, Miriam Sobré-Denton offers "Landscaping the Rootless: Negotiating Cosmopolitan Identity in a Globalizing World" as an opportunity for intercultural communication scholars to reconsider the potential of cosmopolitanism as a concept that can contribute to identity research, pedagogy, and practice. Within the chapter, she promotes the stream of possibilities inherent from adopting and adapting cosmopolitanism in a manner that embraces postcolonial notions of culture in order to move beyond existing conceptions of what it means to be a citizen of the world. More specifically, Sobré-Denton argues for a perspective that situates cosmopolitanism within a number of dialectics—rooted and rootless, global and local, above and below— that work to create spaces for dialogue that can potentially interrupt systemic power structures.

The eighth chapter is titled "Cultural Matter as Political Matter: A Preliminary Exploration from a Chinese Perspective" and authored by Hsin-I Cheng. Cheng's chapter uses ethnographic explorations, namely, participatory observations and group interviews conducted at a university in southeast China in 2010, to broadly discuss intercultural communication scholarship on culture and identity. This chapter focuses on how culture is best understood when conceptualized within contextualized interactions in relation to histories and the present globalized world. In addition, it demonstrates how Asiancentrism, a culturally specific paradigm in inter/cultural knowledge production, represents an important worldview for scholarly inquiry. Through her ethnography with Chinese college students, Cheng illustrates the need for considering contemporary socioeconomic and geopolitical forces in research on culture, and identity and communication.

Kent A. Ono's chapter, "Understanding Immigration and Communication Contextually and Interpersonally," is the final chapter in this section on identity and the global-local dialectic. In this particular chapter, Ono engages the larger geopolitical, economic, and social contexts existing today which proves instrumental in understanding contemporary communication about U.S. politics of migration and immigration. The chapter makes a valuable contribution in that it draws attention to how rhetoric regarding migrants, constructed as aliens, positions them as less powerful in a nation-state that regards them as only capable of doing hard physical labor, within inhumane working conditions, for low pay.

Ono engages multiple questions regarding the production and regulation of difference; these include: Why and how is difference produced? What does the production of difference do? What benefit does the production of difference create, and for whom? Ultimately, this chapter is valuable in the ways that it draws attention to the processes used by groups to map out and articulate racial/national belongingness.

Part IV: Identity and the Liminal

Four chapters focus on *Identity and the Liminal*, the theme of the fourth section of the book. "Postcolonial Migrant Identities and the Case for Strategic Hybridity: Toward "Inter"cultural Bridgework," authored by Nilanjana Bardhan, is the first chapter in this section. This chapter utilizes concepts from the postcolonial studies toolbox to explore the usefulness of hybridity in identity research in intercultural communication. According to Bardhan, identities are increasingly being experienced as hybrid by many, a reality that begs for more nuanced theories of cultural "in-betweenness." Focusing particularly on postcolonial migrant identities, Bardhan argues that performing hybridity strategically, within everyday, mundane levels of intercultural interaction, can represent liberating positions of enunciation and agency for those who traditionally are situated as Others. The chapter is valuable in that it foregrounds the intercultural connective value of theorizing cultural identities in interaction through hybridity (difference) rather than through sameness.

The next chapter, authored by Mark P. Orbe, draws from a series of recent research projects to engage contemporary conceptualizations of biracial and multiracial identity in the United States. "Researching Biracial/Multiracial Identity Negotiation: Lessons from Diverse Contemporary U.S. Public Perceptions" represents an exercise in personal/cultural/academic self-reflexivity that re-engages a typology of interracial family communication that was designed to document the various ways in which people negotiate multiracial identities in a societal context where monoracial identities are normalized (Orbe, 1999). In this chapter, Orbe provides a revised typology that reflects diverse communication orientations that help to provide insight into the complexities inherent within intersections of identity, culture, and communication. The concluding section of the chapter outlines five guiding principles that can help guide future research on biracial and multiracial persons in the United States; these same guidelines are offered as relevant for all scholarship on identity and intercultural communication within local, regional, national, and global spheres.

The scholarship of Jianhua Sun is featured in the twelfth chapter. In "Rethinking Identities Within Globalization Through Chinese American Literature: From Postcolonial to Intercultural," Sun urges intercultural communication practitioners, scholars and educators to find encouragement, insight and inspiration to build communicative bridges in the works of writers who dwell in and write through cultural hybridity. To illustrate the potential in this recommendation, she examines the works of different Chinese American diasporic authors—namely the work of Maxine Hong Kingston, Amy Tan, Jade Snow Wong, Fae M. Ng, and Gish Jen—to reveal the particular ways in which their work emphasizes the complex production of culture as a third space borne out of hybridity that creates unique cultural identities. Throughout the chapter, Sun demonstrates how literary analyses are useful for other intercultural communication scholars seeking to examine intercultural communication identity issues within diasporic contexts.

The English-speaking Caribbean is the topical context of Maurice L. Hall's chapter titled "(Re)Thinking Conceptualizations of Caribbean Immigrant Identity Performances: Implications for Intercultural Communication Research." In this chapter, Hall provides a historical context for understanding why the English-speaking Caribbean is an important location from which to discuss the identity negotiation of people who travel to the United States from the African diaspora. Drawing from and critiquing literature on cultural adaptation and cultural hybridity, the chapter uses performativity as a theoretical framework to promote a conceptualization of identity performances that reflect a menu of choices potentially open to immigrants as they seek to enact identity in different cultural contexts. Hall, careful to situate all options as equally viable choices depending on the context in which the immigrant finds her/himself, regards identity as a process of becoming but never arriving.

Part V: Theorizing "Doing" Identity

The final section of the anthology focuses on *Theorizing "Doing" Identity*. The first, of three chapters, is an chapter titled "Navigating the Politics of Identity/Identities and Exploring the Promise of Critical Love" by Rachel Alicia Griffin. Within this chapter, Griffin embarks upon a journey to make sense of who she is as a critical intercultural communication scholar. More specifically, she works to theorize the promise of critical love—an approach that she characterizes as full of promise and potential—by tracing conceptualizations of identity through the distinctive yet interconnected quantitative, qualitative, and critical paradigms. Through critical articulations of identity, Griffin uses the chapter to locate herself as a critical intercultural communication scholar engaged in the process of identity negotiation who conceptualizes critical love as a productive position in navigating identity politics toward alliance-building across identity differences.

A comment from a student evaluation, "I think you talk to [*sic*] much about your sexuality in the classroom," is the prompt for Keith Berry's chapter. In "(Un)covering the Gay Interculturalist," Berry examines his identity negotiation as a gay intercultural communication teacher-scholar-public servant. He draws specifically from Yoshino (2007) who advocates for recognizing the diverse ways in which LGBTQ persons engage in covering. Different than passing, covering involves making certain aspects of gay culture and identity less obtrusive for the comfort of others. Berry explores how covering occurs in the communication classroom and the impact this identity negotiation has on LGBTQ culture and cultural performers. The chapters concludes as Berry contemplates other areas in which gay covering might occur, and suggests a number of ways the concept of "covering" can strengthen our continuing work as intercultural communication scholars researching identity.

The final chapters in the book is authored by Satoshi Toyosaki. In "Praxis-Oriented Autoethnography: Performing Critical Selfhood," Toyosaki reflects on his understanding of critical selfhood as self-reflexive, purposeful, and conscious materializations of one's subjectivity. In this chapter, he explicates the unstable yet social nature of subjectivity as a means to promote "doing" identity in different ways, personally, relationally, culturally, and politically. In this regard, the chapter extends current research on critical selfhood performance and calls for a particular kind of critical qualitative methodology which he refers to as praxis-oriented autoethnography. Throughout the chapter, Toyosaki advocates for this specific genre of writing that helps to narrate one's path to the hopeful and transformative way of experiencing his or her cultural identity.

CONCLUSION

We began our introduction to *Identity Research and Communication: Intercultural Reflections and Future Directions* by invoking Hall's (1996) question, "Who needs 'identity'?" (p. 1). As articulated in our opening comments, we regard the question as a constant reminder of the continued need to explore the ever-changing nature of cultural identities. Conceptualizing intercultural communication and identity as reflective of a series of dialectical tensions (Martin and Nayakama, 1999) encourages a recognition of how identity remains both individual and cultural, similar and different, historical and futuristic, personal and sociocultural, static and dynamic, and full of privilege and penalty. Each of the individual chapters contained in this volume interrogates these dialectical tensions in productive and meaningful ways; collectively, they synergistically work together to provide readers with a comprehensive landscape for future research on intercultural communication and identity.

I

Identity, Pedagogy, and Praxis

ONE

Performative Pedagogy as a Pedagogy of Interruption

Difference and Hope

John T. Warren and Satoshi Toyosaki

My vision of critical performative pedagogy values the transformative, the critical, the reflexive, the bodily, and the belief that, with possibility, there is hope for all students.

—Warren, 2003a, pp. 110–111

In the space of the classroom, I am accountable in ways that matter— and my . . . our . . . work can take on issues of power and oppression in ways that truly can change the hearts, minds, and spirits of people.

—Warren, 2010b

Social justice is about love, about leading with a critically engaged love that seeks not just community, but community with a purpose, a goal, a hope, a vision of equality that trumps hate and division.

—Warren, 2011b, p. 30

He left us too soon.
He left us these words.
He left us work to do,
the labor of love to love.
We have a lot of loving to learn.

JOHN'S PROJECT

My dear friend and colleague, John T. Warren, passed away from complications related to esophageal cancer on April 2, 2011, nine days before his thirty-seventh birthday. With deep sadness, I write this opening chapter of this anthology, *Identity Research and Communication*. Along with my in-house colleagues here at SIUC, John was instrumental in conceptualizing and planning the intercultural communication conference from which this anthology was born. He was very excited about the opportunity to work with intercultural communication scholars across the United States. Without being able to attend the conference, he passed away.

In this profession, it is not uncommon that our colleagues leave for a while, by taking sabbaticals, research trips, and summer breaks. It is still surreal to me that John will never sit across from me in a faculty meeting. It is still surreal to me that he will not, any more, pop in my office with a smile just to check on me. John's sudden passing after his unfairly short battle with cancer broke my heart. In my broken heart, however, I find conviction that his scholarship will be carried over to new generations of scholars, pedagogues, and students in order to realize its potential in our liberal education. This conviction comes to me, not simply as his friend, but also as an intercultural communication scholar, pedagogue, and student who had the delightful opportunity to see him work on his feet—to move—on the pages that he produced and in the classrooms he taught. This conviction comes to me as a person who finds his work instrumental in thinking of educational possibility, possibility that gives me (and you) hope for helping create a more socially just educational foundation for future children all over the world. His work on performative pedagogy does not simply invite, but earnestly begs for, my, your, and our critical engagement in transforming our oppressive world into a more socially just one.

John and I sat here at this table in this breakfast place we frequented. We opened our laptops and did some morning chores, such as emailing and doing last-minute commenting on our students' papers, while sipping coffee, a necessary ritual for sleep deprivation. Many times in this place, I poured my issues onto him—both personal and professional. With caring eyes and a sharp mind, he responded with kind, affirming words and a hint of tough love. In this place, John and I realized that we had not coauthored and played with some ideas. It is heartbreaking that our coauthorship comes to me in this way. He was my good friend, colleague, mentor, and tennis buddy. I look across this table and only find an empty chair. I miss him so much.

John had many ideas for future projects. One of them was in the making for quite some time. It must have been a couple of years ago. One day, John came into my office:

> John: (He holds onto the office doorframe with his right hand and swings into Satoshi's office. He is holding his yellow notepad in his left hand. His eyes are wide-open, like a little child's in a candy store, full of hope, energy, anticipation, and excitement)
> Satoshi: (He giggles as he thinks John's entry was rather dramatic and funny. While giggling, he responds) Hi? How are you?

His dramatic entrance to the scene! This is how he introduced his new project to me. He held out a yellow notepad with both hands. On the first sheet, he had written down an outline of his new book with a pencil. He was a pencil user. *Performative pedagogy, critical ethnography of the intercultural communication classroom,* and so on; I found interesting and intriguing chapter titles on the page. He asked, "Would you buy this book?" Right after, he rephrased, "Do you think a book like this would be useful?" Of course, he was asking, not how much he would make, but my opinion as an intercultural communication educator/researcher if a book like that could potentially help move our (critical) intercultural communication education forward. He explained the premise of his new book project to me. Looking at his pencil-handwritten outline on the yellow notepad, I confirmed, "Yes, of course." He left my office quickly as if he was going to start writing the book right away.

This is the book about which he talked in the spotlight panel hosted by the intercultural communication interest group of the Central States Communication Association in 2010. This is the book he didn't get to write. As one of the respondents to John's panel, I sat at the end of the table in the conference room in Cincinnati, Ohio, in April 2010, about one year before his passing. He sat in the middle of the table with a bashful hesitant smile of humility. He held onto his presentation manuscript with both hands. Shaking a little, they might have been, I don't clearly remember. But I certainly remember he was nervous. He started,

> Spotlight panels are clearly for old people. That said, it is clear that this high honor comes to me much too soon; my youth and childlike freshness makes a panel such as this seem premature, presumptuous even. But I appreciate the panel nonetheless as it serves as an opportunity for me to continue to work some of the research questions I have been struggling with recently—to workshop some ideas in an effort to gain some traction. (Warren, 2010b)

His introduction was humble; his presentation was rigorous. He was interested in exploring the theoretical and praxiological intersections between his work on performative pedagogy (Warren, 1999; 2003a) and his recent work on difference (Warren, 2008). This intersection was the premise for the book he hoped to write. His fascination with and hope for performative pedagogy came from his conviction that

> critical scholarship needs more than sharp critique in order for it to be useful. Combined with the sharp critical eye, one needs mechanisms of

interruption; places where we can begin to make that critique matter in
ways that provide hope and possibility. (Warren, 2010b)

One crucial place, for him, was and had always been his classrooms,
education. For him, performative pedagogy can be the space full of the
mechanisms of interruption—possibilities. He had labored and he still is
laboring—through the pages he produced, the students he taught, the
colleagues with whom he shared conversations—for social justice in his
pedagogy, a pedagogy that matters and that makes a difference.

John titled his spotlight talk, "Performative Pedagogy as a Pedagogy
of Interruption: Difference and Hope." He was planning to extend the
idea he had workshopped in the spotlight talk and to present it at the
intercultural communication conference; thus, the title of this chapter. I
use his spotlight panel presentation manuscript (Warren, 2010b), his publications, and numerous conversations I had had with him in writing this
chapter. In so doing, I do my best to pull out key ideas and outline his
thinking about performative pedagogy, difference, and identity studies.
Using my specialization in intercultural communication, I do my best in
letting his work and passion for performative pedagogy come to life in
meaningful ways to intercultural communication scholars, pedagogues,
and students. I am nervous as he is not here physically sitting across the
table from me to consult on this chapter. I am nervous because I am not
certain if I can capture his intellectual rigor and passion; however, I am
certain he would have liked me to try. So, I try.

In what follows, I hope to lay out the philosophical and theoretical
foundation for the book John hoped to write. I hope this chapter does the
job for his students, colleagues, and (intercultural) communication educators to gain some traction in continuing, developing, and extending his
project for which he hoped to labor.

TEACHING, LEARNING, AND RESEARCHING DIFFERENCE

The field of multicultural education must develop in ways that are
consonant with its original mission: to challenge oppression and to use
schooling as much as possible to help shape a future America that is
more equal, democratic, and just, and that does not demand conformity to one cultural norm. (Sleeter, 1996, p. 15; also cited in Warren,
2011b, p. 21)

Are we doing a good job in shaping the future America? John would say
that we have a lot more to do. In understanding "change" in our educational practices, we rely on, consciously or not, the notion of difference, as
change is often coded as doing our education "differently." The notion of
difference is tricky in multicultural education and researching/teaching
intercultural communication. Oftentimes, the ways in which we concep-

tualize difference or make the concept work for us are problematic, fundamentally trapping us in the comfort of our dominant, mainstream, and privileged ways of being (Richardson and Villenas, 2000).

In the past—and somehow, still now—multicultural education has been conceptualized as a particular kind of educational initiative and curriculum reform (McCarthy, 1993) in which cultural differences are "'add[ed] on'" (Edgerton, cited in Richardson and Villenas, 2000, p. 263) to the mainstream, dominant, and homogeneous identity master narrative, or who "we" are as "Americans." In this approach, difference manifests as *other* (Apple, 1993; Tanno and Jandt, 1993/1994), *oppositional* (often to norms) (Boler and Zembylas, 2003), *essentialized* (May, 1999), *reduced* (West, 1993), and *static* (Bhabha, cited in May, 1999): Difference is to be, first, marked, second, represented, and third, interpolated to mainstream educational practices. To some degree we, however, cannot escape from these characteristics of difference, or more so our representational activities of those differences in educational contexts. Sometimes, we see these characteristics employed as crafty rhetoric embedded in structural and ideological critiques on culture and power. Hall (cited in Apple, 1993), for example, observes and describes this nature of criticism as "hyperabstraction and overtheoretism" (p. 25), leaving the everyday, actual, and performative process/production of cultural differences behind in theorizing culture and identity.

Along with Richardson and Villenas (2000), I believe that multicultural education has not spoken in a meaningful way, in a way that matters, to social actors in educational contexts. It has not challenged the ideological system that celebrates the very interpolation as a "new" multicultural educational practice. As a result, it recenters and perpetuates the mainstream—or malostream (West, 1993)—educational domination keeping it unchallenged and unchanged. Richardson and Villenas (2000) make a sharp critique on this matter:

> One of the many paradoxes . . . is that the underlying political culture, commitments, and habits of mind are a master narrative rooted in whiteness and yet proposed as a multicultural education. Such a position does not allow multicultural possibilities for a different social and political order or even for a reordering of the current political culture. (p. 264)

We need more careful ways to engage in understanding difference in order to critically engage the political culture in advocating self-reflexive, performative, relational, communal, and structural transformations. Our (multicultural) education is the most important catalyst for those transformations.

Warren (2008) discusses Allen's (2004) and Cummins's (2003) work on culture. He explains how Allen's work pays close attention to details and the ways in which each element of cultural identity (such as race, gender, sexuality, ability, and age) manifests in our relationships. "However, each is discussed independently, divorcing the production of difference from" each other (Warren, 2008, p. 292). Such compartmentalization of cultural identity conveniently serves our teaching, learning, and research productivity or their representational activities, such as lecturing, discussing, writing, and publishing; however, such representation of difference leaves the body—enacting agents and their dynamic contexts—behind in our teaching, learning, and researching, as no one is *just* race, *just* gender, *just* sexuality, *just* ability, or *just* age. Many intercultural communication scholars, including myself, through representational convenience, come to theorize difference distanced from its production within its "natural" and "complex" contexts. "Communication studies (like sociology and education) has yet to fully develop a theory of difference that meaningfully connects the conceptual with the actual, the theory with the social consequences that result from difference" (Warren, 2008, p. 293).

The premature theory of difference permeates even a recent development of an automethodological (Pensoneau-Conway and Toyosaki, 2011a) approach to identity research. Warren (2010b) explains that automethodological work often fails to work across difference. In his own work on deconstructing his whiteness privilege (Warren, 2001a) and his work on his sexual identity as a bi-identified man (Warren and Davis, 2009), "[he] link[s] [his] experience . . . to the generalized manner [in which his] position is marked socially" (Warren, 2010b). My own critical complete-member ethnography (Toyosaki, 2011) does so as well through my examination of my own historical, political, and linguistic privilege as Japanese. These studies politically engage in the social structure of power that enables and perpetuates the privilege with which our bodies are situated. Thus our personal narratives are always already social stories. Here I don't want to characterize this aspect of auto-methodological work as problematic, as I believe this is what makes it good and potentially socially transformative. However, Warren (2010b) points out that "this work, in its systemic focus, positions difference (that is, [his] whiteness as privilege or [his] bi-ness as complicated privilege [or my Japanese-ness as privilege]) as necessarily bad—that which separates us, stands as the site of violence in these tales, the site of discomfort, pain. Difference has a bad rap."

So far, I have identified some symptoms of how we generally understand and put into action the notion of difference. Unsatisfied, critical educators (see Apple, 1993; Fassett and Warren, 2007; May, 1999; McCarthy, 1993; Richardson and Villenas, 2000; Warren, 2008; West, 1993) call for more revolutionary ways to think about identity, culture, power, and education with critical attention paid to how difference might provide more meaningful and transformative modes in which to understand, teach, learn, and research these concepts. West (1993) explains the new cultural politics of difference:

Distinctive features of the new cultural politics of difference are to [critique] the monolithic and homogeneous in the name of diversity, multiplicity, and heterogeneity; to reject the abstract, general, and universal in light of the concrete, specific, and particular; and to historicize, contextualize, and pluralize by highlighting the contingent, provisional, variable, tentative, shifting, and changing. (p. 11)

We need more nuanced ways of engaging difference in our research and education.

REFRAMING DIFFERENCE

Warren (2008) seems frustrated because we appear to trap ourselves in the ways we theorize difference and the ways we deploy it in our multicultural education. In so doing, we find ourselves in the familiar comfort of conformity, power, and oppression, instead of diversity, equality, and transformation, in our educational practices. In current studies of culture, Warren finds two weaknesses in how we theorize difference, or in what is undertheorized. First, the field "fails to advance any theoretical momentum for understanding power *in production*" (p. 293, my emphasis). That is, power is studied and represented as distanced from its actual production in/at/through our bodies and their meetings in the actual contexts. For example, the interpolation approach in multicultural education studies and teaches differences, yet the studying and teaching fail to address the power dynamics on which this approach rests comfortably in the very acts of that studying and that teaching. That is, ways in which the studying bodies and teaching bodies protect and perpetuate the unjust system go unquestioned, unchallenged, and unchanged. Second, difference remains a key point of understanding elements or cultural markers (such as race, gender, sexual orientation, and so on) that define our identities. "However . . . the political and social situatedness of these markers is dramatically undertheorized. . . . The conceptualization of difference still leaves one wanting for how and in what ways these elements affect our lived experiences" (Warren, 2008, p. 293).

From here, Warren (2008) turns to Judith Butler (1993; 1990a; 1990b) and Gilles Deleuze (1968/1994) in offering an alternative model for conceptualizing difference. He (Warren, 2010b) summarizes Butler's notion of repetition in her phenomenological theory of gender, and identity as a stylized repetition of acts.

There is no gender outside of the process of its doing, a process so engrained as to be naturalized and done without much reflection. Butler notes that gender has become so naturalized that we fail to even recognize its genesis. This is important as our notions of repetition allow us to see how what is present to us is a construct, produced through its many enactments.

Warren understands Butler's notion of repetition as the effective, careful analytical tool for deconstructing whiteness and skillfully translates/imports it to his own work on whiteness (see Warren, 2001b; 2003b).

Warren (2008; 2010b), however, argues that Butler's contribution to identity studies is mainly epistemological. In other words, "what matters is how I come to know who I am and how that knowing is reproduced upon the lives and bodies of others around me" (Warren, 2008, p. 294). While Butler (1990b), in her earlier work, discusses the ontology of gender performativity, particularly the notion of becoming, Warren finds Deleuze's (1968/1994) work (in addition of Butler's work) helpful in theorizing repetition and difference in terms of ontology, or what we are.

By introducing Deleuze, Warren (2008; 2010b) makes an explicit and careful shift from repetition as an epistemology to repetition as an ontology of difference. He does this with caution because, in our discipline, ontology is often conflated with essentialism. Warren (2010b) narrates his encounter with Deleuze as follows:

> Deleuze (1994/1968), in *Difference and Repetition,* offers an ontological view of difference, what May (2005) summarizes as Deleuze's attempt to articulate a political ontology that shifts, changes and adapts over time. Part of the struggle with ontology is the degree to which it feels static—the question of being leads quickly into essentialism. Deleuze tries, carefully, to undo this and modifies ontology. . . . Our basic ontology is a repetition of difference.

Through Deleuze, Warren (2008) underscores three important reconceptualizations of difference in understanding identity.

First, difference does not need to be conflated with opposition. Deleuze (1968/1994) argues that "it is not difference that presupposes opposition but opposition that presupposes difference, and far from resolving difference by tracing it back to a foundation, opposition betrays and distorts it" (p. 51). Our oppositional/binary thinking (a perceptual mechanism) functions to conflate difference and opposition. Difference does not have to be understood in the oppositional terms of "you are different from me," a rather negative way of viewing difference which divides the "you" and "me." Instead, difference can be coded as affirmative. Consider the difference between these phrases: "you are different from me" and "you are unique and so am I" (examples used in Warren, 2008). Now consider how subjectivities of the two implicated characters are discursively constituted in these simple yet demonstrative examples. The latter utterance invites intersubjectivity: "You are different but not different." The former marks the departure of two subjects; the latter, a meeting of two subjects—intersubjectivity, yet neither conformity nor absorption.

Second, Deleuze underscores our being as essentially constituted with repetitions of difference. The act of repetition in Butler's sense feels "very much like the doing the same again" (Warren, 2008, p. 297). However, Deleuze reminds us that the act in each repetition is inherently original with its own particularity and contextuality, each act being unique. "Our performances of gender, for Butler, are failed copies . . . where we attempt to emulate the ideal. These failures are inevitable; they are . . . the definition of repetition, always different by nature" (Warren, 2008, p. 299). Thus, our being—ontology—is necessarily transformative and fluid; our identities come to exist through a trajectory—the past, present, and future—of "repetitive acts that are always unique, even if they are historically informed repetitions. Being is fluid, adaptive, and always anew; we are always generating anew, never 'simply' repeating" (Warren, 2008, pp. 296–97).

Third, difference is ephemeral. "For Deleuze, a repetition is an act that disappears as soon as it occurs, an act that once it is, it is no more" (Warren, 2008, p. 299). However, Warren argues, an ephemeral act with its own particularity and unique contextuality becomes processed by our perceptual—reproductive—mechanism, rendering the different as the same or similar with past encounters of the act. I have already discussed this nature of our cognitive processing of difference above. Yet, here again, the ephemerality of difference, so important in understanding and engendering who we are in our everyday life, encounters our cognitive preoccupation with opposition and sameness/similarity, constructing the very significant to "appear" insignificant.

Again, it is not the ontology of difference, but our conceptualization of difference (that is, how we theorize difference and deploy it in understanding the world around us), which gets us in trouble, setting us up for impatient generalizations, lazy opposition, and convenient "hyperabstraction" (Hall, cited in Apple, 1993). Hence, in general, in studies of culture, we leave behind detailed analysis of culture and identity in their actuality, particularity, and contextuality—our actual bodies in particular contexts. Culture, identity, and power become theorized distantly from our actual bodies. What emerges as most problematic for critical intercultural communication studies is that we neglect the ephemeral opportunity for self-reflexive cultural critique and leave behind social agency (or ontological accountability) in our studies of culture and identity. Shifting our way of thinking about difference this way, we can pay, really pay, close attention to details, uniqueness, contextuality, and particularity of our repetitions of "different" acts that constitute who we are. This shift renders the actual, ephemeral moment of doing our identity differently as a site of cultural critique and possibility for change.

Overall, Warren sees difference not as a force that should divide us, but the essential nature of our identity, and understands our identity-rendering repetitions of acts—each act—as ephemeral, as unique and particular, as a site of critical possibility for interruption, critique, and change. This way of thinking about difference dramatically increases our ontological/praxiological grounding from which we rise as identity researchers, intercultural communication educators, and most importantly, everyday social "agents of interruption, critique, and change" (Warren, 2008, p. 300).

PERFORMATIVE PEDAGOGY

> Performative Pedagogy is more than a philosophical orientation or set of classroom practices. It is a location, a way of situating one's self in relation to students, to colleagues, and to the institutional politics and traditions under which we all labor. Performance Studies scholars and practitioners locate themselves as embodied researchers: listening, observing, reflecting, theorizing, interpreting, and representing human communication through the medium of their own and other's experiencing bodies. (Pineau, 1998, p. 130)

This is one of John's favorite quotes to use in his work. I stand along with Pineau (1998) and Warren (1999; 2003a; 2010b; 2011a; 2011b) in advocating for performative pedagogy as an effective site to mount this labor of transforming how we understand difference, theorizing identity in more nuanced and critical ways, and critiquing power and social injustice in our flesh, in our corporeal productions. Warren grounds his vision of this pedagogy in the analytical power of enfleshment (1999), in other words, performance as "a metaphor for everyday life" (Warren, 2010a, p. 217) and a productive methodology "for subjectivity, calling on us to conceive of nuanced ways of seeing identity" (p. 218). His vision of this pedagogy has been introduced under slightly different yet comparable labels, such as pedagogy of enfleshment (Warren, 1999), performative pedagogy of enfleshment (Warren, 1999), performative pedagogy (Warren, 2003a; 2010b), critical communication pedagogy (Fassett and Warren, 2007), reflexive teaching (Warren, 2011a), and critical/performative communicative pedagogy (Warren, 2011b). While these labels and his works under them foreground slightly different angles in talking about pedagogy, his scholarly identity as a performance studies and communication pedagogy scholar comes to life in each. I use performative pedagogy as a term that collectively represents his scholarship on body-centered pedagogy as he recently returned to the label (Warren, 2010b). At its foundation, performative pedagogy asks "students and teachers to take the principles of education (learning content, building skills, promoting intellectual development) and the principle of critical pedagogy (undermining hegemony, questioning power structures, seeking social change) and bring them to the site of body" (Warren, 2003a, p. 94).

Warren (1999; 2003a; 2010b) calls for performative pedagogy to operate along three axes: (1) a performative mode of analysis, (2) a performative mode of engagement, and (3) a performative mode of critique. First, a performative mode of analysis is a body-centered way of studying "how human beings constitute their everyday lives, their identities, their realities through the embodied practices of their daily lives" (Warren, 1999, p. 258). In this mode of analysis, the body is understood as "a performative accomplishment that carries with it the sedimented constructs of privilege, power, and domination from millions of minute acts in the past" (Warren, 2003a, p. 92). Here, the educational bodies—both students and teachers, together—explore the means of complex cultural production, be that their identity, racism, sexism, power, oppression, and so on, by reflexively examining their corporeal participation in their historical productions.

Second, a performative mode of engagement is "a methodology of engaging in education that acknowledges bodies and the political nature of their presence in our classrooms" (Warren, 1999, p. 258) and in our world. A performative mode of engagement calls for the body, our bodies in classrooms, to become a site of knowing and learning, "liberat[ing] the body from the shackles of a dualism that privileges the mind over the visceral" (Warren, 2003a, p. 95). "This is important not just because the body is already a site rich in corporeal knowledge, but because the body, brought to life in the classroom, can be a powerful vehicle for learning" (Warren, 2010b). Through a performative mode of engagement, performative pedagogy "make[s] intellectual content material theories of the flesh—a moving of schooling into a process of the body" (Warren, 2003a; p. 93).

Third, a performative mode of critique is "a critique of and through the flesh that creates dialogic and heuristic way of engaging in students' work" (Warren, 2003a; p. 94). Warren (2003a; 2010b) acknowledges Alexander (1999) for laying the groundwork for this type of pedagogical practice through his notion of critical poetic response. In a performative mode of critique, teachers engage the mode of performance as a way of creating and maintaining the dialogue about students' work. Warren (2010b) laments, "Pedagogical death, it seems to me, is meeting of the life of performance with the same lifelessness of traditional feedback." Through a performative mode of critique, we teachers engage in performative analyses of our own teaching practices, dialogically with our students. A performative mode of critique necessitates our reflexivity in understanding teacherly authority and power in our education system. Our reflexivity should not be done alone (Warren, 2011a). "As members of the dominant culture, we cannot construct socially just educational practices alone; it is arrogant and preposterous to think we can" (Hytten and Adkins, 2001, p. 448; also cited in Warren, 2011a, p. 141). A performative mode of critique engages us teachers to implicate our bodies through our performative modes of analysis and engagement in order to interrogate "our own sense making as teachers" (Warren, 2011a, p. 143).

DIFFERENCE AND PERFORMATIVE PEDAGOGY: PEDAGOGY OF INTERRUPTION

> The performative becomes a site of memory, a location and critical engagement of the stories we tell in assuming our roles as public intellectuals willing to make visible and challenge the grotesque inequalities and intolerable oppressions of the present moment. (Giroux and Shannon, 1997, p. 7)

The focus on the performative in education—performative pedagogy—is a hopeful site where we can labor for transforming our society, actualizing the world as more livable for all. The premise of the book John did not get to write is the very intersection where his work of performative pedagogy (1999; 2003a; 2003b; 2010b; 2011a; 2011b) meets with his conceptualization of difference (2008), education that makes a difference in our bodies, meetings of our bodies, in and out of our classrooms. This is the premise for his project; not yet fully theorized and not yet fully realized. This is the premise from which I think we, critical intercultural communication educators, can benefit in thinking of what we do in our classrooms.

The performative mode of analysis understands that our body is the site of teaching and learning culture and communication. Critically engaged, "the body is re-enfleshed in the classroom through a pedagogy that re-marks and remakes educational subjectivities in an effort to acknowledge the invisible forces of privilege and domination that dwell in absence" (Warren, 2003a, p. 106). Through the performative mode of analysis, we pay close and detained attention to our ephemeral making of our identities, making the invisible visible, carefully analyzing difference with its particularity and contextuality that is constitutive of who we are. Specifically, the performative mode of analysis focuses on how our bodies are sites of power production and how that production takes place through our embodied repetition of difference with its own particularity and contextuality. In this way, the performative mode of analysis helps render a nuanced and careful way of understanding our corporeal productive mechanism of power and injustice. That is, we learn how we, through our repetitions of difference, actively participate in the historically constructed production of power in our everyday lives. The performative mode of analysis teaches us to "really" pay attention to our identity embodiments.

The performative mode of engagement understands our bodies as sites and mechanisms of teaching and learning. Performatively engaged, our educational bodies meet in classrooms. In the meeting, something meaningful happens. Educational participants are asked to be fully present for each other. A collage of educational bodies—the sites and mechanisms of teaching and learning—emerges, inviting "coparticipation" (Warren, 2003a, p. 87) and rendering educational participants simultaneously teachers and learners for each other. The collage invites creative coexistence and cooperation, where students' differences exist as affirmative, not oppositional. The performative mode of engagement nurtures intersubjective collaboration, not division, of differences. Performatively engaged in the classroom, the opposition of the oppressed and oppressors become resituated as a possible collaboration in working together toward a more socially just world. The collage—coexistence, cooperation, and collaboration (in other words, difference as affirmative)—is the very creative force that potentially interrupts our own bodily reproductive system of power.

Finally, the performative mode of critique asks teachers to actively participate in the performative pedagogy that they employ in their teaching. For performative pedagogy to "serve as an interruptive force, calling out the mechanisms of production and imagining possible alternatives" (Warren, 2010b), teachers are to be responsive dialogically to students' presence—their class participations, relationships, and assignments. Again, the difference between teachers and students should not automatically be coded as oppositional, but as affirmative and collaborative. Teachers and students are to nurture a self-reflexive relationship where their own educational practices (their educational identities as teachers and students and cultural identities, such as race, gender, sexuality, nationality, linguistic identities, and so on) can be critically analyzed as an historically informed reproductive system of power. Teachers and students, together, become the collage of existence.

Briefly, I have discussed how I see John's performative pedagogy and his conceptualization of difference co-emerge as a hopeful educational practice that has the potential to make a difference, transforming students, teachers, and our society. As mentioned, this intersection has not been fully theorized. What I have offered here is my initial—premature, maybe—response to his proposal for the future direction of transformative scholarship on difference, performative pedagogy, and identity. "Both flesh and dreams coexist to create possibilities for knowing differently" (Warren, 1999, p. 258). Warren's suggested direction of this line of scholarship certainly invites our curiosity.

> What marks performative pedagogy as more than a set of classroom exercises or activities lies in the combination of analysis, engagement, and critique, each of which, when taken together, constitute a philosophy of educational practice that is transformative, critical, and hopeful. It is this philosophy of education that makes performative pedagogy have so much potential. (Warren, 2010b)

POSSIBILITY IN LOSS: HOPE, LOVE, HEALING, AND MOMENTUM

> Hope gives meaning to the struggles to change the world. Hope is grounded in concrete performative practices, in struggles and interventions that espouse the sacred values of love, care, community, trust, and well-being. . . . Hope, as a form of pedagogy, confronts and interrogates cynicism, the belief that change is not possible or is too costly. Hope works from rage to love. (Denzin, 2003, p. 299; also cited in Warren, 2011b, p. 21)

In his recent publication (Warren, 2011b), John talks about his uncle's death and his experience of attending the funeral. As he and his uncle's sister stand in front of the casket, she says, "I don't recognize him. For his body to look like that, he had to have lived every single day to its fullest—and he did, he lived and loved so much that there is nothing left in his body . . . " (Warren, 2011b, p. 31). He contemplates, "She renews me, as I look past the remains of my uncle and toward the possibility that still lies out before me. I have much more loving to do in this life" (p. 31). In the 2010 CSCA spotlight panel, he narrated his uncle's death and how he was processing it. I cite him at length:

> I am not someone who is good with death; I look upon it too often as an ending, failing to see that a life is measured not in duration but in quality, not in endurance but in effect. I am trying to relearn death, no doubt in an effort to recast this panel as not an ending to my career but rather a pause as I turn toward the horizons of possibility. . . . I'm drawn to a reoccurring ephemerality. My uncle (and, by association, myself) is but for a moment of this world. Difference, as Deleuze offers it, is undoubtedly momentary, a repetition with great complexity that, in its glorious moment of happening, becomes vapor until, finally, nothing but memory. Performative pedagogy is a pedagogy of the moment, the meeting of bodies and spirits and intellects, the generative possibility that, building from bodily meanings, culminates, climaxes and then, with traces of its power, leaves us, changed. As Phalen (1993) might propose, who we are (and, as a result, the moment of our pedagogies) "become itself through disappearance" (p. 146)—ephemerality marks both its loss and its potential. (Warren, 2010b)

I am not sure if I can relearn John's death as he suggests because I am still angry that he is gone. Misguided anger, I know. I miss him so much, and I look for his love in my office and the other kind of love—his tough love. He left us too soon.

At John's funeral, Deanna Fassett, his dear friend and collaborator/coauthor, delivered her eulogy for John. With her permission, I insert her eulogy as it captures John and his day-in day-out, on-page off-page work he had done for us.

> John was my friend for fifteen years—for nearly ten years of this time, he offered to teach me to knit, and each time, I'd refuse. (I'm not very

crafty). But I'd watch him knit, fascinated by how soothing he found it, by how he'd accumulate scarf after scarf. I expect that many of you in this room have something—a scarf, a blanket—John created. (Fassett, 2011)

John offered me to teach knitting as well and told me how soothing it was for him. As Deanna did, I did, too, refuse his offer. I was his tennis buddy, not a knitting buddy. The very last Christmas before his passing, he gave me a scarf. Back to Deanna's eulogy for John:

> When I was on sabbatical, I told John I wanted to learn new things—to master a skill or two that might help me be a better teacher. John asked—again—if I'd like him to teach me how to knit, and, finally, I said yes. What's most important to this story isn't that I learned how to knit and came to enjoy sitting and knitting on our visits and in our travels, but that John had to teach me how to do it on four separate occasions. I would watch him, and then he'd watch me practice, making gentle corrections here and there and listening to swear profusely. Each time I saw John, I would present my practice swatch—irregular, full of small and not-so-small holes from dropped stitches—and explain that I just didn't get it. And he would show me again. What I'd have you take from this small, mundane tale is one of the most important lessons of my life: Love is in the details. In the imperfections. In the paradoxes. While knitting is wonderful, it's the relationships it knots together that matter. Handmade things are beautiful not because they are perfect, but because they are unique—in color, texture, form and function. They are beautiful because of the time and love we put into them. And when I think of my friend John and the time we spent together, which was all too short, it's the imperfections that are the most beautiful. The times we disagreed, the times we gossiped, the times we were confused and didn't know how to proceed—those are the times we grew—together and as individuals. John grappled; he was a grappler. He worked to make sense of his world and his place in it. He was both patient and impatient. He was both sassy and sweet. He was both a prolific writer and an angry, unhappy copyeditor. He was strong and he was vulnerable. In other words, John was complex and imperfect—and therefore unique and easy to love. And though we are imperfect, John knit us together, and that love lives on in and through us. We will miss him terribly, but, with him as the tie that binds, we remain forever connected. (Fassett, 2011)

I still have a difficult time saying that John died. This verb, the past tense intransitive verb, is too sad, to me, connoting, "done, gone, no more, disconnected." I find some comfort—not the kind of comfort I enjoy, but the kind of comfort through which I find myself surviving what is unbearable—in saying, "John left" or "John passed." I think this is so because I can quickly shift the function of these verbs from intransitive to transitive. "John left us his publications." "John passed his book project onto us." In this shift, I can continue feeling his presence in my life. In this shift, I can "try . . . to relearn death . . . to see that a life is measured not in duration but in quality, not in endurance but in effect" (Warren, 2010b).

I neatly put away the scarf John gave me the last Christmas in my bedroom chest drawer. I cannot wear it because, obviously, it is extremely difficult to do so. I cannot wear it because I don't want to mess it up. This is what John would say to that: He would look over his glasses at me, and say, "Satoshi, that's stupid. I made it for you to use it. Use it. I would knit another one if you messed it up. Use it." I know that he would want me to use it, but I cannot, yet. If I would use it, it protects my neck from the cold winter wind and I would look a bit more fashionable. In the use, I find his love. His love is on the words he embodied on the pages he produced. He produced those pages for use, for us to really use. In our use, we find him—his love—again and again. In our use, we are and continue to be connected. In our use, his life gains momentum. I have to relearn how to wear his scarf.

As I complete our chapter, I return to the table at the breakfast place, at which once John and I sat. Maybe I want his affirmation that this chapter does the labor that he is asking for through his scholarship. Maybe I am a sentimental kind of guy. I don't know, but I just wanted to come back to this table one more time before I send this chapter out to the editors. I stare at the empty chair across from me and think, "A footstep." This empty chair which he once occupied and now doesn't (physically)— once there, but no more—is one of the footsteps he took. He inscribed many footsteps—evidence of his life—on pages he produced, on stages on which he stood, in conference rooms he presented, in his students' lives, in his dramatic entry into our offices, in our friendships, in us, in our discipline, and beyond. He is everywhere but nowhere. He is here but not here. Some of us follow or walk alongside his footsteps; some of us might meaningfully walk against the directions towards which his footsteps point. Nonetheless, his footsteps are the evidence of his life. In the body who reads the pages he has produced, in the body who witnessed and experiences his performative pedagogy, and in the body who was and continues to be touched by his friendship, we will continue finding his footsteps, transforming our performativity as scholars, teachers/students, and friends. I treasure his footsteps as a person who had the privilege of witnessing his labor of walking, grabbing the ground with his toes and pushing his body forward. We have a lot of walking—labor—left to do. Yes, that's right: "I have much more loving to do in this life" (Warren, 2011b, p. 31).

> When Freire speaks of a pedagogy of love, a pedagogy of the oppressed, he is speaking about a kind of social action that is based in the most fundamental of all human rights—we all deserve to be more fully human, to be subjects who act upon the world, rather than simply be acted upon. It is a philosophy that cannot end at the classroom wall— we are people in the world and as such, we must be willing to be

transformed, speaking back to the world from this newly humbled and humanized location. It is a vision for being that is worth the effort to actualize. (Warren, 2011b, p. 33)

I know there are complicated issues that are before us—We have considerable challenges as a discipline. . . . Yet the academic community is still ours to craft—and we have an obligation to craft it well or we will lose it. We can stay shut up in our offices or we can become public pedagogues, meeting the world upfront and crafting pedagogical performances that highlight the value of what we do and how what we do is central to building a better world. (Warren, 2011a, p. 142)

TWO

Doing Intersectionality

Power, Privilege, and Identities in Political Activist Communities

Karma R. Chávez

The concept of "intersectionality," though central to understanding identity, power, and privilege within feminist theory, has received less attention in communication studies as a conceptual framework. While some intercultural communication scholars implicitly situate their work within intersectional frameworks, or examine the interlocking nature of race, class, gender, sexuality, ability and nation in a particular case (e.g., Allen, 1998; Carrillo Rowe, 2008; Houston, 1992; McKinnon, 2009; Moreman and Calafell, 2008; Moreman and McIntosh, 2010), few have theorized intersectionality—the interlocking nature of identity and power—within the purview of intercultural communication. In Nakayama and Halualani's (2010a) edited volume, *The Handbook of Critical Intercultural Communication*, for example, intersectionality is mentioned as a theoretical term one time in more than five hundred pages. Moon (2010) writes, "By attending to notions of intersectionality, scholars are more likely to produce knowledge that is specific and local, rather than abstract and overly generalized. In addition, we are more likely to observe how power and privilege may play out in intercultural interactions" (p. 41).

Perhaps Moon's quip and the collection's otherwise silence on intersectionality reflects the fact that intersectionality is a concept so integrated into intercultural communication scholarship that it needs no advancement or theorization. I argue, however, that this is not the case. In this chapter, I offer credence for Moon's claim and argue that intersectionality is a useful tool for critical intercultural and activist scholars to use to understand operations of culture, identity and power. I open by briefly reviewing the discussion of identity within three landmark, meta-theoretical assessments of identity within intercultural communication across the past fifteen years, to show the clear emphasis on singular categories of identity, no matter the approach (i.e., social scientific, interpretive or critical). Next, I define the concept of intersectionality. I then offer a brief case study to highlight the importance of an intersectional approach to the study of identity(ies) in intercultural communication before closing with implications.

IDENTITY IN INTERCULTURAL COMMUNICATION

Identity, particularly "cultural identity," and also nationality/ethnicity, and sometimes race, have persisted as central concepts in intercultural communication. Jackson and Garner (1998) argue that, even as they diverge in significant ways, all the perspectives on identity within intercultural communication pivot from a single tenet: "identity is relational" (p. 46). Identity is not static; instead, it is negotiated with other people, cultures, spaces, and values. Despite this seeming dynamism in the way the field understands identity, Jackson and Garner reveal the ambiguous relationship between "race," "ethnicity," and "culture" within intercultural scholarship, and the conceptual conflation of racial, ethnic and cultural identity. As a result, the authors contend that communication scholars have actually elided a clear conversation about, and understanding of these factors, which would make our scholarship more widely discernible to audiences outside the field. Noting that the three are always, in some ways, indistinguishable (p. 52), their call for conceptual clarity proves curious, and does not provide a method for understanding how these dimensions of identity (not to mention, power) relate to each other, or how they relate to other dimensions of identity like class, gender or sexual orientation. Thus, despite urging for more clarity, and challenging the status of identity in the field, Jackson and Garner reinscribe identity as a singular concept.

Mendoza, Halualani, and Drzewiecka (2002) bring the question of power to the fore in their assessment of identity scholarship within intercultural communication, noting the need to address the relationship between structure and agency and also to move beyond thinking of identity only in terms of nation/ethnicity. More specifically, the authors maintain that "a complex analysis of identity politics and dynamics" involves "a critical interrogation of those sites and practices of articulation (and rearticulation), suturing and unraveling, signification (and re-signification), and other forms of symbolic contestations made manifest through communicative practices" (p. 317). In promoting different approaches to understanding identity, through performativity, resignification, and dynamic translation, these authors complicate the discussion on identity through showing how identity manifests differently in communicative practices, depending on a host of factors such as social conventions, norms, laws and cultural rituals (e.g., Butler, 1999; Collier, 1998; Martin and Nakayama, 1999). They also reveal the necessity of an analysis of power, by keeping structure and agency in productive tension when trying to understand identity. Yet, similar to Jackson and Garner (1998), their sole focus remains on ethnic identity, without attentiveness to the intersections with other dimension of identity.

Despite emerging from an entirely different paradigmatic approach from Mendoza et al., Y. Y. Kim's (2007) assessment of the status of cultural identity research within intercultural communication similarly succumbs to a more or less singular focus. Y. Y. Kim writes, "the term cultural identity is employed broadly to include related concepts such as subcultural, national, ethnolinguistic, and racial identity" (p. 238). Building upon her previous research, Y. Y. Kim concludes that five positions on cultural identity exist within intercultural communication and related fields: "(a) cultural identity as an adaptive and evolving entity of an individual; (b) cultural identity as a flexible and negotiable entity of an individual; (c) cultural identity as a discrete social category and an individual choice; (d) cultural identity as a flexible and negotiable entity of an individual; and (e) cultural identity as a discrete and non-negotiable social category and group right" (p. 242). Even as recent scholarship, such as Ono's (2010), continues to implore the field to rethink the centrality of the nation in our scholarship, ethnicity/nation, and adherent terms race and culture, as more or less singular concepts, continue to prevail as most salient in discussions of identity in intercultural communication.

INTERSECTIONALITY

Much has been said in feminist of color, queer of color, and critical race scholarship about the importance of taking an intersectional approach to understanding identity and how institutions impact people differently. U.S. third-world feminists in the 1970s described the status of women who were marginalized in multiple ways using terms such as "double" or "multiple jeopardy" (Beale, 1970/2005) and "interlocking oppressions" (Collective, 1983; Lorde, 1983). Such ideas emerged in order to articulate the experiences of women of color, lesbians and poor women, who were not always served by the "gender-only" approach of the white feminist movement or the "race- (and to a lesser degree class-) only" approach of racial justice and nationalist movements, as reflected in the title of the famous book, *But Some Of Us Are Brave: All the Women Are White, All the Blacks Are Men* (Hull, Scott, and Smith, 1982). These feminists argued that any focus on only a singular axis of identity or oppression functioned to negate the experience of, and further oppress, those whose lives are constituted by multiple oppressions. Furthermore, thinkers such as Lorde (1984) noted that we must centralize difference, use it as a resource, and understand the ways in which we are simultaneously oppressed and privileged. These feminists, then, called for a complex approach to identity, oppression, and privilege that acknowledged the many ways power functions differently in the lives of different people.

From this earlier theorizing, legal scholar, Crenshaw derived the term "intersectionality" to explain the precarious position of black women in relation to a legal system that acknowledges only (white) women and blacks (men) (Crenshaw, 1989, 1991), and a political and cultural system that perpetually erases black women. Crenshaw carefully shows how the experiences of women of color are systematically erased and denied because of a failure to recognize the ways in which, in her analysis, gender and race both matter and cannot be isolated from one another. What this means is that if a policy is designed to help women who have survived abuse, for instance, but it hasn't taken into account the needs of differently privileged women because of their race, citizenship status, sexual orientation, gender identity, and socioeconomic class, then that policy will likely only serve privileged women (white, middle class, cisgendered, heterosexual U.S. citizens) who are assumed to be the standard upon which such policies are often based.

Similarly, if one wants to comprehend the experiences of immigrants who attempt to acculturate to a host culture, national/ethnic identity is only one factor that helps to understand that experience. As Ong (1999) has shown, new immigrants are more successfully integrated based upon their socioeconomic class and where they fall on the racializing schema which whitens some and blackens others. Romero (2002) has discussed the experiences of female immigrants of color who work as domestics in the United States, and demonstrated the ways in which race, country of origin, gender, and labor status impact these women's experiences in a new culture. Luibhéid (2004) and Cantú (2009) have further complicated immigrant acculturation by identifying how sexuality greatly impacts every aspect of the migration process. Such scholars reveal the necessity of bringing multiple identities to bear upon understanding of people's experience, privilege, and oppression.

As mentioned above, some critical intercultural scholarship already reflects an intersectional approach, to greater or lesser degrees (e.g., Carrillo Rowe, 2008; Cheney and Ashcraft, 2007; Houston, 1992; Meyers, 2004; Moreman and Calafell, 2008; Richardson and Taylor, 2009).[1] Undoubtedly, for instance, Marsha Houston has been an (some might argue, the) unwavering pioneer in advocating that communication scholars integrate race, class, and gender into their analysis of communication phenomena. Similarly, Carrillo Rowe (2008) has worked to carefully show

how women of color and white women understand alliance, friendship and communication very differently as a result of their divergent relationships to power. Some organizational communication scholars such as Cheney and Ashcraft (2007) and Richardson and Taylor (2009) have also worked to integrate an intersectional approach into their understanding of organizational structure, policy, and members' experiences within organizations. Yet, more robust and comprehensive engagement with intersectionality in critical intercultural communication is warranted for several reasons. I'll name some of the most salient ones here. First, if, as Moon (2002) has argued, culture should be thought of as a contested zone, then different tools are required to understand the nature of those contestations, and to push the very definition of "culture" to more adequately account for the power dynamics, ideologies, and complexities that constitute culture (see also Halualani and Nakayama, 2010a). Intersectionality is one important theoretical resource to enable such work. Second, intersectionality challenges the field's emphasis on singularity, by revealing singularity to be always already a fiction, and a tool designed to uphold power imbalances. The Latina feminist philosopher Lugones (2003) has maintained, for instance, that logics of purity (and hence singularity) are colonial logics, tools of the oppressor, even when they are adopted by oppressed people who attempt to challenge their oppression. Intersectionality, or, as Lugones articulates, analysis of "intermeshing oppressions," ruptures such logics, which is imperative for a critical intercultural project. Finally, some have articulated an "activist turn" in communication studies generally (Frey and Carragee, 2007) and in intercultural communication specifically (Broome, Carey, De la Garza, Martin, and Morris, 2005). This activist turn involves both using communication theory to enable activism, which is what Frey and Carragee do, and it also includes working closely to understand activist communities as an important site of theory building in action (Chávez, 2011; Dempsey, 2009; Madison, 2010). As the forces of neoliberalism manifest in political ideologies from the Right to the Left, in the policies of international governing bodies, and federal, state, and local governments around the world, in the funding structures and strictures for social justice causes, and even in the manner in which activists are able to challenge cultural and economic "common sense" that devastates communities, intersectionality is a crucial tool to help challenge these oppressive conditions in a radical way, at their "roots" (Madison, 2010). In the next section, I use a brief case study to illustrate the aforementioned benefits to an intersectional approach to identity(ies) in critical intercultural communication studies.

INTERSECTIONALITY IN PRACTICE

On February 11, 2011, newly elected Wisconsin Governor Scott Walker, a Republican, introduced a "budget repair" bill. Walker declared the state of Wisconsin "broke," and expected to be $137 million dollars in the hole this fiscal year alone. As a result, he proposed a "budget repair" bill, which included many extreme changes to the state budget on issues ranging from Medicaid, prisons, heating plants, and debt restructuring to collective bargaining and pension and health contributions for public employees (n.a., 2011). The entire bill proved incredibly controversial. At the time of this writing, massive protests continue to take place on a regular basis at the state capitol in Madison to denounce this and the fuller budget bill proposed some weeks later. In February, two issues were the primary catalyst bringing people to the streets: the bill's major cutting of collective bargaining rights for public employees, and the increased contribution for pension and benefits that would cost the average state employee hundreds of dollars every month. The only public sector employees exempted from these proposals were police and firefighters, groups which supported Walker in his 2010 campaign.

On February 14, the protests began with more than one thousand members and supporters of UW-Madison's Teaching Assistants' Association delivering thousands of Valentine's Day cards to Governor Walker from Wisconsin residents imploring, "We Heart UW: Governor Walker, Don't Break My Heart." By Tuesday, February 15, more than five thousand people rallied at the capitol, and by February 26, on the thirteenth consecutive day, one hundred thousand people protested the governor at the capitol, while fourteen Democratic State Senators remained in an undisclosed location in the state of Illinois in order to prevent the Senate from having a quorum and voting on the repair bill.

As people all over Wisconsin, and some from other states and countries, expressed their outrage over Walker's proposal in physical protests, others took to their blogs, including Columbia University Journalism Fellow and *Daily Beast* associate editor Dana Goldstein, who wrote a short and provocative statement on February 18. Goldstein noted:

> The Wisconsin GOP's war on public sector unions—except those representing police officers, firefighters, and state troopers—is not only a craven attack on the Democratic base, but sexist, too, since predominantly male professions are deliberately protected while female ones are targeted.
>
> About 80 percent of American teachers, for example, are female; at the elementary school level, nearly 90 percent are women. Nursing is 95 percent female. Nationwide, the majority of public sector union members, represented by AFSCME and other groups, are women.
>
> Meanwhile, over 70 percent of law enforcement workers in the United States are men. Our firefighting ranks are 96 percent male and

over half of all professional firefighting departments have never hired a woman.

Just sayin'. (Goldstein, 2011, para. 1–3)

In the comments of the blog, a number of men chastised Goldstein's analysis by putting up a series of strawperson arguments in place of hers and hurling ad feminam attacks her way. Several women came to her defense, further reiterating points that in 2011 (white) women are still paid only 75 percent of what (white) men are paid across all sectors and education levels.[2] For a very long time, feminists have offered a gendered analysis of labor, but this particular analysis indicates the subtle ways gender identity matters. Even though Scott Walker does advocate a number of policies that could be construed as anti-woman, including proposing that health insurers no longer be required to pay for birth control for women, and defunding Planned Parenthood, it is likely that Walker didn't *intend* for his anti-union bill to target women more than men. It is more likely that he wanted to reward those organizations that supported him before, even as their benefits are more costly than other public employees, and it just so happens this ends up benefiting more men than women. Of course, that unions representing predominantly male professions would be more likely to support Republican policies than other unions that represent a more diverse work force is also a question worth considering. How, even in issues of labor, are policies that Republicans advocate, more beneficial for men? The implication of Goldstein's quip is crucially important, and it demonstrates the need to think complexly about labor and how issues of labor remain very different for women and men, and also different ethnic and racial groups.

Extending Goldstein's analysis even further, *United for a Fair Economy* reports that blacks are 30 percent more likely than the rest of the U.S. labor force to hold public sector jobs (Ali, Huezo, Miller, Mwangi, and Prokosch, 2011). While blacks comprise only 13 percent of the total population, this means that attacks on public sector unions like the ones that are happening in numerous states in the United States in addition to Wisconsin, including Indiana, Ohio, Michigan, New Jersey, and others, disproportionately impact blacks. Considering the specific case in Wisconsin, it would also follow that black women are, in terms of proportions, potentially the most impacted. And yet, black women have not been the face of the labor battle. A number of diverse groups have come out in solidarity, but the racial and gendered analysis of union-busting, especially as it is happening in Wisconsin, has not happened. For example, while the Reverend Jesse Jackson has been notably present at major protests in Madison, his analysis has largely centered on a generic workers' rights platform, and he is often introduced as someone who encouraged Martin Luther King, Jr. to think about the labor struggle. Jackson's unique work challenging racism, and his long-standing (albeit checkered) commitment to coalition building is generally not brought to the fore, by Jackson or those who introduce him. Similarly, while King has also become a regular symbol in the protests, particularly from the American Federation of State, County and Municipal Employees (AFSCME) members—King was in Memphis to support AFSCME union workers when he was assassinated—a contemporary racial analysis, not to mention a gender analysis, of public sector union busting has not been central to AFSCME's (or any other union's) activism.

On the one hand, all of these public sector workers, regardless of race, gender, sexual orientation or ability, are impacted by increased contributions to benefits and limited collective bargaining rights. On the other hand, given the racial make-up of the public sector, and the gendered make up of those targeted in this instance, it clearly seems that some workers, with certain identities, will be disproportionately impacted, and that those workers are also the ones who are already more likely to be more systemically oppressed.

THE IMPORTANCE OF THE INTERSECTIONAL APPROACH

What this case study illustrates about intersectionality is that the interlocking identities of workers matter. Intersectionality, thus proves useful in helping to understand the situation in Wisconsin in several key ways. First, intersectionality reveals how generic or singular identity categories may lead to simplistic understandings of culture and power. A movement on behalf of "workers" as a generic identity category, may fail to interrogate the specific ways this legislation impacts different "cultures" of workers differently. Even as workers have been understood within intercultural communication as a unique culture, that construction has also been largely racialized (as white) and gendered (as male) (Philipsen, 2002). White male workers are also undoubtedly impacted by oppressive economic policies and their plight is important as well. But when "worker" is generically coded as belonging to white male cultural groups, this erases the complexity of the cultural and economic struggle. Intersectionality helps to highlight the complexities and, therefore, to supply a precise description of the different dynamics manifest in this situation, and, for the critical scholar, provides a different tool with which to address the prevailing cultural and economic problem. How might interlocking or intersecting identities be taken into consideration in both understanding cultural dynamics of workers and the experiences of workers themselves?

Second, intersectionality helps to highlight the operation of what Lugones (2003) calls "purity" logics within a given culture or subculture. For example, the primary rallying cry of the Wisconsin protests has been "Solidarity," which is a long-standing mantra of the labor movement.

Solidarity, a potential mark of coalition and alliance building across differences, also suggests that differently positioned groups will be solid, unified, and connected in their collective struggle. Solidarity in this instance seems to refer to issues more than identity, but identity inevitably factors into how the expectation of solidarity operates. In some ways then, solidarity has the potential of being a purifying logic as well. As a form of what sociology of movement scholars call "collective identity," solidarity puts the needs and agenda of the group above all others in order to accomplish the movement's ends (McDonald, 2002). An intersectional perspective highlights some of what gets obfuscated, collapsed, or ignored in claims of solidarity. For example, which workers are imagined to be represented in the solidarity claim? In other words, what identities are these workers imagined to possess, and how is that impacting what people are asked to be in solidarity with?

This question became salient for me in my work with the immigrant rights community in Wisconsin. During a planning meeting in the spring of 2011 with leaders, organizers, volunteers, and state representative Jo Casta Zamarripa (D-Milwaukee) and her staff, we carefully discussed how to ensure that immigrants would not be left out of the workers' rights analysis being offered by union leaders and other activists. While migrant laborers have a long and varied history with unions, the existence of migrant laborers as an important and affected constituency also brings about unique questions and needs for workers' rights, in a similar way that the above discussion of the disproportionate impact on black women does. Multiple dimensions of identity and power, highlighted through intersectionality, complicate acceptance of purity logics and offer resources with which to interrogate them.

Finally and relatedly, an intersectional approach provides analytical resources to investigate and reveal the many dimensions of power and identity that need to be salient as activists and activist-scholars work toward social change. It informs, and is necessarily informed by alliance and coalition work. When Lorde (1984) suggests that difference should not be feared as it is a primary resource for social change, she points to the fact that when people understand their struggles as interrelated, and they have an opportunity to speak openly about differences, those differences can be used productively, without erasing or negating them. An intersectional approach recognizes that people's experiences will vary from one another based on the differing identities and relationships to power. For instance, at several rallies and protests, speakers and protesters with LGBT and queer identities highlighted the importance of considering sexuality and gender in the labor context. Signs I saw including "queers for labor," and "queers are laborers too," point to the need to think in terms of alliance. Wisconsin LGBT organizations, including Fair Wisconsin and Equality Wisconsin, all encouraged LGBT Wisconsinites to join the marches. As one activist put it, "The right to collective bargaining is vital for all workers, and particularly so for lesbian, gay, bisexual and transgender workers and our families" (Neff and Foval, 2011). Even as national LGBT organizations like the Human Rights Campaign often refuse to consider the interlocking nature of identity, and focus only on sexual orientation, these local groups understand the importance of working to build bridges across differences and acknowledging similarities. Also, as this activist's quotation suggests, LGBT people have unique needs as workers as they are not protected by federal workplace protections. Coalition and alliance politics only emerge from acknowledging differences and finding ways to work with and through them toward various ends. In this way, an intersectional approach can both lead activists to coalition building, and coalitions can further aid in developing an intersectional perspective that strikes at the roots of oppressions. Moreover, an intersectional perspective helps to work against "divide and conquer" tactics. In this way, intersectionality is not just an important theoretical tool for unpacking manifestations of culture, identity and power, it also provides practical resources for activists. And the question of LGBT rights and identities is among one of many. Disabled workers, and workers of different ages, for example, have ranging needs that further illustrate the need for coalition and alliance work and an intersectional perspective. Already, by state and federal law, it is perfectly legal to pay some intellectually and developmentally disabled workers under the minimum wage for doing menial labor (Morell, 2011). While these workers are not the public sector workers directly impacted by Wisconsin's state legislation, they reflect a broader system of workplace disenfranchisement that all disabled people experience, an experience completely erased without an intersectional approach to worker identities.

CONCLUSION

As feminists of color and their allies have consistently argued, until we can have dialogue across lines of difference where those most marginalized have a primary voice, and those with privilege listen, no legitimate social change can be expected. The enactment of such dialogue does not always happen even in contexts where activists and others expressly commit to addressing the needs and concerns of the most marginalized. Writing by feminists of color has continued to show that this sort of dialogue is in fact very rare, as adequately engaging in an intersectional analysis of issues that both indicts participants in the analysis and actually gets at the complexities of power, privilege, and domination that constitute the lives of women of color, poor women, and queer women, seems beyond most people's imagination. Without being overly pessimistic, the situation in Wisconsin has certainly created space for people to dialogue and coalesce across lines of difference, even as the singular identity of "worker" has often proved to be the most salient in many people's minds. It is only in taking an intersectional approach to the situation, however, that this fact becomes readily apparent. An intersectional approach indeed provides localized and specific knowledge that attends to the complexities of power and privilege. The intersectional approach then tells us much about the possibilities and difficulties for intercultural dialogue and relating in local contexts.

Yet, the possibility for dialogue and understanding, while important, is certainly only one part of the political project. As my ongoing work with activist communities attempting to build coalitions across lines of difference has shown, a bifurcation between "talking" and "acting" can create additional problems, and this dichotomy also often emerges as a problem of intersectionality. For instance, in an LGBT organization I worked with in southern Arizona, I interviewed one of the only queer women of color in the organization, Geovanna, to ask her about activism, coalition building between migrant and queer rights organizations, and discrimination. She explained to me her frustration with the ways in which activism gets differently construed between people with privilege and those without in activist organizations. She remarked, 'I'm surrounded by these smart people, and my perception is that they talk so much with these big ass words and go in circles, and there's never a point where they act. Mexicans, Latinos, Native Americans, we tend to be more timid and to the point, but we perform action after that.'[3] Essentialism aside, this comment reflected a broader set of conditions where Geovanna perceived activists with more systemic privilege often preferring meetings, emails, and strategizing sessions to organizing in communities or engaging in direct actions, which seemed to be the preferences of those who were most oppressed. From Geovanna's perspective, when coming from a place of regularly experiencing multiple, intermeshed oppressions, activists engaged in different forms of activism than those who did not experience this. Yet, it was often those in the latter group who set the activist agenda. In this way, both dialogue *and* action that actually engages questions of identity and power from an intersectional perspective are incredibly difficult, yet absolutely essential.

The intersectional perspective is equally as difficult and essential for critical intercultural scholars of identity. What I hope to have offered in this brief chapter is an example of how intersectional analysis might look. And I hope to have further shown that understanding of a particular context is far richer when taking intersectionality seriously. Importantly, this call for the centrality of intersectionality in intercultural identity research does not imply that certain identities and systems of power do not predominate in any given situation. It is not hard to think of times when race or gender appear to be the most salient factor in a given communicative exchange. This call also does not demand that every identity needs to be addressed in every given analysis. As I heard the black feminist scholar Brenda J. Allen quip at a National Communication Association panel on intersectionality that Cindy L. Griffin and I organized in 2009, intersectionality is about attending to "differences that make a difference." There are certainly no rules to delineate which differences matter, but it seems vitally important for critical intercultural communication scholars to continue to develop theoretical, methodological and pedagogical tools and resources to facilitate finding out, in vast and varied local contexts.

NOTES

1. While this partial list reflects communication scholarship that engages with an intersectional perspective, it is more difficult to discern which parts of this list properly belong within the purview of "critical intercultural communication," a designation with permeable boundaries.

2. The comments on the blog used the generic term "women," though it is important to note that studies continue to indicate that men of color make less than white men, and the disparity between white men and women of color is far greater than that between white men and white women. Further disparities exist when ability, national origin and sexual orientation or gender identity are considered. For a simple chart breaking down some of these disparities, based on Census and Population Survey data, see: n.a. (2006). "Median Annual Earnings by Race and Sex." Retrieved from www.infoplease.com/us/census/median-earnings-by-race-2006.html.

3. This interview comes from dissertation research. The quotation is in single quotes because at the request of the interviewee, I did not record the interview. Geovanna [her actual first name, at her request], Interview with Author. March 22, 2007, Tucson, Arizona.

THREE

Understanding Identity Through Dialogue

Paulo Freire and Intercultural Communication Pedagogy

Sandra L. Pensoneau-Conway

Intercultural communication pedagogy—indeed, the communication discipline as a whole—has been experiencing a recent trend towards concerted adoption of critical educational philosophies and orientations. This has been most visible with the 2007 publication of Deanna L. Fassett and John T. Warren's germinal work, *Critical Communication Pedagogy*. Inspired by Sprague (1992, 1993) within our own field, along with others who are most noted for their contributions to the field of critical pedagogy (such as Peter McLaren and Henry Giroux), Fassett and Warren offer us a starting point for considering the contributions of communication to critical pedagogy, and the contributions of critical pedagogy to communication. As a foundation of critical communication pedagogy, dialogue as a method, dialogue as a practice, and dialogue as a position deserve continued examination for the ways it contributes to our understanding of identities in the classroom.

Even more relevant here is the relationship between dialogue, identity, and intercultural communication. Dialogue itself has been written about in the context of intercultural communication. Ellis and Maoz (2009) worked to understand the practice of transformative dialogue as a method in which to improve relations between Israeli Jews and Palestinians. Fitzgerald (1993) argues that we must put *culture* and *communication* (as core concepts in dialogue with one another in order to understand a sense of cultural identity. The *Journal of International and Intercultural*

33

Communication even recently (2011) devoted an entire issue to examining dialogue within intercultural communication. Following the precedents of Simpson (2008), Foeman (2006), and others, I wish here to fuse dialogue into intercultural communication pedagogy, though perhaps on more of a philosophical level than on a practical, methodological level. One of the most prominent contributions to the notion of pedagogical dialogue comes from Paulo Freire, most notably in his *Pedagogy of the Oppressed* (1970/2000). While Freire may not have explicitly identified himself as an "intercultural" scholar, Freirean dialogue has much to offer intercultural communication pedagogy.

Freire is perhaps one of the most widely known scholars associated with critical communication pedagogy. His explication of the theory of dialogue is germinal to critical classrooms across disciplines. In this chapter, I explicate Freire's notion of dialogue as outlined primarily in *Pedagogy of the Oppressed* (1970/2000), and examine how it highlights, complicates, and further nuances contemporary discussions of identity and intercultural communication pedagogy. Such a project begs an important set of questions: In what ways can we understand classroom participants' cultural identities through engaging in Freirean dialogue, both as educators and as researchers? What can dialogue tell us about cultural identity? How can these concepts work synergistically to inform intercultural communication pedagogy? I hope to answer these questions by highlighting four fundamental characteristics of Freirean dialogue—namely, dialogue as (1) epistemological; (2) complicating the teacher-student contradiction; (3) subjectifying; and (4) praxiological. In so doing, I provide a foundation for offering dialogue as method for understanding and examining identity within the context of intercultural communication pedagogy.

A FRAMEWORK FOR IDENTITY

Before diving into the implications of a Freirean dialogue for understanding identity in the intercultural communication classroom, I first take a moment to say a few words about identity. Broadly, our *identity* is a way to understand our personhood; it's the meaning we make of our sense of self. We might even say that it's the answer to the question, "Who am I?" However, while helpful for beginning the conversation, this reductive sense of identity is only that—a beginning. To provide a more nuanced interpretation of identity, I turn to two works that most heavily inform my own scholarly interpretation of identity. The first is Calvin O. Schrag's subject constituted in communicative praxis, in his 1986 *Communicative Praxis and the Space of Subjectivity*.

Identity, for Schrag (1986), is an intersubjectively constituted phenomenon.[1] In other words, our subjecthood comes about in relationships with others, and in those relationships, we experience what Schrag calls *com-*

municative praxis. Communicative praxis is "the interplay of thought, [discourse],[2] and action . . . contextualized in a world. . . ." (p. 6). In this space of communicative praxis, subjects are implicated, and identities are formed. An implicated subject is one that arises in the previously mentioned interplay. My very being—a being who engages in thought, discourse, and action—implies my subjecthood and identity. Therefore, my identity is implicated in communicative praxis. Additionally, this implicated identity is undergirded by three elements. The first is communicative temporality. Though the subject is constituted in the present, this present is "a *living* present coming from a past and projecting into a future" (p. 146). Multiplicity is the second element. The implicated subject is never solid and fixed, but contextual, and so multiple. I experience multiple identities simultaneously. The third, and final, element is intersubjective embodiment. I am constituted through my embodiment, which is a response to others with whom I am in relationships. We come to know one another through those embodied relationships, and the embodied practices in which we engage that are situated in a social context. In other words, "I" am never just "I," but I am "I" because I am in a relationship with "you," creating "we." Likewise, "we" are never just "we," because we are situated in a larger social (political, historical, spatial, cultural, and so on) context. Simpson (2008) argues that, "In a pedagogical sense, the process of dialogue is often the primary means to intersubjectivity" (p. 184).

While Schrag does not necessarily identify himself as an intercultural scholar, and while he never (to my knowledge) explicitly discusses cultural identity in the way it is discussed within intercultural communication, his work does have applicability to intercultural communication studies (e.g., see Toyosaki's chapter in this volume). His intersubjective self translates to an intersubjective *intercultural* self. For Schrag, an individual's cultural background is part of the temporality of the subject—our cultural identifications are drawn from our past, performed in our present, and oriented toward our future. Within intercultural communication classrooms, we are called upon to recognize cultural identifications as arising in the space of communicative praxis, in the dialogue of Subjects coming to understand and co-construct the objective world (in the Freirean sense of the term, as I outline more in depth later on in this chapter).

Thought not specifically drawing from, but certainly extending from and relating to Schrag, as well as Butler's (1993) theory of performativity, Fassett and Warren's (2007) *Critical Communication Pedagogy* specifically situates identity within pedagogical contexts through the framework of critical communication pedagogy. Such a pedagogy understands identity as "constituted in communication" (p. 39). Our communicative acts (our language, our everyday performances, our mundane decisions) create the possibilities for our identities, and so identity is who we know ourselves to be, and who others know us to be (the former may not coincide with the latter), within and through communication. More specifically, culture and identity—and therefore, cultural identity—collide with one another in the performative embodiments of both avowing and ascribing identity markers that simultaneously construct cultural categories. For example, by performing "straight" through wearing my wedding right, I simultaneously avow the construct of straight. By avowing the construct of straight, I simultaneously perpetuate and create the category of straight as a performative possibility. However, because identity is constituted in communication and therefore is fluid rather than fixed, my performance of straight can always be performed differently, potentially differently constructing the category of, for example, "straight." Within the classroom, we can look to communication in an effort to understand educational identity (be that of student, teacher, raced student, gendered teacher, and so on). Both mundane and extraordinary acts of communication constitute educational identities. When we come to recognize cultural identity as constituted and negotiated through communication, we can turn to dialogue as one specific act of communication in which persons can engage to know (to know differently, to know better) cultural identity within the classroom.

FREIRE'S DIALOGUE: AN ELEMENTAL APPROACH

I am certainly not the first person to invoke Freire's dialogue in discussions of critical communication pedagogy, educational practices and methods and intercultural communication. So while I acknowledge that what I set out to do might at first glance seem as though I'm reinventing the dialogical wheel, my approach is different in the ways that it intersects dialogue, identity, and intercultural communication pedagogy. There are myriad features that I could point to as a starting point. Indeed, Freire (1970/2000) incorporates essentials such as love, humility, self-reflexion, faith in humankind, hope, and critical thinking as constitutive components of dialogue, and suggests that these, together in dialogue, produce trust and critical thinking. We see here a spiraling quality, in that some of what dialogue requires is also produced through the dialogical process. At its core, though, Freire defines dialogue as "the encounter between men [and women], mediated by the world, in order to name the world" (p. 88).

DIALOGUE AS EPISTEMOLOGICAL

To begin the discussion, I outline four specific elements of Freire's (1970/2000) notion of dialogue that are most salient for this chapter. Each can be found in his brief definition referenced above. First, dialogue is epistemological. This element of Freire's dialogue revolves around the social construction of knowledge, and the classroom as a site of such construction. To say that dialogue is epistemological is to say that it is a way of knowing—of knowing something differently, of knowing something at all. In other words, Freire distinguishes between dialogue and conversation. In his introduction to *Pedagogy of the Oppressed*, Macedo (Freire, 1970/2000) emphasizes that dialogue must be in service of the object of knowledge—the content—and not about the experiences of those engaging in dialogue. One has to strike a balance between simply celebrating experiences and ending it there, and engaging in the object of knowledge. We cannot forget to link the experience to social, political, and cultural issues, but experience is not the endpoint of the dialogical endeavor. We also cannot fall into the trap of confusing mere discussion with dialogue. Allman (2009) explains that in discussion, "people . . . articulate what they *already* [emphasis added] know or think" (p. 426). In a classroom context, discussion serves the purpose of demonstrating understanding or application of previously learned knowledge, but never an active critique or formation of knowledge itself. Hence, we can understand dialogue as epistemology, as a way of knowing. This epistemological project necessitates curiosity not only about the object of knowledge, but also the previously referenced essentials of dialogue (e.g., self-reflexion, love, humility, etc.) (Freire, 1970/2000, p. 18).

For Allman (2009), dialogue as epistemological, however, doesn't end with a focus on the object of the knowledge. Rather, it is about the participants' very relationship to knowledge. We're likely familiar with Freire's (1970/2000) concept of banking education, wherein the educator acts as depositor of knowledge for the depositories that are the students. The students then withdraw the knowledge when they need it (e.g., when taking a test), but never, in the process (if we can even call it a process), engage in active creation and reflection on that knowledge or the process. When Freire outlines banking education, he's not critiquing the method so much as he is critiquing "the teacher's relation to knowledge which now affects how the method is used" (Allman, 2009, p. 426). Banking education ignores and suppresses the intersubjective quality of knowledge, and as its direct counterpart, dialogue takes this intersubjective quality as fundamental. It not only asks us to consider the *what* of our thinking, but also the *why* and *how* of our thinking. It requires us to pose knowledge as a problem.

If we are to understand and practice dialogue as an epistemology, we must attend to its intersubjective nature and realize that it takes place in concert with others. One cannot force dialogue upon an other, nor can one engage in dialogue while that other engages in mere conversation. In dialogue, participants are politically and culturally invested in the object of knowledge, and take it seriously as "collaborative reflection and action upon the world in order to transform our understandings of the world" (Fassett and Warren, 2007, p. 54). Freire (1970/2000) writes that "at the point of encounter" with knowledge, we don't have people who are wholly unknowing (e.g., students), and we don't have people who are all-knowing (e.g., teachers). Rather, "there are only people who are attempting, together, to learn more than they now know" (p. 90). This interactive, collaborative process of problem-posing and answer-seeking (Peterson, 2009, p. 313) informs the second crucial element of dialogue: resolution and reformation of what Freire calls the "teacher-student contradiction" (Freire, 1970/2000, p. 72).

DIALOGUE AS RESOLVING THE TEACHER-STUDENT CONTRADICTION

Freire (1970/2000) describes the traditional relationship between a teacher and students as being a "contradiction" to indicate that these two roles (the role of the teacher and the role of the student) are not to be confused. That is, teachers and students are to remain in contradiction with one another—are meant to be opposed, in a sense, to one another—in order to keep their roles separate. Recall the banking method; the teachers' role is to have the knowledge and to give it to the student. The student's role is to passively accept that knowledge and to give it back, unaltered, when the teacher asks for it. The contradictory nature of this involves the poles at which teachers and students live; teachers are not to be confused with students, and students are not to be confused with teachers. One teaches, and one is taught, and that should always be the order of things. However, Freire calls for a resolution to this contradiction, and instead identifies that "through dialogue, the teacher-of-the-students and the students-of-the-teacher cease to exist and a new term emerges: teacher-student with students-teacher" (p. 80). In this way, classroom participants are simultaneously teachers and students, regardless of their role *prior to* the resolution. The function of this turn of roles, this resolution of the educational contradiction, is that the new (if you will) educational participants "become jointly responsible" for the educational process (Freire, 1970/2000, p. 80).

Seen dialogically, teacher-students and students-teacher together to create and reflect knowledge, so that both are changed in the process. Each comes to understand her/his own world, and that of others, in a way different than before dialogue. In the process, both also gain greater understanding of perspectives and interpretations of reality and of the objects of knowledge. Freire explains in *Pedagogy of Hope: Reliving Pedagogy of the Oppressed* (1992) that such a dialogical, mutual relationship between teacher-students and students-teacher does not negate the process of teaching itself—perhaps in a way we traditionally think of it—but rather, puts teaching and learning in a similar, mutually constitutive relationship. In fact, teaching and learning "both become authentically possible only when the educator's thinking . . . refuses to 'apply the brakes' to the educand's ability to think" (p. 101).

The "ability to think," here, is in fact more than an ability, but is a "right" (Freire, 1992, p. 95). Not only do students have a right to think, but they have "the right to know better than they already know . . . [and the right to share] in the production of the as-yet-nonexistent knowledge" (Freire, 1992, p. 95). Here we return to the epistemological component of dialogue, and understand that resolving the teacher-student contradiction in this way involves a respecification of the relationship to knowledge. A teacher-student's and a students-teacher's relationship with one another changes when their relationship to knowledge also changes (Allman, 2009, p. 426). While a teacher-student may be an initiator of classroom content, the meanings, perceptions, understandings of, along with reflexions about, that knowledge does not stop with the teacher-student. The students-teacher have a right to also consider that knowledge, and offer their meanings, perceptions, understandings of, and reflexions about it, in order for the teacher-student to reconsider his or her initial understandings (Freire, 1970/2000, p. 81). Just as dialogue itself is cyclical in that some of what it requires, it also produces (e.g., critical thinking), this specific component is also cyclical. Teacher-students offer their considerations of the objects of knowledge, students-teacher offer their considerations of those same objects, this (should) lead teacher-students to reconsider and expand their understandings, which should lead students-teacher to reconsider and expand their understandings, and so on and so forth. "It is this educational strategy that supports a problem-posing approach to education—an approach in which the relationship of students to teacher is, without questions, dialogical, each having something to contribute and receive" (Darder, Baltodano, and Torres, 2009, p. 3). And in that act of contribution and reception, we begin to get a sense of the third crucial element of Freire's dialogue: dialogue as a subjectifying phenomenon.

DIALOGUE AS SUBJECTIFYING

Through dialogue as an epistemological journey that resolves the teacher-student contradiction, both teacher-students and students-teacher are made into Subject. Freire (1970/2000) contrasts Subject with objects by explaining Subjects as those who think about, reflect upon, and act in their world, while objects are passively thought about or known, reflected upon, and acted upon. He further contrasts objects with *objective*. The latter, he explains is the concrete reality of existence, the objects that are analyzed in the dialogical process. This is necessary, he goes on to note, in order for liberation to happen. We have to make the world an object of analysis in order for critical reflection to take place. The "world," in this case, is the object about which we dialogue to come to know. "There would be no human action," argues Freire,

> if there were no objective reality, no world to be the "not I" of the person and to challenge them; just as there would be no human action if humankind where not a "project," if he or she were not able to transcend himself or herself, if one were not able to perceive reality and understand it in order to transform it. (p. 53)

The problem with banking education is that it is the students that are objectified, in this sense, and so rather than transcending the self, students are made into a passive, objective reality. The character of the *person* is what is, ultimately, filed away. Students lose their personhood in banking education, and epistemological pursuits are reduced to commodity acquisition.

Our ontological vocation—the function of our being—is to become more fully human, to become and be a Subject (emphasis on the capital "S") who thinks about, reflects upon, and acts in the world (Freire, 1970/2000). Dialogical encounters allow people to create the world, but in order to be a creator, one has to adopt and be recognized by others as a Subject who acts. Through dialogue, we have the opportunity and ability to name the world, and in so naming, to create our selves—our identities. Dialogue is what leads to critical consciousness, and it is critical consciousness that makes Subjects out of objects. "Dialogue is thus an existential necessity" (Freire, 1970/2000, p. 88). To be more specific to practices, Freire (1974) goes so far as to critique elementary school primers because they tell what is happening in pictures, etc., rather than letting the language come from the people using the primers and learning the language, thus objectifying rather than subjectifying (p. 43). When persons are able to participate in their own subjectification process through their coming to critical consciousness, they simultaneously enact praxis, the final critical component in my discussion of Freire's dialogue.

DIALOGUE AS/AND PRAXIS

A key to transformation and liberation for Freire (1970/2000) is praxis. In outlining education as "a practice of freedom," Freire calls upon praxis as "the means by which men and women deal critically and creatively with reality and discover how to participate in the transformation of their world" (p. 34). This brings to bear the duality of the subject and object. Freire writes that authentic praxis is only possible in the dialectic of subjective and objective. That is, Subjects, in the process of cognizing objects, engage in praxis through the process of dialogue. In keeping with the cyclical quality we've seen in Freire's dialogue thus far, he explains that the WORD is the essence of dialogue. It is not simply an instrument of dialogue—not simply the way dialogue takes place—but is a constituent of dialogue itself. This WORD has two dimensions: reflection and action. Every WORD, then, is also a praxis, and every praxis is a WORD.

While this is just a brief description of dialogue, it provides an appropriate point to specifically discuss the intersectionality of these four elements (dialogue as epistemological, dialogue as complicating the teacher-student contradiction, dialogue as subjectifying, and dialogue as praxis). Doing so will not only provide a broader conceptualization of praxis, but will identify the ways that these elements work together in the service of and within the process of dialogue.

Freire (1970/2000) teaches us that the communicative act of dialogue is a condition for revolution and transformation. This transformation comes about through praxis, which is "reflection and action upon the world to transform it" (p. 51). Praxis here is the source of knowledge creation (epistemology) (p. 100). Such knowledge creation can only come about by human beings engaged in their vocation to become more fully human (subjectification). In a pedagogical situation, the resolution of the teacher-student contradiction through dialogue funds this process of subjectification. Indeed, both teacher-students and students-teacher have a right and a responsibility to participate in praxis. As Freire writes, if leaders deny the oppressed their praxis, the leaders deny their own praxis, as well (p. 126). It is in the process of reflexion that human beings become more fully human. Their very Subjecthood—their very humanity—is a condition of their being ". . . *in* a situation. And they *will be more* the more they not only critically reflect upon their existence but critically act upon it" (p. 109). Teacher-students have a responsibility *as teacher-students* to engage in Freirean dialogue with students-teacher. Darder (2009) argues that those who deny students this important opportunity for praxis—and all that the process and action of praxis bring—engage in "disabling the heart, minds, and bodies of their students" (p. 568).

An example may help to clarify how these elements work together. In introductory intercultural communication courses (and even in more advanced-level courses), a popular reading to introduce whiteness is McIntosh's (1989) "White privilege: Unpacking the Invisible Knapsack." I have assigned this article in several of my own courses, and invited the discussion about the article to be guided by both my own and the students-teacher orientation towards it (dialogue as resolving the teacher-student contradiction). In these courses, students-teacher (not necessarily those who appear and/or self-identify as white), often gravitate to item #26: "I can choose blemish cover or bandages in 'flesh' color and have them more or less match my skin" (p. 11). This seemingly mundane choice to have "flesh" color bandages strikes many students-teachers off guard, and oftentimes leads many students-teacher to differently consider the other items on the list, as well as to generate their own lists of the privileges they have at their disposal. This, in turn, oftentimes leads students-teacher—particularly those who appear or self-identify as white—to begin to engage the concept of whiteness not in a defensive way, but in a critical, invitational way. They begin to see their role in the macro-structure and micro-practices of whiteness differently than they did before (and thus to engage dialogue as the process of subjectification). They differently—more, better—understand whiteness on a ubiquitous level, and so are able to chip away at whiteness on a systematic level (dialogue as epistemology). While their obvious behaviors might not be changed immediately, they begin the process of critical reflection, which is likely to lead to a change in behavior (dialogue as praxis). What makes this important is that Freire (1970/2000) says, "Critical reflection is also action" (p. 128). As impactful are the ways my own critical reflection and actions are changed as a result of dialoguing with students-teacher about their experiences with whiteness and the meanings they make of McIntosh (dialogue as resolving the teacher-student contradiction).

In the next section, I argue that those of us in intercultural communication pedagogy are uniquely situated to utilize dialogue as a method in the Freirean sense. I begin by situating Freire specifically within intercultural communication.

PAULO FREIRE AND INTERCULTURAL COMMUNICATION

Though we may never get a clear sense of how Freire conceptualized intercultural communication, intercultural communication pedagogy, or even the concept of "culture," we can certainly get an indirect sense from *Pedagogy of the Oppressed* (1970/2000). This is perhaps most evident in his dialectic of cultural invasion (as an element of the theory of anti-dialogical action) and cultural synthesis (as an element of the theory of dialogical action). In explicating the former (and in drawing upon Louis Althusser), he outlines "culture as a superstructure which can maintain 'remnants' of the past alive in the substructure undergoing revolutionary transformation" (p. 159). Culture, then, is an overarching concept, with a sense of temporality similar to Schrag, and something that persons work with and within to create social change. A thorough read of his work would lead to his understanding of culture as being a fluid, changing, and changeable amalgamation of practices, habits, worldviews, orientations toward the world, language, histories, and so on of a group of people. Within the theory of anti-dialogical action (and specifically, through cultural invasion), oppressors (dominant culture) work hegemonically (and sometimes overtly) to secure the oppressed as adopting the worldviews of dominant culture, and so see themselves (the oppressed) as *necessarily* oppressed. Within the theory of dialogical action (and specifically, through cultural synthesis), the oppressors and oppressed work together, dialogically, to create a sense of themselves anew, as part of a shared culture with changed worldviews so that they further their vocation of becoming more fully human, together. In the process, oppressors and oppressed are subjectified and become cocreators of and coactors within their culture.

IMPLICATIONS OF A FREIREAN DIALOGUE FOR INTERCULTURAL COMMUNICATION PEDAGOGY

As an enterprise concerned with the interrogation of cultural identity, cultural constructs, and the constitutive feature of communication, the project of intercultural communication is in an ideal position to further explore and utilize Freirean dialogue. In part, this is because the intercultural communication classroom presents unique challenges and opportunities, such as: wrestling with the common desire to "fix" culture into a series of labels based on race, ethnicity, gender, social class, ability, sexual orientation, and so on (and so the need to balance the functions of labels with the fluidity of experiences), as well as the tendency to equate *culture* with ethnicity and/or race, though most (even stable) definitions of "culture" wouldn't limit the construct to such categories. I identify four primary implications of dialogue for intercultural communication pedagogy. First, engaging Freirean dialogue reminds us that our goal is not to form friendships with students, in the sense that we become simply casual buddies and risk taking advantage of one another. The goal is to engage in "a process of sensitive and thorough inquiry" (Fassett and Warren, 2007, p. 55). Friendships with students might be an outcome of such a process, but should not be the goal of the process, if we take *friendship* to be of the casual sort. However, Rawlins (2000) does well in reminding us that teaching can be a mode of friendship, in the sense that "the ideals and practices of friendship can provide an edifying ethic for the interactions and relationships of educators and students" (p. 6). The type of friendship that Rawlins advocates as practiced in the classroom can be demonstrated through dialogue. The qualities of *philia* (a genuine care for an other), equality ("equal validity and common humanity" [p. 8]), and mutuality (an investment in the relationship as friendship) all find counterparts in Freirean dialogue, particularly in the element of subjectification.

Second, engaging in dialogue calls and challenges us to examine our intentions as educators specifically, and as communicators broadly. We have to ask ourselves why we make the decisions we do, why we plan the classroom lessons we plan, what we hope to accomplish through the practices in which we engage. Freire (1970/2000) contrasts cultural invasion with cultural synthesis, the latter being a component of his theory of dialogical action. In cultural invasion (a component of the theory of anti-dialogical action), explains Freire, participants (in this case, oppressors) invade the world of others, starting from their own world. In other words, there is an imposition of oppressors upon the oppressed, of one who assumes power over an other, and projects that power from a place of self-centeredness in the suppression of the other's being. This is how educators proceed within the banking system; they know what they think students should know, and simply *give* this knowledge to students without any regard for the worldview, thoughts, reflections, etc. of the students. However, in cultural synthesis, there's a working together through dialogue. The object of knowledge is investigated by a joining of the worlds of the oppressed and oppressors, or teacher-students and students-teacher. The actors come "to learn, with the people, about the people's world" (Freire, 1970/2000, p. 180). In *Pedagogy of Hope: Reliving Pedagogy of the Oppressed*, Freire (1992) reminds us that the democratic, dialogic processes do not permit "teachers . . . to impose on their pupils their own 'reading of the world,'" and use that to frame the content and how that content is approached and investigated (p. 96). This makes dialogue all the more important, then, in challenging us to question and critically reflect upon our intentions in our communicative (and pedagogical) lives.[3]

Third, as critical intercultural scholars and educators, we are required to take seriously the partnership we have with students-teachers in a progressive, liberatory pedagogy. Freire (1970/2000) argues that dialogue is a process of unveiling the world, but this cannot be something someone does *to* or *for* another. If teacher-students attempt to do the unveiling, and assume that students simply accept the unveiling, they rob students of their right to begin from a place of what they know. Even more so, they do not have the opportunity to even *realize* that they know things, and that the things they know matter. Quite the opposite, "They call themselves ignorant and say the 'professor' is the one who has knowledge and to whom they should listen. . . ." (p. 63). Freire identifies as a problem those who "glorify democracy . . . and discourse on humanism," yet do not engage in authentic dialogue (p. 91). He describes dialogue as a "horizontal relationship between persons" (Freire, 1974, p. 83). This resists and negates common top-down models rooted in the banking system, and instead utilizes a partnership model, understanding educational participants as co-constructors of knowledge and as coinvestigators of the world and the situations of those in the world.

Finally, when we believe in and engage dialogue in the classroom, we cannot just pay lip service to the literature's call that we come to know our students as whole people, rather than just who they are in their roles as "students." While bell hooks (1994) is perhaps one of the most prominent scholars to call for a more "whole-istic" pedagogy—understanding educational participants as whole people—Freire (1970/2000) can certainly contribute to this discourse of whole-ism without slipping into the discourse of completion. He sets up dialogue as a way to bridge seemingly vast and uncrossable ideological divides. Dialogue's capacity for "loving inquiry and unflinching self-reflexivity" has the power to "render difference meaningful" (p. 56). In crossing this divide through dialogue, we are better equipped and positioned to understand where cultural difference comes from, how cultural difference is made and actualized, and how our very personhood—both teacher-students and students-teacher—is constructed in and through cultural difference. This involves dialoguing with students-teacher about their cultural identifications, as education is an "interactive process based on the history, experience, and culture of the student" (Peterson, 2009, p. 313). Freire (1992) is worth quoting at length here:

> [I] insist once more on the imperative need of the progressive educator to familiarize herself or himself with the syntax and semantics of the [students]—to understand how those persons do their reading of the world, to perceive that "craftiness" of theirs so indispensable to the culture of a resistance that is in the process of formation, without which they cannot defend themselves from the violence to which they are subjected. . . . Unless educators expose themselves to the [students'] culture across the board, their discourse will hardly be heard by anyone but themselves. (p. 91).

As Orbe (personal communication, June 24, 2011) points out, one of the unique features of the intercultural classroom is that it is the site at which culture, cultural difference, and identity work at two not-always-distinguishable levels: (1) identity forms the course content, and (2) students-teacher and teacher-student "embody cultural identities/differences while in the process of learning about these very same matters." What Freirean dialogue offers intercultural communication pedagogy is multifaceted. First, it offers us a way to co-construct classroom culture, as classroom participants (students-teacher and teacher-student), in engaging in dialogue, develop unique ways of understanding one another, habits of classroom interaction, a past/present/future, a classroom identity (dialogue as resolving the teacher-student contradiction). Second, it offers us space to speak across and about the lived difference—and the lived sameness—experienced by classroom participants as *interdependent* and *co-constitutive* lived experiences (dialogue as epistemology). Third, Freirean dialogue offers intercultural communication pedagogy an opening in which to enact performances of difference that attend to Warren's (2008) desire to recognize difference "as a way to see and talk about the very nature of subjectivity" (p. 292). Finally, it offers us a way to make different matter—to make it important, and to make it material (Warren, 2008, p. 292).

IMPLICATIONS FOR UNDERSTANDING IDENTITY THROUGH DIALOGUE

More broadly than in intercultural communication pedagogy, we are able to use Freirean dialogue to understand identity within the field of intercultural communication. This step is important in connecting what happens in the classroom with what happens in our daily lives, and in the field in which we study.

First, we are called to be cautious of reducing identity to a celebration of experience. In his introduction to the thirtieth anniversary edition of *Pedagogy of the Oppressed*, Macedo (2000) expresses the tendency of "overindulging" in experience, and in so doing, we "fail to move beyond a notion of difference structured in polarizing binarisms and uncritical appeals to the discourse of experience" (p. 18). The danger here is in equating experience with voice; that is, the telling of our experience does not mean we have reached, or are even approaching, critical consciousness. There is not much to dialogue about in experience itself; the discourse of experience must necessarily be situated within a larger sociocultural context. When we can move through experience and go beyond it through dialogue, we have the opportunity to "understand further the richness of . . . differences and the value of what [we] share in common" (Giroux, 2000, p. 210).

Second, we must engage in cultural self-discovery and evolution. Remember that dialogue incites a cyclical process with the WORD. That is, dialogue is constituted by the WORD, and also constitutes the WORD. The word here ceases to be some kind of abstraction, and instead, allows people to "discover themselves and their potential as they give names to the things around them. As Freire puts it, each individual wins back the right to *say his or her own word, to name the world*" (Macedo, 2000, pp. 32–33, italics in original). In this process of naming the world and discovering the self or selves, we recognize the self in context. In working together to name the world—to name our world—we come to an understanding of the situatedness of individuals. Allman (2009) explains that "in dialogue everyone helps each other, and is helped, to explore the historical and material origins of their thought" (p. 427), and these origins are ultimately tied to a sense of self and identity.

Third, we see an effort to focus on ascription of identity rather than avowal of identity. Related to the above, not only are we naming the world, but are also naming the self. Freire (1970/2000) writes that "dialogue does not impose, does not manipulate, does not domesticate, does not 'sloganize'" (p. 168). Through dialogue, Subjects together create space to further come into being as Subjects, subjects that ascribe an identity for the self.

Finally, we realize an empowered selfhood through the intersubjective constitution of identity. Darder, Baltodano, and Torres (2009) turn to dialogue as a method to develop "critical social consciousness" and as a working towards "an emancipatory educational process" committed to empowerment (p. 13). The ways that Subjects meet in cooperation in order to transform the world—to actualize praxis—rather than one Subject conquering another (which, indeed, would not be a Subject in the first place), creates the intersubjective identity formation process. In the "cooperation" component of Freire's theory of dialogical action, the dialogical Subject recognizes that the *I* and the *thou* are interdependent, and *I* would not exist without *thou* (Buber, 2004). Macedo (2000) points to the power of dialogue to bring students—to create paths for students to come—"to a new awareness of selfhood and begin to look critically at the social situation in which they find themselves, [and to] take the initiative in acting to transform the society that has denied them this opportunity of participation. Education is once again a subversive force" (p. 29).

PROBLEMATIZING DIALOGUE

Dialogue is not without its complications, which I address here. We have to understand that if we take dialogue in a more traditional sense of verbal exchange, we fall into the trap of assuming it to be a universal communication construct. How can we rescue dialogue as a position, rather than merely an act of verbal exchange? How can we understand it as a philosophical approach without falling into a position of necessary and required verbal participation? We have to sincerely respect and accept silence as a component of dialogue, especially since there exist various cultural meanings of silence. If we can understand performative silence as a contribution to dialogue, and in so doing, understand silence as an invitation to respectful and critical listening, then we move towards a more holistic dialogue.[4] We also have to remember that embedded within Freire's critique of the banking system wasn't so much a critique of the method, but a critique of the relationship to knowledge. This leaves open the possibility for a liberatory, progressive model of what initially may seem to be banking education (though, admittedly, I struggle to paint a picture of this model).

Additionally, Freire assumed the student to be in a position of powerlessness (or, at least, a position of less power). However, we know from folks like Foucault that power is a fluid phenomenon, never at once located in a singular position, but rather, exists in relationship. Like Schrag's (1986) identity, power is intersubjective. The implications of this for dialogue are that teacher-students, who might generally be assumed to begin dialogue, could at any given moment be in a position of less power. This is especially true as the face of the academy is changing (albeit ever so slowly) and more minority persons are in faculty positions.[5] If we can take seriously the ways dialogue can resolve the teacher-student contradiction, and understand dialogue as "constituted by particular assertions and an accumulation of comments, a negotiation of precise moments located in ongoing relationships and discourse" (Simpson, 2008, p. 187), then we can understand dialogue as being more than what happens in a single class period, begun by one specific person. In this sense, dialogue doesn't have a beginning or an end, but is a continual process of communicative negotiation and renegotiation. It is a process that involves multiple layers of identity, of political agency, of institutional constructs, of mundane communicative acts, converging in never isolated but always already connected dialogical moments. Dialogue here does not exist in a vacuum, but like all communication—and therefore, all identity—is situated in a context of power relations and cultural contestations, including positions of otherness (be that on the part of faculty or student). Even within the dialogic classroom, power can never be eliminated. Rather, power can become at once the object about which participants dialogue *and at the same time* the condition under which dialogue happens. As a classroom culture is cocreated by participants, those same participants will inevitably feel varying degrees of power as both a source upon which individuals members can draw, and a force weighing down upon individual members. For example, in my previous reference to McIntosh's 1989 "Invisible Knapsack" article, participants in that dialogue who appear to be or who may self-identify as white might feel in a position of powerlessness as they are coming to understand the system of whiteness, and participants who appear to be or who may self-identify as racial minorities might feel in a position of power as they enact a different performance of voice in the discourse of whiteness.[6]

CONCLUSION: DIALOGUE, IDENTITY, AND INTERCULTURAL COMMUNICATION PEDAGOGY

I return now to the three questions I posed at the beginning of this chapter, and though I've addressed them throughout, here I attempt to give a concise response to each:

(1) In what ways can we understand classroom participants' cultural identities through engaging in Freirean dialogue, both as educators and as researchers?

Dialogue as epistemological directs us towards coming to understand identity in the first place. Through dialogue, we can establish a sense (even if a contingent sense) of identity, that of ourselves and others. Moreover, if dialogue is the process by which human beings are made into Subjects, then it's through dialogue that we come to know our Subjectivity, our identity. We develop our personhood through dialogue, and so in the intercultural communication classroom, we can wrestle with the tensions of Subjectivity through dialogue. Through that wrestling, classroom participants can get a sense of the messiness and slipperiness of identity, moving through and with identity to situate it within larger group identifications—or, cultural identity. Furthermore, classroom participants understand how cultural identity is not as easy or simple as saying, for example, "People in Western nations tend to place more value on the individual than they do on the group."

(2) What can dialogue tell us about identity?

We have to have an active relationship to knowledge creation—not just knowledge reception—in order to understand the process of identity negotiation and the intersubjective nature of both knowledge and our sense of self. If we have this active relationship with knowledge, then we are able to use dialogue as a method to get a sense of dialogue as a theoretical framework for identity negotiation. That is, we are able to intersubjectively engage with one another (through dialogue) about the intersubjective nature of our cultural identities (that is, their dialogic nature).

(3) How can these concepts work synergistically to inform intercultural communication pedagogy?

When we attend to the Subjectivity our cultural identities and engage in an active relationship with knowledge creation, we can understand Freirean dialogue as informing intercultural communication pedagogy in poignant ways. First, friendship as a classroom ethic (à la Rawlins, 2000) engenders subjectification and moves toward creating a sa*fer* space (because we know we can never be absolutely sure that a classroom is a completely safe space for all participants) wherein classroom participants can broach sometimes-contentious topics involving cultural identity (such as oppression and cultural domination)—dialogue as subjectification. Second, increased self-reflexivity through dialogue on the part of teacher-students effectively promotes a resolution of the teacher-student contradiction, as teachers inevitably understand students' roles as also-teachers, and their own roles as also-students. Third, engaging in problem-posing education through dialogue turns the classroom into an epistemological enterprise, rather than a banking enterprise. Finally, making difference matter (Warren, 2008) engages the process of naming the world, and as such, enacts a sort of praxis.

While the field of intercultural communication is changing as our political and social contexts shifts, we can still work to understand differently methods that have been debated and utilized for decades. The impact of Freire and his notion of dialogue has had a long-lasting impact on pedagogues, particularly in the ways it helps us to appreciate identity constitution and negotiation within the intercultural communication classroom. Simpson (2008) acknowledges that "intercultural communication routinely calls for a kind of dialogical positioning, one which makes demands on how students and teachers see self and others" (p. 182). If we can understand the elements of Freire's dialogue (dialogue as epistemology, as a resolution to the teacher-student contradiction, as subjectifying, and as praxiological), we are better able to also understand the theoretical implications and practical applications of dialogue for understanding.

NOTES

1. For a more detailed account of Schrag's identity and communicative praxis, see Pensoneau-Conway and Toyosaki (2011a).

2. I use "discourse" in place of Schrag's (1986) "language" for two reasons: (1) I read "discourse" to include not only verbal language, but also nonverbal language. (2) Schrag supports the notion of more-than-language. He argues, "Discourse is here understood as a [multifaceted] event, comprised of speaking, writing, and language" (pp. 33–34). He includes nonverbal communication by suggesting, "Speaking . . . also includes the deployment of gestural meaning and articulations through body motility. . . . All of these features of speaking, writing, and language are relevant to discourse as an event of communicative praxis" (p. 34).

3. I point the reader to Jennifer S. Simpson's 2008 article, "'What do they think of us?': The pedagogical practices of cross-cultural communication, misrecognition, and hope." Her article is a reflexive exercise in questioning her own pedagogical assumptions, intentions, and interpretations of classroom dialogue.

4. I thank Richie Neil Hao for this insight into silence.

5. I thank Kent Ono for this insight.

6. However, I continue to emphasize the fluidity of power dynamics. This is merely an example of how power *might* play out in this situation. Without specifically talking to classroom participants about their felt understandings of power here, I can only make assumptions that may or may not be on target as I work to example how power could be salient in a dialogic intercultural communication classroom.

FOUR

(Academic) Families of Choice

Queer Relationality, Mentoring, and Critical Communication Pedagogy

Krishna Pattisapu and Bernadette Marie Calafell

> From shared critical dissatisfaction we arrive at collective potentiality.
> —Muñoz, 2009, p. 189

I came to work with John T. Warren by accident. The faculty mentor with whom I had elected to work during my master's program accepted a job at another university, forcing me to search for a new adviser who could nurture me as I developed my academic voice. As a queer woman of color, I have experienced great difficulty in building connections with mentors who understand and appreciate my experiences in academia. The task of finding another mentor with whom I could have such a powerful relationship seemed daunting.

During the first class I took with him—an introduction to critical communication pedagogy—I began to see John as a strong white ally whose investigations of how whiteness and heterosexism operate in pedagogy enthralled me. He spoke of cross-racial alliances in nuanced ways, echoing scholars of color who have noted the difficulties inherent in such alliances (Allen, Orbe, and Olivas, 1999; Calafell, 2010a; Carrillo Rowe, 2008, 2009; Pérez and Goltz, 2010). As he discussed issues of democratization in schooling (Alexander and Warren, 2002) and whiteness (Warren and Hytten, 2004), John asserted that as a white man, he could never truly get what it means to be a person of color in academia. Instead, like Johnson and Bhatt (2003), he sought ways to utilize his privilege strategically to fight against institutionalized oppression. John was the first white man whom I felt was truly committed to hearing my voice and to helping me articulate my stories.

Eventually, I asked John to be my adviser. I was finally able to release the skepticism with which I have regarded so many white allies. Before John, I had eased too many times into relationships with white colleagues and mentors for whom the concept of coalition involved blatant disregard of difference with harmony as an ultimate goal (Johnson and Bhatt, 2003). Carefully, I stepped toward John, learning to trust him as a genuine white ally. John advocated for queer students and students of color in so many venues. He defended students of color in conversations on the disciplinary listserv and raised difficult questions about how whiteness and heterosexism operate in a popular race critic's arguments. John and I inched toward one another, our difference constituting our complicated coalition and our queerness bonding us together. Like Pérez and Goltz (2010), John and I " . . . challenge[d] and embrace[d] these tensions in this slippery politicized space of coalition—a stance that navigates the ongoing negotiation of critique, love, and difference" (p. 258). John was the academic family I chose, and he chose me back.

We built a durable and multidimensional coalition. John and I served together on committees, working to incorporate critical approaches into training programs and diversity initiatives. Regularly, John called upon me and other students and colleagues of color to speak alongside him. We lifted each other up in the most difficult moments, strengthening each other from the inside out. Our coalition was give-and-take; John nurtured me as a blossoming critical scholar and I supplemented his teachings about institutionalized racism, sexism, and heterosexism with narratives from my own life. He let me speak beside him as an equal, with a perspective that complemented and complicated his own. We became interconnected through our alliance, able to see more together than we could see alone (Johnson and Bhatt, 2003).

When I graduated from my master's program, I honored John at a small commencement ceremony presented by our campus's queer resource center. I spoke of how John had served as a strong queer mentor, showering me with the constructive criticism, love, and support that had helped me to articulate my academic voice. When I faced the most resistance from the racist and heterosexist academic system, I sat in John's office staring down at the colorful laces on his sneakers. Sometimes I sucked back tears. Sometimes I let them flow. And sometimes John cried with me, sharing in the *complexity of my tears* (Allen et al., 1999). We cried the kind of tears that flow from a shared struggle with no end in sight, but which felt a little more bearable when we fought together. That afternoon I gave him a rainbow graduation tassel to symbolize the multiple roles he had fulfilled for me as a teacher, mentor, and queer academic family member. I gave John the rainbow tassel because my accomplishments did not belong only to me—I shared them with him. We built them *together*.

John suggested only one potential doctoral adviser who would be right for me—Bernadette Calafell. He introduced me to Bernadette's scholarship—evocative, poetic, and confrontational in ways that prevent readers from being complicit with oppression. Quickly, I knew I wanted Bernadette to take me under her wing, to help me become a queer, feminist scholar of color who writes and speaks unapologetically about marginalization in academia. I hungered for the opportunity to find community in our shared brownness and queerness, in our desire to use our own voices to push back against erasure. I had learned most of what I knew about culture and communication from white and heterosexual allies; like Calafell (2010b), I awaited an opportunity to theorize *shared* experiences with racism and heterosexism. I wanted to know what Carrillo Rowe (2009) meant when she said that she *became* a queer woman of color through alliances with other queer women of color.

To my delight, Bernadette and her colleagues accepted me into their academic family. Although my heart ached to leave John behind, I knew we had built a lifelong coalition. As my academic family of choice, John provided me with the support I needed as a graduate student in a system that works hard to marginalize and erase my body and my voice. His bravery and considerable accomplishments in the face of overwhelming adversity gave me the courage to push through even the most discouraging times. I knew he would always be there to support me, that he would always catch my heavy heart before it hit the ground.

In this chapter, Bernadette and I chart our shared pedagogical experiences as queer women of color in academia through our relationship with John T. Warren. We draw from the work of identity and pedagogy scholars in communication to highlight the complexity of our cross-racial queer coalitions with John and with each other. We speak alongside critical intercultural communication and communication pedagogy scholars who assert that coalitions are therapeutic, imbued with privilege, and occur across contexts. The concept of queer relationality frames the examination of our experiences and provides opportunities to theorize the possibility of queer futurity in pedagogical and intercultural communication studies.

González (2010) charts the ways disciplinary beginnings of intercultural communication, often created limited definitions of the field. These definitions, in many cases, based in social scientific traditions, often excluded the work of scholars of color. Furthermore, Nakayama and Halualani (2010) in the *Handbook of Critical Intercultural Communication*, argue for the centrality of a critical perspective to the field of intercultural communication. They acknowledge that a challenge for a critical project is to "create new tools and ways of knowing" (p. 596). In this chapter, we work to meet their challenge by bring critical work in studies of identities based in performance, rhetoric, and queer theory, to the fold of intercultural communication. We urge theories of identities in intercultural communication to account for the intersectional privileges and oppressions inherent in such coalitions. By speaking performatively both together and separately, we lift our voices in support of studies of identities in communication that reflect our experiences and the experiences of queer of color in academia.

COALITIONS, ALLIANCES, AND DIALOGUE

In 1981, Anzaldúa and Moraga initiated the first academic dialogue about alliances between "radical women of color" in their feminist anthology *This Bridge Called My Back: Writings by Radical Women of Color*. The authors sought to expand the predominantly white, heterosexual, upper-class feminist movement of the 1970s by emphasizing the importance of coalitions between women across race, sexual, class, national, and linguisticlines. Contributors to the anthology argued that in order to understand and work against oppression, women must reach across identity lines to form stronger, more inclusive coalitions.

Nearly thirty years since Anzaldúa and Moraga (1981) issued this call, critical intercultural communication scholars have just begun to theorize notions of alliance, coalition, and dialogue in pedagogical contexts. Recent identity scholarship presents alliance as an ideal mode of illuminating and transforming experiences with oppression in academia. Through alliances with one another, scholars examine experiences with oppression in ways they cannot alone (Allen et al., 1999; Carrillo Rowe, 2008, 2009; Johnson and Bhatt, 2003; Pérez and Goltz, 2010). Through these alliances, scholars' can understand identities as relational and co-constructed, and engage in critical examination of how intersecting identities construct pedagogical experiences differently (Alexander and Warren, 2002; Carrillo Rowe, 2008, 2009; Johnson and Bhatt, 2003; Pérez and Goltz, 2010).

Alliances can transform oppressive pedagogical contexts by creating possibilities for doing pedagogy differently. Johnson and Bhatt (2003) utilize their privileged race and gender identities strategically in order to become more effective pedagogues (p. 241). Queer alliances open spaces for "queer futurity" through which scholars can re-imagine pedagogical contexts (Pérez and Goltz, p. 266). Although alliances are only one approach to pedagogical transformation, they present us with opportunities to "decolonize love" and to create new representations of ourselves (Carrillo Rowe, 2009, p. 6). Through critical examinations of their similar-but-different pedagogical experiences, Alexander and Warren (2002) push back against invisibility and deploy genuine dialogue as narrative therapy.

Critical intercultural communication scholars understand alliances as contextual, shifting, and multidimensional. Carrillo Rowe (2008) theorizes *differential belonging*, which contends that although alliances often involve great deals of intimacy, they manifest in different ways across contexts (p. 28). Alexander (2005) asserts that his intersectional identities present challenges to alliance-building with black and queer students. Similarly, Pérez and Goltz (2010) rely on their alliance with one another to be more successful pedagogues of race, gender, and sexuality to audiences. For many scholars, using alliances to foreground specific aspects of identities can serve as effective pedagogical tools.

Despite their illuminating and transformative potential, alliances are not without complications. Power inequities threaten the efficacy of coalitions and can reify the same oppressive structures such alliances seek to dismantle. Scholars negate the common idea that alliances are simple and harmonious, seeking instead to illuminate how scholars negotiate intersecting privileged and oppressed identities as they form alliances. Alliances do not rely on undermining difference, but function as a "slippery politicized space" wherein scholars critically examine how differences operate within alliances (Pérez and Goltz, 2010, p. 262). Calafell (2010b) contends that the insistence on coalitions often silences marginalized voices even further by positioning them in direct dialogue with whiteness (p. 244). People of color who resist coalitions in exchange for opportunities to talk amongst themselves often face accusations of exclusivity (p. 244).

In order to push back against these power imbalances, authors insist that alliances follow rules to ensure mutual respect and full recognition of others' experiences. Chávez (2011) asserts that as groups work together to achieve political mobility, they must be fully aware of what is at stake for one another in order to be most effective. Jones (2010) argues that "intersectional reflexivity" must be used when forging alliances; meaning that stakeholders must recognize and name their spaces of disempowerment and privilege. The most effective alliances require that all parties have deep support for one another, are fully engaged, and respectful (Allen et al., 1999; Carrillo Rowe, 2008, 2009; Pérez and Goltz, 2010). Alliances can fail even when individuals follow these rules. However, failed alliances can yield valuable insights about the way power and privilege operate in relationships across contexts (Carrillo Rowe, 2009).

Woven through these themes is the notion that alliances are essentially about love. Hooks (2001) theorizes love as a space of possibility, change, and transformation. Calafell (2007a) writes about love in the process of mentoring, based in reciprocal alliances that acknowledge the multilayered and nuanced levels of power. Authors' multidimensional relationships as teachers, scholars, and close friends create a sense of familial closeness and promote deep investments in one another's experiences (Allen et al., 1999; Carrillo Rowe, 2008, 2009; Johnson and Bhatt,

2003; Pérez and Goltz, 2010). A commitment to cultivating familial love through alliances requires all parties to examine power dynamics with care and concern, never forgetting that their first and most important obligation is to one another. However, as Carrillo Rowe (2008) notes, multidimensional and shifting identities complicate feminist alliances; to create more inclusive critical alliances, feminists must fully consider the ideologies that underlie notions of belonging (p. 28).

THE POSSIBILITIES OF QUEER RELATIONALITY

Queer relationality, which we locate within the realm of queer pedagogy, manifests itself through the mentoring and classroom experiences discussed in this chapter. In defining queer relationality we locate this within the queer use of family. The term "family" itself is often used to refer to a common queer connection (i.e., "he's family"). In using the term, we draw upon the multilayered meanings behind it rather than recentering a potentially heteronormative and oppressive interpretation. As queer women of color we understand the need to often construct families of choice, a practice which also occurs in an academic life, though in many cases driven by a different politics. Muñoz (2009) traces what he terms the anti-relational aspect in a history of queer scholarship, instead arguing for the necessity and importance of relational bonds as a space of "collective political becoming" (p. 189). Similarly, we desire the politics of relation. In theorizing queer relationality we draw on Carrillo Rowe (2005) whose work on feminist alliances across difference argues for a politics of relation. This belonging, Carrillo Rowe argues, is motivated by desire for connection. Commenting on relationality, Blackman (2011), drawing on the work of Simonden, writes "that our individuation is always relational and therefore plural. In other words our very sense of interiority emerges through our relations with other humans and non-human and in that sense we are always more than one and less than many" (p. 184). Each of these scholars speaks to the importance of working toward coalitional politics and a move toward theorizing relationality.

We trace our queer academic families of choice and the hope they offer for the present and the future. We seek to understand and start to theorize how these families also inform our conceptions of identities individually and collectively. Again, our understandings of identities are based in critical and performative dimensions that forefront issues such as power, context, and relations. Thus, our queer families of choice inform not only how we view our identities, but also how our identities are informed by the collectivity of these families. At the center is dynamism, which continuously shifts and contours these identities. These families are homeplaces of reinvention and reinvigoration.

Like Carrillo Rowe (2005) we imagine a relationality driven by desire. We base that desire in the desire for a queer future based in possibility. Explaining queer futurity, Muñoz (2009) writes:

> Queerness is not yet here. Queerness is an ideality . . . queerness exists for us as an ideality that can be distilled from the past and used to imagine a future. The future is queerness's domain. Queerness is a structuring and educated mode of desiring that allows us to see and feel beyond the quagmire of the present. (p. 1)

Muñoz elaborates on queer potentialities: "Concrete utopias are relational to historically situated struggles, a collectivity that is actualized or potential. . . . Concrete utopias are the realm of educated hope" (p. 3). Our queer academic families of choice gesture toward the desire for queer futurity. Blackman (2011) argues: "The concept of queer family allows us to imagine the ties and connections that bind us inter-generationally, and therefore point towards the communities that circulate across space and time" (p. 185).

In theorizing queer relationality, we understand the tensions between identities and collectivities. As queer people we feel the violence of heteronormativity (Yep, 2003a). Similarly, Hill Collins (2008) argues that African American women share a collectivity that is based in shared histories of oppression, but the ways that oppression is experienced is colored differently. In this nuancing is the potential for an honoring of the individual and the collective. Furthermore, we seek to complicate understandings of queerness in ways that are attentive to race, class, gender and other possible markers of difference. Like Cohen (2005), we desire a more complex intersectional queerness that could lend itself to coalitions. As Pérez and Goltz (2010) acknowledge,

> We cannot ever divorce ourselves completely from those strategic and stifling identities, nor collapse or erase the different ways we inhabit history, privilege, and space. Our identities are sutured to bodies that move through the world (and our personal discussions) differently, invoking and contesting differing histories, politics, and significations. Still, our queer alignment grounds our search for a politicized "us," connection along the lines of queer, race, and gender politics. (p. 250)

Similarly, McIntosh (2011) writes of a feminist aesthetic based in a desire for feminist connections across differences that do not downplay these differences, but instead ask that we be accountable to the ways privilege creates spaces that must be affectively acknowledged in the process of coming together. We imagine a queer relationality, a central aspect of our queer pedagogy, as the ambiente—"a common space arising from a reciprocity of praxis" (Richmond Ellis, 2000, p. 3). The ambiente "can be experienced only collectively, even if this collectively is initially private. Reading the ambienteis hence less an act of 'outing' than of 'joining' in a process of generating a social space and infusing it with a sexuality of inclusiveness" (Richmond Ellis, p. 4). Our ambiente is a space of not simply outing or difference, but joining in a social space of inclusive and potentiality across difference.

EXPANDING QUEER IDENTITIES SCHOLARSHIP IN INTERCULTURAL COMMUNICATION

We join scholars who center identities like Johnson (2001), who asserts that queer studies in communication often fail to account for the lived experiences of queer people with multiple marginalized identities. Like Johnson, we contend that a "significant theoretical gap" prevails in queer communication scholarship; failure to attend to the racial and socioeconomic diversity within queer communities renders queer theory incomplete" (p. 3). Similarly, like Moreman (2009), we have felt "homeless" within the field of communication studies, where conversations about queer people of color are few and far between (p. 5). Speaking alongside Muñoz (1999), we are compelled to *disidentify* with articulations of queer theory that do not account for our intersectional experiences as queer people of color.

Additionally, we identify a lack of scholarship in communication studies that accounts for the multidimensional cross-racial relationships within queer communities. We contend that scholarship about coalition-building within queer communities takes on the difficult task of placing diverse queer voices in dialogue. Such studies are, therefore, integral to the future of queer studies in communication. As we build upon this scholarship, we draw centrally from identity theories that speak specifically to the lived experiences of queer people of color. We do this in a strategic move away from queer and identity theories that that gloss over difference, thereby silencing the voices of people of color.

Finally, we theorize queer identities as "moving" in relation to one another (Mendoza et al., 2002). Mendoza et al. (2002) argue that in order to extend theories of identity in intercultural communication, we must examine the interactional, structural, and cultural influences that shape us (p. 324). As we chart our relational queer identities with and through John T. Warren, we contend that we cannot understand our queerness without examining our relationships with one another. With this chapter, we urge queer theory in communication studies to account for the ways in which we come into our queerness through our (academic) familial relationships with one another.

DIALOGICALLY SPEAKING

Taking up Warren's (2011a) call for a reflexive pedagogy that acknowledges how our past experiences build on what we value as teachers and our philosophies, we offer our narratives as spaces to start theorizing how our individual histories come together in our desire for queer relationality and alliance building. We write performatively (Pelias, 2005; Pollock, 1998) as we attempt to evocatively engage the reader in experience. However, we also ask that the reader consider with us the possibility of that experience to actualize Other points of connections, specifically queer relationality. It must be noted that in sharing these narratives we also write from absence. In theorizing queer academic families of choice and the politics of relationality, the person who hinged us together, our friend, colleague, and mentor John T. Warren, recently passed away. This piece is impossible to write without acknowledging and honoring his presence. Thus, we make him present through his scholarship and through our queer politics of relation to him as they continue to shift over time.

Our style in writing this piece is modeled after work by Jones and Calafell (in press), Alexander and Warren (2002), and Fassett and Warren (2007) in that we dialogically come together on the page to demonstrate, work through, and gesture toward possibility. We blend our voices to mirror the dialogic process of coalition building. Langellier (1999) argues that personal narratives do something in the world, while Madison (1998) states that personal narratives offer performances of possibilities. Whether it is a narrative bringing an Other perspective into the dialogue (Corey, 1998), asking an audience to be in dialogue with personal narrative (Madison, 1998), or whether using personal narrative to gesture toward what might be (Madison, 1998), personal narrative and personal narrative performance are central pedagogical tools and spaces to begin theorizing and *actualizing*.

* * *

Long before I met Krishna's mentor, John T. Warren, I knew of him. I knew of him because every time I looked at a journal, he had published something in it. It didn't matter what journal . . . there he was. I finally had the opportunity to "meet" him years ago when the Western States Communication Association conference was held in San Francisco. I distinctly remember standing outside of a convention room waiting to be able to enter for the panel we were both going to. I talked with one of my mentors and John stood to the side holding a bunch of stuff, anxiously waiting to walk in. John was the program planner for the Performance Studies Interest Group that year and he was set to introduce a performance. He watched as a mentor from my master's program and I talked. John and I did not speak. I did not invite him to join the conversation. Even though I knew who he was, I was a bit shy and suspicious.

I do not know if I can actually recall the moment that we finally interacted, but that image of him in the hallway always sticks in my mind as our first meeting. As years passed I continued to see more and more of John's work in the pages of our journals. I began to read his work with a bit of skepticism. Was he really an ally? As a white man talking about his white privilege was he really interrogating that privilege or was he simply recentering it through his work? This is the question I asked myself, and it kept me at a distance from completely embracing John and his work. Scholars such as John himself have acknowledged a history of distrust between white scholars and scholars of color each who study race (Warren, 2003). Elsewhere I have challenged the ways some white scholars have used autoethnography to uncritically center their whiteness under the guise of critical work (Calafell, 2007b; Calafell and Moreman, 2009). My suspicion was based in a history of distrust not only in my own experiences, but in a larger history of the marginalization of people of color.

When I left my job out of graduate school in 2006 and began working at my present position, it seemed that a move to the West became the start of a more meaningful relationship with John. Now when we crossed paths we began to talk, and soon we were collaborating on panels for conferences. Over the last four years John and I had collaborated on many panels, but something else started to happen as well. It began when one of my doctoral advisees joined John as a colleague in his department. Then, one of his advisees joined me as a colleague in my department. I was honored that John had supported one of his students in applying to my department. I was humbled. John had displayed a huge act of faith and trust in sending one of his top advisees to come work at my school. I felt a huge responsibility and wanted to show John that I was worthy of his respect and faith. Later that year Krishna, one of John's master's advisees, applied to and was accepted to our program. John had invited me to write a chapter for the *The SAGE Handbook of Communication and Instruction* that he and Deanna Fassett were editing. Though I did not consider myself a communication pedagogy scholar, I was honored and did not want to disappoint Deanna and John. As I worked on that chapter, I was nervous and worried that my work would not be good enough. It was this piece that John shared pre-publication with his students, including Krishna, and it was this piece that seemed to bond the three of us as Krishna's work intersected with culture and communication and critical pedagogy. But there was also something else. We were queer. A few years ago I had read a piece John coauthored about the experience of bi-men (Warren and Zoffel, 2007). John shared an experience of a student questioning his sexuality and his many layers that informed his response:

I do not tell many people that I am bi. It makes me feel uncomfortable. It makes me uncomfortable because I feel like I am assuming a risky identity which requires no risks—I get the privilege of "really" being married, of "really" being with a woman in public, or "really" appearing in every context, in every moment, as straight, not queer. . . . I question whether it is politically sound for me to remain silent, to not voice my own queer location. It seems like I'm saying I'm queer, I'm not-straight, is to bank on the exoticness, an almost chicness of the identity, without having to walk that line. (Warren and Zoffel, 2007, p. 236)

In 2005 at the National Communication Association convention, John continued this work in a panel we were on together. In the end, he called for a rethinking of sexuality further complicating existing binaries that erase bisexuals. I was inspired and saw much of myself in John's words. His story connected with me and gave me the desire to explore this part of my identity as queer bisexual woman of color, which I did in several publications (Calafell, 2009; 2010a; 2010b; Jones and Calafell, in press). Yet again, John was giving.

In all these experiences my fears about John dispelled as he performed ally. He didn't just talk the talk. He walked the walk. He was kind, giving, generous, and humble. Writing of the work of reflexivity, Jones (2010) differentiates self-reflection versus self-reflexivity: "Self-reflection might scratch the surface, but self-reflexivity, cuts to the bone. It implicates you. Reflexivity is uncomfortable because it forces you to acknowledge that you are complicit in the perpetuation of oppression" (p. 124). John shared Jones' perspective as he wrote reflexively of his positionality and his work,

It is an ethical position that does not deny scholars of color who preceded my voice, but adds my critical voice in harmony with those voices—to attempt to speak a language that moves people constituted in whiteness from a place of ignorance to a place where people question themselves, and their world. This is my ethical responsibility. (Warren, 2003b, p. 157)

This ethical responsibility enabled by John's commitment to acknowledging his spaces of privilege and negotiating them with Others, while also naming the spaces in which he was Othered, allowed for space of queer connection, as he queered our understanding of privilege and oppression in the desire for relationality and coalition.

In February of 2011, I had the pleasure of sitting on a panel with John, Richie Hao, Kate Willink, Bryant Alexander, and Amy Kilgard. The panel was about mentoring. As we sat there I *felt* the politics of relation between us all as our lives had become intimately intertwined, at least in an academic sense. It felt like *family*. I spoke about the trust between us as we shared students and colleagues. The act of this seemed like an act of love driven by an ethic of care. It was the further realization of what I had written about in "Mentoring and Love" (Calafell, 2007a) and how John described his approach to teaching, and by extension mentoring:

> I look to teaching as an act of friendship, an act of love that occurs in contexts of care and trust. I believe that is past of how I developed my ethics of teaching, of caring deeply about what it means to encounter the student as a person, as a whole being that has a history, a story of how they too arrived in this pedagogical moment. (Warren, 2011a, p. 140)

Queerly we had created family in these relations of choice. As John and I sat next to one another at that panel, it was almost six years after that San Francisco conference where we stood in the halls. Now here we were side-by-side; here we were friends. Queerly we were family through our bonds of mentoring. All of my reservations about John had gone, and I felt like a fool for having them. But being the ally that he was, I'm sure John would have understood those reservations.

* * *

Knowing that John will not read the words I write makes composition feel a little too solitary to bear. I have always written with John in mind, anticipating how he would tap his pencils with animal-shaped erasers against his desk as he poured over my drafts. When I exited his office with a newly edited manuscript in hand, I prepared for the challenge of decoding the comments he left in the margins of my pages like gifts. The more excited John was about my writing, the more artistic his script became. I have always wanted to be the kind of writer who would make John proud—whose ideas could turn his handwriting into an indecipherable series of loops and dots.

In the wake of John's passing, my new academic family has wrapped me in the kind of love and support I was not sure I could find beyond John's office. Bernadette and I have sobbed together in the hallways of our department, our hearts heavy with loss. In classrooms and graduate offices, fellow students have offered testaments of how John's scholarship changed the way they think about difference. White colleagues tell me how John's writings about whiteness and pedagogy (Warren, 2003b; Warren and Hytten, 2004) opened their eyes to their own privileged positionalities in academia. Even those who never met John feel his presence in their lives and their scholarship. Much like when John lifted my chin during my deepest moments of self-doubt, his work encourages my colleagues to persevere through difficult scholarly moments. My colleagues and I are dedicated to continuing the conversations John made possible. Because of John, I am in community with so many scholars beyond my daily experience. His contributions have connected us all.

As I struggle to say goodbye to John, the prospect of nurturing a relationship with my new mentor keeps me afloat. I recognize in Bernadette so many of the things I loved about John: her commitment to students beyond the classroom, her straightforward and supportive feedback, and her fearless confrontations of injustices. Bernadette invests in her students' lives beyond the classroom, serving as an out and outspoken role model in campus and community organizations. She recently received a prestigious teaching award for her support of queer students and students of color. As outgoing graduate director, Bernadette has recruited students from marginalized backgrounds who have vested interests in researching issues of inequity. Because of her efforts, I have cultivated deep and multilayered relationships with queer students and students of color. For the first time, I have built a strong community with colleagues who have similar identities and interests.

Most importantly, Bernadette and I have cultivated the type of relationship that is the perfect blend of professionalism and care. Like John, Bernadette is committed to helping her students succeed, even when she must use tough love. She believes in me enough to speak beside me in this chapter, to let her stories stand beside mine as we build community across our shared identities. As a queer woman of color, I never expected that I would receive the opportunity to work alongside a strong queer woman of color like Bernadette. If it were not for John, I never would have realized that I *deserve* such an opportunity, that like heterosexual and white students I deserve the love and support of mentors and colleagues whose identities have shaped their pedagogical experiences in ways similar to mine. By teaching me to place value in my own identities and experiences, John led me to my new family here with Bernadette.

I see John in my professor Richie Neil Hao, also his former student, whose mannerisms and facial expressions echo John's. I hear John's voice when Richie asks, "How might we think about… [the topic at hand]?" Even though I left John behind to continue my graduate education, I found him *here* in the scholarship and in the hearts of my new colleagues and mentors. I found him in all of the students and faculty whose lives he touched through his scholarly activism. John's voice speaks in and through all of us, encouraging us to negotiate our different and shared identities in the way strong families would during times of struggle. With all of our voices speaking together, John will never be silent. Activist scholarship is our family business, and we carry forth John's legacy with great pride.

* * *

Many years ago I sat by myself in my first faculty office. It was after one of my mentors had come to my department to speak. I had just composed an essay on the relationship between mentoring and love for those of who are constructed as Others (Calafell, 2007a). In those moments alone I reflected on the relationships I shared with my mentors and my students. Then it hit me; a thought I had never allowed myself to consider. What do you do when your mentors die? My eyes began to well up with tears. The thought of being without my mentor who had given me so much, and whom I was always trying to give back to in ways that I'm sure would never amount to as much as he had given me, was almost too much to bear. It was incomprehensible to imagine a world without him.

Years later on a Sunday morning, I would come to find out that a friend, colleague, and mentor, John, had passed away. The enormity of that loss was too much. Sitting in my living room feeling the loss I remembered my earlier question. Though John had not formally been my mentor, he was an ally to me who acted in a mentoring way. His loss has been profoundly felt. In that moment of loss Krishna, and those of us who knew and loved John came together. The discussions we had shared at the Western States Communication Association conference less than two months earlier around mentoring and family were at the forefront of my mind.

For years I have been trying to understand the underlying politics of relation between myself and my advisees, particularly those who had been working with friends and colleagues for their master's programs. This year marked a milestone of sorts for me. Four years ago, one of my best friend's master's advisees started in the doctoral program as my advisee. She arrived, after working with my friend, well aware of critical theories of race, gender, class, and queerness. She and I often laugh about what we termed "our family" as the three of us are intricately connected. Seeing each other at Western and NCA was always kind of like a family reunion. We two queers of color who do not want children instead breed ideas. In mentoring my advisee I never wanted to disappoint her or her mentor, and she was always striking the balance between us. She reflects the mentoring of both of us. Now she has completed her degree and she will go on and mentor her own students, perhaps taking a bit of each of us with her.

Just as she began her final year, Krishna began her first. Krishna's voice is so strong, and in its reverberations I hear and feel John. The cycle of mentoring continues. Each of these relationships is connected by a politics undergirded by an Other perspective that gestures towards something more. As Muñoz (2009) writes, we are not yet queer. We desire toward queerness together. As individuals we have sought each other out spurred by a politics of queer relationality based on a shared ethic of hope, love, and care as strategies of resistance against the violence of heteronormativity. I've been struggling for some time to name what exactly it was about these relationships of mentoring that made them feel so different. Anzaldúa and Moraga's (1981) conception of theories of flesh, ways of theorizing through the body informed by years of resistance and survival by Others, underlies our queer relationality.

Debates circle about "identity politics." But the politics we envision are not driven by essentialism or simple theories of identities. They are not driven by binaries. They are driven by queer pedagogies of resistance, colored differentially for each of us, affectively theorized through the body, knowledges that must be passed on as we move toward a queer future. By placing queerness at the center, which is based in disruptions of binaries, and by theorizing through the body, we mark spaces of difference that do not conform to rigid stereotypical conceptions of identities. Identities here are always in motion, always relational, and always informed by reflexivity, a sustained critique that calls for coalitional partners to be aware of their privileges and be responsive to them. Furthermore, our queer and feminist of color perspective call us to locate our theorization squarely on our bodies rather than abstraction which can lead to disembodied and generalized work. Informed by this frame and Nakayama and Halualani's (2010b), we call for other scholars in intercultural communication to be attentive to issues of reflexivity, power, and privilege in their work.

CONCLUSION

By placing our voices in dialogue as queer women of color, we urge studies of identity in intercultural communication to consider the importance of coalitions within and across race and sexuality. In pedagogical contexts where queer people and people of color must negotiate difficult routes toward voice, coalitions provide support and stability. We argue that through dialogue, we establish powerful coalitions with academic families of choice whom help us to queerly navigate pedagogical contexts that attempt to silence and erase us. We believe that the likelihood that queer people and people of color will achieve academic success relies significantly on the establishment of relationships with strong mentors within and across identity lines. Therefore, by exploring our intertwined and multidimensional mentoring relationships with and through John, we highlight the important roles that we have played in one another's lives that have led to our shared and individual successes. We highlight the queer pedagogical moments we have shared.

However, we assert that coalitions need not operate under assumptions of harmony. Like Owens Patton (2005), by portraying our skepticisms and reservations about the idea of cross-racial coalitions, we negate the "guise of civility" that permeates racist, heterosexist, and sexist academic contexts. We validate skepticism as a response to cross-racial coalitions, thereby challenging notions that people of color who resist coalitions are segregationist (Calafell, 2010b). We opt instead to highlight the ways in which coalitions are imbued with privilege and require all parties to be consistently reflexive about their positionalities. Additionally, by showcasing how we have been deeply invested in one another's goals, we further understand coalitions as systems of give-and-take whereby differences are not reduced, but fully acknowledged, celebrated, and respected. We believe that only under these criteria can coalitions reach their full potential, connecting us deeply and genuinely with one another. Both privileges and the chosen sacrifices must be acknowledged if there is to be coalitional politics based in mutual respect, reflexivity, and an ethics of love.

Although we speak specifically about our particular mentoring and ally relationships, the ideas we present in this chapter transcend us and carry larger implications for studies of identity in intercultural communication. We believe that alliances within and across race and sexuality are beneficial for all students and faculty members whose marginalized identities leave them feeling alone and underrepresented in academia. We write this chapter not only to mourn and celebrate John's life and work, but to speak to the larger ways in which alliances like the ones we were privileged to have with John can transform oppressive pedagogical contexts. By acknowledging, celebrating, respecting, and utilizing one another's strengths, we can create widespread coalitions throughout academia that instill in all of us a sense of familial duty to uphold one another through struggle. Additionally, we encourage scholars to begin theorizing identities *relationally* in efforts to produce scholarship that more often reflects the always already co-constituted elements of our identities. We do not purport that either of these tasks is easy; indeed, establishing and theorizing coalitions across identity lines requires deep and careful consideration about our relationships to one another both in this moment and in the histories that have shaped us. As our identities push up against one another in academia, they shape our pedagogical experiences. Through recalling our relationships with John, we ask you to consider how we might hold on to one another in those moments in search of something deeper, more meaningful, and full of love.

Most importantly, we write with a greater purpose than expanding identity theories in intercultural communication: we urge our readers to seek out possibilities for building coalitions in their own lives. We contend that coalitions across all identity lines—queer or not—present opportunities for growth beyond what we can accomplish alone, that both praxiologically and pedagogically we can view our (academic) lives as constellations of opportunities for connecting with one another across difference. By producing scholarship that privileges personal experiences both methodologically and theoretically, identity scholars in communication can build a body of literature that is more inclusive and reflects the myriad possibilities of speaking with one another across identity lines (Alcoff, 1991) in pursuit of more liberated pedagogical experiences for us all. We ask you to join us in this mission so that we might all gain access to voice, so that we might speak alongside one another across identity lines, helping us feel a little less like strangers to one another and a little more like family.

II

Identity and Home/Spaces

FIVE

Cultural Reentry

A Critical Review of Intercultural Communication Research

Richie Neil Hao

It has been seventeen years since the last time I was in Manila, the Philippines. After all this time, I am finally returning to my birthplace that is now somewhat (un)familiar to me. I arrive at Denver International Airport and approach one of the airline self-serve electronic ticket kiosks to print my three boarding passes (from Denver to Los Angeles, Los Angeles to Tokyo, and Tokyo to Manila). What was normally a routine of being able to print my boarding pass(es) when flying domestically is different today. Something unfamiliar flashes on the computer screen: "Please see the attendant to process your request." I follow the screen. I step into the counter closest to me and mention to the attendant that the self-serve ticketing couldn't process my request. She asks me where I'm heading. "Manila," I say to her. In that moment, I realize that I'm not only returning to Manila, I'm returning home.

As I take my seat on the plane and start pondering about my travel to Los Angeles and Tokyo, before arriving to my final destination in Manila, I think about what these places are to me. When the plane arrives in Los Angeles, I feel some (un)easiness as it reminds me of my family who live in the suburbs about forty-five miles away. In Los Angeles, I have to go through another security screening that will take me to the international terminal for my flight to Tokyo. As I embark on this sixteen-hour flight to Tokyo, I experience international travel for the first time since my family and I left Manila for Los Angeles. In light of this, I start thinking about

Manila, even though I haven't been back there since I was thirteen-years-old. Now at thirty, am I a returnee? While I've never considered myself a tourist, given that I was born and raised in Manila, I'm returning to my old home—a place where most of my extended families still live.

My three-week stay in the Philippines makes me think about the current literature that theorizes cultural reentry in ways that doesn't resonate with my experience. Cultural reentry has been defined as the return or transition of sojourners to their home culture (Gama and Pedersen, 1977; Martin, 1984). While I'm indeed returning to Manila, I'm not returning there permanently. In fact, Chang (2010) points out that a gap in current literature on cultural reentry is of "its exclusive focus on permanent returns, disregarding temporary reentries. As a result, we have little knowledge of short-term reentry experiences, which are becoming increasingly frequent" (p. 169). That said, what does cultural reentry really mean? What is "home culture"? What if I have multiple homes? If I'm only in the Philippines—my birthplace—for a few weeks, does my experience count as cultural reentry? These questions motivate me to examine what's lacking in current literature of cultural reentry and offer possibilities in extending future research on this topic. My critique of the literature on cultural reentry is drawn from intercultural communication research, which still relies heavily on other disciplines, such as anthropology, psychology, and sociology. I acknowledge that much of the literature reviewed here can be considered influential, but I have also included recent studies to understand both dominant and alternative interpretations of cultural reentry. In this chapter, I first summarize the themes generated from my literature review on cultural reentry and offer critique by juxtaposing my recent experience of visiting Manila. Then, I discuss the implications of my study theoretically, methodologically, pedagogically and praxiologically for identity related scholarship in intercultural communication.

A CRITICAL REVIEW OF CULTURAL REENTRY LITERATURE

In this review of literature on cultural reentry, I examine the following themes for my critique to fill the gaps in current literature: host/home binary, and reverse culture shock and deculturation. These two themes are the most prominent in the discussion of cultural reentry where I offer critique and possibilities in extending the conversations in the literature.

Host/Home Binary

The first prominent theme I find in the current literature on cultural reentry is that of the host/home binary, which is exemplified in studies that focus on the experiences of U.S. college students returning home from host countries (Martin, 1986; Rohrlich and Martin, 1991; Smith, 2001; Wilson, 1993), non-U.S. international students who go back home after their schooling experiences (Brabant, Palmer, and Gramling, 1990; Chang, 2010; Rogers and Ward, 1993), and business executives returning home after working abroad (Adler, 1981; Black, Gregersen, and Mendenhall, 1992; Harvey, 1989). For instance, Martin's (1986) study "examined 173 student sojourners' perceptions of their communication in three types of reentry relationships (with parents, siblings, and friends)" (p. 183). The student sojourners were surveyed to "(1) evaluate their current communication and (2) describe specific communication changes in these relationships" (p. 183). Martin's study focused on the role of communication, since most of the extant research on cultural reentry then primarily examined it from a sociopsychological process of individuals adapting to the home culture. While Martin acknowledges the "fluidity and ever-changing nature of human relationships" (p. 184), her work on cultural reentry draws primarily from relational communication literature that tends to understand cultural reentry experiences through interpersonal communication theories (e.g., uncertainty reduction theory) that emphasize that there are "stages" that returnees experience in order to accomplish successful cultural transition.

Contrary to Martin's study, Y. Y. Kim's (2000, 2002) theory of cross-cultural adaptation examines adaptation as something that is more cyclical rather than linear, which means that through communication returnees experience multiple feelings and behaviors; as a result, they are interculturally transformed in the process. Y. Y. Kim's theory of cross-cultural adaptation has become influential in reentry studies and it emphasizes the notion that adaptation is complex and should be understood contextually; however, the main drawback with Y. Y. Kim's theory and several studies on cultural reentry is that they tend to discuss sojourners who return to their homes permanently, which reinforces the notion that there is one, and only one, home that one returns to. It reminds me of Clifford (1992) problematizing the need to distinguish local from global: "Some strategy of localization is inevitable if significantly different ways of life are to be represented. But 'local' in whose terms? How is significant difference politically articulated, and challenged? Who determines where (and when) a community draws its lines, names its insiders and outsiders?" (p. 97). Perhaps that is why Chang (2010) emphasizes that it is important to examine short-term reentry because "the duration of stay may influence returnees' motivation to readapt to their home culture, which may affect their interaction with others and, hence, their reentry experiences" (p. 169). To fill these gaps, Chang's study "explores the experiences of mothers of study abroad students in China interacting with their returnee children during their short-term reentries" (pp. 169-70). As part of her analysis, Chang cites Simmel's work on the notion of strangers in which Chinese mothers saw their returnee children as strangers because they are "physically close but psychologically differ-ent" (p. 172) based on their perceived changed values and behaviors.

I appreciate Chang's (2010) emphasis that short-term reentries do oc-cur, as I experienced when I went to visit the Philippines for three weeks. While my reentry to the Philippines is considered as such since I came back to the place I was born and raised, I did not go back "home" perma-nently. The drawback of current literature on cultural reentry is that it tends to frame reentry as something that is permanent, and home as the destination to which one ultimately returns. But, what if one has more than one home? In my own personal example, I have multiple homes: the Philippines (birthplace), Los Angeles (parents' home where I lived for several years), and Denver (where I currently live and work). As I travel back and forth between these places, it's hard for me to categorize, for example, Los Angeles and Denver as host cultures and the Philippines as home. As the literature suggests, the Philippines is my only home be-cause that's the place where I originated. Therefore, if and when I return to the Philippines, I'm returning home. Yes, the Philippines is my home, but I'm eventually returning home to Denver. As for Los Angeles, I re-turn there at least once or twice a year to visit my family and the place where I grew up and spent most of my schooling years. Therefore, it is not easy to simply categorize one place as home and the other as host. Instead, I argue that the Philippines, Los Angeles, and Denver are all my homes; they are homes to me in different ways—each of them has a different cultural significance for me. Given that many people, such as immigrants, now live in multiple homes (including birthplace and cur-rent residence), it is imperative to problematize the predominant litera-ture on reentry as a very linear concept according to which one place has to be "host" and the other "home." As Clifford (1992) points out, "Every-one [is] more or less permanently in transit. . . . Not so much 'where are you from?' but 'where are you between?' (The intercultural identity ques-tion)" (p. 109). In a sense, Clifford's point suggests that we enter in and out of a place or cross borders to create a space where multiple identities are negotiated.

Even though Chang's (2010) study makes an important point that short-term reentry does occur, the fact remains that there is still the di-chotomous relationship between home and host cultures. As a result, multicultural individuals experience the categorization of "strangers" when they come "home." This begs the question of who is the stranger and in what ways? Is one's stranger status based on the fixed notion of where "home" is? According to Berry's (1998) assimilation strategy in acculturation, one's changed values can be performed in different ways, such as altering one's physical appearance and changing norms or rules in social interactions. An example Chang (2010) gives is that Chinese student returnees' "personal style of communicating with their mothers was not satisfactory to the mothers [,]" even though the student returnees "had learned basic social courtesy for interacting with others in society" (p. 174). Chang's study makes me think about how I had to negotiate my Chinese Filipino and American identities when interacting with Chinese Filipinos in the Philippines. While I grew up learning some of the basic mannerisms, my "cultural slippage" was evident when I handed out my business card to a Chinese Filipino interviewee with one hand.[1] As soon as I did that, my aunt called me out for being impolite while joking that I had forgotten my cultural manners while being away in the United States for so long. In that moment, no matter how much I had to negotiate or code switch my body, I slipped through the cracks as someone who is different. However, I do not see myself as a stranger in the Philippines. I was able to communicate in local languages with different people who actually commended me for not "losing myself" (perhaps in midst of the process of acculturation in the United States). In fact, some of my interviewees and relatives thought that I am more Chinese than their children who are about my age, since they didn't seem to make an effort to learn Hokkien (Chinese dialect spoken in the Philippines) and the Chinese culture.[2] I was surprised to find out that I fit right into the Chinese Filipino culture for being able to speak Hokkien and Tagalog effectively among my participants and other people I interacted with. In a sense, I was not a stranger as a returnee to the place where I used to live seventeen years ago.

Upon reflecting on the moment of being able to claim myself as a member of the in-group, I started wondering about whether or not my parents' efforts to make sure that my siblings and I retained our Chinese Filipino culture, which included but was not limited maintaining language proficiency, was a cultural tactic on their part to preserve our cultural identities in the dominant white U.S. culture. Is that one of the reasons why I am able to still speak my native tongues well enough to "pass" as one of the Chinese Filipinos without them being able to consider me a "stranger"? I suppose my own upbringing in Los Angeles allowed me to maintain language proficiency in part because my family and I continue to communicate in our native tongues in addition to English while at home. On the other hand, technological changes and globalization continue to influence Chinese Filipinos in the Philippines to become more "American" by following "American" ways of being. I theorize that one way for Chinese Filipinos to become more "American" is to speak more English than local languages. So, in the Philippines, I am not the strange one, but it is those whom I find can no longer speak Hokkien in the way I could while I was brought up in the Philippines and the United States. In essence, they are not the Chinese Filipinos I remember growing up. Yet, at the same time, I think they are becoming more like me in terms of speaking more English than our native tongues, which perhaps could also explain why I am not a stranger to Chinese Filipinos in the Philippines.

Upon returning to the United States, I started "slipping" into my Tagalog and Hokkien tongues when speaking to people who don't speak the languages. For instance, I started uttering Tagalog and Hokkien words and expressions to my spouse during conversations at home. Had I become a stranger in a place that I have called my home for at least half of my life? Having lived almost about the same amount of time in the Philippines and the United States, where is my real home? Which one do I consider as home and which one as host culture? In some ways, if I was only in the Philippines for the duration of three weeks, wouldn't the United States (more specifically, Denver) be my home? But, I was born and raised in the Philippines, so wouldn't that be my home too? Even though each has different meanings for me culturally and personally, both the Philippines and United States have become my homes. Halualani (2008) reminds us, "If indeed migration is conceptualized by many groups as a distinctive cultural act, we shouldnow explore how 'culture' and 'cultural identity' have incorporated globalized change and become a shifting dynamic field that refuses geographic specificity yet remembers a cultural past" (p. 19). Unfortunately, in the current literature on cultural reentry, "home" culture is typically understood as the "original" culture where one was born and raised. There is still an assumption that one has to be a stranger and the other a "local," which reinforces the binary of being at home and being elsewhere.

Reverse Culture Shock and Deculturation

Much of the literature on cultural reentry tends to emphasize that returnees experience reverse culture shock and deculturation when they return home from abroad (Adler, 1975; Austin, 1986; Berry, 1998; Clifford, 1992; Ford, 2009; Gaw, 2000; Gudykunst and Y. Y. Kim, 2003a; Martin, 1986; Storti, 1997). First, according to the literature I reviewed, returnees typically go through reverse culture shock. Koester (1984), for example, notes that

> international sojourners often experience feelings of helplessness, withdrawal, paranoia, irritability and a desire for home which have been identified as part of "culture shock." But those concerned with international exchange have also documented "reverse culture shock" which occurs when the individual makes the transition from foreign to home culture. (p. 251)

Culture shock has been generally defined as an individual's feeling of discomfort in an environment due to its unfamiliarity (Adler, 1975; Bennett, 1998; Clifford, 1992). By contrast, reverse culture shock occurs when returnees experience uneasiness or discomfort in their home environment after coming back from abroad (Adler, 1975; Gaw, 2000). Scholars, such as Brislin and Pedersen (1976), point out that the "readjustment back home is likely to be even more difficult than going abroad in the first place . . . " (p. 16). One reason that reentry can be difficult is because family, friends, coworkers find the changes in sojourners' attitudes, behaviors, and interaction rules that have been acquired while abroad to be disruptive (Chang, 2010; Koester, 1984; Smith, 2001, 2002). Another reason is that the sojourners find the original culture has changed in terms of its physical characteristics, as well as changes in linguistics, social, relations, religious practices, and family orientations (Callahan, 2010; Jansson, 1975).

More importantly, others' perceptions toward the returnees may have changed, given the assumption that the returnees have changed while abroad. As Jansson (1975) explains,

> In most cases, there is a shift in values, a portion of "history" that is not mutually shared, and behaviors which differ from those expected within the social system. The re-entrant is in the minority and is, in a sense, defined by those who remained in the group. (p. 136)

What is fascinating is that Brislin and Van Buren (cited in Koester, 1984, p. 252) state that sojourners who are most successful in adapting to the foreign culture may experience the greatest difficulty in adjusting back to the home culture. Because many returnees do not expect to have the need to adjust when they return home, they experience additional pressures during reentry (Martin and Harrell, 1996; Smith, 2001, 2002). Many returnees also face difficulty in adjusting to their lives, which include but are not limited to matters related to housing, schools, finances, and jobs (Koester, 1984; Storti, 1997). Koester (1984) adds that returned sojourners generally perceive themselves as

> "changed" and unique because of their intercultural experience. Because of the separation from their home culture they have a new perspective on themselves as products of a particular culture. Furthermore, returned visitors often express a recognition that understanding of the culture of their international visit continues to grow and change. (p. 252)

In light of this, sojourners have to adapt to the cultural expectations of the host culture and/or maintain their home culture (Berry, 1998; Callahan, 2010; Gudykunst and Y. Y. Kim, 2003a). More specifically, sojourners may employ integration strategies in which host and home cultural systems are integrated, assimilate to the host culture completely, or perform separation strategies by not adapting to the host culture and maintaining home culture. These cultural strategies could affect how returnees experience identity shifts. An identity shift occurs when sojourners choose to integrate two cultural systems discussed earlier (Sussman, 2000). An affirmative identity shift is experienced by sojourners when they maintain their home culture and do not adapt to the host culture successfully. By contrast, "sojourners who choose to identify with the host culture and are

good at adapting will undergo significant cultural self-concept distur-
bance; they develop an additive identity shift. Upon reentry, these returnees tend to have high levels of distress" (Chang, 2010, p. 169). In this
sense, "reentry experiences have been explained in terms of the cultural
identity shifts of returnees as a result of their entry experiences (i.e.,
acculturation). That is, their cultural identity shifts prior to reentry may
influence their reentry experiences. . . . " (p. 168).

However, Martin's (1986) study demonstrates that "not all reentry
relationships are problematic [,]" (p. 194) as discussed in much of the
literature on cultural reentry; this is because communication between
student sojourners and their parents, siblings, and friends could influence whether or not they would have a positive or negative reentry experience. In essence, Martin problematizes literature that tends to frame
cultural reentry as a difficult experience for returnees. Y. Y. Kim (2002)
also confirms that experiencing culture shock is not necessarily bad, but
rather it is necessary for one's own individual growth. As Ford (2009)
asserts in his study of Japanese student returnees enrolled in mainstream
Japanese schools, we should not "presume that all returnees are over-
whelmed by negative experiences on their return to Japan and their re-
integration into its educational system" (p. 65). In light of my own experience of cultural reentry in Manila, communication with my relatives and
childhood friends allowed me to have a positive experience while I was
over there. Although I had to readjust to certain communication norms
and practices, I did not face significant challenges in being able to communicate with people I know. In fact, as I mentioned earlier, family,
friends, and people I got to meet while in Manila thought that I spoke in
my native tongues (Tagalog and Hokkien Chinese dialect) more so than a
lot of younger people (my generation and younger), which actually allowed me to create a sense of cultural affiliation that I thought I had lost
since I have been living in the United States for the last seventeen years.
My cultural reentry experience shows that each person's experience is
different; therefore, it is important not to essentialize that all returnees'
experiences are the same in which they have difficulty in adjusting and
communicating with family and friends (e.g., Callahan, 2010; Y. Y. Kim,
2002; Koester, 1984; Smith, 2001). Y. Y. Kim (2002), in particular, specifically notes that reentry experience depends on the role of environment in
which members of the cultural group could make it easier or more difficult for the returnee to adjust culturally, which demystifies the notion
that returnees seem to always experience difficulty in adjusting from host
to home culture and vice-versa.

Despite the fact that " . . . not all returnees will experience similar
levels of distress upon reentry because of their acculturation experiences"
(Chang, 2010, p. 168), many scholars who write about cultural reentry
state that returnees experience deculturation, also called "reacculturation" (Martin, 1984), which is experienced when returnees have to un-

learn the original or old cultural patterns (Callahan, 2010; Gudykunst and Y. Y. Kim, 2003a). The assumption here is that returnees typically experience deculturation because they have been immersed into the host culture and may have forgotten how to behave in the home culture. Berry (1998), Gaw (2000), Martin (1984), LaBrack (1993), Storti (1997), and Sussman (2001), among others, have documented in their studies that returnees typically experience deculturation. For instance, Sussman (2001) found that American managers who spent from six months to four years overseas found reentry difficult due to the significant cultural identity changes they experienced. In Gaw's (2000) study, American students who had studied abroad felt major reentry shock and experienced isolation as a result of their perceived inferiority in the home culture. Contrary to different studies' findings of returnees experiencing deculturation, Koester (1984) argues that many returnees actually feel that they can incorporate both host and home cultural experiences perhaps because

> often individuals returning to their home culture are able to see the routine day-to-day messages conveyed by their countries' social systems in a new way. Commonly accepted understandings of cultural value symbols, political terms, social roles, and foreign policies are questioned and reinterpreted. Also, individuals in the reentry phase of the international experience can look at their host cultures and reevaluate their understandings of the dynamics of those social systems. (p. 255)

Therefore, not all returnees experience the same kinds of negative feelings and emotions when they return home. As also demonstrated in Callahan's (2010) study of returned missionaries from the Church of Jesus Christ of Latter-day Saints, he argues that returnees do not simply socialize themselves into another culture, but rather they integrate the combined experiences. That said, none of Callahan's participants actually "lost" their home culture (deculturation). In fact, 85 percent of Callahan's participants reported having little or no difficulty during reentry into the United States. This reminds me of my own Chinese Filipino identity which I have managed to maintain even after living in the United States for so long. Did my Chinese Filipino identity change? Absolutely, but, like Callahan's participants, I simply evolved over time culturally having multiple identities in which I am able to integrate my Chinese Filipino with my American identity.

Koester (1984) also posits that an intercultural/international experience could actually be beneficial for returnees for the purpose of reflecting upon their experience internationally and making sense of that experience in relation to where they currently live. When we think about it, technological advances have bridged the gap in bringing people from all over the world together even closer than before (Shome and Hegde, 2002a). As a result, there are a growing number of individuals who would consider themselves as transnational or hybridized (Hegde, 1997). During my visit in the Philippines I couldn't believe that U.S. popular media have influenced so much of the Filipino lifestyle; they are so prominent that many Filipinos are extremely familiar with U.S. television shows and films. In that sense, Filipinos' identities continue to change and develop over time. The Philippines I visited is no longer what I remember it to be while I was growing up; the world is changing and becoming smaller, and the Philippines is no exception. Upon returning to the United States, my experience in the Philippines where cultural familiarity with what I have in the United States shows that I did not have to deculturate.

Reflecting on my visit to the Philippines and travel back to the United States, I can say that the notion of reverse culture shock and deculturation cannot be generalized as something that can be experienced by every returnee, especially for those, like me, whose "home" and "host" cultures are arbitrary in that they do not necessarily fit into the either/or approach. It is difficult for me to categorize what I'm supposed to experience in both countries in regards to identity negotiation. By using such an explicit categorization of the Philippines and the United States as either "home" or "host" culture would only stabilize how my body and identities could be situated. Perhaps at first glance, the reverse culture shock and deculturation theories make sense, and I certainly do not disregard that such experiences do exist. Yet, I would like us to simply take into consideration that people who are multicultural and have multiple homes do not necessarily experience reverse culture shock or deculturation the way that the literature suggests.

DISCUSSION

Literature on cultural reentry tends to freeze (multiple) identities and simplifies the concept of home as a destination to which one must return permanently. Thus, it is important to understand reentry beyond a long-term return basis; understanding reentry on a short-term basis allows us to understand they "may involve different patterns of social interaction between significant others and returnees, which may further shape reentry experiences" (Chang, 2010, p. 179). As I have critiqued current literature on cultural reentry, I have discussed how returnees do not necessarily go back home permanently, but rather sometimes they go back for a short-term visit, as demonstrated in Chang's (2010) study on Chinese international students' short-term visit to China to see their families. Reflecting from my own short-term visit in the Philippines after seventeen years since my family and I immigrated to the United States, my experience does not support current literature on cultural reentry that seems to reinforce the "host" versus "home" binary, as well as stabilize returnees' experiences as problematic or negative. In this concluding section, I want to turn our attention to my chapter's theoretical, methodological, peda-gogical and praxiological implications for identity related scholarship in intercultural communication.

In my chapter, I critiqued both influential and current literature on cultural reentry by focusing on how the literature tends to emphasize the home/host binary, which is problematic for those who have multiple homes, especially given that many of us now live in a world that contin-ues to get smaller due to technological changes and heightened immigra-tion in different parts of the world. As Shome and Hegde (2002a) point out, "Globalization as a phenomenon produces a state of culture in trans-national motion—flows of people, trade, communication, ideas, technolo-gies, finance, social movements, cross border movements, and more" (p. 174). More importantly, "globalization is not something that occurs in opposition to the national, or is discrete from the national. Rather, the conditions and contradictions of, and within, the nation intersect with the global, and vice-versa. . . . " (p. 174).

As migrations and different social and technological changes occur, it is imperative for us to reconsider how we make sense of current reentry models that tend to freeze constructions of home and host cultures and assume that all returnees experience same levels of reverse culture shock and deculturation. While experiences of reverse culture shock and decul-turation may occur, not all returnees experience them similarly, or at all. In particular, according to Callahan (2010), deculturation may not hap-pen due to many reasons. First, returnees do not have enough time to completely adapt to their new culture. After all, the longer the sojourner stays in the host culture the more deculturation occurs. Second, individu-als can delay or eliminate deculturation altogether if they knew that they will return to their home culture at a specific time. Finally, it is likely that deculturation does not occur given that cultural experiences are never really lost, but rather they are hidden as we negotiate our identities in different contexts. As Callahan (2010) puts it,

> Future studies concerned with the theoretical description of the contact process should be more concerned with how this is taking place. Stud-ies of this sort would identify movement and types of movement and their impacts on the contact process. Additionally, more work needs to be done to identify how cultures respond internally to increased media and technological pressures. Does the increase in communication tech-nology warrant a change in the way we view the phenomenon? Are the older studies based on outdated models of movement and research? (Conclusion section, para. 2)

Like Callahan, I agree that few studies on cultural reentry (e.g., Chang, 2010; Y. Y. Kim, 2002) actually take into account different factors, such as media and technological changes in economically developing countries in particular, that could affect one's experience with reverse culture shock or deculturation. Y. Y. Kim (2002), for example, specifically writes about the importance of media in reducing one's experience with culture shock and reverse culture shock. She provides an example of news media allowing the traveler to adjust to the host culture and refamiliarizing with one's home culture when returning home. In her study, Chang (2010) gives an example of how a Chinese college student returnee did not significantly experience reverse culture shock because he could easily watch both Chinese and U.S. television programming online. In sum, it is necessary to take media and technology into account to better understand cultural reentry experiences within conditions of transnational connectivity.

Many recent studies (e.g., Gaw, 2000; Storti, 1997; Sussman, 2001) on cultural reentry still rely on outdated models of identity, culture, and movement that communicate identities as fixed and stable, which could explain why much of the cultural reentry literature continues to construct returnees as homogenous because of the assumed similar experiences. As Chang (2010) attests, "What happens during reentry are complicated processes of relating between people with many different identities" (p. 179). As I have discussed in this chapter, the home/host binary dominates the current research on cultural reentry, which reflects culture from a nation-state perspective that treats diverse cultural groups as "homogenous and static collectives" (Halualani, Mendoza, and Drzewiecka, 2009, p. 21). Halualani et al. further add,

> To accept cultures as nations as inherently and naturally truthful and accurate at a surface level would be to risk reproducing external framings of cultural groups advanced by colonialist governments, dominant nationalist parties, and ruling power interests that benefit from such "status quo" thinking. (p. 24)

Therefore, it is critical to reframe culture as a contested site where meaning is historically, politically, and socially produced (Collier, Hegde, Lee, Nakayama, and Yep, 2001), which is why we should not reduce the study of cultural reentry simply to the nation-state paradigm. Going beyond the nation-state approach allows possibilities for multiple understandings of how cultures and identities are never static, but continue to evolve and change over time in place-based and space-based ways.

Experiences of cultural reentry should also be reframed in ways to make it applicable to experiences of multicultural individuals. Like much of the literature on cultural reentry, literature on identity in intercultural communication tends to "unproblematically . . . use the following as boundary markers of identity: nationality/ethnicity, presumed group membership, identified shared meanings, stable social context, and purportedly self-evident empirical behavioral manifestations of shared cultural practices" (Mendoza, Halualani, and Drzewiecka, 2002, p. 313).

Even though much of literature on identity that operates from a functionalist paradigm has "contributed great insights into the boundaries of identity and its behavioral/speech enactment" (Mendoza et al., 2002, p. 313), it doesn't look at historicities and power relations. Perhaps understanding identity as performative would be beneficial because it "enables us to take seriously and push further the notion that ethnic identity is emergent" (Mendoza et al., 2002, p. 318). As Callahan (2010) notes, "while sojourners may never be able to 'go home' in the psychological sense, . . . upon returning migrants are *more* than who they were when they left, not less" (Conclusion section, para. 3, italics in original). Ayumi, one of Ford's (2009) Japanese international student participants in his study who spent six years in the United States, confirms Callahan's point as she reflects on her bicultural identity as a student returnee in Japan:

> Gazing through the two countries, I have experienced many things. I have seen my country of origin from the outside viewpoint. On the other hand, I have seen many differences in culture, and how people react to strangers to that country. Still, I find that at times I really identify with my Japanese side, but other times, my American. Living there for a long time turned me into an American. Perhaps that is how things will always be like for returnees, that I will be forever caught between two worlds. (p. 71)

In so many ways, I can relate to Ayumi's experience of being in-between, which can pose challenges in negotiating my identities in different cultural contexts. As Kanno (2000) notes, identity should be seen from "multidimensional view" in which it is changing, fragmentary, and contradictory (p. 3). In her study of Japanese returnees, Kanno (2000, 2003) states that her participants expressed the desire to be a member of the mainstream Japanese society, yet they wanted to maintain their uniqueness. The notion of "authenticity" poses so many questions of how one struggles to navigate what it means to be "authentic" in various cultural spaces. Mendoza et al. (2002) argue that using performativity in understanding identity "directs our attention away from the misleading notion of 'authenticity' to a more interesting question of how particular conventions are transported across borders, infused with new meanings, and practiced in specific locations" (p. 319).

CONCLUSION

This review of the literature on cultural reentry demonstrates that more work is needed to specifically address the complexity of returnees' multiple identities. Perhaps Y. Y. Kim's theory on cross-cultural adaptation has provided us a starting point to understand that returnees are becoming more intercultural and multicultural. Other intercultural communication scholars (e.g., Drzewiecka and Halualani, 2002; Halualani, 2008; Hegde, 1998; Mendoza, 2002a) have also written about identity and diaspora, and their work helps us better understand how multiple identities are becoming more common and the need to conceptualize immigrant identities as space-based rather than just place-based. In a transnational world marked by more frequent travel and image/information flows, this has implications for how reentry is conceptualized. As Halualani (2008) states,

> Driven by the momentum of neocolonialism, global capitalism, and the spread of industrial economies, internationalizing changes have occurred both as a sweeping pattern across the globe and as a concentrated move "at home," or within specific national boundaries. These dramatic shifts have disrupted and challenged the presumed certainties of culture. . . . For example, we can no longer presume that cultures—as homogeneous entities—eternally reside and remain within specific geographic boundaries. (p. 4)

As Halualani's (2008) demonstrated, it is imperative for scholars who examine issues of cultural reentry to include multicultural voices to elicit different understandings of reentry experiences. One way to expand and reframe existing literature methodologically is for scholars to do more qualitative examination of cultural reentry. Moreover, even though there have been some recent studies on cultural reentry that utilized interviews (Chang, 2010; Ford, 2009; Isa, 2000), a critical perspective would provide additional layers in investigating power relations that exist while in spatial transitions.

I hope that my critique of literature on cultural reentry allows us to rethink pedagogy and praxis. In academic and non-academic contexts, it is crucial for intercultural communication scholars today to practice what we teach and make it applicable in everyday contexts. When we talk about cultural reentry in the intercultural communication/training classroom, teachers should critically examine with their students and participants why we need to understand the complexity of cultural reentry in the age of transnationalism and globalization. It is also important to consider the following: Who is privileged enough to move and in what ways (Shome and Hegde, 2002a)? Why must short-term reentries be distinguished from long-term reentries? Why is it necessary to go beyond the home/host dichotomy? Besides negative experiences of reverse culture shock and deculturation, why do we need to look beyond these types of experiences? These questions allow teachers, students, and other participants to acknowledge that cultural reentry is complex and returnees' experiences should not be lumped as being all the same. After all, each returnee is unique in how she or he understands home spaces and what these spaces mean—culturally, socially, and politically.

As I continue to cross different borders and spaces, I seek to locate my homes. While current literature on cultural reentry forces me to locate a home, I find it difficult to name one home. As a permanent resident of the United States who still holds Filipino citizenship, am I supposed to only claim one home? I simply cannot choose; like Ayumi, "I will be forever caught between two worlds" (Ford, 2009, p. 71). Each place—the Philippines and the United States—carries special meaning for me personally, historically, socially, culturally, and politically. Both places inform me of who I am today. This just shows that identity is more about the "process of becoming rather than being: not 'who we are' or 'where we came from', so much as what we might become, how we have been represented and how that bears on how we might represent ourselves" (Hall, 1996, p. 4).

Upon returning to the United States, I remember the moment driving away from Manila right before the sun was rising when the streets were near empty, except for a few folks running along the Manila Bay as a morning routine. I could not help but stand still and look at the people and the bay. I do not think I have ever paused that long to look at something or someone. I was having one of those feelings of not knowing when I would be returning home again; it took me seventeen years to come back home, so when would I be back again? I was finally getting used to the place again and (re)familiarizing myself with the people, place, and culture. I was not ready to leave yet. But there was also a moment in which I thought of my other home in Denver to which I was excited to return. While there was some sense of sadness in leaving Manila, there was also some happiness as I was returning to another home— the one I will call home for the years to come.

NOTES

1. As part of my visit to the Philippines, I also conducted interviews of Chinese Filipinos for a research project on Chinese Filipino diaspora.

2. Hokkien can also be alternatively called "Minnan," another dialect variant in the Southern Chinese region, but Chinese Filipinos commonly refer to their spoken Chinese dialect as "Hokkien."

SIX

Performing Home/Storying Selves

Home And/As Identity in Oral Histories of Refugees in India's Partition

Devika Chawla

FIELDWORK/HOMEWORK

Anilji and I have spent two hours combing various corners of his retirement flat. The birth certificate must be found, because Anilji[1] says, "We must begin at the beginning." We eventually find it well preserved between two old photographs from Karachi. It establishes Anil Vohra as a "British Subject" born in Karachi in 1930. "Why is it important?" I naively ask this seventy-seven-year-old man. He says it's not important, but it establishes where he's from. He wasn't born in Pakistan; there was no Pakistan, he was Indian, and a British subject. Home can be about origins.

Harbansji, an eighty-two-year-old lady, also returns to origins. She says, "It's very heartrending, you've left your birthplace. We are Indian citizens, there is no doubt about that, but it's the birthplace you always think about." Home is the mother, Harbansji tells me, "the real mother is where you are born . . . it is like losing a limb . . . like you've lost a life that you would love to live over again . . . but, would I be where I am or be what I am, had I not lost this home? I don't know the answer to that." Home—coterminous with the body. Its material loss can be a gain.

I am late for every meeting with Dadaji (granddad), a ninety-two-year-old once-famous radio artist from Lahore. Dadaji chides me about it during every visit. "The traffic has become awful, Dadaji," I apologize after every late arrival. Dadaji's days are regimented; he awakens at 5

87

a.m., takes his morning walk at 5:30, and brews *chai* for the entire house-hold by 6:15 a.m. Today he is in a mood to recite *shairi* (Urdu sonnets) sung by him and aired on All India Radio in the 1930s. After a few hours when I am ready to leave, Dadaji asks his daughter-in-law to look for the invitation from the Queen. "Of England?" I ask. "Yes, of course," he replies. His son, a surgeon who lives in England, is being awarded with the *Most Excellent Order of the British Empire* for his service to medicine. Dadaji, as the sole surviving parent, has been invited. And he is flying to attend the ceremony. "Have you ever been to England?" I ask. "No, this will be my first time, I never saw the queen when she ruled us, but I get to see her now," he announces proudly. I think this is some sort of a homecoming.

"I went to Sibbi last night," Arjunji announces. I'm confused. Sibbi is his village in Pakistan. He laughs, his wife laughs, and they explain that every few days he "goes away" to Sibbi in his *sapne* (dreams). "I wake up and my wife and I discuss all the details of my dream, where I was playing, which room in the house I was in, and what we were doing—it's almost real," he smiles. Sibbi/home can be visited, imagined. Sibbi lives.

Mrs. Chopra will not sit still. Every visit is a tour around her home in south Delhi. She is a sprightly eighty-three-year-old who does not stand on too much formality. One day she takes me on a tour of the bedrooms, "See this table and this cupboard, and this bed, they are so old they're from Lahore, but my daughters—and none of them have even been to Pakistan—they won't let me throw these." She laughs, "These are so old, I don't know why they like them, I hate them." The nostalgia seeps into generations, unknowingly. You can miss home, even if it was not home.

Sheilaji will not return to her birthplace. For her, there is nothing to see and there is nothing she wants to see. "Don't you want to see your old home?" I ask. "No, my memories of that home are all about terror, it does not seem like home." People often invite Sheilaji to go with them to revisit Lahore, but she always refuses saying, "The bad memories are more than the good ones, I don't want to see it." I ask curiously, "Your children? You don't want them to see where you are from?" "No, they don't need to see or know." Yet her grandson has joined a cricket club and travels to Pakistan to play the game. Sheilaji disapproves. Home can be about the terrors of belonging.

LOCATING HOME IN/WITH IDENTITY

What is home and why do we seek it? Is it about origins? Or is it a poetic space that unleashes the imagination? Is it an un/homely idea that gener-ates the terrors of belonging? Or is it a state of becoming and unbecom-ing? Is home coterminous with our bodies? Or is its material and emo-tional loss necessary to gain a semblance of a self? Are home/s—as places or states—almost unnecessary and disposable? What is the relationship between physical and emotional homes and the selves that we perform?

In this chapter, I focus on the intersections between identity and home in the oral histories of refugees in India's Partition of 1947. This chapter is a small excerpt from an ongoing project entitled, "Un/homely partitions: Mobilities of home in oral histories of India's Partition," for which I began ethnographic oral history work in 2008. My project is a storied contemplation on the nexus of home, travel, dwelling, and identity, an emergent complex thematic in the stories of my participants. This nexus is comprised of a series of tensions along which home is often experienced—as a space/place/state/idea that is stayed in (here-native), traveled to (there-Other), inhabited (or colonized), domesticated (or subjugated), felt (or not), and arrived at (or departed from). I position home as a spatial, discursive, poetic, and contradictory imaginary that enables (and is enabled by) multiple narrations of individual and family identity.

The overarching framework through which I engage identity in the south Asian family context is a flexible narrative approach. That is, I address identity as a narrative, communicative, and performative process, defining it as the story that we tell about ourselves to both ourselves and to others (Carr, 1986; Freeman, 1998; Ricoeur, 1992). And, in telling stories we create selves, cultural understandings, and a world (Bakhtin, 1981; Mannheim and Tedlock, 1995; see also Alexander, 2004; Langellier and Peterson, 2004, 2006; Pollock, 2005, 2008). Specifically, I am forwarding the idea that in telling, performing, and embodying visions and versions of un/home, Partition refugees claim, reclaim, and invent new selves and multiple subjectivities. I posit an understanding of a narrative life and a narrated self as a life-in-culture lived historically because a human life is life history ". . . an historical phenomenon stretched out in time between birth and death" (Freeman, 1998, p. 174; see also Freeman, 2002).

Complementarily, here and in the larger project, I rely on contemporary transnational understandings of home for my use of the word "un/home" because it includes "elsewhere spaces" and conditions that might also be experienced as home (Bhabha, 1992, 1994; Lewis and Cho, 2006; Straight, 2005). I am proposing that in these narratives of these particular persons, performing un/homes becomes an exercise in performing selves. In other words, these performances show us that identity, in a transnational and postcolonial context, might be understood as emergent, narrated, performed, and un/bound to categorical notions of selfhood.

INDIA'S PARTITION

The Partition, or what is commonly referred to as the *batwara* in Hindi, is India's bittersweet accompaniment to independence from British rule in

1947. It led to India's division into secular India and the Islamic state of Pakistan (East Pakistan became Bangladesh in 1971). Its human cost was the loss of one million lives and the displacement of about eighteen to twenty million persons on both sides of the border. As a watershed event that re/shaped the political, social, and geographical topography of the Indian subcontinent, the Partition has periodically drawn scholarly attention. A review of literature on Partition reveals that that subject has been pursued along three thematic domains: (1) High politics and statist literature that emphasizes larger national dialogues about the historical, political, and religious aftermath of Partition (see, for instance, Hasan, 1993, 2000; Khan, 2007; Zamindar, 2007); (2) fictional and film literature that includes short stories, films, documentaries, novels, and poetry—in short, Partition told from the standpoint of artists and writers who experienced its aftermath (see, for instance, Desai, 1980; Rushdie, 1981; Sidhwa, 1991; Singh, 1956); and, (3) oral and life history work that engages local and everyday narratives of ordinary persons displaced and replaced by the event (see, for instance, Butalia, 2000; Kaur, 2007; Menon and Bhasin, 1998).

My research falls within the third domain since I am interested in exploring how the Partition *lives along with* and *in* family discourse across three generations of refugees on the Indian side of the border.[2] I began fieldwork trying to understand how ordinary people organize their lives and families as a consequence of politically and religiously motivated displacements. Through their oral history narratives, I wanted to consider how identity (individual and familial) is negotiated when political, economic, emotional, and social resources are either scarce or simply unavailable. Not surprisingly, my engagement with these questions has come to be charted by routes navigated by my participants who—in story after story—un/define, long for, reject, and, sometimes, found home in Other locales that were unfamiliar, uncanny, unsettling—un/home. Admittedly, my ethnographic work did not begin with this search for home, yet when narrations of politically enforced postcolonial displacements became narrations of un/home, I took note.

UN/HOME

Increasingly, discussions of home occur against the backdrop of travel (Ahmed, Castañeda, Fortier, and Sheller, 2003; Clifford, 1992; Kaplan, 1996). Home, migration (forced or otherwise), and travel can no longer be characterized as distinct conditions, and instead it is more constructive to interrogate how, "uprootings and regroundings are enacted—affectively, materially, and symbolically—in relation to one another (Ahmed et al., 2003, p. 2). Even so, a consistent thread that runs through contemporary cross-disciplinary thinking on home and travel is a modernist version of home whereby home is projected as "a stable center of safety and domestic virtue" (Straight, 2005, p. 1). In these discussions, home connotes a safe (often feminine) space that can stand for "community; more problematically, it can elicit a nostalgia for a past golden age that never was, a nostalgia that elides exclusion, power relations, and difference" (Kondo, 1996, p. 97).

In his classic and popular study, *Home: The History of an Idea*, Rybczynski (1986) traces an emotional and material genealogy of home positioning home as both a physical place as well as a state of being-at-home that embodies love, security, safety, and dwelling. The roots of these ideas can be traced back to Heidegger's (1993) classical ruminations, "Building dwelling thinking," and Bachelard's (1964) phenomenological commentary, *The Poetics of Space: The Classic Look at How We Experience Intimate Spaces*, wherein home is associated as familiar, as a physical location, as a state of being at home in the world, as a question of arriving at meaningful selfhood, and as a space of the imagination. Heidegger (1993) proposes that humans build to dwell and in dwelling we may find traces of being human, or as he states:

> I dwell, you dwell. The way in which we are and I am, the manner in which we are humans on earth, is *Buan*, dwelling. (p. 147)

Heidegger is concerned with mystically explicating what it is to live and be at home in the world—a question of arriving at meaningful selfhood. His notion of dwelling can be, "regarded as a sort of ideological statement in favor of rigid and traditional identities . . . home as a distinct human space in contrast with the spaces of mobility and labor . . . dwelling is the constitutive relationship through which space is opened up and subjectivity is comprised" (Lopez and Sanchez-Criado, 2009, p. 349). Heidegger's key contribution is to disassociate "dwelling" and "being-at-homeness" with a specific place.

Bachelard's (1964) work on home, imagination, poetics and space complements most of the ideas proposed by Heidegger wherein, he associates home and the house, ". . . as our corner of the world. As it has been said, it is our first universe, a real cosmos in every sense of the word" (p. 4). Yet, Bachelard's conceptions differ (in degree) from Heidegger's, in that he is most interested in a topo analysis of the space that is the house and how this topography

> . . . shelters daydreaming, the house protects the dreamer, the house allows one to dream in peace . . . therefore the places in which we have *experienced daydreaming* reconstitute themselves into a new daydream, and it is because our memories of former dwelling-places of the past remain in us for all time. (Bachelard, 1964, p. 6, italics in original)

Undoubtedly, in both these modernist iterations of home, home is not just a physical location, but also a space of the imagination. The home of modernity can survive its material loss because it can be imagined and poetically excavated. Moreover, home-owners and home-makers "constitute themselves as inhabitants of their homes" and define themselves through home, "whereby moving into another living space and another dwelling is a change of life itself" (Lopez and Sanchez-Criado, 2009, p. 351).

Such ideas about "homely" homes are utopian, idealistic, and indeed Eurocentric—a critique rightfully leveled at modernist understandings of home, habit, and place's relationship with subjectivity (see Behar, 2005; Bhabha, 1994; Friedman and Randheria, 2004; Lavie and Swedenberg, 1996; Martin and Mohanty, 1986; Straight, 2005). In this era of forced and continuous global migrations we know that homemaking can also be experienced as destabilizing, terrifying, disabling, and disembodying (Straight, 2005; Zirbel, 2005). In fact, home may be experienced as "unhomely," a strategic translation of Freud's notion of *unheimlich* (the uncanny) by postcolonial theorist Homi Bhabha, who astutely positions unhomely as a postcolonial space that relates the "traumatic ambivalence of a personal, psychic history to the wider disjunctions of political existence" (Bhabha, 1992, p. 144). The unhomely reveals "the forgotten but familiar strangeness of home as a site that elicits enigmatic longing, control, or outright violence" (Straight, p. 2; see also Appadurai, 1996; Bhabha, 1992, 1994; Vignes 2008a, 2008b). In postmodern, postcolonial, and transnational conversations, home can be a space (or an idea) that is unfamiliar and unsettling, and embodies the potential to provoke intimate terrors. In short, home may never have been home, yet it continues to be intricately linked to our subjectivity in its un/homeliness and absence.

To enter the oral histories of displaced persons is to inevitably enter the history of a material loss of house and home because the displaced "view home with a more urgent longing" than the secure (Straight, 2005, p. 2; see also Spivak, 1988). In that sense, the thematic for my larger project is neither unusual, nor novel. What is notable, however, is that this conceptual approach has not received sustained analysis in the specific context of the subcontinent's Partition. Also noteworthy is the fact that in "speaking and voicing home" in the stories they co-constructed with me, my participants seemed to experience their subjective positions in the world thereby challenging me to engage the inductive nexus of home and identity. In acknowledging their choice to own their subjectivity/s in this particular way, I have taken seriously the call of contemporary social researchers who note that it is crucial, even necessary, that marginalized (displaced) persons craft home (discursively and materially) in/outside of the modernist imagination (Kondo, 1996; Martin and Mohanty, 1986). For, if home is so central to these (our) stories and if our stories are a means for claiming the space of home, then crafting home can enable newer capacities for self-making.

The stories performed in my broader project enter a space outside/inside/alongside homes of modernity to show how home may be imagined against its antithesis; how people tell stories of home as a place made present by departures and action; how unhomely homes, even as they destabilize, may be the only resource from which we claim our selves; how home is, perhaps, best approached as movement and motion, rather than rootedness and stability; and, how modernist homes may still be, ironically, the "rightful" homes that we want to achieve. In the next pages, I briefly discuss one set of family oral histories to illustrate the nexus of home, travel, and identity. Home, in this set of stories, is "domesticated" into a modernist ideal by cross-generational family members. It is my contention that this family's way of "speaking home" and storying the Partition experience in *this* way enables and engenders a different sense of self (for different purposes). This is one story of how identity is "narratively" *arrived at* and *stayed in*.

DOMESTICATING (THE IDEA OF) HOME/SELF

I came to be interested in the idea of "how stories travel" after being involved in the stories of the Khanna family from east Delhi. This is my encounter with how a Partition story travels across three generations of women in a middle-class family. I experienced this family story in three movements—(how) a story travels; (how) a story struggles; (how) a story (is forced) to find home. In this cross-generational account I address how, in this particular family, the narrative account of the ailing patriarch is "held," and indeed domesticated, by female family members (and by this ethnographer/me) in narrative homemaking practices in order to discursively rescue a modernist idea of home, and thereby preserve a family identity.

(How) A Story Travels

The field story begins with my travel into the field site with Labbi Devi's (Mrs. Khanna's) daughter, Asha. I started my work with all families by first interviewing the oldest surviving members of the family who experienced Partition. I settled into a routine wherein I would be escorted to meet the first generation members by their children or grandchildren who would invariably proceed to tell me "their story" of their parents'/grandparents' stories. The storytelling process was labyrinthine and taught me to understand how narratives/experiences/subjectivities, especially within families, travel and remain in constant daily negotiation with one another.

My experience of every interview with Labbi Devi was similarly circuitous, but more so for other reasons. First, all our meetings were moderated by other family members—her daughter (Asha), her daughter-in-law (Rani), and her daughter (Kavi). Moreover, we were always in the presence of Labbi Devi's husband, Lalaji. In short, I was never granted any private moments with Labbi Devi. I was reconciled to the situation and simply began to refer to the narrators as multiple interlocutors and to Labbi Devi's oral history as the "family oral history." In my initial interpretation of this experience, I was enthusiastic about how engaged the family seemed to be in the collective storytelling. I named it a process of "lively remembrance," co-narrated by all involved and present. This very live performance was "showing" me how this family story had traveled and was staying alive in the back and forth of multiple interlocutions. After all, as Pollock (2008) notes:

> . . . the oral history is itself a repetition without stable origins. It is a form of cultural currency that flows among participants. As such it does not "belong" to any one teller. Its vitality lies in the exchange of teller and listener. . . . In a horizontal economy, a performance of oral history is a tale told *alongside* another. It enacts the intersubjection of interview partners, and their mutual becoming in the fraught negotiation of subjectivity, temporality, memory, imagination, and history. (p. 128, italics in original)

I convinced myself that this process of oral history performance was both repetitive and "homely." But my enthusiasm was short-lived because I realized that another process was at work. In revisiting, rereading, relistening to the Khanna oral history record, my approach to the story was shifting. I felt that I had submitted (or been forced to submit) to the memories of Lalaji, Labbi Devi's husband, who had been diagnosed with the neurological condition of Alzhiemer's ten years ago. I began to (painfully) note that all our conversations were constantly interrupted by Lalaji's invocations of "his big house and shop" in Lahore—what I call the "house and shop story"—as well as his continuous recitation of Urdu poetry. The women in the family would defer to every remnant of the patriarch's memory, so much so that Labbi Devi's story about the family's trajectory of rehabilitation was bypassed. It is important to note that she was/is the only lucid/able surviving member of the family who directly witnessed Partition. Yet, the ailing patriarch's account was held center stage by all of us. We succumbed to this discursive/paternalistic/patriarchal authority and aided in sacrificing Labbi Devi's account. Indeed, this is why I call this movement—(how) a story struggles.

(How) A Story Struggles

When I encountered this "rich point" in the transcribed oral histories, my first instinct was to attempt a feminist analysis wherein I would proceed to deconstruct how Labbi Devi was being silenced, left un-voiced, and disallowed from entering her own family history. Since I was unsuccessful in "enabling" voice, I began to wonder if I was failing as an ethnographer and an oral historian. I was troubled by many questions: Was I not doing enough to "elicit" her account? Was I re-subjugating her by passively entering an already ongoing family dynamic? Was I complicit in the process of silencing this woman who was already subjugated by historical forces, and then re-subjugated by family discourse because the patriarch's story—fleetingly remembered—needed to *stand in* and *stand for* family remembering? Had I encountered, what Geertz had long ago predicted of anthropology, "as a task at which no one ever does more than not utterly fail . . . all ethnographic descriptions are homemade, that they are the describer's descriptions, not those of the described" (1988, pp. 143, 145)? Well, then what of the story that "has" been performed alongside the researcher? Under such representational dilemmas what must the ethnographer do? Does she relegate all materials to the archive?

In worrying about the failure of feminist ethnography, Visweswaran[3] (1994) warns that to try and re-interpret failure as a success by refining one's method does not necessarily mean better results. In other words, should I have insisted on meeting Labbi Devi alone, should I have insisted on getting "her" story of the Partition? Instead, Visweswaran asks that ethnographers must track failure at the epistemic level or via Spivak's (2003) notion of "cognitive failure"—when projects are faced with their own impossibility (see also Spivak, 1988). Visweswaran contends that feminist ethnographers—similar to historians—fail because they continue to see women as women as and not as historical subjects sometimes primarily constituted by race, class, and sexuality. She asks that we look at failure as both an epistemological crisis and an epistemological construct because "failure might signal a project that may no longer be attempted, or at least not on the same terms" and that the ethnography must hold in tension the "desire to know and the desire to represent" (Visweswaran, 1994, p. 100). Ultimately, a failed account can engender new kinds of positionings. In my case, I arrived at what I consider a failed account and instead of a movement from failure to success, my analysis moved from success to admitting failure.

What must I do? It is entirely possible to conduct a deconstructive transnational feminist analysis of the family story and indeed show how female subjects are subjugated in historical discourse and that women may, and often do, become the instruments of their own oppression. In undertaking such an analysis, I can reinforce and reify the disciplinary mechanisms of the gendered nation-state and position my participant as an unwelcome and marginalized subject of historical discourse (see Butalia, 2000; Menon and Bhasin, 1998). However, how far can such an analysis take me? What can it tell me about these interlocutors and their experiences? Instead, my decision is to take another route—to attempt to hold sway with how the story "is," why it "stays" where it does, and ultimately what it might tell us about our narrative quest to feel at home and find home amidst the chaos of forced migrations.

So I decide to stay inside the "home and shop" story and instead consider these questions: Why does this family entrap its story in a circuitous repetition that is encouraged by everyone including this ethnographer? I revisit segments of Labbi Devi's account and find (again) that she is unafraid and in fact enthusiastic to tell the story of the family's post-Partition struggle since she was an active participant in the family's economic mobility in the last five decades. But she is passively persuaded to stay outside the intricacies of narrating that struggle because remembering the "home and shop" appear to be crucial to the family identity and selfhood. I want to argue that this seemingly "unconscious" maneuver allows the family to "hold" the story and thereby preserve a stable sense of the idea of home. And when a home is preserved, then subjectivity, in this case the family's identity, can be salvaged from becoming an identity that gets lost in the "conversation of struggle." The "conversation of struggle" is sacrificed because in that story the family must acknowledge the trauma of displacement that means an inevitable loss of footing, a loss that they want to dis/un-remember. All this is achieved by subjugating the subject and muting her voice/story.

(How) A Story (is Forced) to Find Home

The only way that the story can enable home, indeed find a home, is for the interlocutors to perform the rules of domesticity by controlling both the story and the subject. The story has traveled and is forced to find roots in "the home and shop" image of the patriarch through the encouraging machinations of the female family members (and myself). This un/conscious strategy is a "narrative home-making practice" that relies on repetition—the image of "the home and shop" must be repeatedly evoked to bring home into relief, to maintain home, and so replenish a family identity.

This narrative home-making practice is a performance of domesticity that coincides with the modernist visions of home and dwelling that these/us women want to preserve in this story. It stands parallel to modernist domestic practices whereby domesticity is understood as a "set of ideas that over the course of nineteenth-century Western history have associated women with family, domestic value, and home, and took for granted a hierarchical distribution of power favoring men" (Hansen, 1992, p. 1). In studies that trace the modernist history of home, the evolution of home into a private and intimate sphere coincides with domestic arrangements being taken over by women making it not only a feminine space, but also a place under feminine control. Such control gave rise to the idea of domesticity as, "a set of felt emotions . . . domesticity has to do with family, intimacy, and a devotion to the home, as well as with a sense of the house as embodying—not only harboring—these sentiments" (Rybcznski, 1986, p.75). Homely domesticity was the result of women's role in the home. Lukacs considered domesticity one of the most crucial achievements of modernity, and Rybcznski (1986) calls it above all else a "feminine achievement" (p. 75). In the second half of the twentieth century the idea of domesticity has been critiqued, deconstructed, and reinvented leading to rearticulations of domestic roles. Even though I address this change in other portions of my larger project, I am interested here in how traditional domesticity circulates in this family story.

Labbi Devi, Asha, Rani, and I, discursively perform conventional domesticity and our "home-work" enables the narrative dominance of the patriarch's "home and shop" story over Labbi Devi's "conversation of struggle." We safeguard the patriarch's romantic version of home, even though "new" home/s came to "be" because of Labbi Devi's labor in the "new world." We privilege the "old home" according it both narrative and imaginative stage.We reproduce ideology by disallowing the new home/s from becoming an achievement. In anchoring his story, we anchor home and self.

I stand short of emphasizing that our "home-making" strategies are conscious. Rather, I want us to realize how pervasive and persistent homes of the "old world" are, and how easily a patriarchal and modernist adaptation of home can come to be. For this family, circulating the patriarch's construction of home seems to become crucial to its identity in the process of the telling of Labbi Devi's oral history, so crucial that women in the family take upon themselves the task of keeping alive and favoring the Alzhiemer's-ridden patriarch's rendition.

Perhaps this family story, (forcefully) told collectively with its patriarchal, modernist, ideological reproductions of home notwithstanding, is really about *homewell*—the desire to belong in and with something—to recover the fragmented self lost in national fragmentations/Partitions. In short, the maneuvers are all about achieving the semblance of a stable family identity and so a stable sense of self. After all, home, as Daniels (2003) in his essay "Scattered remarks on the ideology of home" states:

> . . . is, among other things, the desire to go on living without transforming changes; the wish for the ongoing reduplication, the endless repetitive loop, of one's everyday life, idealized, even sacralized; the desire for things to stay as they are, and to consider them right and just; the wish for the end of history. Home is also the desire to be at home with oneself, as well as the deep wish to have a unified originary "self" to begin with. (p. 191)

CONCLUSION

I believe that this brief summary account of one refugee family's desire to preserve one image of home to retain a stable sense of self, anchored in a modernist tradition, is *not* representative of either my fieldwork or the transnational condition. While it is certainly true that home, travel, and identity are an emergent conceptual nexus in the oral histories I have been gathering over the last three years, I want to caution that this must/ should not *become* the story of identity for postcolonized displaced persons. To encourage this interpretation to solidify/settle is dangerous because as Clifford (1992), notes, "diasporic conjunctures invite a reconception—both theoretical and political—of familiar notions of ethnicity and identity . . . unresolved historical dialogues between continuity and disruption, essence and positioniality, homogeneity and difference (crosscutting "us" and "them") characterize diasporic articulations" (p. 108; see also Bhabha, 1994). To me, the theoretical and praxiological purchase of this interpretive analysis coincides with the transnational identity project that continuously seeks newer ways of looking at how the displaced and the marginalized "story" their selves outside of received notions of identity, specifically those frameworks that ask us to situate our "selves" in ethnic, religious, racial, economic, gender, and nationalist categories (Appadurai, 1996; Friedman and Randheria, 2004; Kaplan, 1996). By employing home as a unit of analysis, this project stretches our understanding of how postcolonized/transnational subjects in an increasingly globalized world might experience/live their identity/s. It also forces us to realize how some persons communicate and sketch their "selves" in stories that center locality, habit, and space. Engaging the nature of locality in a globalized world (separate from national or ethnic identity) is a project that remains under discussed in intercultural communication identity research. This project can, therefore, provide an impetus for intercultural identity researchers to engage "habitality" in future research with transnational populations. Ultimately, contextually and methodologically, my project focuses on a population and research methodology (oral history) that also remains marginal within the field of intercultural communication identity research—reinforcing the notion that more work on identity with Other populations must continue in order to understand the distinct and disparate ways people narrate their "selves."

More specifically, this project can contribute to the field of intercultural family communication and identity research. As my analysis here illustrates, for the Khanna family, a modernist sense of home remains crucial to its selfhood and this process is embodied in family storytelling betwixt and amongst the participants and researcher. From a narrative and communicative standpoint, this work clarifies, "how meaning and identity are negotiated communicatively as stories are told amongst family members and the researcher (Kellas, 2005, p. 366). Indeed, it must be noted that the researcher's/my engagement with the story is a crucial part of the interpretive analysis (Pollock, 2008). It is in this back and forth between family members and researcher that a family identity narratively emerges. It also shows how one pattern in a story "can generate larger contexts in which all patterns, all constructed forms of lived experience can symbolically converge" (Goodall, 2000, p. 41). We see how family stories (told jointly) become sites of identity negotiation and creation (Langellier and Peterson, 2004, 2006). Finally, in this particular case, we are privy to how home *becomes* and *is* the unit of analysis for the storied self. For, it is the story of "home and shop" where the Khanna family identity converges and is performed, and that is the story I/we must listen to.

NOTES

1. All participant names are proceeded with a "ji" which is an honorific addendum commonly used in north India as a sign of respect for older persons or persons of higher stature. All participants have been given pseudonyms.

2. Persons from each successive generation were accessed using the following guidelines: Generation I refers to family members who were born in 1937 or before; generation II comprise family members born approximately between 1945–1957; generation III includes refugee family members born after 1970. Forty-five particpants across three generations of ten families were interviewed for this project.

3. I am using a small portion of Visweswaran's (1994) argument on de-centering the subject here. I am interested in merely looking at ethnography and failure and not so much at the de-centering of the field. I do, however, take up some of her discussions in other portions of this project.

III

Identity and the Global-Local Dialectic

SEVEN

Landscaping the Rootless

Negotiating Cosmopolitan Identity in a Globalizing World

Miriam Sobré-Denton

Through my own experiences, travels, and academic work, I have become intrigued by the construct of cosmopolitanism (Appiah, 2006) in intercultural communication teaching, research, and praxis. This term, with its nascence in Greek philosophy and subsequent use in the social sciences such as anthropology and sociology, has rarely been applied to intercultural communication scholarship. I am using "cosmopolitanism" as an umbrella term to address the construct as it is studied as a whole (see, for example, discussions by Beck and Sznaider, 2006). But what does it really mean to have a cosmopolitan identity? Can this be "achieved"— and by whom? What is communicative about this phenomenon? Is it possible to reappropriate and reconfigure this term from the colonizing and elitist connotations it may be associated with? This chapter seeks to understand what it means to have a cosmopolitan identity in the context of intercultural communication, whether this construct can be taught, and what a cosmopolitan perspective on identity can add to intercultural communication theory.

KEY CONCEPTS

Before delving into these issues at greater depth, it is important to begin with some definitions. This chapter draws from socially constructed perspectives on identity, through which identity is viewed as being negotiated and contested through dialogue and context (see the work of Hecht, Collier, and Ribeau, 1993). I posit here that identity is neither wholly a part of nor apart from either the realms of negotiation through social interaction or the contextual and systemic issues which engage intercultural communication, such as language rights, citizenship, colonialism, and globalization (Mendoza, Halualani, and Drzewiecka, 2002). Finally, identity is understood through the construct of hybridity (Bhabha, 1994) where individuals construct their sense of self through multiple influences in a dialogue of dialectical tension.

Identity entails a sense of who we are, socially, culturally, nationally, ethnically, racially, religiously, sexually, and as "mediated by family, peers, friends" (Appiah, 2006, p. 231) and its systemic limitations and influences. This perspective entails embracing identity as socially constructed through communicative relationships embedded in linguistic, cultural, religious and racial contexts. However, just because it is a social construction stemming from dialogic processes across multiple realities does not make it false or ideological (Friedman and Friedman, 2008, p. 241). Identities are rooted in cultural space, in that we are socialized into our sense of self through cultural communicative practices. However, as cultural spaces themselves become increasingly and recognizably hybridized, identities shift. They are swayed by multiple, often paradoxical influences (Werbner, 2008), negotiated through dialectical tensions that lie "in between the designations of identity . . . [opening] up the possibility of a cultural hybridity that entertains difference without an assumed or imposed hierarchy" (Bhabha, 1994, p. 4).

Cosmopolitanism[1] is defined by Hannerz (1996) as a state of "identity without borders" that is accessible to those who engage in regular negotiations of multiple cultural spaces and the subsequent identity processing of such experiences. This could be specified as an ethical engagement and dialogical conception of identity, negotiated by straddling the global and the local cultural spheres in terms of personal and social identities (Beck and Sznaider, 2006). Fisher (2008) conceptualizes cosmopolitanism as a focus on an ethical obligation to all others in the world that transcends national citizenship ties (Fisher, 2008, p. 48). Cosmopolitanism is often presented within the context of globalization, and compared to related terms such as multiculturalism.

Cosmopolitanism versus Multiculturalism

Multiculturalism involves an orientation towards cultural diversity; however, it has been criticized as oversimplified and for conflating the cultural boundaries of ethnicity, race, and nationality (Hollinger, 2006). Cosmopolitanism promotes tolerance and cultural diversity, but explores identity from a less polarizing perspective; that is, cosmopolitanism allows for identities to be hybridized, shifting across more "traditional" cultural boundaries that multiculturalism espouses (Hollinger, 2006). The difference between the two seems to lie in the move beyond "cultural bridging" or facilitating of cultural contact within the boundaries of the nation-state to a sense of belonging to the world. That is, whereas multiculturalism is based on preserving inherent differences *within* pluralistic societies (nation-states), cosmopolitanism is based on *bridging* them.

This perspective can be seen in Sparrow's (2008) critique of Adler's (1977) "multicultural man." Adler (as cited in Sparrow, 2008) describes a multicultural man as someone who might "embody the attributes and characteristics that prepare him [*sic*] to serve as a facilitator and catalyst for contacts between cultures" (p. 239). This perspective is quite similar to traditional definitions of cosmopolitan identity (see, for example, Hannerz, 1996).

Sparrow (2008) discusses having taught the "multicultural man" construct for years to her intercultural students and noted increasing questioning and even rejection of such an elitist (and male-centric) perspective on multiculturalism. Specifically, Sparrow found in her interview study that Adler's multiculturalism mostly reflected only the experiences of Anglo-American males. The men and women of varied ethnic and cultural backgrounds in her research described their identities as going beyond Adler's conceptualization to include issues of power, racism, prejudice, stereotyping, and gender (Sparrow, 2008). In particular, this sense of belonging *bridges* cultural differences (creating home through associations with others who identify as rootless) rather than simply facilitating cultural contact. One of her students notes: "I think of myself not as a unified cultural being but as a communion of different cultural beings . . . I have developed several cultural identities that diverge and converge according to the need of the moment" (Sparrow, 2008, p. 252). Cosmopolitans go beyond embracing diversity; they take from this orientation to the world an ethical stance that moves beyond constraints of the nation-state. They empathize to a greater extent with difference than with sameness, and act out moral cosmopolitanism in just such a manner.

Cosmopolitanism as a Communicative Phenomenon

The creation of a cosmopolitan identity involves a profoundly communicative phenomenon, in which cosmopolitan perspectives are socially constructed through communicative interaction with other border crossers, often about various aspects of border crossing. That is, cosmopolitanism is communicative because it centers on the manner through which individuals negotiate their identities through relationships with members of their "home" cultures, as well as the spaces through which they travel, live, and leave pieces of themselves. Further, notions of home and belonging are all communicative, particularly from Martin and Nakayama's (2008) theory of dialectical tensions, which involves "letting go of the more rigid kinds of knowledge we have about others and entering into more uncertain ways of knowing about others" (p. 85).

Cosmopolitanism requires negotiating multiple contradictory ideas simultaneously, in order to transcend cultural allegiances while living and maneuvering through rooted cultural and social life. For example, cosmopolitan identities are negotiated through communicating simultaneously from global and local perspectives, representing a dialectical tension, and "holding two contradictory ideas simultaneously" (Martin and Nakayama, 2008, p. 82). As dialectics "are not discrete, but always operate within relation to each other" (p. 84), cosmopolitans exist in a communicative space of constant tension, between belonging and isolation, between privilege and disadvantage, between self-exploration and other-orientation.

While I advocate for cosmopolitanism as an important construct that has value for intercultural communication theorizing, this chapter must also acknowledge the broad critiques of cosmopolitanism as being violently colonial and only accessible to the Western elite (Harris, 2003; Vertovec and Cohen, 2002). Buescher and Ono (2009) criticize Appadurai's modernity (a precursor to the notion of cosmopolitanism as discussed in the current chapter) as centering on "consumption, the purchase of products, access to television, film, tapes and the physical ability to migrate, to cross borders, and occupy space" (p. 80), thereby assigning a colonizing aura to the very term cosmopolitanism. Such critiques maintain that cosmopolitanism is only accessible to those who can engage in voluntary (i.e., privileged) border crossings and have the intellectual tools to analyze their experiences. I do not intend to refute these critiques, but rather to dialogically revisit cosmopolitanism and attempt to point out its usefulness for the discipline. I acknowledge that cosmopolitanism is a culturally contested term, but I hope that in this chapter I can take steps towards loosening some of its negative connotations, something scholars in related fields are doing. This begins with a discussion of how cosmopolitan identities are negotiated.

NEGOTIATING A COSMOPOLITAN IDENTITY

According to Appiah (2006) and Werbner (2008), a cosmopolitan identity entails connection with others, intercultural mindfulness, and an overall strong sense of ethical global stewardship. Such positionality can provide a situating space for cosmopolitan identities as existing in a constant state of (re)construction, one that could ideally lead to individuals who take what is rooted across multiple cultures and internalize it in a manner that transcends culture-specific allegiances, i.e., they become culturally rootless.[2] This means that cosmopolitan individuals identify as different from those rooted in any one specific culture and are open to—to the point of willingness to engage in critical self-transformation —the cultural other through "kindness to strangers" (Appiah, 2006). Cosmopolitanism does not necessarily conflate cultural identity with that of identification with the nation-state. Rather, it can entail any kind of cultural identification movement, including movements across/through race and ethnicity, social class, sexuality, religion, spirituality, etc. This entails "local" intercultural engagement within culturally diverse spaces within or beyond national borders, as well as a sense of global communitarian responsibility, or the idea that all of humanity belongs to a single planetary community, in which identities are shared across a global universe at the global and local levels (Nussbaum, 1997). There is the sense that, since cosmopolitans identify as being at home in the world, they are required to engage themselves in promoting its well-being. This can be seen in work that promotes overarching ideals for education, humanitarian work, environmentalism, and philosophical movements (Appiah, 2006; Reimers, 2009), creating opportunities for service and social justice.

Gunesch (2004) identifies seven areas of personal concern to the negotiation of cosmopolitan identity: simultaneous straddling of the global and the local; competence that displays a respect for local cultural diversity wherever possible; an engaged openness towards cultural diversity; the ability/mobility to cross cultural boundaries regularly; a rejection of the typical tourist approach towards travel (i.e., travel as cultural commodification); a postmodern notion of home; and a critical attitude towards the nation-state (pp. 15–17). Not all individuals who cross borders regularly are considered cosmopolitan, nor would all self-identify as having a cosmopolitan identity. As Appiah (2006) notes, "you can't have any respect for human diversity and expect everyone to become cosmopolitan" (p. xx). In order to negotiate cosmopolitanism, one must recognize that not everyone can, will, should, or would want to negotiate this identity.

What happens to those who seek this ideal of cosmopolitanism but can never achieve it—or alternatively, those who live in hybridized spaces but cannot, will not, or do not wish to be forced into such an ideal? The benefits of cosmopolitanism "on the ground" should be contextualized through an orientation towards communication competence that stresses humility. This kind of communication competence is well-defined by Tervalon and Murray-García (1998) in the area of multicultural training for physicians. The authors describe communication competence not as a static outcome (or, to contextualize for this chapter, a cosmopolitan state), but rather as "a commitment and active engagement in a lifelong process that individuals enter into on an ongoing basis with patients, communities, colleagues, and with themselves" (p. 118). This process negotiates a space between humility through self-reflexivity, and critique of and empathy for power imbalances across diverse communities. If this kind of orientation can be folded into the definition of cosmopolitanism, this allows it to become less of an end-state than an ongoing process, which treats individuals with respect and humility regardless of their socioeconomic status, race, mobility, gender, sexual orientation, or nationality (but without trivializing differences).

Dialectical Tensions of Cosmopolitanism

Theorizing about cosmopolitanism often entails negotiations between global and local (see Beck, 2006; Kaufmann, 2003). The dialectical nature of cosmopolitanism's pull between global and local creates an interesting tension between the rooted relativist and the rootless universalist. As such, those with a cosmopolitan orientation to the world feel both allegiances pulling at their sense of self-concept in relation to others. It is this very tension which creates the cosmopolitan identity in those cultural border crossers.

Cosmopolitan identities represent further dialectical tensions, and as such can be well-informed by using Martin and Nakayama's (2008) concept of intercultural dialectics. This also links identity to hybridity as negotiating multiple paradoxical forces coexisting within one individual. In this manner, then, several other dialectical tensions might well describe the kinds of both/and (rather than either/or) orientations of cosmopolitanism. These could include orientation-to-self/orientation-to-other, insider/outsider, universal/particular, cultural/individual and privilege/disadvantage (Martin and Nakayama, 2008). For example, drawing from Tervalon and Murray-García's (1998) discussion of humility and self-reflexivity, one dialectic of negotiating a cosmopolitan identity could entail an orientation of critical honesty with the self in order to orient with sensitive openness to the other (orientation-to-self/orientation-to-other). Here, it is imperative to examine one's own preconceived notions; to critique these in a humble way; to acknowledge the need to act knowledgeable, correct, and professional; and to remain open to the unique experiences of every individual—even as these experiences and identities are steeped in context and must be understood as such. This simultaneous critical orientation to self and other engages in constant reevaluation of communicative processes. Additionally, it creates a space of tension that can and should be constantly revisited and renegotiated.

Another dialectical tension to be navigated when negotiating a cosmopolitan identity involves the simultaneous existence as an insider/outsider. That is, cosmopolitan identity involves also a feeling of being more at home in the world than in any one part of it. This creates a sense of interconnection and mindfulness, but also fosters isolation and homesickness for a non-existent home. This may be viewed as moral universalism but can also be seen as empathetic relativism. Cosmopolitans may be able to judge all cultural groups on their own unique terms through shared empathy [see Appiah's (2006) discussions of female vs. male circumcision or Gunesch's (2004) respect for local cultural diversity], *or* focus on some universal model of idealized humanitarian goals, which would break down the very idea of the nation-state.

While globalization dictates that borders are blurring, particularly with regard to nation-state identity, the unique cultural markers that create cultural identities cannot and should not be shirked in the name of cosmopolitanism. Alternatively, cosmopolitanism need not be limited to the privileged, Western elite. Werbner (2008) finds that non-elite and non-Western cosmopolitanism is possible, although this is often largely due to the pressures of globalization and postcolonial migration (p. 347). Furia (2005), who uses the World Values Survey to evaluate whether cosmopolitanism is elitist and Western, finds that the United States "... is arguably the *only* 'privileged' society to rank among the top five most cosmopolitan societies . . . [joining] Jordan, Brazil, the Dominican Republic, and Mexico in ranking the highest in terms of the societal prevalence of 'moral cosmopolitanism'" (p. 354, italics added). So, in order to negotiate a cosmopolitan identity, one must neither be elite nor Western, and can have allegiances to local cultural diversity as well as a sense of global citizenship. Can cosmopolitanism be taught in a pedagogical context such as a classroom or workspace, similar to Tervalon and Murray-García's (1998) lifelong learner model? Or is it something one learns through the course of life and environmental circumstances, combined with one's unique orientation to the world, upbringing and experience? Must one be privileged in order to have a cosmopolitan orientation to the world?

Teaching Cosmopolitanism

Several of Gunesch's (2004) criteria can be adapted to a rubric for teaching cosmopolitanism. These involve empathetic mindfulness, willingness to embrace difference, curiosity about other ways of life to the point of being willing to change some fundamental paradigms, global/local engagement, and humanistic responsibility. Each of these can be situated within intercultural communication literature in different ways.[3]

A cosmopolitan educational framework lays out the criteria to create citizens of the world, through recognizing that "previously isolated groups now live in close proximity, and this new reality gives rise to significant new opportunities as well as new challenges to be confronted and overcome" (Waks, 2010, p. 590). Reimers (2009) describes three dimensions of global competency (or a cosmopolitan educational framework) that can be taught: acceptance (beyond mere tolerance) of cultural difference and "a framework of global values to engage difference" (p. 2); verbal and nonverbal proficiency, since the link between empathizing with another culture is made the strongest through linguistic compe-

This leaves out a lot of people who are never given the opportunity to normally learn these things ↓

tence; and a "deep knowledge and understanding of world history, geography, and global dimensions of topics such as health, climate, and economics of the process of globalization itself" (p. 2) and the ability to be critical of these processes. While this may be a problematic framework for identity change, it provides a starting point through which to negotiate the tensions described above.

However, several barriers also exist for teaching cosmopolitanism. To begin with, the very notion that cosmopolitanism as a perspective can be imparted in a classroom setting invites problems and critiques. The criteria described above have not been tested and are not understood to actually lead to an outcome of being "more cosmopolitan." Indeed, cultural humility and self-reflexivity both entail lifelong learning processes as opposed to discretely defined outcomes. So in today's world of assessment, cosmopolitanism may not lend itself to the kind of specified, testable knowledge that must be learned in schools. Additionally, cultural awareness and reflexivity must be developed over time, ideally through exposure to difference that emphasizes both the ability to articulate one's own identity and to openly engage with others about theirs (Reimers, 2009). Without resources and time within the curriculum through which to mindfully expose students to difference, teaching cosmopolitanism can easily become another oversimplified way through which to deal with diversity. In an era where schools are cutting funding across curricula from elementary schools to universities, teaching cosmopolitanism in a nuanced manner that represents non-Western, non-elitist, vernacular viewpoints may not be given the time nor the attention needed—particularly if it is at the expense of other subjects such as math and sciences. Using extracurricular activities to teach cosmopolitanism is an option (which will be discussed in more detail below); however, as many after-school programs such as the Girl Scouts and the Boys and Girls Clubs of America are already underfunded, there is, again, a question of time, money, and resources.

Cosmopolitanism provides an educational agenda that acknowledges "the ubiquity of change and the presence of difference, but it also perceives these conditions as promising rather than merely problematic" (Hansen, Burdick-Shepherd, Cammarano, and Obelleiro, 2009, p. 590). Thus, at a surface level, aspects of cosmopolitanism can be taught, under the rubric of educating for global competency, which emphasizes the intercultural communication competence model (see Hansen et al., 2009; Reimers, 2009). Intercultural communication competence involves acquiring "in-depth knowledge, heightened mindfulness, and competent communication skills—and, most critically, applying them ethnically in a diverse range of intercultural situations" (Ting-Toomey, 1999, pp. 265–66). Ting-Toomey describes five competencies that are imperative to bridge cross-cultural differences in communication: global perspectives on politics and culture; the ability to take multiple perspectives in relationships; skill in communicating with multiple cultural groups, the ability to adapt comfortably to living in other cultures, and the necessity of equal treatment and respect for multiple points of view. Such competencies increase knowledge, mindfulness, and skills in intercultural interactions (see also Collier, 2005).

Cosmopolitanism can be viewed as a conceptual framework through which to understand intercultural communication competence. However, this approach assumes that multiple perspectives are skills that can be taught, with outcomes that can be measured. Shifting from a more traditional model of intercultural communication competence (such as Ting Toomey's) toward notions more similar to cultural humility (Tervalon and Murray-García, 1998) and relational empathy (Broome, 1991) might prove useful. This shift focuses less on specific measurable outcomes and more on reflexive synthesis of experiences that can lead to a lifelong process of cosmopolitanism. A practical example of this kind of curriculum is provided below.

In a current research project, a colleague and I are working with Hostelling International (HI), whose mission is "to help all, especially the young, gain a better understanding of the world and its people through hostelling" (www.hiusa.org). Through this mission, HI-USA works to bring education for global competency to individuals who might not ordinarily have the opportunity for such exchanges. Through experiential and project-based learning (Gibson, Rimmington, and Landwehr-Brown, 2008), HI-USA has created global-learning opportunities for individuals who often have not left the four-block radius of their home cities. In other words, this can be seen as an illustration of bringing cosmopolitan values to those who may not engage in regular border crossings.

One example of this programming includes Cultural Kitchen, where middle-school students spend ten sessions learning about another culture, spend the night at the hostel and cook a meal for their families, friends and hostellers that represents that culture. The hostellers may eat their meal for free as long as they discuss their own travel experiences with the students. This gives opportunities for its students to communicate about a culture entirely new to them, and to explain and discuss their own experiences with travelers. It provides exposure to multiple cultural groups and gives the students a window into a lifestyle traveling might make available to them, and shows them how this can be achieved on a shoe-string budget. Another sample program, Exchange Neighborhoods, "pairs two high schools to host the other school in an exploration of each other's cultures," and through this, teaches high school students in inner city schools to "build pride around their own culture, while opening their minds to learn about a new neighborhood and culture of their peers" (www.hichicago.org/community_ens.shtml). A third program is called Community Walls, where students paint murals of their neighborhoods and then are required to self-reflexively explain their murals, which are put on display in public places such as Chicago's Midway Airport.

These three sample programs attempt to create new learning experiences for their students in various ways. Exchange Neighborhoods provides a site for learning relational empathy, not only through putting students in one another's shoes over an extended period of time, but by asking them to self-reflexively compare their own ways of life to those of their counterparts through free writing, dialogue, and in the end, a group presentation. Cultural Kitchen gives participants an opportunity to learn (somewhat) extensively about a nationality different from theirs (thereby assisting intercultural knowledge growth). It also provides a third cultural space (Broome, 1991) through which participants can learn about multiple cultures and describe their own, which could promote cultural curiosity. Community Walls focuses on cultural self-awareness, encouraging students to not only illustrate their homes and neighborhood spaces, but to do so in a reflexive manner, knowing that they will have to share this information with an unknown audience. All of the programs include debriefing, writing activities, and often simulation games beyond the experiential learning. Further, all three programs contain a component that asks participants to develop their knowledge beyond their local spheres, to a more global level awareness. The goals for these programs include teaching students what it means to be both insider and outsider, how they can be simultaneously privileged and disadvantaged, and most importantly, how to orient to the world in a manner that includes self-reflexivity and humility as well as openness and tolerance. To help HI in their endeavor of providing such programming, we are using a cosmopolitan educational framework (Hansen et al., 2009) to examine and assess the educational programmers, educational programming, and student outcomes for programming at Hostelling International, Chicago.[4] The results from this study should help illuminate whether or not cosmopolitanism can be taught, and how teaching can focus on process rather than outcome.

While I remain optimistic that certain aspects of cosmopolitanism can be taught, this doesn't necessarily mean that all people can and should want to cultivate a cosmopolitan identity. Nor does it mean that simply learning about another culture's language and customs is enough to create embodied cosmopolitanism. Indeed, much of the discussion above could be reconceptualized to sound like teaching cosmopolitanism equates to teaching intercultural communication competence. While part of a cosmopolitan perspective may include intercultural competence, it should be noted that those two terms are not interchangeable. The sense of rootlessness, the lack of home, the potentiality for involuntary, vernacular cosmopolitanism stemming from postcolonial shifts in population and power—these are ways of being that do not necessarily fit into the rooted positionalities assumed by the literature on intercultural communication competence.

Further, critics would note that the privilege to voluntarily cross borders often enough to gain a sense of global citizenship is a prerequisite for cosmopolitan identity (see Harris, 2003); and simply crossing a neighborhood to learn about one's own and other cultures is not enough to change an orientation towards the world. Cosmopolitanism as a disposition may not have anything to do with exposure to an intercultural mindset; even if it does require this exposure, that exposure may not necessarily be voluntary. Examples of this include those who have been colonized and are forced to learn the ways of the colonizers so as to function in those societies (such as the people of Papua New Guinea following Australian colonization; see Strathern and Stewart, 2010); and those who have been involuntarily and violently displaced throughout their histories, and are required to learn and relearn new cultural customs in order to survive and thrive repeatedly across the world (such as rootless cosmopolitan Jews; see Azadovskii and Egerov, 2002).

So even though certain aspects of cosmopolitanism can be taught, the larger answer to the question of whether or not this is a teachable phenomenon is that the complexity of teaching an orientation to the world may not be achievable—and further, it may not be ethical. As Appiah (2006) notes, cosmopolitans should understand that cosmopolitanism should not—indeed, cannot—be forced. The next issue to address in this chapter, then, involves who actually does identify as having a cosmopolitan identity. What kinds of people embody this phenomenon and why? Why are some people more likely to identify as cosmopolitan than others?

WHO HAS A COSMOPOLITAN IDENTITY?

Many scholars (see, for example, Calhoun, 2002; and Harris, 2003) would posit that in order to be "eligible" for a cosmopolitan identity, individuals must have the privilege to voluntarily cross cultural borders on a regular basis and a presence of mind and intellectual training that enables them to engage their transition experiences at the cosmopolitan level. This locates cosmopolitanism as Calhoun's (2002) "rich-man's" doctrine, embodying "the class consciousness of frequent travelers" (p. 86). While this position should not be discounted, I believe that it oversimplifies what it means to have a cosmopolitan identity, limiting the construct to little more than an indictment of (white) male privilege, globalization and the tourist industry.

When examining who embodies a cosmopolitan identity, dialectical tensions must be explored for their nuances across and within cultural spheres. To utilize Martin and Nakayama's (2008) intercultural dialectics, cosmopolitan identities are negotiated within the spaces of the cultural and the individual, the personal and the contextual, the privileged and the disadvantaged. For example, a cosmopolitan individual is constantly negotiating identity as idiosyncratic and at a distance from any one cultural affiliation. She or he sees her or himself as a member of any number of multiple larger cultural groups, whether these entail where that person was born, currently resides, or what race, ethnicity, religious affiliation and sexual orientation s/he identifies with and how this shifts as s/he crosses borders. Personal identities must be negotiated through constantly shifting contextual influences.

Rather than imagining that a cosmopolitan identity is a privilege available only to those with sufficient economic, social, and cultural capital to become frequent border-crossers, I contend that it is more useful to conceptualize this as both an orientation to the world and a communicative phenomenon, which engages both experiential and dialogic processes. Individuals are more interconnected as a result of globalization, and as such, all of us have more intercultural experiences and cross more cultural borders everyday—through technology, media, global economics, and demographic flows—than our ancestors had the opportunity to. Therefore, globalization is symbiotic with cosmopolitanism (Roberts, 2008). Mobility, as a construct, should not presuppose privilege: "people, commodities, cultures, and technologies are all mobile . . . mobilities are not just flows but networked relations and are globally organized in new kinds of spaces and temporal processes" (Delanty, 2006, p. 32). Therefore, the argument that cosmopolitan identities can only be experienced by the privileged elite contradicts Martin and Nakayama's (2008) notion of simultaneously coexisting privilege and disadvantage. Hall and Werbner (2008) aptly note that identity is not a "free-floating smorgasbord . . . [but] is always tied to history and place, to time, to narratives, to memory and ideologies" (p. 347). However, they go on to state that identity is also always in process, through social, historical and cultural constructions. As such, we are all exposed to more difference than ever before, and it is our reactions that determine whether or not we have a cosmopolitan orientation.

If cosmopolitanism can be conceived of as discursive, transformative, translative communicative space (Delanty, 2006), then it is elitist to assume that only the privileged Westerner has access to this perspective and space. The very dichotomizing of the world into East and West, for example, takes a decidedly *un*-cosmopolitan, non-dialectical stance. Further, according to Furia (2005), Appiah (2006) and Delanty (2006), cosmopolitans don't necessarily have to self-identify as cosmopolitan in order to take this orientation towards the world. Delanty (2006) describes cosmopolitans as "people who construct their lives from whatever cultural resources to which they find themselves attached" (p. 30). This can just as easily apply to African-Americans, who "show up as more cosmopolitan than U.S. Caucasians on *every one* of the thirty-two indicators of cosmopolitanism" (Furia, 2005, p. 353, italics in original) as do Jordanians, Brazilians, Dominican Republicans, and Mexicans.

So why do some people identify as cosmopolitan and not others? Why is it that a graduate student of mine who was raised in a small town in Germany and now lives in Carbondale, Illinois, has a deep interest in cultural connections, and has traveled to five continents of the world, while her sister—indeed, her entire family—has rarely left their town to travel outside of Germany? When this student read Appiah (2006) and Hannerz (1996) in preparation for her MA thesis, she described the theory (both in class and later on to me in my office) as the clearest conceptualization of her experience she had encountered throughout her studies. While it may be true that those with exposure to multiple cultures from a young age may be more likely to identify as cosmopolitan than those who have never left the vicinity in which they grew up, this is certainly not always the case. Further, just because an individual travels a great deal does not necessarily make them cosmopolitan. Just as cosmopolitanism may not necessitate the literal crossing of boundaries [see McEwan and Sobré-Denton's (in press) discussion of virtual and socially mediated cosmopolitanism], cosmopolitanism need not only apply to those with travel experience, even from a young age. Cultural curiosity and an interculturally oriented mindset could lead to cosmopolitanism, particularly when added to intercultural experience (corporeal or virtual) and skilled, mindful intercultural communication competence. That curiosity can drive individuals with little or no cosmopolitan influences to develop a cosmopolitan orientation to life; conversely, those who experience a life of constant cultural border-crossing may yearn for nothing more than a stable location to call home.

CRITICAL ETHICAL COSMOPOLITANISM

So how do cosmopolitan-identified individuals grapple with issues of systemic power? Delanty (2006) defines critical cosmopolitanism as "the cosmopolitan imagination [that] occurs when and wherever new relations between the self, other and world develop in moments of openness" (p. 27). This calls attention to multiple forms of cosmopolitanism, including moral, political, and cultural cosmopolitanism. As such, Delanty reappropriates cosmopolitanism as "a cultural medium for societal transformation that is based on the principle of world openness" (p. 27). This world openness provides the ethical mandate to resist systemic oppression through transformative mutual implication of the global and local in the largest system of all—that of the world. This entails a learning process in which human agency is recognizable as having the potential to transform present systemic oppression into an imagined future of reflexivity, cohesion, and a sharing of the burdens of globalization. Those individuals who identify as cosmopolitan, according to Delanty (2006), engage in opening dialogic spaces that move beyond ethnocentricity through internalizing the following values: irony (an affective distancing from one's home culture that allows for critique); reflexivity (an understanding that cultural affectations are learned through social conditioning); skepticism towards ideological grand narratives that reify power structures; empathy towards other cultures; a dialectical orientation towards cultural hybridity; a commitment to open dialogue with other cultures; and a sense of displacement or homelessness (pp. 42–43). Cosmopolitan identity entails an embracing of the ethical implications that shared global responsibility makes salient—regardless of whether the individual agrees with other members of this world system, cosmopolitan or not.

CONCLUSION

I maintain that a cosmopolitan identity or disposition is an overwhelmingly communicative phenomenon, stemming from discourse, dialogue, empathy, and constant negotiation and renegotiation of the self, other and the world. I wonder why intercultural communication scholars have arrived so late to the application of this construct which has been fruitfully cultivated by sociologists, anthropologists, political theorists and philosophers. This may be due to concerns about the inherent violence of utilizing a term that has been (rightfully) perceived in the past as elitist, colonizing, and critically problematic (Harris, 2003). However, communication scholarship—while it must be responsible and self-conscious in its choice of channels of communication (such as language choices)—is young enough and innovative enough to be able to take certain contested terms, purposively divest them of their negative connotations, and with those in mind, reconfigure them with new meanings. Examples of similar reappropriative moves include the viability of the word "queer" as a term of empowerment (Berlant, Warner, Clarke, and Denisoff, 1994; Fox, 2007; Jagose, 1996); the Black is Beautiful movement and its revaluing of the connotations of the group label "black" (Smith, 1992; Turner and Tajfel, 1986); reappropriation of stigmatizing labels such as "geek" and "nerd" (Galinsky, Hugenberg, Groom, and Bodenhausen, 2003). These kinds of reappropriation, while not discounting the difficult history of contested terms, allows for the reimagining of such terms by cultural communities as a form of empowerment, a means for undoing past violences, and reapplying language in more empowering and useful ways. As intercultural communication scholarship embraces postcolonialism and hybridity theory to an increasing extent, cosmopolitanism, if it can be extracted from its colonizing and elitist connotations, can provide a multifaceted, dialectical/dialogical framework through which to better understand communicative processes in a world where boundaries are increasingly porous.

The implications of this chapter span pedagogical, theoretical, methodological, and praxiological spheres. The pedagogical processes of cosmopolitanism are one direction for this research to take, i.e., identifying how cosmopolitanism can be understood and conceptualized for the intercultural communication classroom. As such, I call for intercultural communication scholars to use this framework in teaching about issues of globalization, transnationalism, postcolonialism, and mindful intercultural communication. It should be noted here that this call also entails teaching students about the colonial roots of cosmopolitan theory, in an attempt to understand both the implications of what came before (e.g., Kant, the Sophists, the violence of colonialism) in order to better understand and reconfigure cosmopolitanism for more positive, postcolonial and critically transformative intercultural efforts.

In terms of theoretical and methodological implications, engaging cosmopolitanism in intercultural communication scholarship includes grappling with critiques of cosmopolitanism as Westernized and elitist, and learning how to better operationalize it as a framework for research. Cosmopolitanism can be engaged at the individual identity level, but should also be explored in terms of interpersonal interactions, social networks, and global cultural flows such as migration and pop-cultural/media influences. Finally, praxiologically, this chapter raises the importance of understanding cosmopolitanism as a rubric for transformative critical pedagogy and praxis. In order to do this, it is imperative to continue to explore how the term "cosmopolitan" can be loosened from its problematic and colonial roots, in order to create space for work that involves social justice and bridge building at local and global levels. In other words, the central question is: How can cosmopolitanism be harnessed to engage the global good rather than reifying currently existing injustices?

In short, this chapter provides only the first steps in a stream of possibilities that can be gleaned from the adoption and adaptation of this perspective in a manner that engages postcolonial notions of culture, as a means of moving beyond the modernist conceptions of what it means to be a citizen of the world. An orientation towards the world as entailing an embracing of difference, kindness to strangers, and a positionality that engages empathy, reflexivity and mindfulness are all more than fitting goals for the future of identity studies in intercultural communication scholarship. A perspective that locates cosmopolitanism within the dialectics of rooted and rootless, global and local, above and below, can create spaces for dialogue that can potentially interrupt systemic power structures through teaching, research, and community service.

NOTES

1. Much of the literature used in this chapter tends to engage cosmopolitanism as a universalist term, as an embodiment of a utopian cosmopolitan figure completely freed of local attachments and epistemologies that frame the relational aspect of identity. While I draw from this literature and therefore some of these views are echoed in this piece, I would like to acknowledge that my own dialectical and negotiated perspective on cosmopolitanism assumes that it has multiple forms (at the individual, social, cultural, and global levels) and that these forms are constantly renegotiated throughout transnational and postcolonial cultural shifts and global flows.

2. This chapter does not necessarily advocate for the notion of identity-as-rootless as a desirable state. In terms of negotiating identities, loosened cultural ties can make this process much more problematic and confusing. However, the argument that Appiah (among others) is making here is that, due to the influences of globalization, hybridized identities are becoming more prevalent, and as such, an understanding of how identities are constructed and flow when cultural selves become more rootless than rooted bears consideration.

3. See, among others, Broome's (1991) work on relational empathy and how it can be used in the intercultural classroom; Collier's (1989) discussion of mindful intercultural communication; Casmir's (1997) positioning of third culture theory; and Evanoff's (2006) nuanced treatment of ethic responsibility through intercultural dialogue.

4. I am aware of the conflict between cultural humility as process-based learning and the assessment-based skills more present in communication competence models, and that this current project seeks to assess the very process-based learning that may not lead to measurable/discrete outcomes. However, we are still interested in understanding whether students experience paradigm shifts, and intend to use participant/observation, interviews, and other qualitative data collection methods to "see what happens" to these students.

EIGHT

Cultural Matter as Political Matter

A Preliminary Exploration from a Chinese Perspective

Hsin-I Cheng

The content and scope of intercultural communication research continues to be a focal reflection in the field (Leeds-Hurwitz, 1990; Moon 1996; 2010; Shuter, 1990). Leeds-Hurwitz (1990) and Moon (1996; 2010) re/locate the scope and development of intercultural communication research agenda. Their studies provide a historicized account for the ways in which "culture" has been investigated in the U.S. academy with considerations of political, economic, and social movements. In terms of seeking localized understanding, Shome (2010) advocates for expanding research foci on "the connections between cultural power and larger geopolitical relations and international histories as they come to inform unequal power relations between different cultural groups and identities, and their practices and imaginations" (p. 150). This chapter explores how culture is perceived and experienced in Chinese contexts. By focusing on how culture is conceptualized within contextualized interactions in relation to histories and present globalized world, this study aims to explore the impact of intercultural communication knowledge on culture, identity, and communication. First, this chapter broadly discusses intercultural communication scholarship on culture and identity. Specifically, it introduces Asiancentrism, a culturally specific paradigm in inter/cultural knowledge production. Next, an example based on ethnographic work and group interviews with Chinese college students is provided to illustrate the need for considering contemporary socioeconomic and geopolitical forces in research on culture and communication. The chapter concludes with implications for future research.

CULTURAL KNOWLEDGE IN THE FIELD OF INTERCULTURAL COMMUNICATION

The conversation about how "culture" has been conceptualized in the field of intercultural communication began decades ago. Examining the origin and development of the research foci in the field, Leeds-Hurwitz (1990) points to Edward Hall's collaboration with the U.S. Foreign Service Institute during the 1940s and 1950s. In her tracings, micro-level analyses of interactions in particular national regions were found in major research on cultures. As Moon (1996) points out, the scholarly treatment of culture during the 1980s and 1990s was fed by the international political atmosphere in which culture was represented by national identities and reduced to a set of characteristics influenced by distinct cultural values. Much research on cross-cultural comparison works to facilitate cultural adjustments often between two societies, one of which often is English-speaking and the other is not. Meanwhile, Shuter (1990) provides critiques on how research from the 1980s to the 1990s could be furthered with more focus on the unique communication patterns within a particular cultural group. He further promotes intracultural communication research in building theoretical investigations. The call for specific attention to localized practice deserves our attention for it relates to how culture is materialized in everyday life. However, its reliance on geographical descriptions and seeming assumption of the unity within cultural groups suggests a somewhat static view toward "culture" and its "land referent" association (Jackson and Garner, 1998, p. 43). Our present life is full of interactions unbound by physical relocation such as that of im/migrants. This dynamism invites further consideration of seeking how one's identity, namely, making sense of one's relations to the world, is accomplished through everyday communication.

The need to problematize the notion of cultural references as naturally and neutrally given characteristics ascribed to individuals within a nation-state boundary was suggested in the late 1990s (Ono, 1998). Too often, historical and power relational contexts are omitted in discerning interactions between peoples with heterogeneous backgrounds. Jackson and Garner (1998) conclude that racial, ethnic, and cultural research is often indistinguishable from one another in the field of communication. In fact, culture is often conceptualized as less contentious and "categorically inclusive of ethnicity and race" (p. 51). Further, they critique the superficial binary conceptualizations without historicized and multifaceted understanding of identity experiences prevalent in the field of communication scholarship.

Y. Y. Kim (2007) generates five themes of cultural identity research in communication scholarship based on "ideological messages" that promote "assimilationism, pluralism, integrationism, and separatism" positions (p. 239). The article concludes that intercultural communication scholarship can be divided into two broad "philosophical-methodological" knowledge bases including "the assimilationist and integrative side" and the "pluralistic and separatist side" (p. 249). The assimilationist and integrative scholarship with the premise of individual cultural identity is "more 'universalized' and 'individuated'" (p. 248), and it is "consistent with the 'melting-pot' view of cultural identity" (p. 244). The other side is what Y. Y. Kim refers to as "the pluralistic and separatist side" where "critical researchers'" advocacy of pluralistic ideals is reflected in the conception of cultural identity as largely ascription-based and a monolithic entity" with "an implicit message that gives cultural identity a nonnegotiable moral and political imperative" (p. 249). This perspective risks to "overlook the potential 'dark side' of a rigid, categorical adherence to cultural identity, that is, the tendencies of collective ingroup glorification and outgroup denigration" (Y. Y. Kim, p. 249). Kim's article points to an important issue which is the tension between the individual and group based perspectives toward cultural identity while it alludes to a historically contained or/and geographically bound context with a pre-existing "pot" for individuals' cultural identity to universally melt into. Further the article seems to suggest that research focuses on the role of historical and sociopolitical conditions in which cultural identity is transformed and negotiated in negative or even divisive ways. Such a perspective may risk fixating demarcation of cultural "ingroup . . . [versus] outgroup" (Y. Y. Kim, p. 249) and creating a static view toward the "broad social histories, critical personal antecedents, and subjective interpretations of others that encase our realities" in forming and negotiating identifications (Jackson and Moshin, 2010, p. 348).

Over the years, research on how cultural identity as social reality is communicatively experienced by groups of various power locations in U.S. society has been published (e.g., Halualani, 2002; Nakayama, 2004; Warren, 2003b). Orbe's (1998) co-cultural theory focuses on lived experiences and communication strategies enacted by co-cultural members to achieve particular interactive outcomes. Aoki (2000), Flores (1996), and González (1989), along with many others, have contextualized and interrogated rhetorical construction and communication codes of Latino/a in the United States. Attention has been paid to the ways in which class identity serves as a cultural marker intersecting with other identities such as ethnicity and gender that demarcate in-group and out-group members (Moon, 2001; Philipsen, 1975; Wong, 2004). Kinefuchi (2010a) and Cheng (2008) study the complicated ways in which recent immigrants from fareast and south-east Asia strategically make sense of their lives in the United States pending on their status and available resources. These are just a few examples where intersectionality serves as the analytical lenses where class, gender, able-bodiness, nationality, legal status, age, linguistic ability, sexual orientation, and race/ethnicity are accounted for in one's negotiation of cultural identity.

In this regard, we have witnessed exciting scholarship that has paid special consideration to how power structures are implicated in the processes of identity negotiations, specifically in U.S. contexts. Meanwhile, Shome (2010) reminds us that it is imperative to recognize "the connections between cultural power and larger geopolitical relations and international histories as they come to inform unequal power relations between different cultural groups and identities, and their practices and imaginations" (p. 150). In the flux of shifting emphases on nuanced understanding of contextualized intercultural communication, Shome further encourages an expansion of "intellectual imagination" by moving the analytical sphere to the global arena (p. 151).

In tracing various driving forces behind the legitimacy of claiming cultural imagination and representation of the self and other, intercultural researchers continue to point to the need to examine the impact of European-based knowledge production on various ways of lives. Afrocentric (Asante, 2006) and Asiancentric (Miike, 2007) paradigms are two exemplars where cultural understanding is decentralized and relocated within a culturally specific perspective. Further, claims are made with assumptions from those capable of knowledge dissemination and control, and they impact cultural identities created and consumed. One such example is the extolment of "aggressive individualism" (Asante, 2006, p. 156) in "Eurocentric theories of communication" (Miike, 2007, p. 273) as the cultural ideal promoting "triumphalism over others" (Asante, 2006, p. 156).

Conventional concepts used in intercultural communication research such as individualism versus collectivism also have begun to be reexamined. Wong and Liu (2010), for example, cogently critique how Confucius societies are labeled as collectivistic and deemed irrelevant to modernity in which individualistic Western societies belong. Such scholarship points our attention to nuanced cultural understandings which have been largely blindsided by applications of theoretical concepts without scrutinizing contexts and consequently creating misrepresentations. Specifications to the process in which local knowledge is lived provide multilayered understanding toward cultural experiences. For the purpose of this chapter, I discuss Asiacentrism and its implications for understanding culture, communication, and identity, particularly in contemporary Chinese contexts.

ASIACENTRICITY AND CULTURAL KNOWLEDGE OF IDENTITY

Critiquing the heavy reliance on Europe and U.S. centered knowledge, Miike (2007; 2010) proposes Asiacentrism as a "meta-theoretical" and analytical paradigm for intercultural communication research on "Asian" cultures from linguistic, religious-philosophical, and historical dimensions. Such a paradigm advocates centering on non-Western women and men's lived experiences within its history during academic scholarship production (Miike, 2010; Yin, 2009). "Asiacentricity as a metatheory concerns itself more with *how* we theorize that with *what* we theorize" (Miike, 2010, p. 201, italics in original). Asiacentricism highlights cultural salience such as Confucian practice in many Asian societies, and asserts that by locating our understanding locally (e.g., keeping harmonious relationships in the Confucius teaching) better intercultural communication may be reached (Miike, 2010). This paradigm encourages contextualizing cultural meanings in traditional wisdom embedded in linguistic and philosophical teachings rooted in shared history within a cultural group. Yet, in the present, interconnected world histories are re/created in geopolitical power nexuses that are regionally and globally unbalanced. As Clifford (2000) explicates, the future is imagined when "people selectively mobilize . . . [and articulate] tradition[s]" that do not "fundamentally threaten the dominant political-economic order . . . in a productive game of identities" (pp. 97–100). Overlooking the political and socioeconomic relations particular to a location risks perpetuating the dominant knowledge that produces structures that the paradigm sets out to interrogate. The impact of societal and ideological structure on cultural identification, and how including this analytical perspective may enhance academic understanding of intercultural communication, is left unknown.

Kuo and Chew (2009) critique Asiacentrism as an oppositional, polarized and ethnically divisive paradigm in which a dichotomy of "East" versus "West" is created. They call for a more harmonious and integrated model that builds "theories that transcend regional applications" (p. 428). Such a theoretical stance, they argue, would be "humanocentric" (p. 430), and would focus on finding the "universalism" of cultural-centric paradigms for similarities among various cultural groups (e.g., using *guanxi/* connections to explain social networking in Western societies). With the intention to harmonize, this critique seems to negate historical, political, and material differences brought upon by specific experiences.

Promoting "universal" value integration may compromise particular meanings for those who have been marginalized and silenced in "universalism." An agreement, for example, advocating openness such as that made possible through the North American Free Trade Agreement (NAFTA) has different consequences for people in Mexico, the United States and Canada. Even within the same nation-state, people in various social positions have experienced it differently (Burfisher, Robinso, and Thierfelder, 2001; Malkin, 2009). The sociopolitical atmosphere each society affords its residents brings forth the distinct cultural expressions that might share similar meaning on the surface level and yet carry drastically different logics underneath. In searching for a delicate balance between cultural universalism and specificism, both "Asiacentrism" and "human-ocentrism" paradigms seem to view culture as an inclusive concept void of current forces of geopolitics. Further, they suggest that it is possible to address current intercultural communication issues by separating the cultural from the political. This chapter attempts to seek how culture can (not) be separated from the political realm from the perspective of a group of Chinese college students in our contemporary interconnected world. This referential study is described and presented next.

CULTURAL SPECIFICITY IN TRANSNATIONAL CONTEXT

This study is an ethnographic exploration using participatory observation and group interviews which I conducted at a university in southeast China during November and December, 2010. I attended and took field notes on formal and informal discussions with roughly forty students.[1] In addition, four focus group discussions were conducted and each lasted from two to two-and-a-half hours with a total of twenty-seven participants. All were born in the late 1980s, a decade after Dong's economic reforms in 1978.

When I first asked the participants to describe what culture meant to them, they initially had identical responses. For example, one participant explained that "culture is everything that is created in the course of human development, and that it includes two levels. One is the material level and the other is more of the spiritual level." They explained that historic relics in Rome, paintings like Mona Lisa, would comprise materialistic culture, and religions such as Islam and traditional rituals comprise the spiritual level of culture. When I asked them how they came to the definition, they all laughed and one participant said, "From the textbooks in high schools." One commented, "I hope I didn't memorize the definition wrong." One shared "I know it is sad [that we only think based on textbooks and exams, but that is what happens here]." There was overwhelming agreement on how, as Chinese, they themselves are collectivistic people who are less inclined to be critical thinkers than those in the United States. When I further asked about their most recent experience with culture as a concept, each time the discussion became lively with much uniqueness and critical depth beyond the given definition. They explained it from the perspective of how they understand themselves and want to be understood by others. From re/reading the field notes and transcripts, patterns emerged suggesting that the more the conversations occurred, the more the pronounced role of sociopolitical structure was revealed in these young Chinese students' daily experiencing of culture and ways of relating to their realities.

Culture as Politics

For these participants, a sense of politics at the national and global levels permeates discussions on culture. When speaking of Chinese culture, participants often brought up Confucianism as the featured or selected identifying representative of Chinese culture to help foreigners understand the culture better. In "making it easier" for those who have "little understanding of the Chinese culture," Confucianism serves as a token symbol for promoting Chineseness outside China. A student described how "there is misunderstanding of what Confucianism is. It is different from what it was in the past because of many interpretations and societal conditions." Several mentioned how they themselves might not be as heavily influenced by Confucianism since it was revitalized only within the last couple of decades. One participant stated that "culture is never separated from politics" and the influence of Confucianism has waxed and waned in history pending on the given political will.

In discussing Makeham's work on the development of Confucianism in the People's Republic of China (PRC), Tan (2008) points to the role of "cultural nationalists" in the revitalization of Confucian "traditional values" after the end of the Cultural Revolution which lasted from 1966 to 1976. In addition to the PRC, governments in Singapore and Taiwan have heavily sponsored academic scholarship in hopes of claiming Chinese cultural identity even earlier (Tan, 2008). These students' critiques resonate with Makeham's statement on "culture as deployed for the purposes of defining a particular sort of political identity" (cited in Tan, 2008, p. 580). For example, conventional Confucianism is perceived as a deterrent to modernization and democratization of the new Chinese cultural nationalism movement which was led by the Chinese intelligentsia against Western imperialistic powers after the Treaty of Versailles created post-World War I. Since then, Confucianism has been appropriated in various Chinese societies to serve particular purposes by highlighting its different doctrines. One of the most distinct examples is the contemporary framing of the "commercial or market economy" (Wong, 1997, p. 58) with "*ru* (Confucian) entrepreneurs" (Makeham, 2008, p. 323) to set it apart from capitalists in Western societies. As such, political and cultural influences are inseparable in understanding contemporary Chinese culture.

In our interactions, these students described a Confucianism that is deeply rooted in the Chinese ways of life such as harmony and role-abiding behaviors in relationships. All conversations went further when they unpacked the driving forces behind these values. For example, in the eyes of these students, the need to "follow the crowd" to keep harmony reveals more of an adhering to the environment than performing collectivistic characteristics of being easily influenced (Wong and Lui, 2010, p. 53). By pointing out "feeling the pressure to follow the crowd," the students showed their awareness of the struggle they experience when behaving in a culturally and politically appropriate manner. Such a keen critique of cultural values derived from their everyday political and social experiences was common in my interactions. One student mentioned how the most disrespectful insult for a Chinese is "go and greet your mother." It was explained that this statement indicates that the mother had an extramarital affair. A couple of students further questioned whether such an insult would work if a woman makes the statement about one's father because of the unbalanced gender power and rules in traditional teachings and current society. The level of analysis seemed quite strong and ironically juxtaposed in these students' frequent self-description as being "Chinese collectivists who do not think critically." Moreover, societal and political power relations were imbued in their unpacking of the meaning of part of their cultural identity.

Culture as Growth

The participants discussed how they experience culture from an active perspective through assimilation within political realms. Several participants used "Sinocizing" and "Americanizing" to explain their sense toward Chinese and U.S. American cultures. This is similar to viewing culture as "organic systems [that] . . . strive to affirm life so as to evolve and expand" (Rodriguez, 2002, p. 2). That is, they view culture as a process of "becoming" in accordance with the geopolitical structure of the world. Stockman (2000) stated that it is imperative to better understand Chinese society given China's economic and strategic powers. China is viewed as an emerging "soft power" in the world in these discussions, and these students recognized the growing Chinese cultural influences around the globe. One participant explained her hopes for "the Chinese language to be as influential as English so people all over the world have to learn it." As Zhang (2009) points out, Chinese identity construction is closely intertwined with its linguistic expressions, especially in the post-Mao and globalized era.

Through these interactions, I learned that Confucian Institutes established in 2004 are set out to do just that. They are designed to teach Chinese (i.e., Mandarin) to the world with the vision to "increase the development of cultural diversity and create a peaceful world" ("Confucius Institute Headquarter," n.d.). As projected on the homepage of the Confucius Institute Headquarter, the estimated number of Chinese/Mandarin learners would be one billion in 2010 globally. In October 2010, there were 322 Confucian Institutes and 369 Confucian classes in 96 countries across all continents. The goals of these nonprofit educational institutions lie in "increasing people all over the world's understanding to Chinese language and culture and furthering cultural exchange and collaboration" ("Confucius Institute Headquarter," n.d.). When the conversation went on to what counts as Chinese language, all participants agreed upon Mandarin. Two protested by asking: "What about Cantonese that is spoken more widely here in this region? Can you say that it's not Chinese?" Cultural politics permeated their sharing of immediate identifying experiences. The ways in which global influence is perpetuated through acts of disseminating cultural knowledge through linguistic expansion is articulated by Tan (2008) who points to the role of "cultural nationalism" in the state promotion of *ruxue* (Confucianism) scholarship in the PRC. The interconnectedness of China's national and global strategies and the ways these participants experience culture are inseparable.

At the same time, all participants separated cultural influence from political and economic power within the current and future China by stressing cultural pride instead of strategic positioning operated by the nation-state. The dynamic in their expressions was somewhat conditioned to the context in which they reside. For example, when discussions on cultural diversity within China occurred, participants returned to textbook definitions once again by stating the importance of respecting minority groups' clothing, rituals, and foods. One student mentioned Tibetans and made an explicit disclaimer: "I am not supporting its independence, but their ways of life is totally different from ours." This statement speaks volumes about the necessity of separating politics in order to discuss cultural representations. Zhang (1997) describes the tendency for the post-Mao Chinese intelligentsia to be part of the state and adopt the "cultural-political strategy" where the "[apolitical] high culture" has served as their refuge (p. 12). The line between being cultural and political is a delicate one to walk. These students are clear about both the local and global practices and ideologies. In this way, the ways they view their cultural identity are more or less becoming aligned with that of the growing powers locally and globally.

Culture as Knowledge

With the prevalent scholarly dissemination and representation of how Chinese culture is collectivistic (Wang and Liu, 2010), many of the participants mentioned their recently gained knowledge on "individualistic versus collectivistic" values from college courses. They explained to me how "it is true that Chinese people do not challenge authority and lack of independent thinking." Yet at the same time, these participants expressed strong opinions during these conversations. They demonstrated their independent and critical thinking while explaining their lived experiences. For example, one participant shared that during her internship, she witnessed how Western business people focused on establishing *guanxi* with their Chinese business partners. After explaining her understanding of the economic motivations, she questioned "how come *guanxi* was the only aspect that Westerners see in Chinese people" and protested "It is different now. Things are changing. We [Chinese] are not just that but it seems that they [the Westerners] are only interested in understanding that."

The study of *guanxi*, roughly translated as "connections," has gained great academic attention, particularly in the West, and this Chinese term has been incorporated into English usages (Gold, Guthrie, and Wank, 2002). Within this body of literature, some researchers view *guanxi* as inextricably a Chinese "artifact of historical and institutional conditions," while others deem it similar to that of one's social capital (Gold et al., p. 9). What made the student's comment significant does not lie in whether *guanxi* exists in Chinese culture or not. Rather it was the participant's poignant cultural analysis of her daily experiences in relation to the geopolitical arrangement. Asante (2007) cogently argues against the contaminated imagination of Africa in the minds of Chinese people caused by European domination of "media institutions, universities, churches and other organs of opinion" (p. 72). He warns how theories and knowledge produced about those under examination create a cultural reality for the very ones being studied and trapped in the "language imprisonment" (Asante, 2002, p. 98). The ways in which these Chinese students self identify with cultural constructs developed from European and U.S.-centered scholarship resonates with Afrocentric and Asiacentric critiques by Asante (2006) and Miike (2010). However these students' quest for the forces behind the high interests in this particular cultural phenomenon suggests their critical understanding of sociopolitical influences over cultural representation.

On several occasions, students described communicating with their friends who live outside China by engaging in *Renren*, a Facebook-like social network forum. They learned about the unfair treatment toward the Chinese in other countries. Few shared that in many European and U.S. sightseeing places popular among Chinese tourists, there are warning signs of "No Spitting" written in Chinese characters. Another topic brought up was how, as one participant said, "the Chinese consumers do not have rights to return their purchased items in some market places (shopping malls). . . . I can't remember where exactly in the United States, but it's about Chinese people are good at taking advantages." An ambivalent feeling toward the representation of the Chinese culture was expressed. On the one hand, the participants felt disheartened that "people in the West think that Chinese being the only group needed to be reminded" because of their own behaviors. On the other hand, some questioned the appropriateness of being treated as less desirable visitors, and connected such a treatment to the less powerful global position China currently occupies.

These special, or rather exclusive, regulations positioning the Chinese in Europe and the United States as backwards are similar to the "Orientalized imaginations" of the Chinese found in the *New York Times* (Ono and Jiao, 2008). In the students' critiques and reflections, such cultural representations were promptly connected to the rising economic and political influence that China now carries in its relationship with the "West." Searching for localized understanding of cultural knowledge has to be performed against the backdrop of imperialist history and present transnational relations. These participants discussed Chinese culture via making connections of their lived experiences with the academic scholarship and market practices inside as well as outside China. The political, social, economic, and historical forces all intersect in the ways cultural identity is materialized in their sense-making and interactions.

Summary

Overall culture is experienced and expressed through how the participants' understood identities within particular considerations toward contemporary power relations. Culture and identity are experienced politically in their expressions of how they live their reality and relate to the world. In their struggles to capture meaning in their experiences, the fluidity, uncertainty, and possibility within the dynamic global conditions are underscored. When multilayered power relations are omitted from the analyses of (inter)cultural communication, the deeply felt emotions and localized contexts may be excluded. At the same time, those were the very moments where the participants as cultural actors had visceral reactions and struggled to communicate. In the process of unpacking their knowledge consumption, these students demonstrated how they were taught to approach culture by negating their lived experiences and sense of realities. Meanwhile, they seemed to be acutely aware of the necessity or benefits of separating the cultural from political arenas. The sociopolitical environment that they exist in provides a uniquely different experience to study the concept of Chinese culture and identity, which cannot be explained simply with representative ancient philosophies such as Confucianism.

CONCLUSION

I share Shome's conviction (2010) that intercultural communication research needs to engage in the transnational context from a critical perspective that includes historical and current local/global nexuses. While a culturally specific perspective such as Asiacentrism de-centers the conventional U.S.-European epistemology and focuses on unique linguistic, religious-philosophical, and historical dimensions (Miike, 2010), it pays little attention to the political environment that deeply influences people's cultural experiences, visions and sense of self. For instance, how do recent global events such as the Jasmine Revolution in North Africa and Middle East affect academic research on Chinese cultural identity?[2] As an article in the *New York Times* described, since February 2011, the Chinese government has tightened control with actions such as detaining the artist Ai Weiwei,[3] has been closely watching the appearance of Jasmine, a cultural symbol of popularity, and ridding the Qing dynasty paean *Mo Li Hua* (Jasmine) from the internet (Yin, 2011). What might the understanding toward Chinese culture be like when the researcher is not solely focused on the Confucius-centered values and instead incorporates and anchors the analysis in the sociopolitical/socioeconomic forces in how cultural identity is experienced, formed, and approached? A cultural-specific paradigm like Asiacentrism will be further enhanced by including particular structural environments (i.e., sociopolitical contexts) in analyses. When contemporary transnational relationships are included, the ways in which culture is experienced via identity expressions may be more comprehensive. As these students' sense-making illustrated, the integrations between the local/political and global/cultural are far more fluid in their ways of life.

Seeing the evolving global and local relations as possibilities for growth in gaining intercultural knowledge, as Rodriguez and Chawla (2010) suggest, allows multifaceted understanding of the volatile relationships between self and others. Asante's (2002, 2006) Afrocentrism and Miike's (2007, 2010) Asiacentrism advocate cultivation of agency in history re/making by relocating international/intercultural communication theoretical lenses to specific cultural practices and wisdom as a way to challenge knowledge subjugation many non-Euro-American groups have experienced. With this focus in mind, this chapter points to the necessity to further include contemporary sociopolitical condition for its imperative influence over the continuation of cultural identity development. As Ang (2000) reminds us, the making of our history depends on "how we conceive of ourselves as active, changing subjects, in ways that generate meaningful links between how we have been represented and how that bears on how we might represent ourselves" (p. 1). Culture is a site replete with identity negotiations that enable us to become political agents struggling to narrate self-worth and self-representation. Academic knowledge production on international and intercultural communication research ought not to exist outside this effort.

NOTES

1. All participants in both ethnographic and interview research granted consent to be included in this study. Group interviews were conducted and recorded in Mandarin. The author later translated and transcribed them into English.

2. This refers to the anti-government protests, which occurred December 2010 through January 2011, in which Tunisian President Zine El Abidine Ben Ali was driven to resignation due to the public anger over unemployment and corruption under his twenty-three-year rule. Jasmine is Tunisia's national flower and many media organizations referred to this uprising as the Jasmine Revolution (Eltahawy, 2011).

3. After being detained for several months, Ai Weiwei was released in June 2011 (Branigan, 2011).

NINE

Understanding Immigration and Communication Contextually and Interpersonally[1]

Kent A. Ono

The contemporary political, social, economic, and cultural context surrounding immigration should directly affect the kinds of theories of immigration and communication we construct within both intercultural communication and the larger field of communication. When approaching the study of immigration and communication, we should not simply import methods and theories we have honed to perfection and successfully used in previous studies, despite the appeal and convenience of doing so, because doing so does not always help us address some of the most pressing research questions we face, such as: When considering undocumented migration, what values should guide our thinking? What has produced the conflict between immigrants and citizens and immigrants and nation-states and thereby affected communication about migration? How should communication scholars respond to immigration policies they may regard as inhumane? How should they study discourse that constructs migrants as different and alien, and hence draws a line between friend and foe and citizen and non-citizen? And, can interpersonal conflicts and tensions be best understood and resolved through micro or macro approaches to the study of intercultural communication?

These kinds of questions are much too important to presume existing tools we have been trained to use are by default necessary and sufficient for answering such vital research questions, for forming questions to begin with, and beyond that for being ethical actors in the world. This chapter argues we need new theories and new approaches that may take time to build and then learn through study, application, analysis, theory building, and even activism. Key to this argument is that theories adapted to our research questions, because they are suited to the questions, have the greatest likelihood of helping produce relevant answers. More specifically, I argue that an understanding of the larger geopolitical, economic, and social contexts existing today is needed in order to understand contemporary immigration and communication, as well as relations, and that understanding conflicts surrounding immigration, such as in Arizona, can be helpful in forging such a perspective. I begin the chapter by discussing two primary ways immigration has been researched in the field of communication—critical and intercultural. Then, I suggest both approaches are necessary but require further inquiry into social, political, economic, and cultural—hence contextual—dimensions of immigration and communication.

THE STUDY OF MIGRATION IN (CRITICAL) INTERCULTURAL STUDIES

The field of communication is a relative latecomer to the study of immigration, having only recently begun to address the issue in a serious manner (Ono and Sloop, 2002). Most of the research that has been conducted so far has been from rhetorical, critical cultural, and critical intercultural perspectives. For instance, work has focused on California's Proposition 187 (Hasian and Delgado, 1998; Jacobson, 2008; Ono and Sloop, 2002), undocumented migration (Mehan, 1997), Chicana/o history and identity (Flores, 2000, 2003), the Minutemen (DeChaine, 2009; Holling, 2006; Justus, 2009), symbols of migrants (Pineda and Sowards, 2007), citizenship (Calafell, 2008), discourse (Amaya, 2007; Holling and Calafell, 2011), metaphors (Cisneros, 2008, 2011; Santa Ana, 2002), sovereignty, and borders (Chávez, 2001; Cisneros, 2008, 2011; DeChaine, 2009; Flores, 2000, 2003).

While some critical intercultural scholarship has addressed immigration in a serious way, for the most part intercultural communication as a field has not taken up the issue of immigration with as much fervor or energy as have critical scholars. Indeed, one might argue that research in intercultural communication has largely and inadvertently treated the issue of immigration as an interpersonal issue—thereby emphasizing individual and interpersonal aspects of immigration, rather than social, political, economic, or cultural ones. Perhaps recognizing this, in Chapter Eight of *Intercultural Communication in Contexts*, Martin and Nakayama (2010) bring interpretive and critical frameworks into conversation with earlier work on immigration that focused on issues of cultural adjustment (Adelman, 1988; Nwanko and Onwumechili, 1991; Rohrlich and Martin,1991), transition (Adler, 1975), culture shock (Bennett, 1998; Oberg,

1960; Ward, Bochner, and Furnham, 2001), acculturation (Berry, 1992; Berry, U. Kim, Minde, and Mok, 1987; Kashima and Loh, 2006; M.-S. Kim, 2002; Onwumechili, Nwosu, Jackson, and James-Huges, 2003; Ward, 1996), sojourners (Chen, 2000; Martin, 1984, 1986; Martin, Bradford, and Rohrlich, 1995; Weissman and Furnham, 1987), adaptation (Y. Y. Kim, 2005b, 2006; Zimmerman, 1995), identity (Ruggiero, Taylor, and Lambert, 1996), and assimilation (Telles and Ortiz, 2008). Thus, Martin and Nakayama's (2010) approach recognizes the value of both "contextual influences" such as "institutional, political, and class influences" on the study of immigration and interpersonal ones (p. 336). In this way Martin and Nakayama concentrate not only on experiences new migrants face such as culture shock, economic difficulties, discrimination, identity conflicts, feelings of being different, and a lack of self-confidence, but also relations of privilege and relative disadvantage between migrants and established members of society, and relations of power between sending and receiving societies, voluntary and involuntary migration, and the politicization of employment, language, and citizenship relation to immigration and communication, as well. Through their dialectical approach, they offer a more comprehensive model for studying immigration and communication and in the process helpfully define key terms associated with the study including assimilation, segregation, separation, integration, marginalization, hybridity, cultural adaptation, the psychology of adaptation, liminality, and transnationalism, and multicultural identity.

Whereas critical cultural studies have primarily addressed immigration as a socioeconomic/sociopolitical issue, and intercultural communication has primarily addressed it as a psychological and interpersonal one, Martin and Nakayama's work uniquely crosses both in order to produce comprehensive understanding of the issue, and to encourage reflexive awareness of interdisciplinary approaches to problem solving. In the name of better theory construction, yet some scholars unfortunately may take up a defensive posture, and in doing so reproduce binaristic thinking rather than seeing the mutual benefits of multiple approaches and perspectives to intercultural communication research.

For instance, Y. Y. Kim (2007), in defending her own approach to the study of communication, has labeled critical approaches in unfortunate ways, thereby suggesting they are less useful for researchers. She has suggested that critical approaches to intercultural theory fall under the categories of "pluralist" and "separatist." Such theories, she argues, conceive of "cultural identity as a discreet and non-negotiable social category and group right" (p. 246). This description of critical work simplifies it and makes it more likely to be rejected as a legitimate theoretical approach to research. Nevertheless, she (Y. Y. Kim, 2008) also offers useful categories and an important goal of seeking a "world that is more open, flexible, and inclusive" (p. 366). She advocates a world in which we get along, where we attempt to work together, which is a valuable and useful attitude. What is less helpful is suggesting that those studying adaptation theories and the like are the ones trying to get along and build a better world; whereas, those doing critical work are somehow inhibiting that goal. Moreover, at times (e.g., in her discussion of "acculturation" and "deculturation") it appears she conceives of adaptation as something that is inevitable vs. something that takes a lot of hard work to do. Her approach does not seek to recognize the need for awareness of differing relations of power in order to address inequality and seek ways power can be distributed more fairly.

My own approach in this chapter falls under the category she describes as the social in terms of "language, behavior, norms, beliefs, myths, and values, as well as the forms and practices of social institutions" (Y. Y. Kim, 2007, p. 241). More specifically, my emphasis is on the latter part of this, the "forms and practices of social institutions," but I would argue these dimensions of studies of migration communication are not simply incidental but in fact function in a more determinative way that might initially be imagined.

This chapter theorizes the way social, political, economic, and cultural conditions pertain to contemporary immigration policies and regulations, addresses such issues from a rhetorical and critical intercultural position, and does so in an attempt to contribute to the contemporary theorization of critical intercultural communication, theories of identity, culture, difference, and otherness through the study of migration discourse. Since my approach emphasizes the social, political, historical, and economic and assumes power is not supplementary or epiphenomenal but formative of communication, I am less interested in cultural identity, specifically, here than I am in (1) the contexts in which identities are formed; (2) the pressures and demands placed on what cultural identities can be; and (3) the processes by which identities are formed—hence not in what culture *is* but in how people live it and what leads to identities changing. Furthermore, my approach emphasizes an understanding of cultural difference, autonomy, power, and rights as a means of getting along, of living together peaceably, and of helping improve the lives of others and the world more broadly—lofty goals indeed.

Before moving to a discussion of contemporary immigration policy, it is useful to note briefly the particular view of ideology I am drawing upon in order to theorize contemporary immigration and communication. This theory of ideology grows largely out of the writing of Althusser (1967). Particularly useful is Althusser's notion that the social is overdetermining, that ideology is formed across different strata of social and institutional life, is reproduced across different sectors, such as schools, churches, families, and therefore has the cumulative effect of *overdetermining* social experience. Ideology, in its most powerful guise, therefore, is not easily localizable, since it so often transfuses social and cultural life. For instance, while violence may be discouraged as a means for solving problems in schools and in homes—what Althusser would consider to be "ideological apparatuses"—the very same lesson against violence may be reinforced, albeit sometimes by mere threat of enforcement by what Althusser calls "repressive apparatuses" such as the police, the military, and the prison and larger carceral system. In this way, ideology is experienced as being natural, in part because it is so widely accepted, and in part because, whether directly or indirectly, it is promulgated cross-institutionally to the point of social saturation.

I now describe the current state of immigration policy before expounding upon a theory about the relationship between globalization and migration and its relationship to immigration relations, specifically in the case of Arizona.

THE CURRENT STATE OF IMMIGRATION POLICY

Changes in immigration patterns and immigration policy in the United States fundamentally affect how we think about culture, cultural difference, the production of deviance, and our notions of self and other within society: indeed, the very basis for humane relations and interactions. A flurry of legislative proposals about migration have emerged since at least the spring of 2010 that affect what it means to be a citizen; how those living within the boundaries of a nation-state relate to others; and how we conceive of constitutive relations between groups, especially relating to health, hospitalization, education, criminality, imprisonment, labor, and economics.

Policy proposals ranging from the revocation of the citizenship of children born in the United States, to the investigation of the immigration status of school children and prospective patients in hospitals, to the limitation of educational content and programming in public schools on the basis of race and ethnicity were all seriously considered (and some passed) in Arizona during the past two years.[2] In fact, the one-year anniversary of the signing of Arizona's Proposition 1070—which legalized the observation, inspection, and questioning of those suspected of being undocumented migrants by police—was April 23, 2010.

Additional Arizona legislation, such as HB 2281,[3] makes it possible to remand public academic programs and curricula focusing on race and ethnic identity perceived to be distorting historical facts. While ultimately failing to pass this last legislative session, five additional pieces of legislation aimed to deny health and education benefits to undocumented migrants and U.S. citizens born of undocumented parents. SB 1308 and 1309 were crafted to take away citizenship from children of undocumented migrants. SB 1405 sought to have prospective patients prove citizenship before being admitted to a hospital. SB 1407 attempted to require schools to check student citizenship status. And, omnibus bill SB 1611, combined efforts to mandate citizenship checks in schools, deny undocumented migrants marriage licenses, and prohibit undocumented migrants from driving.

What arguably began in California more than fifteen years ago in a haunting fashion today has recurred in California and this time has spread to Arizona. But, these matters are not just ones relating to region or state but are, as bell weather trends so often are, precursors to legislation threatening to spread across the country and be considered at a national level.

What becomes clear when examining this context of immigration policy is that understanding macrosocial and political contexts integral to the production of immigration policy is necessary for comprehending intercultural relations and inequitable relations between citizens and immigrants. Awareness of the larger political context not only helps us understand the theoretical issues that pertain to immigration and intercultural identities, but also informs the investigation of the topic of immigration itself, allowing us to reflect back on the very notions of what we consider intercultural communication to be. In short, it is for intercultural communication to think through the social, political, economic, and cultural contexts in which current immigration policy has emerged.

Now that I have briefly described the crisis that is facing the nation-state, if not its states, in relationship to intercultural communication, next I venture to discuss the forces of globalization as they relate to migration. Knowledge and awareness of such contexts are essential to an understanding of racial and cultural identity, power relations, and the way difference is produced through and in communication processes.

THE GLOBALIZATION OF MIGRATION

During the last two to three decades, there has quite possibly been an imperceptible and slow but nevertheless steady shift away from emphasizing individual rights to migrate toward the privileging of rights of nation-states and corporations to migrate and to surveill and control individuals and individuals' rights and power to migrate. Given that migration has come to function today within a context of rapid modernization, industrialization, and nation-state consolidation, it is sometimes difficult to recall that *migration* as a human practice has always been fundamental to life and living and that, ideally, the ability to move globally should in theoretical terms be conceived of as a fundamental human right (Nevins, 2008).

This is all to say that migration is a freedom. Or, is it? It is rarely listed among other freedoms humans have such as "freedom of speech" and "freedom of expression." On occasion, "freedom of movement" *within* a nation-state context is affirmed. For instance, there is a distinction made in the United STates: moving across the fifty states is accepted and often encouraged, but moving between the United States and Mexico is acceptably regulated (with movement between the United States and Canada being regulated less intensely). If migration is a foundational human right, then ideas, rules, regulations, laws, and theories should, first, take the freedom to migrate as a given and, then, be developed with the assumption that the ability to move about is just how it is. But, this by no means is the case.

Paradoxically, just as freedom of movement across borders for individuals neither is expressly guaranteed nor envisioned as a fundamental human right, corporations and governments have systematically and continuously sought such freedoms for themselves and acted as if such rights are or should be, if not unconditional, then at least unquestionable. Furthermore, the rights of migration of individuals have been subordinated to the needs and desires of nations and corporations for individuals to migrate. In other words, people cannot freely move about of their own accord, but corporations and nation-states have sought to move both people and goods for their own purposes more fluidly.

This dialectic I am describing between the freedom of individuals to mobility and that of nation-states and corporations to cross borders, as well as the power of nations and corporations to determine individual mobility, is not only antinomic—opposing phenomena existing simultaneously and in relation to one another—but also paradoxical. This paradox between individual rights and corporate and national rights of migrancy is fundamental to our current historical moment, and it should cause us to reflect on the rights guaranteed in such cherished documents as the Declaration of Independence, the Constitution of the United States, and the Bill of Rights. To what degree were non-sentient "entities"—businesses and organizations (both national and extra-national)—meant to be endowed with a thing called "rights," and were those rights meant to supercede rights afforded to individuals, especially people with limited capital or limited capital interests? It is more conceivable that a person sometimes functions like a corporation (e.g., Rupert Murdoch) than that a corporation sometimes has the inalienable rights and freedoms of a person? To make this subject/object substitution is, in essence, to equate people with objective social relations.

This paradox emphasizing corporate and national mobility and the strict control of human mobility is definitive of neoliberalism—the unfettered flexibility of corporations and nation-states to move freely in and outside of hemispheres, while working ceaselessly to moderate control or to gain control of the flow of people, laborers, and goods in and outside of sovereign nation-states. The forces of globalization dramatically seek to create maximal flexibility, while the rights of individuals to migrate are necessarily tied to the strategies and policies of globalization forged by companies and nation-states. Individual rights to migrancy are an effect, sometimes an after-effect, of state and organizational policy, not the basis for it: hence, the ability to pass the North American Free Trade Agreement (NAFTA) but the inability, thus far, to pass the Dream Act, which in part seeks to make undocumented migrants who have lived and worked in the United States for a long time citizens, demonstrates that the interests of transnational free trade and commerce takes precedence over the desires for citizenship of hardworking and taxpaying undocumented migrants.

In a sense, when human migrancy *is* addressed, it is less about humans' right to migrate and more akin to the right of employers to move them, not unlike the movement of goods, products, and objects. In a loose sense, when workers are needed, immigration laws are relaxed or ignored in order to accommodate corporate and state needs for labor. When there is no longer any need for such workers, immigration laws are constricted and enforced (Davila, 1986; Portes, 1977), because the capacity of companies and the state to take care of (non-laboring) bodies requires resources and capital.

Of course, however, immigration and economics map onto one another unevenly, producing not only contradictions but also illogics in capitalism. These breaks in logic should ultimately serve as evidence of a larger potential to *challenge the logics* of capitalist desires and actions. In other words, while there exists a logic to the relationship between immigration and economics, there are always exceptions, e.g., when immigration regulations are too tight to allow for a requisite number of workers from outside the nation-state to migrate and hence to fill a labor need and when workers needed for labor are denied a drivers license to transport them to do that work.

As numerous scholars over the past decades have documented, the neoliberal logic of global economics has privileged the flexibility of movement for companies and nations to cross borders (e.g., Hardt and Negri, 2000; Miyoshi, 1993; Ong, 1999). The World Trade Organization (WTO) and the vast commercial entities and organizations that benefit from it, including nation-states, seek new, more efficient ways to create, market, and sell commodities to newer and more extensive markets. Alternatively, within nation-states, there is tremendous effort at the national level to control the movement of subjects, to document the whereabouts of bodies and their circulation, and to map the location and dispersion of bodies that cross national, maritime, and jurisdictional boundaries.

In their *tour de force, Empire,* Hardt and Negri (2000) brilliantly lay out the parameters of what they call global *Empire*—the loosely organized, complexly articulated, interweaving of vast forces of capital, labor, and infrastructure to consolidate energy, resources, and ideology in such a way as to ensure the flexible acquisition, manufacture, circulation, and sale of capital, labor, and resources. This way of thinking about globalization as a force with the logic of efficiency, flexibility, consumption, afflu-ence, and the consolidation of power has guided noted scholars of culture for the last two decades, at least since the Public Culture group at the University of Chicago first began publishing on the subject. Figures such as Arjun Appadurai, Ben Lee, Saskia Sassen, and the like all drove home these broader notions of economic flexibility and the cultural transforma-tions they implied.

Ong (1999), too, in her work emphasized the reality of flexible capital-ism, in part to suggest not only ways migrants took advantage of neolib-eral circumstances but also to explore ways nation-states were changing as a result of having to address the needs for efficient uses of labor, resources, and capital.

Miyoshi (1993) and Rouse (1995) began to offer more critical insights into the globalization processes and the downside of globalization, and they did so in part through a critique of nation-state policies such as the NAFTA, the General Agreement on Trade and Tariffs (GATT), the Asian Pacific Economic Agreement (APEC), etc. In part, their critical observa-tions recognize that as neoliberal globalization strategies were employed to free up the movement of capital, labor, and resources, and while, through technology, greater efficiencies would continue to be sought, the control of people, unlike mere products, could be difficult, which is per-haps why Hardt and Negri (2004) followed their book, *Empire*, with their book, *Multitude* (Hardt and Negri, 2004).

Basic to humanity, after all, is the impulse, desire, and necessity of movement out of, into, and across places, spaces, geographies, and lo-cales. The relationship between the desire for mobility and the vast ef-forts to control humans, their bodies, and their labor must be, at least at times, conflictual. The interests of capital at times are in contradiction with those of the interests of humans. In order to control humans, a process, very often a violent process, transpires. This is precisely the heated context at the border—raised to boiling point levels—that we see taking place today: the forces and interests of globalization coming face-to-face with the needs and desires of human subjects requiring and desir-ing migration. At this intersection, identities and differences are pro-duced through communication, and these, along with material conditions have real-world consequences.

SHIFTING SOCIAL AND POLITICAL CONDITIONS

In this section, I discuss what has happened at the U.S./Mexico border over the last two decades, and I offer a theory of the rhetoric of migration as it relates specifically to the construction of racialized identities and the relationship of all of this to critical intercultural communication.

When writing the book *Shifting Borders: Rhetoric, Immigration, and California's Proposition 187* with John Sloop (2002), and following Berg (2002), I was convinced that there was a palpable psychoanalytic relationship between popular cultural representations of aliens, as in *Close Encounters of the Third Kind*, and the conception of migrants, undocumented and documented. Certainly, one can read our book and see the fears of ostensibly undocumented men from Mexico climbing border fences and rushing to freedom in the United States which were replayed over and over on television prior to voters passing Proposition 187 in California as parallel to that of aliens invading Earth, the United States, and U.S. communities in science fiction alien films, as Berg (2002) so provocatively and compellingly suggests.

And, while that may have been more or less right relating to Proposition 187, this new move to mark Latinas/os and Mexicanas/os as alien has less of a direct referent, is less (in my view) about a cultural condition tightly interwoven with popular cultural representations and more of an assertion of raw power based on tremendous anxiety of U.S. citizens and nativists about their own position of power within the world economy. What is happening in Arizona can be understood as resulting from uncertainty about the position of the United States within the global economy. As such uncertainty increases—augmented by such things as China's rapid economic liberalization and modernization—the greater uncertainty is experienced by those on the ground experiencing and/or imagining future political, economic, and personal conditions. Furthermore, the greater the anxiety around the United States' position within global economic and power relations, the greater the likelihood rhetoric and policies will target those seen to be contributing to this prospective massive shift of resources and relations, such as undocumented migrants and their children who are U.S. citizens.

There has certainly been a shift in rhetoric since Proposition 187, and this shift is evidence not only of a change in states' concerns about migration (shifting the central concerns about migration from California to Arizona), and a shift in circumstances, of massive bolstering of energies at the California border to less adequate ones at the Arizona border, but also of a level of desperation as evidenced by the hyperbolic nature of the discourse.

Indeed, the shift in tactics, the level of desperation and anger, and the radical nature of solutions proposed relating to immigration seem ever-so-much a part of the broader shift in U.S. conservatism that, if one had to name a starting point, could be traced to the election of Hollywood actor Arnold Schwarzenegger as the governor of California and before him the election of professional wrestler Jesse "the Body" Ventura in Minnesota, if not the election of Hollywood actor Ronald Reagan before them. Arguably, because of their elections, Sarah Palin can *become* a media celebrity (like them) as a result of this collapse of politics into entertainment and

[handwritten marginal note, left margin: "so spot on for what is happening in the US right now"]

entertainment into politics. After their elections, it was as if in conservative politics there were no "holds barred," as if one could shoot for the moon. Any outlandish idea was worth considering, even possibly the Republican presidential candidacy of former member of the Ku Klux Klan and Louisiana representative, David Duke. Any tactical pursuit could not be rejected out of hand. The limits of U.S. politics then become only the limits of the conservative imagination.[4]

In the twenty-first century, the appearance of the Minuteman Civilian Defense Corps, Sarah Palin and Michele Bachman, the Tea Party, and now Arizona's Jan Brewer have taken the open field of political drama to theatrical absurdity. For instance, before being fired, Mark Williams, the leader of the Tea Party Express, went so far as to call the NAACP racist, saying in a July 14, 2010, exchange with *CNN* correspondent Roland Martin, "Racists have their own movement. It's called the NAACP. . . . A bunch of old fossils looking to make a buck off skin color." Before that of course were the much watched comments on television by former *Fox News* newscaster and ideologue Glenn Beck, calling President Obama racist. The absurdist theater—like Edward Albee's poignant attention to the degree to which everyday life verges on absurdity and even horror—closely approximates the experience of many of us witnessing the shift in contemporary popular conservative politics today.

So absurd is it with regard to race that people seem unphased not only that President Obama could be pictured as a baby monkey but also that the picture could circulate virally across cyberspace. So absurd is it that in Champaign, Illinois, near where I live, the former and longstanding mayor continues to question President Obama's citizenship. And, Donald Trump who made Obama's citizenship his major campaign issue ultimately then gave up his bid for the presidency once Obama "officially" produced his long-form papers. This trend toward the more dramatic, desperate, and cynical is evident not only in responses to and rhetoric about immigration and politicians' off-handed comments, but also in policy proposals—proposals that sometimes become law—to take away the citizenship of children born in the United States or to legalize racial profiling by checking the citizenship of people simply because they "appear" to the person hired to enforce the law to fit the profile of an "undocumented" immigrant.

CONCLUSION

Needless to say, cynical discourse that reaches the level of absurdity described above is not self-reflexively aware of its relationship to globalization or to social policy. The discourse does not address the broader context of North-South hemispheric relations, i.e., the unequal economic and trade relationship between the global north and global south. Nor does the discourse address, for the most part, the histories of the U.S. acquisition of land and territory over time, even as economics is an over-determining theme throughout the discourse about politics and migration.

In brief, the discourse leaves out the social, economic, political, and cultural context, and this is one thing critical intercultural communication scholars can provide. Thus, following the early 1990s recession in California, Proposition 187 passed in California, after which there was a massive mobilization of border interrogation, security, and enforcement during the mid-1990s as evidenced by Operation Gatekeeper in San Diego, Operation Safeguard in southern Arizona, Operation Rio Grande in southern Texas, and Operation Hold the Line in El Paso, Texas. These efforts, supported by federal financing, for instance more than doubled the number of border agents nationally from 4,226 in 1994 to 9,212 in 2000 (most of which were at the U.S./Mexico border).[5]

The effect of this work, which included creating a literal steel wall that extended into the Pacific Ocean below the city of San Diego, was to create a pathway for undocumented migrants into Arizona through the very dangerous Sonora desert. From 1992 to 1999, border apprehensions declined in San Diego, California, from 566 in 1992 to 146 in 1999. During that same time period, apprehensions increased in Tucson, Arizona, from 71 to 352 (Manning and Butera, 2000). In a sense, whereas migrants came to the United States through San Diego before Proposition 187, following it, they came through Tucson, Arizona.

Not only does rhetoric about the California and Arizona borders for the last two years leave out sociopolitical/socioeconomic and cultural context, but it is heightened and desperate—much more so than it was twenty years ago when heated rhetoric about Proposition 187 inflamed passions in and outside of California.

I see it as my role as a scholar to call attention to these dimensions of the discursive in the larger context of the politics of migration. My sense is that people underestimate the degree to which discourse plays a role in constructing migration, identities, and difference. In our book, Sloop and I (Ono and Sloop, 2002) argued that migration discourse actually shifts borders and that borders themselves have no inherent meaning prior to their representation, that borders are not distinct lines of demarcation prior to communication saying they are, but borders are, rather, more importantly concepts that when discussed come to have real meaning and material effects.

If this chapter makes a contribution, it is to help draw attention specifically to global and economic processes and relations that impinge upon policy making and thereby shift intercultural relations and the identities of migrants. Constructing migrants as aliens is part of producing difference, positioning migrants as responsible for the economic conditions people experience and recognize, and positioning those with rights or longevity within the nation-state as in power over those doing hard physical labor for low pay and inhumane working conditions. Right before completing this chapter, a district judge ruled that an Alabama law allowing officials to determine the immigration status of public school students and police to check the immigration status of those they imagine might be undocumented to be legal, although the initial law had even more problematic dimensions to it. This ruling unfortunately illustrates well the role of the state in helping regulate migration, while limiting the rights of migrants and laborers, and surveilling and then potentially marking them in the process.

John Warren was fully aware of the role communicative processes play in the constitution of racial identity. His recent essay (2010) in the *Handbook of Critical Intercultural Communication* (Nakayama and Halualani, 2010a) emphasizes his career-long struggle to understand his own embeddedness within the structures of racialized power, as well as his effort to theorize, rethink, and re-perform racialized identities in ways that approximate an unlearning of the socialization that so fixes socialized identities within racialized logics.

This chapter draws attention to the processes used by groups to map out and articulate racial/national belongingness on a continuum of inclusion to belongingness. The less different one is, the more one belongs and should be included. The more the same, then the more one should be a member. As DeChaine (2009) has argued about borders as apparatuses for the construction of differences: "They are bounding, ordering apparatuses, whose primary function is to designate, produce, and/or regulate the space of difference" (p. 44). But, this regulation of difference first requires a production of difference. Why and how is that difference produced? What might the production of difference do? What benefit does the production of difference create, and for whom?

While people may *be* different, or *interpreted* as such, it is a very different matter to *mark* them publicly in this way. Marking people as different in discourse is one step beyond simply noting their difference, or understanding them as different, or even treating them as different interpersonally or institutionally in social relations. Rather, marking someone as different (or "making them alien") requires a great deal of energy, a commitment to making public, notifying others, using a loudspeaker to call attention to differences one notices. This has the effect of giving into and contributing to the very inequities that our present condition of globalization creates. As Shome and Hegde (2002a) argue: "This is because in our current times global capital is producing inequities of culture by articulating (and disarticulating) spaces and places that are often geographically discontinuous in similar (and dissimilar) ways. Thus, inequities of power are now increasingly becoming a matter of inhabiting different and unequal spatial fields of power—that cut across national and racial boundaries—through which global capital travels and utilizes" (p. 180).

At issue is the degree to which empire and, relatedly, neoliberalism, have become naturalized, an acceptable global condition of being, one fully accepted in policy, attitude, memory, and praxis. The forces of globalization have created the conditions for the maximization of capital flow, the efficiency of capital flow across borders, but at what expense? With this fundamental logic driving the system, to try to explain precisely what the logic of globalization is sometimes would be made easier simply by conducting an empirical study of the WTO's rhetoric, policies, and activities. For, who better knows precisely how capitalism can be made to work more effectively at the global level than the WTO?

The institutional and rhetorical strategies to figure documented and undocumented migrants as "alien" illustrate anxiety and frustration about the changing world, as well as the degree to which a discourse of differentiation, exclusion, and control continue to be critical to the production of nations, citizens, and subjects. Yet, despite these vast processes of labor, trade and tariffs on goods, open market policies, a seemingly unstoppable use of transnational force responsive to a multiplicity of political conditions globally, as well as heightened rhetoric, the fundamental fact of migration frustrates these conditions; it is knowing this—and understanding these institutional and rhetorical forces as in relation to each other and from that perspective—that might set us on a different course. Thus, context is crucial to the study of identity and difference. This chapter is a call to intercultural communication scholars to critically interrogate the disparate contexts and their force in constructing conflict relating to migration, the subsequent discourses of differentiation that follow and the identities and relations that are materially remade in the process.

NOTES

1. I would like to thank Nina Li for her research assistance and Sarah Projansky and Tom Nakayama for helpful advice and feedback. I would also like to thank Nilanjana Bardhan and Mark Orbe for their very helpful and supportive comments.

2. For a rundown of these bills, please see org2.democracyinaction.org/o/5262/t/0/blastContent.jsp?email_blast_KEY=1156551 Last accessed: September 8, 2011.

3. Signed into law May 11, 2010, not effective until December 31, 2010.

4. Some will likely think of Marilyn Davenport's, member of the Orange County Republican Central Committee, circulation of an image of President Obama as a baby ape via e-mail, because of its recency. See "Calif. GOP official emails Obama ape 'joke,' says it's not racist." *New York Post* (April 17, 2011). I include reference to this specific article because it republishes the image, which reflects on the problematic editorial policy of that organization as well.

5. See Nevins (2008), Appendix F.

IV

Identity and the Liminal

TEN

Postcolonial Migrant Identities and the Case for Strategic Hybridity

Toward "Inter"cultural Bridgework

Nilanjana Bardhan

What is theoretically innovative, and politically crucial, is the need to think beyond narratives of originary and initial subjectivities and to focus on those moments or processes that are produced in the articulation of cultural differences. These "in-between" spaces provide the terrain for elaborating strategies of selfhood—singular or communal—that initiate new signs of identity, and innovative signs of collaboration, and contestation, in the act of defining the idea of society itself.

—Bhabha, 1994, p. 2

Our goal is not to use differences to separate us from others, but neither is it to gloss over them.

—Anzaldúa, 2009a, p. 245

We perform our cultural identities in various ways that are marked by historical and contextual factors, by how we perceive difference and power relations between self and other, and by the goals we want to achieve through communicative interaction. There are, therefore, many possibilities for how identities may be performed. Given this reality, our theoretical toolbox must contain an array of tools for conceptualizing and understanding diverse forms of intercultural identity interactions.

This chapter utilizes tools from the postcolonial studies toolbox (e.g., Anzaldúa, 1987; Bhabha, 1994; Godiwala, 2007; Krishna, 2009; Pratt, 1992;

Sharrad, 2007; Spivak, 1993) to specifically address intercultural communication praxis that involves postcolonial migrant identities. Our world is marked by diverse postcolonial spaces inhabited by equally diverse postcolonial subjects. Postcolonial migrant identities are hybrid identities that have been worked over by forces of colonialism and migration. In this chapter, I argue that performing hybridity strategically, at mundane levels of intercultural interaction, could be a possibly liberating position of enunciation and agency for those who identify as postcolonial migrant subjects (see Bhabha, 1996). I further argue that along with accomplishment of self-empowerment, such performances could also aid in intercultural bridgework. After addressing extant critiques of hybridity as a cultural phenomenon, I utilize hybridity and its attendant notions of transculturation, ambivalence, and mimicry to make the above case. I foreground the intercultural connective value of theorizing cultural identities in interaction through hybridity (difference) rather than through sameness. Overall, my goal in this chapter is to theorize cultural difference productively and dialogically, in the service of agentic and communicative identity building which can aid in healing colonial/postcolonial trauma and (cultural) transformation angst.

Before moving on to the rest of the chapter, I would like to begin a personal narrative, an "accented tale about identity," to which I will return at the end of the chapter. This narrative is an account of performance of strategic hybridity in the classroom, and is illustrative of the main arguments I present in this chapter. What started as an unselfconscious identity performance on my part has now turned into a self conscious (or strategic) one. The experience of this narrative is a recurring one for me, and the different outcomes have helped me think through the value of strategic hybridity in intercultural praxis.

"*You don't have an accent!*" I have received this reaction from American students on numerous occasions in the classrooms of the two large U.S. midwestern universities at which I have taught. This usually doesn't happen right away, but after a good number of weeks into the semester when the students and I have developed rapport and a degree of familiarity. I have received this comment from several others as well—acquaintances, colleagues, and even strangers. But I will stick to the specific context of the classroom for this story since context is key in performances of strategic hybridity.

Sometimes the student adds "*You don't speak like the other Indians* [read: East Indian] *I've met.*" I always wonder what they expect my reaction to that comment to be. I could respond to what seems to be their genuine (but reductive) surprise in several ways. I could get into the didactic mode and talk about how everybody has an accent, what an accent is, and why accents do or do not change. I could get into detailed possible explanations of why I "don't have an accent." Or, I could get into and say something like, "All Indians don't speak the same way." I have tried the above approaches before (except for the snippy one!), and they haven't felt adequate. Something is still missing—it is the connection across difference.

What kind of an identity performance would I need to engage in to "interrupt" (see Warren and Toyosaki in this volume) their sedimented notion of how someone who looks like me "should" speak and, simultaneously, open up an invitation for intercultural bridgework? I will return to my serendipitous discovery on this matter at the end of the chapter.

THEORIZING IDENTITY IN INTERCULTURAL COMMUNICATION

Intercultural communication involves the study of cultural identities in interaction in various contexts and spaces. Scholars, over the past few decades, have studied this central concept of identity from functionalist/post-positivist, interpretive/constructionist and critical perspectives (Martin and Nakayama, 1999; Yep, 2004). Research so far has mainly focused on how being a member of a particular culture (or possessing a particular cultural identity) impacts communication behavior (here culture and identities are conceptualized somewhat objectively and prediction is a key goal) (e.g., Gudykunst and Hammer, 1988; Imahori, 2001; Ting-Toomey, 1993); how members of a particular culture, through everyday communication, construct a relational sense of identity and belonging within that particular culture (here culture and identities are conceptualized as co-constructed through communication and social interaction) (e.g., Carbaugh, 1990; Collier and Thomas, 1988; Hecht, Collier, and Ribeau, 1993; Pratt, 1998); and how oppressed cultural identities are historically, ideologically, and discursively produced as an effect of unequal power relations (here culture and identities are conceptualized as sites of contestation) (e.g., Holling and Calafell, 2007; Jackson, 1999; Nakayama and Martin, 1999).

In all of these trajectories of research, identity is positioned as an individual and/or group accomplishment, or theorized critically with the aim of enabling resistance or identitarian politics against ascribed and oppressive identities (Shin and Jackson, 2003). While such theorizing of identity is no doubt necessary and valuable in the larger repertoire, the issue is that groupness (sameness) and resistance (opposition) are the two recurring options offered (see Pascual, 2012). There seem to be no strong alternatives outside this binary in the landscape of intercultural communication identity research. Furthermore, culture is often theorized as functioning naturally in terms of wholeness and sameness, with deep roots, clear-cut boundaries and static characteristics. Consequently, cultural identity tends to be theorized in originary and sovereign fashion.

Collectively, the above lines of research have not yet paid sufficient attention to the "in-between" spaces of identity or to affirming non-unitary identities and communicative interactions that heal rather than suppress colonial/postcolonial trauma and transformation angst. More recently, scholars have emphasized the need to study intercultural communication and identity from a postmodern/deconstructive perspective, and to infuse postcolonial theorizing in this area of work (Chuang, 2003; Collier, 2001; Gershenson, 2005; Mendoza, 2002b; Rodriguez, 2003/2004; Shin and Jackson, 2003; Shome and Hegde, 2002). A postcolonial move can help us productively address the colonizer/colonized binary in intercultural communication. It can help us theorize culture (as it relates to identity) as a "traveling" (Clifford, 1992), deterritorializing, and mutating variable in postcolonial conditions, and identities as routed and non-sovereign rather than rooted and sovereign. As Rodriguez (2003/2004) suggests, it's time to move from "culture" to "culturing" and treat the concept as a verb rather than a noun since "cultures are always in flux, that is, always reckoning with instability and change" (p. 9). Such theorizing can enable us to move beyond the dualism inherent in *either-or* binaristic approaches to identity, and into the spaces of *and-both*.

Furthermore, interrogating identity through the lens of postcolonialism can assist with theorizing the space of the "inter" in intercultural communication, a space that cries out for more scholarly attention (Carrillo Rowe, 2010a). In turn, focusing on the "inter" can help us problematize the primary conceptualization of difference in the study of identity and intercultural communication, i.e., difference as *pure* (oppositional) difference that needs to be tamed and overcome, or as something negative that oppresses. As Rodriguez and Chawla (2010) have recently noted, the assumption in most intercultural communication literature is that

> . . . our differences are what ultimately make for strife and conflict. Our differences as cast as a set of dangerous and perilous rapids that demand vigilant and sensitive navigation. Any wrong act, movement, behavior, or word can presumably send us crashing into the rocks and currents of discord. (p. 29)

This chapter heeds their call to develop more creative and less defensive assumptions about difference in our scholarship in a world where differences are intersecting at a faster pace.

In fact, the play of difference is becoming more common not just in our interactions with cultural others, but also within our own embodied senses of self. For some, such as those who perpetually reside on cultural borders (e.g., postcolonial migrants), the experience of difference and displacement is presumably greater (e.g., see Hegde, 2002). Perhaps difference and "in-betweenness" can be made into a source of intersticial agency (Bhabha, 1994; 1996) and catharsis (Holling and Calafell, 2007) for those who seem to experience it more. When perceived as a source of agency and self-empowerment, difference may be performed to accomplish intercultural bridgework that may not have been conceivable before.

BRIDGEWORK

By focusing on difference not as pure difference but as an interactional effect whose meaning keeps sliding (Hall, 1996), it may be possible to better study (and imagine) how to accomplish intercultural bridgework, and how to creatively perform difference in the space of the "inter." According to Anzaldúa (2009a),

> To bridge means to loosen our borders, not closing off to others. Bridging is the work of opening the gate to the stranger, within and without. . . . Effective bridging comes from knowing when to close ranks to those outside our home, group, community, nation, and when to keep the gates open. (p. 246)

Mendoza (2010) writes, "To bridge is to straddle worlds—whether by choice or by force—and to be compelled to find a way of connecting the two in ways that make sense" (p. 100). Bridgework enables entry into the space of the "inter" in intercultural communication. It opens up the possibility of intercultural praxis and identity work that aims to rupture oppressive binaries and bring about transformation. Bridgework focuses on the in-between spaces of identities in interaction in order to deconstruct cultural authority. According to Carrillo Rowe (2010a):

> The inter of intercultural communication is a capacious site of unfolding interactions across lines of difference. It gestures towards the unknown and unknowable space between unevenly located subjects. The inter points to a process vexed with contradictions: a generative site of learning and yet one that can never be mastered. . . . This is to say that the inter marks a process of becoming that is constituted *between* subjects, who, in engaging the inter are, in turn, reconstituted through their exchange. (p. 216, italics in original)

Writings about bridgework are not new. In *This Bridge Called My Back: Writings by Radical Women of Color* (Moraga and Anzaldúa, 1981), we learn through the narratives and poems of women of color about the work they do to create connections between disparate groups. This work can often be painful but it demands that we do not give up hope about the possibility of building alliances across seemingly incommensurable differences.

Thus the goal of bridgework is not to simply create happy and "equal" meeting places between self and cultural others, but to create possibilities for transformation and intercultural alliances. Such bridgework is hard work because it deploys the embodied non-unitary self, usually located in a non-dominant position, to perform an intercultural politics and praxis of multiplicity on an everyday basis. Such praxis attempts to simultaneously connect with the other (its goal is not to simply negate the dominant other) as well as reconfigure hegemonic codes and colonial assumptions. It is marked by a fertile tension that opens up opportunities for individuals from non-dominant and dislocated cultural groups (such as postcolonial migrants) to imagine, enunciate and enact agency in creative ways that affirm their split identities, and simultaneously invite (maybe compel) the unevenly located cultural other on to the bridge to jointly engage in possible transformation. The communicative construction of this fertile tension is the first step toward possiblizing connection across difference.

Thus a move away from thinking of identity in terms of sameness and wholeness, and toward difference and performances of the "inter," can enable postcolonial migrants to harness the cultural power of their double seeing selves despite unequal power relations. It could help affirm that self-empowerment is a legitimate form of power, and that power and agency can work in contradictory and oblique ways in identity performances. And while there are no guarantees that such identity performances will always have desired outcomes in moments of intercultural praxis, there are no guarantees either than they will *not* lead to empowering transformations of self and other (Kraidy, 2005). Location, context, histories, the subjectivities involved and power configurations are, of course, key, in every moment within the space of the inter.

Within postcolonial theory, hybridity (along with its attendant concepts of ambivalence, mimicry and transculturation) is one conceptual domain that carries potential for further enriching conceptualization of such proactive bridgework in intercultural communication. This concept has been celebrated effusively and critiqued vehemently, and I next track its value for this chapter.

CRITIQUES OF CULTURAL HYBRIDITY

The term hybridity and its use in cultural critique make some uncomfortable because of its semantic history. In the nineteenth century, at the height of European colonization, the term was transferred from the natural to human sciences and deployed in the enterprise of scientific racism that pushed theories of racial purity and hierarchy (see Young, 1995). In current times and in postcolonial theory, hybridity has become a celebrated theme and its meaning has been reconfigured from a negative term or producer of border anxiety and contamination to a politics and perspective that is capable of producing subversion and transgression of dominant canons (Brah and Coombes, 2000; Kraidy, 2005; Nederveen Pieterse, 2009; Papastergiadis, 1997). Some of the critiques against hybridity are worthy of note, while others seem to be guided by limiting conceptualizations of culture and cultural politics.

While hybridity is about cultural mixing and mingling, it also entails the production of a different (i.e., non-oppositional) kind of difference as a result of transculturation. Most of the critiques, however, tend to ignore the intersticial agency and empowering potential of the difference produced. Some of the main critiques of hybridity are as follows (Anthias, 2001; Friedman, 1999; Nederveen Pieterse, 2009, pp. 101–9):

- Hybridity's value lies only in its ability to critique essentialism
- Hybridity is a dependent notion that, instead of combating essentialism, simply hybridizes it
- It is trivial to assert that all cultures are mixed
- Hybridity matters only at the level of self-identification
- Hybridity talk is the privilege of a new postcolonial elite class, and less privileged border crossers live in real fear of the border
- Hybridity is not parity
- Hybridity logic supports neoliberal globalization which works through exploiting difference
- Hybridity remains at the level of a fuzzy cultural descriptor, and is under theorized in terms of what it can accomplish in an unequal world.

Nederveen Pieterse (2009) responds convincingly to these charges by noting that hybridity as a critique of essentialism is necessary because there is plenty of oppressive cultural essentialism at work in our world. Foregrounding hybridity, he notes, is a mode of cultural politics that helps rupture naturalized boundaries and canons that are divisive. Hybridity is dependent on essentialism only to the extent that cultural essentialism continues to exist and oppress. The critique that hybridity is meaningful only at the level of self-identification is actually not a weakness but quite relevant from the perspective of intercultural communication. How we self-identify is inextricably linked with how we relate with others. The charge that hybridity is a privilege and can be positively experienced only by elite postcolonial migrants is, according to Nederveen Pieterse, "at odds with common experience" (p. 108). Citing the example of Turkish migrants in Berlin, he argues that there are plenty of spaces in this world that engender mundane hybridity. Regarding the argument that hybridity is not parity, the comeback is that there exists no cultural politics that guarantees parity. Hybridity, at least, could be a strategic move towards deconstructing cultural inequality.

The charge that hybridity is complicit with consumption practices fueled by neoliberal capitalism which manifest in various forms of cultural fusion is a worthy one to a certain extent. As Hall (1997) has noted, unlike previous forms of globalization such as territorial colonization, which worked through strategies of total domination, current neoliberal globalization works through incorporating, even celebrating, difference in its onward march in the service of decentered capital. However, reducing hybridity to surface level fusion of cultural products and practices does not do justice to a phenomenon that is quite complex (Kraidy, 2005). Perhaps the real issue is the last critique listed: hybridity's critical potential remains under theorized. It remains a fuzzy and somewhat static cultural descriptor. Prabhu (2007) notes that an array of disparate works are lumped under the hybridity label, and that they do a poor job of distinguishing between the different forms and modalities of hybridity. There is obviously work to be done in this area, and according to Kraidy (2005), the critical potential of hybridity needs to be carefully mined:

> . . . agency must be grasped in terms of people's ability to accomplish things in the world they inhabit. If culture represents the meanings, ways of action, and ways to evaluate the value of actions in a society, and if cultural hybridity entails a change in those meanings and actions, then attention ought to be paid to hybridity's ability or inability to empower social groups [or individuals] to have influence over the course of their lives. Ultimately, then, the value of a theory of hybridity resides in the extent to which it emphasizes human agency. (p. 151)

In this chapter I pursue one line of argument within the rubric of hybridity that emphasizes human agency for a non-dominant group. The question that I am specifically interested in is: *Does hybridity have the potential to offer a critical perspective on how culturally displaced postcolonial migrants may accomplish agentic bridgework through intercultural communication?* I choose to focus on this specific group and its cultural and historical modalities (while acknowledging that postcolonial migrants are not a monolithic group) to somewhat avoid the lumping that hybridity work is often guilty of. However, I hope that what I am attempting in this chapter will have heuristic value for other forms of hybrid cultural identities and their specifically located (inter)cultural politics.

HYBRIDITY AND ITS ATTENDANT NOTIONS

In order to delve productively into the above question, a more detailed explication of how hybridity has been theorized in postcolonial studies is in order. What hybridity is *not* is benign and flat cultural fusion or joining. It is form of splitting (Bhabha, 1994), and carries with it attendant notions of cultural translation, transculturation, mimicry and ambivalence. Also, as Sharrad (2007) emphasizes, "there are all sorts of hybridity, and each types does different cultural work in its particular context" (p. 101).

Within postcolonial studies, Homi Bhabha's work on hybridity is salient. He theorizes hybridity as a mode of cultural engagement *through difference* which opens up the possibility for "newness to enter the world" (Bhabha, 1994, p. 303). Postcolonial subjects are hybrid in the sense that they are (dis)located in cultures that have been worked over during colonial contact, and they tend to possess a sense of self that does not comfortably fit into originary narratives of identity. The hybrid is formed "out of the dual process of displacement and correspondence in the act of translation," and "hybridity is the process by which the discourse of colonial authority attempts to translate the identity of the Other within a singular category, but then fails and produces something else" (Papastergiadis, 1997, p. 279). Identity, in this case then, is not a matter of simple fusion, but a tense and ongoing negotiation of differences, within and without; it is about a sense of self defined by contradiction. In the case of postcolonial migrants, the dislocation is doubled in the physical shift away from the postcolonial homeland. The migrant finds herself to be (dis)located in the hostland, engaged incessantly in the continuous and always incomplete process of hybridity (Hall, 1990) and negotiation of contradictions.

Consequently, in the process of identity negotiation between the self and cultural other, postcolonial hybrids are in a position to performatively interrupt binary logics through which oppositional and unequal forms of identity differences are produced (Bhabha, 1994), and thereby decenter the essentialism associated with each cultural identity. This decentering occurs in the space of the "inter" in intercultural communication, is marked by cultural translation, and holds the possibility of transformation of attitudes. According to Bhabha (1994), "Translation is the performative nature of cultural communication. . . . Cultural translation desacralizes the transparent assumptions of cultural supremacy . . . " (pp. 326–27). Translation's outcome is the shift in meanings, and herein lies some of hybridity's critical potential.

The notion of transculturation (Pratt, 1992) further helps explain the formation of hybrid subjectivities. According to Pratt, transculturation is a phenomenon of the contact zone. A contact zone is a space where cultures previously separated intersect, usually in the context of colonization. These are spaces of "copresence, interaction, interlocking understandings and practices, often within radically asymmetrical relations of power" (p. 7). It is in these spaces that transculturation occurs. As Pratt explains: "While subjugated people cannot readily control what emanates from the dominant culture, they do determine to varying extents what they absorb into their own, and what they use it for" (1992, p. 6). While agency is oblique in such cases, it is nonetheless present. As Rogers (2006) notes, "Power dynamics are an intrinsic part of these hybrid forms, but not as simple, one-sided formulas of powerful-powerless" (p. 497). Transculturation produces hybrid identities and the cultural skills to survive tactically, and subvert when possible. It produces the embodied realization that cultures and identities are not sovereign, that they are always caught up in the play of hybridity.

Mimicry and ambivalence are also attendant notions to hybridity. Mimicry arises out of the desire to be like the colonizer in order to gain power, but it is never complete because the colonized wants to simultaneously hold on to the position of the avenging colonized. According to Bhabha (1994), mimicry "is at once resemblance and menace" because it produces a hybrid subject that is *"almost the same, but not quite"* (pp. 122, 123, italics in original). This resemblance, then, instead of bolstering the identity and power of the colonizer, produces the effect of disavowal of its authority and purity since it produces an ambivalence that mocks the very idea of an original or essential identity (Godiwala, 2007). *Without essentialized identities and pure difference, there can be no cultural superiority or hierarchy.* Godiwala (2007) points out that the colonized hybrid subject is different from the postcolonial migrant in that the hybrid identity of the migrant creates ambivalence not just through mimicry but also through a non-oppositional modality of difference. This is a difference that is able to inhabit two or more cultures "with the ease of long acquaintance," and it "arises from the valorization of self, which does not have to conflict with the appreciation of the Other" (p. 71).

Thus the postcolonial migrant is doubly dislocated, hybrid, and in a vexed position when it comes to claiming a pristine, continuous or originary cultural identity. As Hall (1990) writes, it is not by focusing on who we are but "'what we have become' . . . can we properly understand the traumatic character of 'the colonial experience'" (p. 225). To this I would add that in coming to terms with and valuing the enunciative and cultural power of one's hybrid self, the postcolonial migrant may find herself in a position to accomplish agentic bridgework in the space of the "inter" in intercultural communication through performances of strategic hybridity. And in this process, she may find ways to take better stock of the angst of cultural displacement and transformation set in motion during colonial times.

PERFORMING "INTER"CULTURAL BRIDGEWORK THROUGH STRATEGIC HYBRIDITY

In this part of the chapter, I make a critical shift from the idea of hybridity to that of *strategic hybridity*. As Sorrells (2010) notes, "intercultural praxis may manifest in a range of forms such as simple or complex communication competency skills; oppositional tactics; and creative, improvisational, and transformational interventions" (p. 184). Strategic hybridity is an option for accomplishing transformational interventions. Positioning hybridity as a strategic performance can address the charge that hybridity is often treated as a static cultural descriptor that goes nowhere. Furthermore, such a positioning figures in the possibility of agency, puts hybridity into critical motion, and equips it with the potential to accomplish something in the world (Madison, 1998).

Strategic hybridity can be thought of as a form of intercultural praxis that is performative, agentic, interventionist and about accomplishing something in the present. It is a concept that has been suggested by Sharrad (2007) (see also Noble, Poynting and Tabar, 1999) who notes that strategic hybridity might answer the needs of those who have been worked over by colonial forces and wish to maintain an *and-both* identity stance somewhere between assimilation and the right to be recognized as different. The cultural politics involved here is not so much about "overcoming in the hereafter" but more about what can be accomplished in the moment (Krishna, 2009, p. 92). Strategic hybridity follows a path somewhat similar to that suggested by Spivak (1993) in her notion of strategic essentialism, but with a focus on hybridity instead. Spivak notes the value of a *self-conscious* performance of essentialism in cultural politics, in particular situations, which aims to achieve social justice for the subaltern. Similarly, hybridity may be performed self-consciously and strategically with the goals of transgression and intercultural bridgework in mind. Here, the choice of the term "strategic" hinges not on a "power over" (i.e., domination) view but more on the self-conscious nature of the cultural politics involved in performances of hybridity—a cultural politics that focuses on self-empowerment and "power with" the other. According to Bate and Bowke (1997), empowerment occurs through "power to" interactions (in my argument, the "power to" move is intrapersonal), and the "power with" approach is synergistic in nature and "power emerges from and resides in mutuality between partners" (p. 77). A combination of both would be necessary in performances of strategic hybridity emerging from non-dominant identity positions. Furthermore, the self-consciousness involved is crucial, whether one is committed to a strategy of essentialism or hybridity, since it stops us from dogmatically naturalizing either position.

Drawing upon Bakhtin, Werbner (1997) describes two forms of hybridity: organic or unconscious hybridity and intentional hybridity. Regarding the former, she writes that "despite the illusion of boundedness, cultures evolve historically through unreflective borrowings, mimetic appropriations, exchanges and invention" (pp. 4–5). Intentional hybridity, on the other hand, works off of the ground prepared by organic hybridity in order to aesthetically "shock, change, challenge, revitalize, or disrupt" through deliberate acts and/or representations that "fuse the unfusable" (p. 5). Werbner, too, notes the value of a "new form of self-consciously hybrid politics" (1997, p. 8).

Since performances of strategic hybridity involve mimicry, it is necessary to remain in the self-conscious and critical mode so that mimicry does not slip into internalization of colonial ideologies (Godiwala, 2007).

According to Bhabha, a decentered hybrid self is an "everyday practice, a way of living with oneself and others while acknowledging the 'partiality' of social identification; it becomes part of one's ethical being in the sense that such a 'decentering' also informs the agency through which one executes a care of self and a concern for the 'other' . . ." (cited in Krishna, 2009, p. 93). The decentered hybrid self, for Bhabha, is a source of creativity, intervention and possibility.

Within intercultural communication praxis, the creative work of mundane strategic hybrid performance would involve surprising the other by yoking together unlikely things that would normally seem contradictory. Such cultural performances, as Conquergood (1998) suggests, could be especially empowering for non-dominant groups. Referring to Bhabha's enumeration of the performative nature of cultural acts of transgression, he writes that he prefers to think of performance "as transgression, that force which crashes and breaks through sedimented meaning and normative traditions and plunges us back into the vortices of political struggle" (p. 32). Madison (1998), in a similar vein, writes: "In the *performance of possibilities*, I see the 'possible' as suggesting a movement culminating in creation and change" (p. 277, italics in original). Drawing upon Anzaldúa's work, she underscores the importance of moving beyond the oppressor/oppressed dualism by "critically traversing the margin *and* the center" and "opening more and different paths for enlivening relations and spaces" (p. 277, italics in original). In fact, performances of strategic hybridity that aim to accomplish intercultural bridgework hold the possibility of accomplishing something more than just transgression (i.e., an oppositional disruption): they aim to build connections and bring about transformation *while* performing transgression.[1]

I now return to the question I posed earlier: *Does hybridity have the potential to offer a critical perspective on how culturally displaced postcolonial migrants may accomplish agentic bridgework through intercultural communication?* If hybridity is envisioned as strategic and performative, following are some possibilities.

First, performances of strategic hybridity can help validate the doubly dislocated cultural identities of postcolonial migrants who often struggle between the impossible desires to belong completely in the new home, recreate the old home culture, and maintain a pristine and unitary narrative of the self that suppresses the transformations of colonization and migration. This struggle can rob one of agency and a positive sense of self, and manifest itself in fractured, confused, or overly defensive and essentialist identity positions during intercultural praxis. Taking the lead in initiating bridgework through strategic hybridity itself could generate a sense of empowerment, affirmation, and agency. As Bhabha (1996) notes, "hybrid agencies find their voice in a dialectic that does not seek cultural supremacy or sovereignty" (p. 58). While outcomes are never guaranteed, the very process of engaging in the performance could result in catharsis in relation to colonial and migration trauma and angst. If desired bridgework and some transgression of cultural authority is achieved, then the reward could be even greater. Thus, the postcolonial migrant may be able to chart out a path from a reactive (i.e., negative) to a proactive identity stance, and in the process develop a high tolerance for ambiguity (Anzaldúa, 2009b) and a lesser need for (an impossible) pure identity.

For example, Holling and Calafell (2007) describe how performance artist Guillermo Gómez-Peña stages his personal narratives in ways "that not only bridge communities, but also point to the contested and con-structed nature of identities [and culture], critiquing the authenticity games played between Chicana/os and Mexicans by blurring the line between the two" (p. 73). Such staging of identities is also possible in the space of the "inter" in mundane everyday intercultural communication praxis.

Second, the postcolonial migrant may enter into intercultural bridge-work with various goals in mind, such as: to educate, transform attitudes, subvert binaries upon which pure and hierarchical difference are usually constructed, problematize normalized stereotypes, reconfigure hegemon-ic codes, challenge divisive essentialisms, demonstrate that culture is a traveling variable, highlight the difference-similarity dialectic of intercul-tural communication (Martin and Nakayama, 1999), and to build unlikely alliances across seemingly incommensurable differences (Carrillo Rowe, 2010a). These are all possibilities that can be tapped by performing differ-ence in ways that demonstrate that there is always a "connective tissue" (Bhabha, 1996, p. 54) between seemingly different cultures and identities.

For example Pascual (2012), in promoting hybrid cultural politics in intercultural communication praxis, notes that such politics can help us move beyond the perspective that intercultural communication involves an *either-or* choice between assimilation or resistance to dominant cultural ideology. She describes her work of procuring funds from a European-based international organization for distribution in Latin American of-fices in terms of daily strategic performances of her hybrid American and Mexican identity positions through which she traverses the margins *and* the center to incrementally bring about social change. She explains that by working in this space of the "inter" she learns daily about the "ambig-uous and multidirectional" properties of power, and the transformative value of bringing together systems operating on contradictory logics (p. 304).

Third, Cooks (2010) recently observed that focusing on power and privilege just at macro levels "have in many cases prevented a detailed analysis of the multiple status moves present in any interaction" (p. 121). She writes that overly zooming out the critical lens "simplifies differences where their construction is often more complicated, and layers of privi-lege and oppression are uneven" (p. 121). Strategic hybridity takes a nuanced "zoom in" view of identity differences in intercultural interaction. Performances of strategic hybridity could also induce incremental change in micro-macro dynamics. In other words, such intercultural praxis may gradually orient us towards more macro level bridgework and alliance building, and thereby increase possibilities for changes in dominant attitudes and power configurations and reduce intercultural animosity at the planetary level.

Connected to the above point, we can hope that identity performances of hybridity, if gradually normalized, may lead to less charged and more positive relations between postcolonial immigrants and host cultures at larger structural and discursive levels. A possible outcome could be growing acceptance and incorporation of the logic of interculturalism in place of multiculturalism in national or transnational policies and structures (e.g., immigration). Policies steeped in the logic of multiculturalism envision cultures and identities as essentialist and separate, which makes it difficult to argue effectively against historical inequalities (Bhabha, 1996; Werbner, 1997). On the other hand, policies guided by the logic of interculturalism would envision cultures as *separate yet connected*, and take into account the play of history and power inequities (Nederveen Pieterse, 2009). The ways in which we envision culture and difference are directly related to how we envision change and parity. In current conditions of transnational complexity, such a shift would be meaningful to postcolonial migrants or any non-dominant subject position, and could lead to a world where straddling two or more cultures is seen more as part of the norm rather than an exception (Anzaldúa, 1987).

AN ACCENTED TALE ABOUT IDENTITY (CONTINUED)

I now return to my narrative regarding accents. I left off wondering how to perform intercultural bridgework with American students who ask why I don't speak with, what in their perception is, an "Indian accent." Quite by accident, I have discovered a way.

One time, when I received the comment *"You don't speak with an accent"* in one of its varied forms, I resorted to an identity performance the result of which took me by surprise (and I ended up surprising my students as well). I started explaining how I don't have a fixed accent, that my border-crossing lived experience has made me travel through various modes of accent switching and, for example, when I am back visiting in India, my accent changes significantly (but temporarily). Towards the end of this explanation, I performed a gradual accent switch, and then switched right back to the accent with which I had started. This unexpected arrangement of my "no accent" and "accented" selves in one continuous enunciative movement produced a moment of non-unitary identity performance, a straddling of two cultural worlds. It was also, simul-

taneously, an invitation to see difference differently, i.e., as non-oppositional.

This performance, or doing of hybridity, always produces a reaction,
and of course the make-up of the classroom audience is key in eliciting
different reactions.

"*Wow, how do you do that*???" (Okay, the performance has had some
sort of an impact.)

"*Can you do that again?*" (Oh dear, let's not make this into a curiosity
act.)

"*You know, now that I think about it, it's funny how my boyfriend's accent
changes when we drive down to visit his family in South Carolina. It actually
starts getting all southern during the drive itself!*" This came from a white
woman who has spent most of her life in rural southern Illinois (Ah, here
is a "connective tissue" among our differences, and I don't feel like the
outsider who can perform interesting tricks. We may have accomplished
a little something in this moment because she willingly entered into the
"inter" with me).

Although I am usually the only postcolonial migrant in the classroom,
I am in a relative position of power because of my role of teacher (also,
students' minds are probably more open and accepting of new ideas). I
have an advantage here which I recognize as I narrate. Outside of the
classroom, the story and power dynamics might be very different. And
the same performance may not help me draw my interlocutor onto the
bridge and into the space of the "inter." In that case, a different mode of
intercultural praxis might be necessary.

This narrative is a tiny example of mundane strategic hybridy in the
context of the classroom, and by no means is it radical. I share this story
because it affirms to me that there lives possibility, however little or big,
in exploring the potential of strategic hybridity in everyday intercultural
praxis. Every little step of transformation and connection across difference is an incremental step towards bigger change. As Allen (2002) notes
with regards to intercultural alliance building efforts, we must "acknowledge and celebrate victories, however small they may be" (Allen et al., p.
316).

CONCLUSION

The concept of hybridity, as it has been developed in postcolonial studies,
has not been sufficiently explored for its usefulness in identity research in
intercultural communication. Identities are being increasingly experienced as hybrid by many in a rapidly reconfiguring world, and we need
more theories of cultural "in-betweenness" in our theoretical toolbox in
order to grapple with and come to terms with our postmodern and postcolonial selves. And in so doing, we have to continue to find ways, when-

ever possible, to connect across differences in order to build a more humane world.

This chapter is a small contribution in the larger project of theorizing
communicative "strategies of selfhood" (Bhabha, 1994, p. 2) that could
empower those who do not fit neatly into clear-cut identity boxes. More
generally, it is also an invitation to intercultural communication scholars
to further explore the potential of postcolonial theory in intercultural
identity scholarship. Furthermore, it is a knock on the door of models and
theories of cultural transition that do not take into account specific migrant subjectivities, possibilities of agency, and how migrants may incrementally change the societies they enter. In terms of intercultural praxis,
it is a call to extend ourselves to build bridges across difference and
consciously be open to possibilities for communicative intervention and
transformation. The bridges may break, or they may endure. They may
be short or long ones, weak or strong ones. But any connection is worth
the effort. Pedagogically, the better we can teach ourselves to be open to
various views on intercultural identities and interactions, the better we,
as educators, will be able to teach our students how to live well in a
world in which multiple identity positions and possibilities for alliances
and transformations exist. Instead of fearing difference, we can teach
ourselves and our students that ". . . we can transform our world by
imagining it differently, dreaming it passionately via all our senses, and
willing it into creation. As we think inspiring, positive, life-generating
thoughts and embody these thoughts in every act we perform, we can
gradually change the mood of our days, the habits of years, and the
beliefs of a lifetime" (Anzaldúa, 2009b, p. 312–13).

In conclusion I would like to note that while I have made a case for
strategic hybridity and intercultural bridgework in this chapter, I also
acknowledge that there are no guarantees of outcomes. In the same
breath that I argue for strategic hybridity, I also maintain that it will not
be an appropriate strategy in all cases and contexts. In some cases, strategic essentialism, or a mix of both (or maybe even non-engagement) may
be the more effective route. These might involve situations where any
move toward performing hybridity might endanger, physicially and/or
emotionally, the already marginalized. But I do believe that we should
have an array of strategies in our repertoire of intercultural praxis, and
judiciously and ethically perform bridgework whenever possible.

NOTE

1. I thank Hsin-I Cheng for this insight.

ELEVEN

Researching Biracial/Multiracial Identity Negotiation

Lessons from Diverse Contemporary U.S. Public Perceptions

Mark P. Orbe

Biracial and multiracial Americans, a diverse group of individuals whose parents are from different racial and ethnic groups, have always existed within the United States (Orbe and Harris, 2008). Historically these individuals were described with very specific labels (e.g., mulattos, quadroons, and octoroons) used to delineate different gradations of enslaved blacks (Davis, 1991). However, the one-drop rule, whereby a single drop of black blood meant a person was black, made the existence of multiracial Americans nearly invisible (Rockquemore and Laszloffy, 2005). The rhetorical power of the "one-drop rule" is embedded in the historical, legal, and social fabric of the United States. Yet the increasing number of individuals who embrace biracial or multiracial identities and the prevalence of several high profile persons continues to challenge societal traditions that regard racial and ethnic identity in uni-dimensional, distinct forms. As such, historical conceptualizations of race and ethnicity are being challenged by a growing number of biracial and multiracial Americans, resulting in reconfigurations of historic racial designations (James and Tucker, 2003). Unlike the past, increasing numbers of multiracial Americans refuse being "boxed in" one racial category, and instead affirm multiple sources of their racial identities (Root, 2001). As Orbe and Harris (2008) write, this includes individuals whose identities reflect two different races (Frazier, 2002; Lewis, 2006; Walker, 2001), as well as those whose lineage encompasses complex racial and ethnic combinations (e.g., Tiger Woods's identification as Cablinasian, a term he created to refer to his Caucasian, black, American Indian, and Asian ancestry).

These biracial and multiracial identities can be juxtaposed against the communicative identity of President Barack Obama who has emphasized his biracial ancestry—being the son of a white woman from Kansas and a father from Kenya—but does not identify as a biracial person (Jones, 2010). He does not identify as white but aspects of his identity are located within his close relations to white family members, belongings, and affiliations (Carrillo Rowe, 2010b). However, within the United States, a rule of hypodescent has historically existed whereby a monoracial identification associated with the racial group with the least social status has been assigned to racially mixed persons (Root, 1996). Consistent with this principle, Obama implicitly identifies as African American complete with multiple signifiers of blackness (Moffitt, 2010). Yet his communication is seen as "less about being biracial and more about being bicultural" (Jones, 2010, p. 104), something regarded as much of a gift as a burden (Smith, 2009). Several scholars point to President Obama's negotiation of multiple racial identities as a compelling motivation for re-examining issues of culture and identity which ultimately will lead to a greater understanding of who we are and who we are becoming as individuals, a society, and a global community (Asim, 2009; Jones, 2010).

An African proverb states: *The way out is back through*. This chapter applies the principle captured in this proverb by providing a scholarly-personal chapter that uses self-reflexivity, defined by Fasset and Warren (2007) as "an important motion, back and forth, between one's actions and how those implicate one in social phenomena" (p. 48). In this regard, self-reflexivity regarding my scholarly and personal lived experiences with biracial and multiracial identity negotiation serves as a launching point to provide direction for future research geared toward exploring issues of identity and intercultural communication. More specifically, I draw from data from a series of recent research projects (Drummond and Orbe, 2010; Orbe, 2011; Orbe, Bradford, and Orbe, 2011; Orbe and Drummond, in press; Orbe and Drummond, 2009) that offer insight into contemporary conceptualizations of biracial and multiracial identity in the United States to reengage a typology of interracial family communication that was designed to do the same (Orbe, 1999). This self-reflexive process ultimately leads to guiding principles that promise to maximize the potential of future research that seeks to explore the inextricable relationship of identity, culture, and communication.

One important acknowledgment before I proceed: My chapter focuses on the communicative identities of biracial and multiracial individuals currently living in the United States. Yet, as a sociopolitical creation, race is constructed in many different ways in different parts of the world

(Orbe and Harris, 2008). Some scholars, like Shome (2010), critique inter-cultural communication scholarship for privileging U.S.-centric concep-tualizations of race, and in doing so, marginalizing the racialized experi-ences of others around the world. While the topical focus of this chapter may contribute to this problematic issue, I hope that by making this important acknowledgment explicit it works—at a minimum—to disrupt the "frequently unmarked U.S. nation-centeredness" (Shome, 2010, p. 152) of race scholarship.

BIRACIAL AND MULTIRACIAL IDENTITY NEGOTIATION

For many years, biracial and multiracial identity development was understood via frameworks developed for U.S. racial and ethnic minor-ities (Orbe and Harris, 2008), something that reinforced the one-drop rule (Rockquemore and Laszloffy, 2005). Yet, these identity development models are less than ideal for three reasons. First, these models are limit-ed in that they portray identify development as a linear process with a clearly articulated goal (Spencer, 2006). Second, bi/multiracial identity has no clear-cut ultimate outcome that makes identity formation highly ambiguous and tentative (Nance and Foeman, 2002). Third, biracial and multiracial identity negotiation is found to take on an even greater spiral-ing process when compared to monoracial identities and oftentimes can change over time, place, and context (James and Tucker, 2003).

Several models of biracial identity development appeared in the 1990s (e.g., Jacobs, 1992; Kich, 1992; Poston, 1990). Of these three, Poston's (1990, p. 153) "new and positive model" of biracial identity appears the most innovative. Specifically, it extends earlier models by suggesting that biracial identity follows five stages: personal identity, group categoriza-tion, enmeshment/denial, appreciation, and integration. In the final stage of biracial identity development (integration), individuals are able to carve out an identity that reflects their complete selves with no pressure to prioritize certain aspects of their identities over others. While models of identity development provide some insight into identity formation, they are largely limited in that they portray a linear formation of how identity develops via pre-determined, ordered stages (Orbe and Harris, 2008). The realities of identity, however, are typically not easily captured in neatly formatted stages (Nance and Foeman, 2002). Contemporary communication theories that are grounded in interpretive and postmod-ern worldviews reject the idea that identity is something that can be "achieved"; instead they embrace the idea that identities are constantly negotiated via cultural contracts, multiple locations, or similar points of contact (Hecht, Jackson, and Ribeau, 2003).

I am a *product* of a biracial marriage and *participant* in a multiracial marriage that has created children who are African, European, Asian,

and Native American (and have a Spanish surname). Consequently, issues of culture and identity negotiation—and not identity development—remain a fixture in my communicative life. Reflecting on my own
experiences, as well as those around me, I wrote about how interracial
families communicate about race to their children. This piece (Orbe, 1999)
features a typology that describes four different communicative orientations found in interracial families: (1) Embracing the black experience; (2)
Assuming a commonsense approach; (3) Advocating for a color-blind
society; and (4) Affirming the multiethnic experience.

According to the original typology, embracing the black experience is
based on three ideas: (a) parents believe that it is important to prepare
their children for interactions in society that define them as black regardless of their appearance; (b) a black identity allows biracial children to
benefit from the strength of African American communities, and (c) interracial families regard the black experience as positive, affirming, and
inspiring. The second communication orientation, assuming a common-
sense approach, rejects the one-drop rule as antiquated and illogical. Instead, families work to form identities that make the most sense for them
in terms of family composition (e.g., presence and/or absence of parental
influence), appearance (e.g., skin color, hair, other body features), and
larger environment (e.g., neighborhoods, schools, places of worship). In
this regard, racial identity is seen as connected to, yet independent of,
one's biology.

Advocating for a color-blind society reflects the third orientation of
multiracial family communication. Within this approach, families downplay racial differences and focus on the realities that humans are all part
of one race, the human race. This communicative stance resists racial
classifications that are manipulated to separate different groups based on
distinctions that are social and political—yet unscientific—in nature
(Orbe and Harris, 2008). Advocating for a color-blind reality is an important step toward diminishing the saliency of race in the United States.
Affirming the multiracial experience is the final element of the typology.
It focuses on how families work to make sure that children appreciate all
of the various cultures that they are a part of. For many families, this
approach includes teaching children about all aspects of who they are
and ultimately encouraging children to make their own self-designations
about race, cultural, and racial identity.

This initial typology reflects the multiple ways in which multiracial
families communicate about race. It holds significant insight into how
familial socialization influences individual identity negotiation, and is
presented in a way where one orientation is not positioned as "more
correct" or "authentic" than others. Recently, I have engaged in several
research projects that have focused on issues related to identity, race, and
communication. While only one of these projects focused specifically on
biracial and multiracial persons, I found powerfully insightful articula-

tions of lived experiences that spoke to the challenges, tensions, and beauty inherent to bi/multiracial identities. After providing a brief description of each of these projects, I utilize different voices to critically engage the four orientations described in the 1999 typology. Ultimately, this process generates several implications for future research on identity(ies) and intercultural communication.

SELF-REFLEXIVITY IN MOTION

Fasset and Warren (2007) differentiate between essays that are *reflective*, which suggests an accounting or mirroring, and those that are *reflexive*, which features a process of going back and forth to ultimately move forward. This chapter is not about accounting for existing work as it is about a process of re-engagement of a particular social phenomenon. Several recent research projects prompted this self-reflexive chapter on biracial and multiracial identity negotiation. First, I engaged in a coauthored research study that explored several communicative issues related to race and ethnicity: Identity, racial and ethnic labels, and ingroup/outgroup perceptions. Data was collected from one hundred individuals from diverse backgrounds via thirteen focus groups, during September 2006 through May 2007, in a large southeastern U.S. metropolitan area. Details regarding the methods of the study can be found in existing publications (Drummond and Orbe, 2010; Orbe and Drummond, in press; Orbe and Drummond, 2009). Second, I conducted a national study of public perceptions of President Obama as communicator, with a particular interest in investigating how individuals from diverse backgrounds make meaning out of his rhetoric regarding race matters. From June to December 2010, I spoke with 333 individuals who participated in forty-two focus groups across thirteen different U.S. states. Analysis of this large qualitative data set is being published in book form (Orbe, 2011) with specific focal points on communication style, race matters, and the media. Participants' comments focusing on President Obama's biracial ancestry, as well as their own multiracial identities, were analyzed for this current chapter. The third research project is a collective autoethnography designed specifically to explore how three individuals, from different generations, describe the impact of President Obama's emergence as a world leader on their biracial and multiracial identity negotiation (Orbe, Bradford, and Orbe, 2011). Treated as secondary data, the insight generated through this scholarly inquiry is invaluable in understanding the dynamic nature of identity.

Collectively, these research projects were meaningful in capturing the diverse communicative experiences of people from mixed ancestry. Some were consistent with the four orientations described within the 1999 typology summarized earlier; however, other descriptions worked to clarify and extend the work in meaningful ways. The next four sub-sections illustrate this for each of the four approaches to communicating about biracial and multiracial identities.

Embracing the Experience of a Person of Color

Initially, this communicative approach was termed "Embracing the Black Experience" because the one-drop rule was unevenly applied to biracial and multiracial individuals with African American ancestry so that social separation between white and black worlds could be maintained (Davis, 1991). While this may remain largely true for some, the data reveals that individuals from a multitude of backgrounds also communicate in ways that embrace the identities of their parents of color. Given this, a shift in more inclusive terminology is appropriate.

The majority of participant comments that illustrate this particular communicative approach were found in the largest data set (Orbe, 2011). In particular, comments from older African Americans were most likely to describe biracial individuals, like Barack Obama, in monoracial terms. For example, consider the comments of one forty-something-year-old African American man who was born and raised in Alabama but is currently residing in southern Virginia. Within his comments, he acknowledges President Obama's biracial ancestry but relinquishes to the historical power of the one-drop rule:

> [His blackness] is all they see, but it is kinda ironic. It is weird because we are in 2010, and it's the same. Back in the day, someone who was mixed was mulatto, but all that they saw was that they were black. If you had brown skin, the white part faded off. You were black. And even now, 2010, all that they see is his brown skin. That's all that matters. The fact that he had a white mother, and was raised by white people, it doesn't matter. They don't see any of that!

Similar comments are heard from other older African Americans across the United States. Another older black man from Alabama echoes the sentiment here by identifying the racial dichotomy that oftentimes forces choices related to biracial identity. In referring to President Obama, he says:

> I understand that he is multiracial, but people don't always see that. Even when you look at his multiracial background, America views things as black and white. I acknowledge that he is multiracial, but I define him as being black. And I think that a lot of people would say the same. Because it has been the standard, or the norm, that people have to fall under one of those two categories.

Some examples of younger biracial people embracing identities of a person of color (e.g., African American, Native American, or Latino/a) exist across different data sets. Most of these individuals' comments mirrored those of older people of color and spoke to the tendency of humans to categorize. This is the case with one young multiracial woman from Florida who describes her family by saying:

> We can trace back our white ancestry, but we just describe ourselves as black . . . Because walking down the street, people are going to describe you as black. They're not going to be like, "Oh, she's half white and half black." They're always doing that . . . because they just want to put you in that one category. The way I see it, it is not right to divide people, but you do have to do some sort of classification. It's just in our human nature to be that way.

Several of these young people explain how their perspectives are directly informed by those of their parents. This is seen in the comments of one black woman in Massachusetts when she says: "My dad would say that biracial doesn't exist. Because of the one-drop rule—if you have one drop of black blood, then you are black." Another young person, a twenty-something-year-old Caucasian woman from West Virginia, describes how her views are an extension of older relatives. Specifically, she says: "I have always been told that if you have a black parent, then you are black. Yes, there are biracial people, but I have always been under the impression that being biracial is a sub-group of being black."

Some of these articulations of identity go uncontested, however, other instances surface as individuals challenge the rationale behind such an approach. Such is the case when the topic is discussed within an all-white focus group held in Florida (Orbe and Drummond, 2009). Specifically discussing his experiences with Hispanics, one young white male reacts to individuals who embrace the experience of a person of color:

> [With some Latin-Americans] I'll identify them as a fellow white person; then I'll find out somewhere along the way that they're part Cuban or something like that and they think of themselves as completely Hispanic. And I'm thinking to myself, you're a white person or at least part white.

This set of comments illustrates how identity is constantly negotiated via different cultural contracts (Jackson, 2002a; Jackson and Crawley, 2003) or identity gaps between "self" and "other" perceptual frames (Hecht, Warren, Jung, and Krieger, 2005). Jeffries (2002) acknowledges efforts to move beyond the one-drop rule, but she forcefully resists any attempts to strip her of a racialized identity that she embraces with vigor:

> We have played by your rules and now you want to change them. How can you tell me "one drop" means I'm black, and for hundreds of years make me proclaim that as my identity? Then when it is "chic" to proclaim a multiracial heritage demand I select a more exotic title for myself thus stripping me of my only true identity as black? If I don't look black by your standards, that's just too damn bad. You and your rules created me. Your back door entrances, your separate water fountains,

and snotty looks create me. So deal with it. I am a proud black woman, and yes, perhaps I could be something different, perhaps I could be mixed, but your rules say one drop and thank God I qualify. (p. 51)

Assuming a Contingency Approach

The initial typology describes the second communication orientation as "Assuming a Common-Sense Approach" in light of biracial and multiracial individuals whose identities are informed by family composition, physical appearance, and/or larger environments. The rationale behind this orientation is that when people engage in sense-making processes (Weick, 1995) regarding their identities it occurs within situational contexts that multilayered and complex. Within this re-conceptualization of the typology, I continue to hold to the core idea that biracial and multiracial individuals identify in ways that make the most sense to them. However, a shift in terminology is warranted given that each of the four communication orientations included in the typology *makes sense to the individuals who embrace them.* Consequently, this second orientation has been re-named to emphasize the salient function that situational context serves in identity negotiation (Harris and Sim, 2001).

Assuming a contingency approach highlights how the identity negotiation of some biracial and multiracial individuals depends on other factors. Within this orientation, racial identity is contingent on a number of factors including racial ancestry, early socialization experiences, cultural attachment, physical appearance, social and historical context, political awareness and other social identity markers like age and spirituality (Wijeyesinghe, 2001). Issues like social and historical context, for example, are important given that younger biracial and multiracial people appear less willing to follow the one-drop rule. This is evident in the collective autoethnography (Orbe et al., 2011) where the influence of this form of social and cultural norm increasingly reduced the younger the person was. Jones (2010) reminds us that biracial and multiracial individuals must be understood as "situated selves—products of particular times, places, and personal experiences" (p. 137). One particular example that stands out as a vivid illustration of this involves an eighteen-year-old multiracial woman from Michigan. She describes how her identity is negotiated differently depending on situational context. For instance, her self-articulated identity as a multiracial person is challenged at her urban high school where most of her classmates receive free or reduced lunch. However, in her estimation, socioeconomic status has a huge influence on racial identity:

People at school do perceive me as a white girl, and sometimes I feel that no matter how much I explain to them my actual history. Race perception is closely mingled with socioeconomic status. They are thinking I am too rich to be black, too proper, too smart, etc. I "dress white" and I engage in "white activities," like playing soccer. I think that they say I'm white because they think I fit in with more white people. And that doesn't bother me because I am white.

This example reflects how assuming a contingency approach recognizes that biracial and multiracial identity does not exist in a vacuum; instead a person's identity is formed at the places where categories of identities intersect (Crenshaw, 1991).

Assuming a contingency approach embraces identity as a dynamic fluid process steeped in the idea that different aspects of one person's identity may take on greater salience in different contexts. This is consistent with Root (1996) who includes "the right to identify myself differently in different situations" (p. 7) within her *Bill of Rights for Racially Mixed People*. The most vivid illustration of this orientation is seen within the comments of a biracial woman whose black and Puerto Rican identities take different forms in different situations. Specifically, she describes her reality as follows:

> When I was living in Maryland, I went to high school there [and] lived in a really Hispanic neighborhood. And all my friends were pretty much Hispanic. And I do have some Hispanic descent in me. I mean I don't speak Spanish. And some people when they look at me they think I am. Others, they think I'm black. So, when I was hanging out with my Spanish friends and somebody would ask me what my race was, I'd be quick to say, "Oh, I'm Puerto Rican and Black." But I've noticed down here I mean there are still a lot of Hispanics, but most of my friends are African American or black . . . When people ask me my race, I automatically go, "I'm black and Hispanic." I'll flip it. It's weird. I notice I'm doing that, but I guess it's like the same thing but the ordering, you know, clearing changed . . . So, I mean I guess that's just me, and my friends understand and accept me.

This particular quote points to how various factors—such as levels of family identification, physical appearance, friends, relations with extended family members, and composition of neighborhood—are salient to decisions on label preferences for multiracial persons (Rockquemore and Brunsma, 2002).

Advocating for a Color-Blind Society

As briefly described earlier, the third communicative orientation of multiracial persons downplays racial differences and focuses on the realities that humans are all part of one race, the human race. Individuals whose communication reflects this stance resist racial classifications that are based on distinctions that are social and political—yet unscientific—in nature (Orbe and Drummond, 2009). Within this approach, racializing a person's identity is problematic because it works to reinforce the myth of race (Montagu, 1997). Consequently, advocating for a color-blind society leads biracial and multiracial people to identify as *humans*; this act of agency is seen as an important step toward diminishing the saliency of race in the United States.

Re-examining the data from recent studies reveals numerous sets of comments reflecting this particular approach to identity in general, and biracial/multiracial identity in particular. In data collected in a large southeastern U.S. city (Drummond and Orbe, 2010), a substantial number of participants describe their understanding of racial identity in these terms:

> I don't agree with all that because what I think is that we are all human beings . . . there is no point of someone being white or someone being black . . . God made us all equal, and we are the ones who are making the differentiation and we shouldn't be.

Similar comments are seen in comments illustrating diverse public perceptions of President Obama's racial identity (Orbe, 2011). Many individuals describe him as a "post-racial" public image, one whose eclectic life experiences allow him to transcend race in productive ways that reduce its ability to divide and conquer. Given the historic and structural dimensions of racism in the United States, numerous scholars challenge the notion that Obama's election marks the emergence of a "post-racial society" (Gavrilos, 2010; Joseph, in press; Orbe and Urban, in press). In fact, Squires, Harris, and Moffitt (2010) consider such declarations as naïve and self-congratulatory (p. xviii). Individuals from biracial and multiracial ancestry who advocate for a color-blind society do not necessarily embrace a pollyana existence that denies the realities of racism. In fact, their identity negotiation is seen as a rejection of a racist system of classification based on oppressive designations.

For some, this communicative orientation includes critical rejection of social-political constructions of race. Criticisms of the U.S. racial and ethnic classification system are most apparent in the comments of first generation immigrants who were quick to point out that racial differences are not real and were something that they had to learn after arriving in the United States. For many from Latin American countries where race is conceptualized in less rigid ways (if at all), negotiations of racial identity(ies) in the United States are "flawed." One man born and raised in Colombia and currently living in Florida says: "I just think that the whole notion of categorization is flawed in that it reinforces this notion of we are all different and we need to exploit those differences, and then of course, that can lead to one group is better. . . ." Within these discussions, many individuals acknowledge that reality of race in the United States which is a challenge for people who want to embrace a color-blind society. Within the collective autoethnographic process, I also identify this issue which has been an ever-present tension since becoming a parent of multiracial children. Specifically, I write:

> Here's the catch-22: I want for my children to live in a color-blind society but feel like I need to prepare my children to succeed in a society where race still is a salient issue. This means preparing them to deal with the overt and covert prejudices and discrimination that they will face. However, in doing so, maybe I'm giving them all of the racial baggage that are part of my generation but not necessarily theirs—so in preparing the next generation about the realities of race, we may be weighing them down with the burden of race that no longer exists as we've known it.

Communication scholars conceptualize a number of intercultural communication dialectical tensions that offer fresh perspectives on biracial and multiracial identity negotiation (Martin and Nakayama, 1999). Within this framework, identity is inherently situated within a series of tensions including person-social/contextual, static/dynamic, and present-future/history-past. Such an approach might also lead scholars to investigate the tensions within, and between, each of the four communication orientations described here.

Affirming the Multicultural Existence

Affirming the multicultural existence is the final approach of the typology. It reflects how biracial and multiracial persons embrace all aspects of their identities. Consequently, *multicultural existence* has replaced *multiracial experience* in the label to illustrate how race is one of many cultural factors that are inherent to a person's identity. Within this communicative orientation, individuals resist social pressures to identify in monoracial terms (e.g., black or white) or as "half-of-this and half-of-that." Instead, a biracial or multiracial identity is defined as encompassing of all aspects of one's multifaceted heritage. Collins (2000) describes such an orientation as reflective of a "doubled identity," one that is enhanced by multiple selves rather than fragmented into halves, thirds, or other forms of racialized human fractions. In this regard, racial allegiance is not limited to one group (Harris and Sim, 2001).

Of the four communicative orientations of biracial and multiracial identity negotiation, affirming the multiracial experience is the one that is most represented in the secondary data re-analyzed for this chapter. Given the advances since the typology was first conceptualized in the late 1990s, this should not come as a surprise. Of particular significance is the change in the 2000 U.S. Census that allows individuals to describe themselves as being of two or more races for the first time. According to James and Tucker (2003), almost seven million people self-identified as multiracial—the majority of which were young children—a number that will grow exponentially (Orbe and Harris, 2008).

Within one research project (Drummond and Orbe, 2010), one young woman from Florida shares how embracing a multicultural experience includes the tendency to resist a singular label:

> There's not really one term that I prefer. I think that different people assume different things. I don't mind being called Indian, but a lot of people call me English because I was born there and have an English accent. I'll have that the rest of my life . . . By blood, I'm Indian. My grandparents were born there. But both my parents were born outside India, my mom in England, my dad in the Philippines, me and my brother and sister were all born in England.

Within these comments, her racial and ethnic identities (i.e., Indian) are situated within cultural identity markers like nationality and age. Struggling with labels that capture the complexity of multicultural identities is difficult. Several people across data sets share how their self-descriptions vary from "short quick-fix answers" (e.g., mixed) to more in-depth explanations. While these articulations may vary, the multidimensional aspects of individuals who embrace a multicultural experience remain intact. One young woman explains:

> My mother is Colombian. My biological father is Cuban. But I was raised by a Dominican stepfather. And then in the area we grew up in, there were a lot of Puerto Ricans, Dominicans, and Mexicans. So, now people are always guessing, "You're Puerto Rican. You're this. You're that." I don't know how to describe myself with a simple term. I know I identify myself mostly as Latin, but it's not that simple . . . there's always a title but it never fits.

Multicultural persons, like the woman who is quoted here, are more likely to resist traditional racial and ethnic labels and cocreate new ways of self-identity (Drummond and Orbe, 2010; Hecht et al., 2003). This assertion appears to reflect on a larger transnational worldview, one which acknowledges that race remains a salient contemporary issue but believes that traditional cultural divisions can be transformed through an appreciation of cultural similarities and differences (Orbe and Drummond, in press).

IDENTITY AND INTERCULTURAL COMMUNICATION:
IMPLICATIONS FOR FUTURE RESEARCH

As an exercise in self-reflexivity, this chapter provides an invaluable opportunity to landscape the future of communication-based scholarship on biracial and multiracial identity negotiation. The revised typology—Embracing the Experience of a Person of Color, Assuming a Contingency Approach, Advocating for a Color-Blind Society, and Affirming a Multicultural Existence—reflects diverse communication orientations that help to provide insight into the complexities inherent within intersections of identity, culture, and communication. The framework is situated within the idea that biracial and multiracial individuals have the right to identify themselves in ways that make the most sense to them personally, culturally, and socially. As such, it embraces the values as articulated by Root's (1996) *Bill of Rights for Racially Mixed People* which includes the right: Not to justify my existence in this world; not to keep the races separate within me; not to be responsible for people's discomfort with my physical ambiguity; not to justify my ethnic legitimacy; to identify myself differently than strangers expect me to identify; to identify myself differently than how my parents identify me; to identify myself differently than my brothers and sisters; to identify myself differently in different situations; to create a vocabulary to communicate about being multiracial; to change my identity over my lifetime—and more than once; to have loyalties and identify with more than one group of people, and to freely choose whom I befriend and love (p. 7).

I initially envisioned this final section as a place to articulate how several lessons learned from a self-reflexive and scholarly/cultural/personal process can inform future research on biracial and multiracial identity negotiation. However, during a recent collective autoethnography, one of my coauthors made an insightful observation that shifts my focus here. Specifically, this thirty-something-year-old biracial man from Michigan writes:

> In regard to being denied these rights, it happens just about every day. As I was just told last week (by a good friend, even) that I am a haircut away from being white. Basically, he was taking away my right to identify as black or multiracial. To tell me that the only thing that makes me "non-white" is my dreadlocks is a silly opinion and rather offensive. . . . I have been looking at this list for quite some time now. I like the list a lot and will most likely post it in my classroom. But I should also comment that this Bill of Rights also seems to extend to all people, not just people of mixed race. The high majority of them are about identity and self-identity and I believe all people have the right to self-identify. Even when these self-identities have bothered me or annoyed me in the past. I now fully understand the importance of self-identification.

As I quickly reviewed Root's list, his comments immediately made sense to me. Through the self-reflexive process that was a part of authoring this chapter they also allowed me to understand the universal nature of certain "lessons" that hold local and more global relevance. In fact, I began to wonder how this *Bill of Rights for Racially Mixed People* is negotiated overtly and covertly in different communities across the world. As an intercultural communication scholar-educator-activist, I am dedicated to exploring the similarities and differences of lived experiences and the negotiation of racial identities within various cultural contexts. This appears to be an especially rich area of scholarly inquiry.

Consequently, I close by articulating five guiding principles that are specific to the lessons learned from my research on biracial and multiracial persons in the United States, but have relevance for all research on identity and intercultural communication within local, regional, national, and global spheres. My hope is that they will help to landscape a future of scholarly inquiry that resists explorations that fail to acknowledge how human agency exists within structural and oppressive conceptualizations of race and culture. First, identity is better conceptualized as a lifelong negotiation (Jackson, 2002a; Orbe and Harris, 2008), not a developmental process with a clear end-point. Second, identity is a communicative phenomena and is best understood and studied as such (Collier, 2005; Hecht et al., 2005; Imahori and Cupach, 2005; Jackson, 2002a; Ting-Toomey, 2005). Third, identity is a social-cultural construction that is both influenced by, yet separate from, biological and genetic composition. As such "it is important to distinguish between racial ancestry and racial identity" (Jones, 2010, p. 137). Fourth, identity is a complex, messy process; consequently intercultural communication identity research must incorporate multiple points of intersectionality (Crenshaw, 1991) and other influential factors (Rockquemore and Brunsma, 2002). Communication scholars must push forward and engage in research that is "multifocal and relational" in its exploration of "race as it intersects with other factors, such as gender, socioeconomic status, age, sexual orientation, and nationality" (Orbe and Allen, 2008, p. 211). Fifth, and finally, identity research needs to recognize, engage, and negotiate intercultural communication tensions both in terms of research and practice. Martin and Nakayama's (1999) conceptualization of intercultural dialectics offers a fresh alternative to understanding how cultural tensions exist amidst oppositional, but not necessarily polarizing, contradictions. Identity and intercultural communication researchers would be wise to utilize the communication-based model, and others like it, in their attempts to advance existing scholarship.

TWELVE

Rethinking Identities Within Globalization Through Chinese American Literature

From Postcolonial to Intercultural

Jianhua Sun

Much research on cultural identity has been published in the field of communication, yet only in the past two decades (indeed during this century) has work begun to discuss diaspora specifically (see Drzewiecka and Halualani, 2002; Gajjala, 2010; Halualani, 2008; Kinefuchi, 2010b; Mendoza, 2002a; Mendoza, Halualani, and Drzewiecka, 2002; Rinderle, 2005). Additionally, while much research addresses *cross*-cultural identity, very little of it addresses third space identities (Bhabha, 1990a), identities borne out of hybridity that are syncretic, unique, and not equivalent to an additive theoretical model that simply sees an immigrant's culture, for instance, as the sum of the etic plus the emic culture.

Less research in the field, still, looks at literature, specifically, as a communication form. Early communication research saw literature as communication, and certainly fictional and non-fictional works of prose fiction and poetry are not only communicational but mediated by processes similar to those that produce newspaper articles and arguably visual culture as well, if not oral communication, which utilizes language, as literature does (Horner and Gaillet, 2010).

Specifically, in this chapter, I examine Chinese American diasporic authors' works, namely the work of Maxine Hong Kingston, Amy Tan, Jade Snow Wong, Fae M. Ng, Gish Jen, and David W. Louie. I do this specifically in order to understand the particular way their work emphasizes the complex production of culture of a third space, a space borne out of hybridity that creates unique cultural identities. My approach ultimately may be useful to other intercultural communication scholars seeking to examine identity issues within diasporic texts.

DIASPORA AND HYBRIDITY

A much discussed term by critical cultural studies theorists over the last two decades, the term "diaspora" often means a dispersion but sometimes, as Hall (1990) suggests, difference and hybridity resulting from change. When referring to dispersion, or movement, either migration is forced, hence people become refugees or exiles from their homeland; or, the migration is voluntary, meaning people choose to leave of their own will and volition. Of course, economics conditions most decisions about whether or not to move, and, thus, these categories are by no means clear cut. Diasporic immigrants, therefore, not only include those who are away from home because of political and religious conflicts, colonization, and slavery, but also because of entrepreneurship, information acquisition, research, and study, although some have argued that not all forms of movement should be labeled diasporic (Butler, 2001).

Homesickness is a common effect of diasporic immigration. Depending on the type of migration, homesickness can be soothed through crossnational travel back and forth between homes, as well as by transnational communication, e.g., through the internet, telephone, or technologies such as Skype. Migrants may even have houses in more than one location, which may ease their entry into and exit out of a given location. Eventually, those with more than one cultural background may no longer be considered part of the diaspora (e.g., this disappearance of the diasporic attribution often takes place for the children of migrants). This transformation from being diasporic and migrant to being a more permanent member of a society (or simply nomadic) changes the terms of intercultural subjectivity, such that even sad stories relating to migration may, ultimately, be replaced with those of a nomadic interculturalist in a globalized time.

This notion of *nomadological migrancy*, a term I am coining here, is in part, dependent on loosening and giving up the fixity associated with identity (e.g., national identity and the inherency of cultural identity). To cross boundaries without those boundaries being determinative of identity suggests a renewed sense of subjective agency, and more importantly a refocusing on the positives of transnational and global migrancy, versus only the negative and socially determining dimensions that nevertheless affect, reflect, and organize social identity.

Changes in the ways we think of identity have evolved in part as a result of the end of the Cold War which opened up new possibilities for and dimensions of globalization. But, what is the exact meaning by globalization? Is it the international chain supermarket, such as Trader Joe's, full of relatively inexpensive multicultural goods? Or are name brand companies like McDonald's or the ubiquitous sushi bars in every major city definitive of what globalization means? Certainly, we see evidence of globalization in the first class museums of Europe and the United States that both hold and exhibit art from Asia, South Africa, and the Middle East. All of these give the general appearance of globalization, or are, at the very least, symptomatic of it.

But, perhaps more toward the core of what globalization is and means is the notion of *cultural flexibility*, following Ong's (1999) notion of "flexible citizenship." I suggest that at the core of globalization is the potential for flexibility, not only in the sharing of culture, but also in the crossing and overlapping of racial, national, gender, and sexual identities. In the face of globalizing forces, the potential for new cross identifications is multiplied. Certainly, it was the potential of globalization that drew a generation of scholars like Appadurai (1996) and others to note positive and transformational cultural potentials within globalization.

But, rather than have global capitalism and corporate globalization pave the way for what globalization is, centering postcolonial theorizing is key to developing theories that address the significance of cultural flexibility. Bhabha's (1986) theory of cultural hybridity is certainly one of the most influential theories to evolve out of postcolonial thought. Having had a problematic history, hybridity (as a term) was historically associated with biological mixing and as a result was often associated with anti-miscegenation—the fear of mixing blood lines and the derogation of people who did so and of their offspring. For instance, Young (1995) writes that both hybrid languages such as creole and hybrid children produced from sexual relations across the races "were seen to embody threatening forms of perversion and degeneration" (p. 5).

But, in an historical context in which talking about being "pure bred" is associated with problematic racial theories of bygone eras, the notion of hybridity has, in part as a result of Bhabha, become a term that is no longer associated with "race suicide" and "mixed breeds," but with the consequences of globalization, as well as globalization's future potential. In *The Location of Culture*, Bhabha (1994) sees hybridity not as a means of erasing colonialism and its histories nor "as the *source* of conflict—*different* cultures—but as the effect of discriminatory practices—the production of cultural *differentiation* as signs of authority—changes its value and its rules of recognition" (p. 114, italics in original). While hybridity and cross-cultural exchange are now appealing terms (at least in postcolonial thought), they also symbolize the potential for new-found creativity across both ethnicity and culture. Hybridity theory is among those theories central to intercultural communication scholarship with the greatest potential to break down long standing divisions and hierarchies, linear thinking, and essentialisms related to identity.

In order to address the way hybridity functions, it is useful to look at the mediated communication form of literature to see how hybridity (in this case between China and the United States, and more specifically in the form of Chinese American hybrid culture) works to resist the power of colonial forces to assimilate and yet to create culture anew.

WORDS AND TABOO—HYBRIDITY AND MAXINE HONG KINGSTON'S WORKS

You must not tell anyone . . . what I am about to tell you.

—Kingston, 1989, p. 3

Maxine Hong Kingston begins her exploration of cultural identity with the story of her aunt. Ironically, the first thing we read is her mother's warning about not telling "anyone" what she is about to tell. Of course, keeping silent is exactly what Kingston is not doing. She cannot remain quiet about her story, because she cares more about exploring how her Chinese cultural history can be reconciled with her emerging sense of being as a Chinese American. She tells her story, despite having told her audience not to repeat it. It is, therefore, an imperative for Kingston to uncover what her Chinese cultural history is, and one way of doing so is through the very act of telling the stories about her family's Chinese past. To express her desires by bursting forth with words is a brave action for a young girl directed to remain silent.

Kingston is famous for her autobiographical non-fiction and has attracted much attention from international literary critics in the late twentieth century. Among her many notable works, her most influential ones are: *Thewoman Warrior: Memoirs of a Girlhood Among Ghosts* (1976), *China Men* (1980), and *Tripmaster Monkey: His Fake Book* (1989). These three books integrate her ancestral Chinese tradition with American culture, lifestyle, and literatures. The first book won a National Book Critics Circle Award for non-fiction, and was enthusiastically acclaimed.

The Woman Warrior is Kingston's autobiography. It is the story of a Chinese American girl's difficult childhood experiences growing up with two cultural backgrounds. While one culture is encountered with the other, the narration offers a kind of transition from the Chinese world (culture) to the American one, by means of metaphor, imagination and cultural inversion. The book opens with a chapter on the "No-Name Woman," a story about a nameless aunt in old China, who brought disgrace upon the family by having an illegitimate child and then killed herself and the newborn baby in the family well, after villagers raided her house. No-Name aunt's story is a cautionary tale meant to discourage the young Kingston from engaging in premarital sex when she starts to menstruate, and she is asked not to mention it again. "Don't let your father know that I told you. He denies her. Now that you have started to menstruate, what happened to her could happen to you. Don't humiliate us. You wouldn't like to be forgotten as if you had never been born. The villagers are watchful" (Kingston, 1976, p. 5).

The young Kingston, however, has difficulty making sense of her mother's story, because her mother's messages are difficult to adapt or apply to her immediate American reality; actually what Kingston combats in Chinese culture is the feudal and patriarchal ideology and social practices "pre-provided" by Confucian "roundness," which forces the individual into a given model that has been agreed upon by all members of the society. Out of a strong desire, Kingston breaks the taboo her mother has passed on to her and rewrites the story from her own hybrid understanding. For example, as Su (1989) notes, Kingston relates No-Name aunt's romantic inclinations to a "Western tradition" (p. 15). Besides, she reconstructs the woman warrior role model FaMulan to respond to that of the victimized aunt in the coming chapter. In doing so, she takes care to reconcile her Chinese past and her U.S. present, which then helps her locate her own "in-between" cultural identity.

In Confucian patriarchal ideology, a woman is required to obey her father before marriage, her husband during marriage, and her sons in widowhood. She is also required to obey four rules of virtue, namely to at all times maintain fidelity, physical charms, propriety in speech, and efficiency in needle work. Among these, fidelity is considered one fundamentally important virtue for a woman (Dainian and Yishan, 1990). No-Name aunt was attacked because her action—adultery, as evidenced by her pregnancy—threatened socially acceptable behavior for women tacitly enforced through centuries of tradition. "Adultery, perhaps only a mistake during good times, becomes a crime when the village needed food" (Kingston, 1989, p. 13).

All members of the family kept silent about the transgression of adultery, including No-Name aunt herself. If speaking could be seen as a spiritual experience, obviously women, in this context, had been deprived of the right of expressing their innermost thoughts, feelings, and desires. From the point of view of most readers, who know little about Chinese feudalism, No-Name aunt is but a decoration. Her appearance as a character simply adds a level of spice to the story; she is a mere exotic ornament, adding to the overall pleasure and atmospherics of the book. But, who is No-Name aunt? What is her personality, actually? No one cares. She is only a victim, or a beautiful vase—she has no position or meaning at all.

Although No-Name aunt's story seems like a report of a far-away event in China, Kingston presents a variety of cultural influences which will eventually have effect on Kingston's personality as it emerges through the novel. She uses the story of her aunt to question rigid cultural models ("roundness"), to indicate some strategies of reaction (e.g., individualism), and introduce some basic metaphors (e.g., food, money) by which little Kingston will have to mediate between traditional China and the reality of U.S. culture. Kingston's intention of imaginatively reconstructing her aunt's story displays moral circulation, in which values are not imposed on, but changeable, by the narrator. Moreover, in the last part of the novel, the title "A Song for a Barbarian Reed Pipe" itself signifies the production of two cultures merging into one voice. But more importantly, Kingston presents American cultural influence in the description of a Chinese story, and the narration at this point may be called intercultural. As a creative artist between two cultures, and a word warrior and creative negotiator who transforms "revenge" into "word report," Kingston uses the cultural sources which are handy. This, in turn, makes her work accessible to all despite ethnicities, nations and cultures.

On a biographical note, Kingston was born to Chinese immigrant parents in Stockton, California, in 1940. Her parents ran a laundry house to support the family, despite the fact that her father was a scholar in China. Kingston was a trained teacher of English and American literature. She was drawn to writing from a young age. After relocating to Hawaii in 1967, she began writing extensively, often reflecting on her cultural heritage through a blend of fiction and non-fiction. Her work points sharply to all kinds of conflicts: between Chinese culture and American culture, men and women, depression and desire, publicity and confidentiality. In addition, her book seeks to cross social divides, and thus emphasizes communication in the process.

Kingston received the National Book Award in 1981 for her second book, *China Men*, and was nominated for the Pulitzer Prize. *China Men* is a companion to *The Woman Warrior* and received more controversial reviews. It is a saga about Kingston's family history, and represents the mental battle and physical obstacles that faced her male ancestors, who were themselves early immigrants to the United States.

Motivated by knowledge of her father's silence in the family, Kingston gives voice to her immigrant ancestors, while she rewrites a mythic family history. In *China Men*, Kingston celebrates men's lives, specifically their efforts toward westward expansion, but nevertheless also represents them as victims, not victors. For instance, when the men complete work laying the transcontinental railway, they are then driven out of the towns in which they live.

In *China Men*, Kingston questions the validity of the existing history by rewriting the Chinese legend of Tang Ao and the Western story of Robinson Crusoe by developing a Chinese American style of storytelling. In the revised myth of Tang Ao, a story originally from a classic Chinese novel *Flower in the Mirrors*, Tang Ao searches for Gold Mountain and arrives to a land full of women, and assumes that, as a man, he would be in good position. Unexpectedly, the women chain him, pierce his ears, break and bind his feet, and paint his face. They make him serve food at a banquet. The guests comment on his feminine charms. There are no taxes and no wars in the land of women, and the location is in North America. Kingston highlights the interchangeability of cultural tales by conflating two very different versions of the myth.

Kingston's third book, *Tripmaster Monkey*, is many things. The title itself suggests various possibilities the book exemplifies. The Chinese hero Monkey King overturns the divine orders of both ocean and heaven in China and is now a long-time citizen in California; in this tale, the historic Chinese migration journey to Gold Mountain is now a transformational trip. Wittman Ah Sing, the young male protagonist, is an English major, but works at a toy store. He is bored with his job and wishes to stage a phantasmagoric play that brings together traditions of all ages. He quits his job and begins to pursue life as a stage actor. The book ends with a theatrical performance of his work that lasts not for hours but for days.

By portraying a new image of the human being through the character Ah Sing, the book offers a viewpoint about identity: that it is changeable and that one can creatively conceive of it. A given identity does not conquer another; rather, like the play created by Ah Sing, identity is the result of interanimation and crossover—more of a combination than the production of hierarchical relations—of identity between two cultures— neither purely "East" nor purely "West," but a compound—or "hybrid"—novel cultural identity. As Ah Sing, the protagonist, says about his work, "I'm including everything that is being left out, and everybody who is no place" (Kingston, 1989, p. 52). In writing this, Kingston has created a hope for a connection to be established between the two separate worlds of her past and present life. In a sense, then, she is an intercultural artist—belonging neither wholly to China nor to the United States. More accurately, she is an observer, delving deeply into both cultures, but not beyond or above both.

CHINESE FOOD—ALWAYS ATTRACTIVE

Jade Snow Wong is another international artist who burst onto the literary scene in the 1990s. Wong was born in San Francisco and grew up in an immigrant, Chinatown family, which maintained traditional Chinese customs. Having been educated both in Chinese and American lifestyles, she grew up to be a successful ceramicist, as well as Chinese American author. Wong's first work, *Fifth Chinese Daughter* (1950), was translated into several Asian languages through sponsorship by the U.S. State Department's "Leaders and Specialists" project in 1951, and excerpts appeared in *The Literature of California* in 2000 (Hicks, 2000). Kingston went so far as to call Wong "The Mother of Chinese American Literature."

As a Chinese American female, Wong writes about her personal experiences of growing up in a Chinese immigrant family of nine children, and about how she is taught Chinese traditions and legends at home. She combines old lessons she learned from her parents with the new education and initiatives of the Western world. Through her writing, she reaches her goal of bridging two cultures and showing that a woman could be successful by writing books.

Wong devotes a lot of space in *Fifth Chinese Daughter* to descriptions of Chinese food habits, customs of weddings and funerals, China town daily life, as well as business dealings intending to reveal the "mystery" of the Chinese community. Chinese food is a significant topic throughout the entire book. In fact, there are at least forty different food items described in the book. Besides required daily foods, such as rice, a New Year's Eve dinner, a mid-autumn festival moon-cake, a happiness pie for a wedding, and a red egg drink prepared for a baby's first month of life, instructions on how to make and prepare Chinese food (such as how to clean chicken) are described. These descriptions draw from Chinese culture and are, in effect, examples of the culture of food and its movement to new locations, and the author's specific inclusion of such details within the novel are part of her diasporic agency.

The *Fifth Chinese Daughter* reflects Chinese cultural values that Wong's parents nurtured in her. However, living in the United States, Wong finally accepted the American lifestyle in achieving self-renewal with her own efforts while she was brought up true to her parents' ideal of a good Chinese daughter and future mother. Self-determined, Wong started her favorite pottery career to support herself at the age of twenty-three, which was contrary to her parents' will. As for her writing, Wong mentioned in an interview (Ziqing, 2003) in China that the initial motivation for composing *Fifth Chinese Daughter* came from the racial prejudice she had experienced. She accepted Elizabeth Lawrence's (editor and publisher of the magazine *Harper's* at that time) invitation to write her first book because she had found many misconceptions about the Chinese culture in the United States. A Western person could be an expert about Chinese arts but at the same time, s/he may know little about how the ordinary Chinese lives and thinks. She hoped that readers would respect her family culture by reading the story of her daily family life and education (Ziqing, 2003). But she didn't realize then that her book would remain attractive to readers for years to come.

Twitchell-Waas, a white American scholar and critic, notes that Wong's *Fifth Chinese Daughter* focuses on the positive similarities the author saw between very different cultures in order to generate sympathetic understanding from mainstream white America. Wong's intention was to promote the sympathetic recognition of Chinese Americans by emphasizing how well they fit in with mainstream American values (Twitchell-Waas, 2004). This observation definitely points out the function of Wong and her book in intercultural communication.

FROM POSTCOLONIAL TO INTERCULTURAL

Like Kingston and Wong, Amy Tan, Fae M. Ng, Gish Jen, and David W. Louie also are key Chinese American literary figures. Along with discussing their work briefly, I make the argument that they have been successful because of the notions of diaspora and postcolonialism with which they engage. Furthermore, I ask: Have they satisfactorily challenged the hegemony of nation-state narration from a globalized perspective? And, what influences have they had on contemporary artistic practice?

The achievements of these Chinese American writers owe much to the preoccupation with multiculturalism in the 1990s, and the social changes and ideology relating to an emerging interest in globalization. Their work encourages readers and artists to boldly imagine utopic identities, ones based on exploring cultural and political resources for themselves, the people they represent, and even their nations, crossing boundaries in a way that emphasizes an overall free and open attitude toward culture, sharing and cultural exchange. Such intercultural qualities both contain elements that could be said to be postcolonial in origin, but rather than only through critique, these works transform, through praxis, and hence do the cultural work necessary to move from postcolonial critique to intercultural praxis. Specifically, as Bhabha suggests (1994), the experience of colonization remains, yet hybridity functions as a recognition and a critique of colonization. Additionally, however, a third space is created that is unique and cannot be said to have been an intention of colonialism but rather a novel and unintentional but nevertheless powerful cultural form that emerges out of the colonial context.

Such praxis should not be understood just at the level of individual agency, but rather as social transformation. It is not just in the individual acts of intercultural exchange assumed by each author that the significance of these works lie, although the specificity of their intervention is certainly significant, noteworthy, and maintains its own style and uniqueness. Rather, the real significance of the works lies in the collective dimension of the intervention that is made obvious by each individual contribution—thereby moving our way of thinking about it from the individual (or subjective) to the social (or transformative) level. Thus, for intercultural communication, this means moving from more of a focus on the individual, or individual communicative acts, to that of an understanding of individual praxes as having broader social meaning, hence de-emphasizing the individualism that is often so much a part of intercultural identity scholarship.

The Joy Luck Club (1991) by Amy Tan, *Typical American* (1991) by Gish Jen, and *Pangs of Love* (1991) by David W. Louie, for example, are works that exemplify this growing cultural context of globalization. Each book not only illustrates the uniqueness of the author's own racial and national culture and politics, but also shows the contradictions and possibilities between the West and the East. Jameson (1998) defines globalization as "an untotalizable totality" that intensifies binary relations between nations, but also between regions and groups. These binary relations continue to operate as if the logic of national identities continues to exist and as if national identities remain foundational to, if not constitutive and regulative of, international relations. Hence, nations are seen always as individual nations in binary relationships with other individual nations. These nations then coordinate and work together, but no substantial change occurs to denationalize nations as an automatic effect of globalization to make them less nationalist or more cosmopolitan.

Continuing with Jameson's logic, globalization is not simply a collection of binaries, or point-to-point relations, that are already different from some plural constellation of localities and particulars. Globalization also includes relations that are first and foremost binaries of tension or antagonism when they are not outright exclusionary altogether. In the process of working to define itself against its binary counterpart, each offers a transformation of sorts through the self-recognition of binary relations. Such relationships are symbolic and, therefore, manifest themselves differently, yet constitute an overall impression of the reality of global social relations.

Standing on U.S. land, Chinese American authors retell Chinese stories through an American perspective and thinking that helps them reexamine Chinese culture. Just as scholar Belle Yang says, the Asian American has a wider world, because s/he is not only a pure Chinese but also a pure American, and s/he observes from multiple angles (Yuqiu, 2003).

For instance, Chinese American authors receive both Chinese and American language training, which suggests not the embracing of one culture over another, a way of thinking that is hierarchical and linear, but rather a *doubling* of culture, a twining of cultural knowledge. To give an example of the benefits of intertwined language knowledge, one can turn to the work of Fae M. Ng, who also often discusses how Chinese culture plays an important role in her work. This can be seen, for instance, in the Chinese name of her book, *Bone* (Ng, 1993). She suggests three ways to think about "骨": as a glyph, as a meaning, and as a pronunciation. She says "骨" in her dialect sounds like "good" in English, such as when someone nods her head and says "good." As a fourth generation Chinese American, Ng remains thoughtful and interested in the connection between the title of her book and Chinese culture and identity, both honoring and maintaining Chinese tradition in one sense and creating the potential for understanding by older generations of Chinese people, on the other. It is the reality of many U.S.-born Chinese to function as a bridge between immigrant parents who cannot speak English fluently and the broader U.S. culture and society. While they help their parents understand U.S. culture and society, they also, in reverse, convey ideas about Chineseness to Americans, e.g., pronunciations in Chinese and Chinese ways of thinking. This intercultural *translational labor* can be arduous but often is a necessary condition of the position of children of migrants. Furthermore, the role of cultural translator informs their own self identities in such a way that they learn about their parents' way of living, as well as their parents' cultural traditions.

Such is the case with Lela Liang and her family in *Bone*. She is the voice of her parents as well as of U.S. society. She encourages and helps her stepfather to apply for social salvation. But she nearly collapses when her sister commits suicide, and she has to explain how her parents understand death to the police many times, using different languages to do so. But, she uses her bilingualism and biculturalism in order to filter, add and omit, alter, and reframe in order to make things understandable and communication possible.

Similarly, Kingston imagines a hybridity cultural model in *The Woman Warrior*. The young girl in the novel imagines that she sees the world from the perspective of a gourd. After a series of painful thoughts, she attempts to view things from a new global perspective, and to go beyond a simple binary way of thinking from the perspective of the East *or* West: "We belong to the planet now. . . . Wherever we happen to be standing why, that spot belongs to us as much as any other spot" (Kingston, 1989, p. 107). Furthermore, the story of FaMulan in *The Woman Warrior* is a typical combination of Chinese legend FaMulan with another male heroic legend YueFei, who is remembered by the four characters on his back tattooed by his mother.

Gish Jen entitles her first book *Typical American*, indicating Chinese Americans' struggles for survival in the United States. Her approach is a profound one, for she sees racial minorities not as outsiders, but as insiders whose worldviews originate within the syncretic cultural context of the Americas. In a sense, then, Jen defines "diasporas" as individuals or families who gesture forth to a new location and, from there, create new cultural identities within their newfound cultural conditions and social circumstances. Chinese American culture, therefore, through the stories of these Chinese American authors, exemplifies a model of hybridity borne out of the struggle for a syncretic identity and circumstances that, together, transform cultural conditions through hybrid experience and performance, thus remaking postcolonial identities through the articulation of such identities within transnational spaces. Hence, they cannot simply be read as a representation of either Chinese or American culture, but are reflective of a unique and creative combination of elements with characteristics from both cultures. In this regard, they weave both cultures into a the specific context of time, place, and space—an original possibility within unique features, at times complementary of, and at times divergent from, both cultures understood individually.

CONCLUSION

Nomadological migrancy is a lived performance, suggesting not only the practical employment of intercultural skills within situations, but also a dynamic lived experience that lasts and continues on. Culture and identity cannot be taken off and put on like a glove, and are manifested through complex lived experiences. Trans-culture authors are able to represent what a habitual eye may fail to see, and think, what conventional thinking may miss, with their multi-angle vision. They are able to challenge the hegemony of the nation-state, and their writings help us imagine the dynamic forms culture and identity take when they are somewhat released from the grip of nation-state-centric thinking.

With the rapid pace of globalization, there appear more opportunities of interaction and cooperation between regions, nations and cultures, and this offers many possibilities of exchange and communication. Intercultural communication practitioners, scholars and educators may experience dilemmas, misunderstandings and may even complain at times. One place they can look for encouragement, insight and inspiration to build communicative bridges across seeming cultural (and postcolonial) divides would be the works of writers who dwell in and write through cultural hybridity. Such work of art exists everywhere, and they can help us envision a move from the postcolonial to the intercultural in how we think of identity and intercultural communication. Political power structures and the market economy may limit their space of work and presentation range, but they still keep on exposing the realistic problems and possibilities in globalized society. The field of intercultural communication can imbibe much, theoretically and praxiologically, from the study of such "in-between" literary texts.

THIRTEEN

(Re)Thinking Conceptualizations of Caribbean Immigrant Identity Performances

Implications for Intercultural Communication Research

Maurice L. Hall

Areas of research focus in intercultural communication such as cultural adaptation (e.g., Gudykunst and Kim, 2003b; Y. Y. Kim, 2002) and cultural hybridity (e.g., Bhabha, 1990b, 1994; Kraidy, 2002) provide some analysis of the communication implications of moving from one culture to another through lenses as varied as history, geopolitics and social behavioral theory. For example, scholars analyzing cultural hybridity from postcolonial theoretic frameworks (Hegde, 1998; Shome and Hedge, 2002b) have analyzed the importance of foregrounding history and geopolitics as a significant context for understanding how issues of power, race and ethnicity are implicated in immigrants' communication strategies in a new host culture, but they also set out to problematize conceptualizations of race, ethnicity, colonizer/colonized as fixed and/or binary identity constructs (see also Collier, 1998; Shome 1998). In a similar vein, scholars debate the assumption of "nation" as a fixed construct with stable cultural meanings (e.g., Cheseboro, 1998; Drzewiecka and Halualani, 2002; Ono, 1998) while also analyzing how large concentrations of immigrants can reconstitute the boundaries of the nation-state beyond its borders (Patterson, 1995; Robotham, 1998).

In this chapter, I use the English-speaking Caribbean[1] as a context within which to discuss how and why issues central to understanding

and theorizing about the communicative implications of the movement
of people between cultures are impacted when those people are arriving
in the United States, from small, developing countries, such as those in
the Caribbean.[2] In this chapter, first, I provide some historical context for
understanding why the English-speaking Caribbean is an important location from which to discuss the identity negotiation of people who travel
to the United States from that part of the African diaspora. Second, I
present a brief review of two prominent areas of research in intercultural
communication: cultural adaptation and cultural hybridity.[3] For each of
these two scholarly approaches, I briefly discuss how some scholars have
used these approaches to analyze communication and identity negotiation. Finally, using performativity as a theoretical framework, I present
suggestions for conducting intercultural communication research in the
context of Caribbean immigrants that encompass some of the specific
issues outlined in this chapter, but that also have implications for broader
issues of understanding identity negotiation.

THE ENGLISH-SPEAKING CARIBBEAN

Some thirty-four million people live on the islands of the Caribbean,
islands that have, at varying times, been colonized by the French, the
Spanish, the English and the Dutch. The island states of the Caribbean
exist in an archipelago that runs north from the coast of Venezuela and
stretches roughly 2,500 miles ending south of Florida, separating the Caribbean Sea and the Gulf of Mexico from the Atlantic. Most of the inhabitants of the Caribbean are ex-slaves of black African descent, but the
cultures of these islands are composite mixtures of European and African
influences with current significant North American market dominance.
Geographically, the islands of the Caribbean are, literally, in between two
large continents to the north and south.

The islands are most recognizable to North Americans as a tourist
destination. Since the islands are largely dependent on the United States
(and to some extent on Western Europe) for tourism, they market themselves as a pre-modern paradise, where the quality of life is the antithesis
of that found in large industrialized countries that privilege technological
sophistication, market-driven economies and assumptions of the primacy
of material progress. The Caribbean states are small and are unable to
sustain any meaningful production of local resources (Louisy, 2001). European, African, Indian, and other populations negotiated the rich cultural mixtures that have come to characterize the Caribbean (Bhabha,
1990b). From this perspective, the geographical location of the islands has
resulted in a crossroads in which a variety of cultures and nationalities
from across the globe are represented. Almost every aspect of cultural
life—food, music, dress, and religion—has been impacted.

The negotiation of racial identity in the Caribbean has always been more complex, however, than the simplistic notion that a wide variety of cultures have come to intermingle there and are all equally celebrated. Although most of the residents of these islands share African ethnic ancestry, they have always been dealing with negotiating the dominance of white identity in the face of the violent subordination of African (and Indian) identities. The majority of the population that was black and poor was relegated to providing the small farmers and field workers who harvested the sugar canes and bananas to be sold as exports. But the stubborn survivalist attitudes that characterize these people who refused to give up in the face of the odds stacked against them (Patterson, 1995) led to large scale migratory patterns that, according to Patterson (1995), have linked the fate of the Caribbean inextricably with North America.

Jamaican scholar sociologist, Orlando Patterson, analyzed the extent to which the decades between the 1960s and the 1990s represented a boom for Caribbean immigration to the United States. More than 95,000 immigrants arrived in the U.S. more than 100 years ago with another 290,000 arriving in the first three decades of the last century (Patterson, 1995). By the end of the 1960s, Jamaica, for one example, was sending more than 100,000 people a year to North America. These migration patterns have had a dramatic effect on the cultures of both the Caribbean and the United States. In the United States, these new immigrants became a major component of the black population in states such as New York, New Jersey, and Massachusetts, with more than half of all blacks from the Caribbean living in New York (Patterson, 1995). More than two thirds of these immigrants are of English-speaking ancestry, with Jamaicans being the largest group. Overall, Patterson (1995) estimates that of the black population in the United States during the 1990s, at least 6 percent (roughly two million people) are of Caribbean, black, non-Hispanic ancestry, of whom 86 percent are foreign born. These estimates exclude undocumented immigrants.

These immigrants have reformed and moved boundaries and borders that marked well-defined nation states. Political reforms in islands like Jamaica in the 1990s created a whole new trading class that travels constantly between the Caribbean and North America to buy and sell various kinds of goods and merchandise. Affordable jet travel has led to frequent travel back and forth between Caribbean countries and the United States and Canada both for people living in the islands and for immigrants (Hall, Keane-Dawes, and Rodriguez, 2004)). The flow of American cultural products and technology has resulted in a very dramatic and constant presence of American cultural and political life in the Caribbean. In essence, these events have created a transnational Caribbean community that exists in the United Kingdom, North America, and the Caribbean (Hall et al., 2004; Patterson, 1995). In other words, as people move freely between these countries, Caribbean culture no longer exists geographically within the borders of the island states; the culture also exists significantly in major U.S. and Canadian cities. People live, work, and travel in both geographical spaces (Hall et al., 2004).

BRIEF REVIEW OF CULTURAL ADAPTATION

This case example of migration from the English-speaking Caribbean is meant to illustrate the inextricable linkages between the United States and its Caribbean immigrants, and is but one example of how globalization has resulted in constant traversing of national boundaries as students, business professionals, diplomats and journalists (to name a few) travel frequently between countries for varying lengths of time (Onwumechili, Nwosu, R. L. Jackson, and James-Hughes, 2002). These continuing patterns of migration between countries have also led to significant political and social upheaval in countries like the U.S. For example, large scale temporary travel and immigration between several Caribbean states and the United States in the 1990s was linked to several large cities in the United States facing the issues of gangs from the Caribbean called "posses" that featured devastating episodes of drugs and violence in and among Caribbean immigrant communities. The unresolved issues of class, race, and power in the aftermath of colonialism that brought these immigrants to the United States were the impetus for much of the social unrest that occurred in the United States once they started living here.

With immigrant groups from the English-speaking Caribbean, the issue of cultural adaptation is never unlinked to the issues of class, race and nationality that brought these immigrants to the United States in the first place. For that reason, theories of cultural adaptation should take the complexities of history and geopolitics into account as part of the analysis. The issue of facilitating effective cultural adaptation received a lot of scholarly attention, in part, because scholars in intercultural communication tended to treat cultural adaptation as a prerequisite for psychological health (Gudykunst and Y. Y. Kim, 2003b; Y. Y. Kim, 1997, 2002; Onwumechili et al., 2002).

One reading of the classic literature on cultural adaptation assumes that immigrants arrive in the host culture almost as blank slates whose success in acculturation largely depends on their motivation to adapt. There was no sense that racial tensions, historic animosities, long-held cultural stereotypes and gendered, cultural and other power inequities also influence immigrants' willingness and/or ability to adapt as well as the host culture's willingness to receive them. By adaptation, most of these scholars meant cultural transformation: what Gudykunst and Y. Y. Kim (2003) referred to as de-culturation and acculturation. The immigrant (Y. Y. Kim, 2002) must first relinquish the native culture and its attendant communicative practices and patterns, and fully embrace the communicative practice of the host culture. This process leads to "communicative competence" (Gudykunst and Y. Y. Kim, 2003b) in the host culture. More recent work by scholars like Y. Y. Kim (2008) has begun to address the fluidity of cultural identity in a world made increasingly complex by unrelenting media exposure as well as increased global mobility. Y. Y. Kim (2008) makes an argument for *intercultural personhood*, by which she means an orientation to identity negotiation that rejects fixed, dichotomous cultural boundaries in favor of openness to cultural flux and change enabled by globalization and the ubiquity of electronic media. Conceptualizing identity in this way, then, calls for a fluid interplay between acculturation and de-culturation, and acknowledges that cultural adaptation can occur even if one continues to reside in one's native country (Y. Y. Kim, 2008).

Of course, there needs to be caution in assuming that adaptation or cultural transformation (however fluid) is simply a matter of learning to adjust to a new culture; cultures are not neutral: cultures are raced, gendered and hegemonic spaces that impose hierarchical value judgments of the worth of the human beings who occupy them (Goldberg, 1993). Immigrants, then, are always negotiating their cultural identity in the context of the scripts, stereotypes and power dynamics that characterize their particular group in the imagination and in the racial discourse of the host culture.

BRIEF REVIEW OF CULTURAL HYBRIDITY

A second, prominent scholarly response to the problematics associated with negotiating cultural identity in the context of transnational migration is cultural hybridity. While hybridity is a contested scholarly term and scholars in intercultural communication and communication studies have questioned the meaning, relevance and deployment of this trope in studies of communication and culture (Kraidy, 2002; Shome, 1999, 2003), there is utility in exploring how cultural mixture can lead to cultural innovation, transgression and transformation. Hybridity assumes a "Third Space" of identity negotiation, as Bhabha (1994) conceives of it, a space of identity negotiation that exists in and through the complex social interactions that attend the contact and mixtures of two or more different cultural formations.

Bhabha (1994) has used hybridity as an analytical tool to explore the cultural aftermath of the colonial encounter. He has argued against simplistic binaries such as oppressor/oppressed, colonizer/colonized, pointing instead to the ways in which innovative cultural forms have resulted from the interstitial spaces of colonial encounters that combined, but were very different from, the original cultural formations that existed. Scholars have used hybridity as a trope to analyze the creative cultural artifacts, expressions, behaviors and art forms that have been the result of globalization and immigration with its attendant, pervasive mixing of cultures (Kraidy, 2002). Unlike the fundamental assumptions of scholars working from the cultural adaptation framework, scholars who analyze cultures through the lens of hybridity celebrate the creation of new cultural expressions that represent neither of the original cultures. From this perspective, cultural transformation is not the requirement; instead, there is an assumption that cultures eventually morph into that which negates the uniqueness of each of the original cultures.

The term "hybridity" has rightly been subjected to rigorous scholarly examination and critique. For example, Bhabha's (1994) work on hybridity has been very influential, but also very controversial. He uses the metaphor of "in-betweenness" to articulate his conception of identity as highly contingent and ambiguous, a discursive production that is designed to interrupt and unsettle fixed, "originary" discourses of gender and race, among other forms of identity. Bhabha's (1994) sense of the ambiguity associated with the colonial encounter is also imbued with a sense of hope, even celebration, at the creative and transgressive opportunities present in communal re-articulations of identity. But Bhabha's (1994) articulation of the trope of hybridity has come in for heavy criticism. Ania Loomba (1998) challenges the overly broad scope of how he uses the terms and the discursive emphasis in his conceptualization. She argues that Bhabha's work "generalizes and universalizes the colonial encounter" (p. 178); the colonial subject seems to be universal and homogenous, unlinked to very specific contexts of race, class or gender. In part, this may derive from Bhabha conceiving his work in purely "semiotic or psychoanalytic terms" (Loomba, 1998, p. 179) without focusing on specific histories or locations. The discursive emphasis in Bhabha's work seems to ignore or sideline the very real, material conditions of poverty, violence and domination that were hallmarks of the colonial enterprise and its aftermath (Loomba, 1998).

Communication scholars provide an even more specific analysis of the ways in which attending closely to the discursive features of cross-cultural negotiation provide nuanced, sophisticated approaches to understanding how identity is simultaneously a product and a process related to social interaction across lines of power and difference. For example, Shome (2003) emphasizes the limitations of the undergirding spatial metaphors associated with hybridity and other tropes used to analyze culture, power and identity: metaphors such as center-margin, location-dislocation or borders and in-betweenness. These spatial metaphors are problematic if they assume a fixed, static, unproblematic reality rather than a material, structuring context within which cultural power is enacted in ways that have implications for identity and agency.

Similarly, Orbe and Drummond (2009) and Drummond and Orbe (2010) have undertaken a complex research program in which they investigate the complexity of identity negotiation as a socially constructed process that has implications for understanding the role of power and privilege in identity creation. Drummond and Orbe (2010) draw on Cultural Contracts Theory to argue for the ways in which cultural standpoints frame co-construction of identity between and among groups of difference, particularly where difference is mediated between marginalized versus privileged groups. Arguing that social identity groups are always already implicitly involved in social contracts that influence identity negotiation, they assert that willingness to cocreate identity and engage in more fluid identity performances is often linked to issues of power, privilege, and positionality in social groupings.

Orbe and Drummond (2009) also make an argument for the discursive nature of identity construction among groups they have studied. Language both frames and mediates the social reality that social groups inhabit; therefore, the language of race and cross-cultural interaction itself dichotomizes the very reality it purports to objectively describe. The work of these two scholars provides sophisticated analysis of the ways in which communication is inherent in creating, defining, and engaging social difference.

CULTURAL IDENTITY NEGOTIATION AND CARIBBEAN IMMIGRANTS

The uniqueness of the process of cultural identity negotiation when the immigrants are from developing countries calls for a different approach to conceiving of cross-cultural communication; especially when the developing country is located in the African diaspora. The designation, "Third World," coined initially by the French demographer Alfred Sauvy (Goldberg, 1993), was initially used to politically position the world's nation-states during the Cold War. The aggressive conflicts between the First World (developed Western countries and some Asian countries such as Japan) and the Second World (then communist-dominated nation-states) prompted a categorization of countries that were not immediately involved in the conflict as aggressors—the Third World. The racial symbolism of coming from the Africanized Third World is not insignificant when thinking of and theorizing about immigrant identity negotiation in the United States. Specifically in the context of the English-speaking Caribbean, the black and brown bodies that left their homelands to escape the subordination of their culture and the resulting lack of economic opportunities in the years following the colonial aftermath and political independence on many of these islands are met with an equally implacable racial hierarchy when they arrive in the United States. Orbe and Drummond (2010) explore the complex ways in which immigrants from developing countries, such as those in the Caribbean, negotiate their identities in complex ways that align their performance of self-identity in multifaceted ways with those citizens of color born in the United States. The negotiation of cultural identity is not neutral, but deeply raced. How, then, can researchers study and theorize about immigrant identity negotiation so as to capture the complex layers of race, class, nationality, and agency? The constructs associated with performativity offer some conceptually rich tropes that yield some creative ways of thinking about immigrant identity negotiation.

PERFORMATIVITY AND EMBODIMENT

The concept of performativity has roots in Speech Act Theory (Madison, 2005; S. Jackson, 2004). Embodiment is a theoretically rich construct in performance studies that has significant utility in analyzing issues of immigrant identity negotiation. In many approaches to performance scholarship, the body is a site of knowing and experiencing (Madison, 2005), a site of performing the ordinary "everydayness" of daily life (Stucky, 2002) and a site of cultural inscription that exists within very specific sociohistorical contexts (Pineau, 2002). Postcolonial scholars have long recognized the body as a useful metaphor for theorizing about the violence inherent in colonial encounters (Kanneh, 1995). The feminized body has often been used as a synonym and also a metonym for the powerlessness of the colonized to resist the colonial oppressor, and the body as ideological and political metaphor has a significant history in postcolonial literature (Dash, 1995). Goldberg (1993) argues convincingly that as a systemic construct, racist exclusion finds its authority in the discourse of the body, thus forging an underlying unity for the discourse of race: "As a mode of exclusion, racist expression assumes authority and is vested with power, literally and symbolically, in bodily terms . . . human bodies . . . are classified, ordered, valorized and devalued" (Goldberg, 1993, p. 54).

R. L. Jackson (2006) traces the history of the ideological and cultural scripting of the black body in the United States, particularly the black male body, from slavery through to current popular cultural expressions, arguing that "since the emergence of race as a social construct, black bodies have become surfaces of racial representation" (p. 12). Jackson (2006) concludes that "race is about bodies that have been assigned social meanings" (p. 12). Any analysis of cross-cultural identity negotiation, then, would be incomplete without an analysis of embodiment, and for the purposes of this chapter, embodiment linked to performativity.

Performativity provides a lens for analysis of cultural micro practices (Allen, 1990; Ashcraft, 1998), mundane, everyday performances that inscribe or write against oppressive raced or gendered social, cultural and institutional structures. Embodiment provides a context for examining the communicative constitution of these performances. By way of illustrating the link between embodiment and performativity I want to draw on and extend Pineau's (2002) use of *enfleshment* and *refleshment*. Pineau's (2002) use of these two constructs is focused on the educational context. Enfleshment refers to the process by which the body acquires certain habits over time that seem to become natural rather than culturally constructed. Refleshment refers to the process by which the body learns alternative behaviors. In the educational context, enfleshment and refleshment speak to the competing and contradictory social norms that often must be negotiated in the process of schooling; these terms also speak to the ways in which students come to explore and learn new, productive modes of being. But Pineau's (2002) sense of embodied pedagogy has significant utility for making an argument that links embodiment and performativity in the context of discussing immigrant identity negotiation. The body spends a significant, formative period learning behaviors in the native culture that seem taken for granted and natural, rather than culturally constructed. In a new cultural environment, these ways of knowing and being are significantly challenged and often interrupted. The body may adapt to these new norms and learn new cultural performances and behaviors, or may indeed enact hybrid cultural performances that are innovative mixtures of the native and host cultures. Either way, the body becomes a site of knowing, learning, and experience when it comes to immigrant identity negotiation. The focus on embodiment is also important because in a white-dominated society, black and brown bodies are marked in ways that make them, paradoxically, hypervisible, yet invisible.

EMBODIMENT AND IDENTITY PERFORMANCE: IMPLICATIONS FOR RESEARCH

Never passive in the face of oppression, the people of the Caribbean have developed strategies of resistance that are significant, transgressive language and gender performances aimed at writing against the well-practiced mimicry of the white, European colonial body. Concepts of embodiment and performativity are intriguing in their continuing potential to help scholars analyze how oppressed peoples write against their own oppression and reconceptualize and engage with their worlds on terms that are their own and not those of their oppressors. The silencing of the black and brown speaking body enabled the voice of the white colonial master and, later, a white (and black) postcolonial middle class elite to prevail in speaking on its behalf. But, through immigration, and other forms of location and relocation, these black and brown bodies reconstituted new centers of national culture outside the Caribbean, thereby extending the boundaries of national cultures to New York, Miami, Philadelphia, and Washington, DC. There are entire sections of New York and Miami, for example, that are so populated with concentrations of immigrants from the English-speaking Caribbean that these areas have, for all intents and purposes, become an extended location of the Caribbean (Patterson, 1995; Robotham, 1998). With extending the boundaries of the native culture, the impact on the host culture is significant as exemplified through an exuberant orality through music such as reggae and dancehall (with heralded artists from Bob Marley and Peter Tosh to more contemporary artistes such as Sean Paul), and a vibrant intellectual and cultural heritage as expressed through well-known personalities as varied as Marcus Garvey, Colin Powell, and Louis Farrakhan (Hall, 2010).

I am not arguing here that cultural transformation or the development of hybrid cultural forms are irrelevant to the process of cultural identity negotiation for English-speaking Caribbean immigrants; rather, I am arguing that a focus on performativity and embodiment allows for the foregrounding of agency and resistance. In the context of moving to a white, Western, capitalist culture, black and brown bodies from the Africanized Third World are never sites of neutrality; instead, given the complex history of cultural inscription and the black and brown body in the United States, theories of cultural transformation or developing hybrid cultural practices fail to account for the significance of history, race, class and power in cultural identity negotiation. In the social and cultural context of the United States, authoring any meaningful cultural identity for residents of Caribbean descent must, of necessity, first involve writing against deeply raced concepts that inherently position blackness as the subordinating social condition upon which the very definition of whiteness depends (Goldberg, 1993).

For English-speaking Caribbean immigrants, cultural transformation (Gudykunst and Y. Y. Kim 2003b), enacted uncritically, would seem to entail a process of refleshment (Pineau, 2002), a learning of new bodily performances that could easily amount to an appropriation of a white or nearly white identity. Resisting uncritical appropriation of mainstream, raced American cultural performances would seem to be crucial to maintaining psychological health.

I concur with critical intercultural scholars such as Hegde (1998) that assuming a stable, fixed, coherent self is problematic when seeking to discuss the complexities associated with negotiating cultural identity in a new country. One of the challenges with the assumption of a fixed self is that this allows for the conceptualization of selves as dichotomous entities positioned in oppositional relationships each to the other; it is also, therefore, a logical consequence to assume identity negotiation as fairly linear, moving in a trajectory between binary states such as acculturated/ not acculturated, native/stranger, or categorizing identity negotiation in terms of sequential spatial metaphors such as First, Second and Third Space. Based on these assumptions, one's negotiation of identity in a new host culture is seen in terms of movement that is progressive, but linear. One must move from A to B: fixing identity at any place short of B is regarded as failure. In other conceptions, one may exist in the space between A and B (or even C?) but never fully inhabit either one. It is not that the conceptualizations of identity listed above are somehow inaccurate or lacking analytical value, but that they do not fully account for the increasingly complex realities of the social construction of cultural identity. There is also an implied determinism in these conceptions of how identity is socially constructed.

Pineau's (2002) use of *enfleshment* and *refleshment* is premised on the conceptualization of identity as always in the process of becoming but never arriving, and is meant to be seen as reflecting fluid, multiple, sometimes contradictory identity performances. Conceptualizing identity negotiation in terms of performance not only captures the fluidity of identity, but foregrounds communication in identity negotiation through the construct of the moving, speaking, performing body. This allows for researchers to conceptualize immigrant behavior in terms of options that may help researchers continue to complicate the thinking around how immigrants, particularly those from the Caribbean, engage in identity negotiation in the United States.

Most importantly, there is a need to bring together emergent theoretical frameworks in communication studies—postcolonialism, hybridity and performance—to develop new approaches to theorizing about cross-cultural communication that capture inevitable changes in the disciplinary focus of intercultural communication, reflecting the growing presence and influence of non-white populations in the United States. I would like to suggest that researchers, using interpretive, qualitative methods such as ethnography, autoethnography, and performance ethnography (Denzin, 2003) investigate a range of performative responses of Caribbean immigrants in relating to the American host culture, ranging from total disengagement to selective, critical appropriation of performances that reflect conformity with the host culture.

Central to conceptualizing identity negotiation in terms of performance is agency: that is, this conceptualization of identity negotiation assumes that immigrants consciously, constantly, and knowingly choose from a menu of performance options characterized by an ambivalent, dialectic tension of resistance and assimilation (Hedge, 1998). This ambivalence, very well captured and noted by Hegde (1998, 2002) in her studies of Asian immigrant women, reflects the complexity of the immigrant relationship with the host culture. This ambivalence can be conceived of as a continuum represented by a vertical axis in which the immigrant moves between extremes of engagement and disengagement with the host culture, intersecting with a horizontal axis representing the immigrant's choice of identity performances that reflect movement between more fixed and more fluid identities. Within these intersecting axes there are options for a range of behavioral responses in relating to the host culture, ranging from total disengagement to selective, critical appropriation of performances that reflect conformity with the host culture. What is more, there is no linearity implied in this model since the immigrant can move at will between these performance choices. The immigrant dwells within the permanent tension of this menu of performative options, thereby resisting the determinism implied in *only* conceptualizing identity categories as fixed and dichotomous. Indeed, it can be argued that the very binaries discussed earlier in this chapter of black/white, domination/subordination that characterizes many Western democracies such as the United States necessitated an examination of how to develop more complex theorizing about how immigrants choose to respond.

Engagement-disengagement

In this conceptualization, *engagement* with the host culture is perhaps best characterized by Y. Y. Kim's (2002) model of intercultural transformation. The immigrant displays performances consistent with full communication competence in the host culture and is therefore seen as "functionally fit" (Y. Y. Kim, 2002) and "culturally transformed" (Gudykunst and Y. Y. Kim, 2003b). The communicative behaviors displayed are seen as appropriate for successfully negotiating the host culture. Examples of these kinds of performances could be as simple as competently executing host culture greetings and leave-taking rituals to displaying a willingness and competence in negotiating the scripts associated with a wide variety of more complex social, cultural, and religious rituals. *Disengagement* from the host culture is characterized by performances that are inconsistent with, ineffective, or inappropriate for achieving communication competence in the host culture. Examples of these kinds of performances would include withdrawal from social interaction with members of the host culture and perhaps even downright shows of hostility to members of the host culture. It is important to note that these are performance options and not descriptions of permanent states. Immigrants could choose performances anywhere along the continuum as relevant to context, frame of mind, etc.

More Fixed-More Fluid Identity Performances

The use of the comparative here is designed to suggest that these performances are evaluated in relationship to each other as opposed to an evaluation based on a stable, external norm. *More fixed* identity performances reflect less flexible behavioral responses that limit the immigrant's options for moving beyond her own conceptions of essentialized identity categories. An example of this kind of performance would be insistence on holding fast to rituals or practices such as methods of disciplining a child out of perceived loyalty to the native culture, even though these methods are inconsistent with socially accepted norms in the host culture. *More fluid* identity performances reflect very flexible behavioral responses that are designed to transgress or even disrupt previously essentialized conceptions of identity. An example of this kind of performance would be choosing to dress or behave in ways that contradict taken-for-granted assumptions of "correct" gender behavior in the native culture. Representing these two continua as intersecting axes suggests a variety of performance options for the immigrant that combines behaviors reflecting the underlying assumption that they are constantly wrestling with the tension of resistance and assimilation.

CONCLUSION

The conceptualization of identity negotiation reflects a menu of choices potentially open to immigrants as they seek to enact identity performances. All of these are equally viable choices depending on the context in which the immigrant finds herself; none is "better" than the other because any choice or combination of choices could be "right" for a given context. This conceptualization, premised on the conceptualization of identity as always in the process of becoming but never arriving, is meant to be seen as reflecting fluid, multiple, sometimes contradictory identity performances. These are not meant to be fixed, stable performances; rather, immigrants may choose from between and among these performances as often as needed—even enacting different choices of performance several times a day. Consistent with the conceptualization of immigrant identities as multiple and fluid (Hegde, 1998, 2002), these performances choices are meant to reflect some of the contradictions and complexity associated with identity negotiation.

I concur with Hegde (1998) that immigrants of color are often faced with contradictory discourses as to what it means to be assimilated. This arises from the deep ambivalence in the United States to the very presence of people of color, and particularly black and brown people, whether native or foreign born. Such conditions call, then, for a flexible menu of performance options for immigrants. The contradictory tensions of assimilation and resistance often mirror the ambivalence in the United States about the presence of various immigrant groups of color, particularly those from the African diaspora. All options for response, including no engagement with the host culture, must, therefore, be seen as viable responses; however, it bears repeating that none of these performance options reflects a permanent, stable, ongoing performance.

Finally, conceptualizing identity negotiation in terms of performance, not only captures the fluidity of identity, but foregrounds communication in identity negotiation through the construct of the moving, speaking, performing body. In this conceptualization, immigrants continually make conscious choices and so are conceptualized as actively writing against their potential marginalization or oppression. This conceptualization of identity performances sets out to propose options that may help researchers continue to complicate our thinking around how immigrants, particularly those from the Third World, engage in identity negotiation in the United States. Consistent with the conceptualization of immigrant identities as multiple and fluid (Hegde, 1998, 2002), these performance choices are meant to suggest options for researchers to investigate some of the contradiction and complexity associated with identity negotiation and, as a result, complicate and add to some of the underlying assumptions of some of our current theoretical concepts about the performance of identity in intercultural communication research.

NOTES

1. I have focused on the English-speaking Caribbean to avoid focusing on other issues in cross-cultural communication such as language differences, which need a discussion that is outside the focus of this chapter.

2. As opposed to arriving from a "Second World" developing country, such as countries in Eastern Europe or the former Soviet Union, or from another developed country, such as those in Western Europe or parts of Asia such as Japan.

3. There are many additional tropes that could be the focus of study such as diaspora, transnationalism, border, globalization, etc. Some of these may be touched on, but the focus will be on cultural adaptation and cultural hybridity as two examples of prominent programs of research in the literature that deal with identity negotiation.

V

Theorizing "Doing" Identity

FOURTEEN

Navigating the Politics of Identity/ Identities and Exploring the Promise of Critical Love

Rachel Alicia Griffin

[Survival] is learning how to stand alone, unpopular and sometimes reviled, and how to make common cause with those others identified as outside the structures in order to define and seek a world in which we can all flourish.

—Lorde, 1984, p. 112

I must begin with the questions that have brought on sleeplessness: What does it mean to identify as a critical intercultural scholar? What does the embodiment of a critical intercultural identity look like on an everyday basis? If being and becoming a critical scholar is risky and tinged with vulnerability then what will sustain me for years to come? These questions have kept me awake at night jotting down what one might call "nighttime confessions" (Tuitt, 2006, p. 29) of a critical intercultural scholar, an identity that for me is always stamped with a bright red "in progress" and situated somewhere in relation to hope. Sometimes I feel hopeful, at other times I feel hopeless. As a biracial black and white woman who was raised by my lower-working class white mother amidst a white extended family, always attending traditionally and predominantly white schools,[1] I was born into a world that requires a "critical eye" (Pelias, 2000). However my academic introduction to the critical paradigm occurred in 2004 at the University of Denver in a course taught by Mary Jane Collier. Interestingly, this course also marked the first time that I ever really understood Kuhn's (1996) *The Structure of Scientific Revolutions* even though I had read it twice two years before.

In our course, Collier traced the major paradigmatic shifts in intercultural communication from quantitative to qualitative to critical, and we discussed the implications of each shift with regard to how culture and identity(ies) are understood. In hindsight, I wonder if there are words to express the awakening that her class incited or if I can clearly articulate how I immediately began to understand myself, my place in the world, and others differently. Embarking upon the journey to do so, this chapter narrates how I make sense of who I am as a critical intercultural scholar, how I understand our field, and most importantly why I believe that love can further the theorization of identity and our efforts to build coalitions across identity differences. To theorize the promise of critical love, I begin by tracing conceptualizations of identity through the distinctive yet interconnected quantitative, qualitative, and critical paradigms. Then I forefront critical articulations of identity to locate myself as a critical intercultural scholar engaged in the process of identity negotiation. Finally, I conceptualize critical love and position this concept in service of navigating identity politics and building alliances across identity differences.

TRACING IDENTITY IN INTERCULTURAL COMMUNICATION

Rooted in the quantitative paradigm, when academic inquiry in the field of intercultural communication emerged full force in the early 1980s, identity was largely understood as a measurable and fixed phenomenon (Gudykunst, 1983). Through social science research, scholars identified specific characteristics, symbols, and cultural meanings that pertained to distinct identity groups (Mendoza, Halualani, and Drzewiecka, 2002). Quantitative scholars also drew comparisons among identity groups that relied on firm categorizations. For example, Collier (1988) compared intracultural and intercultural competencies among Mexican, black, and white Americans. Importantly, such work allowed for the establishment of possible boundaries between identity groups and explored foundational topics such as identity salience, cultural competence, and intercultural adaptation (Collier, 1988; Collier, 1989; Ellingsworth, 1983; Mendoza et al., 2002). Following the surge of quantitative research that largely established the field, the emergence of the qualitative paradigm called for identity to be understood as socially constructed, relational, and negotiated rather than objectively measurable and fixed (Jackson and Garner, 1998; Ting-Toomey, 1986; Ting-Toomey, 1999). Ting-Toomey's (1986) creation of the identity validation model, and later on identity negotiation theory (1999), marked strong turning points toward qualitative research. In alignment with Ting-Toomey's (1986) work, Hecht, Collier and Ribeau (1993) proposed the communication theory of ethnic identity which positioned identity development as contextual and continual. Following the interpretive turn which deeply challenged the positivist roots of the field, identity was communicatively understood as fluid, multifaceted, subjective, and socially constructed.

In the 1990s, critical approaches to identity emerged that embraced the strengths of the interpretive stance while advocating for the "intricate politicization of identities in communicative contexts" (Jackson, 2002b, p. 247). Articulating how to do so, Mendoza et al. (2002) call for us to theorize "the ways in which [identity constitution, performance, and negotiation] are enacted via communicative practice . . . not only meaning interactions on the interpersonal or even inter-group levels, but also communicative practice as it operates on other levels of the symbolic or the structural" (p. 324). Positioned in relation to, but different from, quantitative and qualitative approaches to identity, the critical paradigm strongly emphasizes power, ideology, macro-contextual factors, and agency as essential to the theorization of identity (Halualani and Nakayama, 2010; Mendoza et al., 2002). Taking a critical approach to identity, scholars deconstruct how systemic privilege and oppression manifest during identity negotiation and performance, and also theorize how intersectional identities (i.e. ability, gender, religion, etc.) are constructed and expressed in relation to power and dominance (Asante, 1980; Jackson, 1999; Jackson, 2002a; Mendoza et al., 2002; Nakayama and Krizek, 1995; Yep, 2003a).

Approaching identity critically yields several benefits that are often unattainable from quantitative and traditionally qualitative approaches. First, a critical approach is more attuned to revealing processes of identity "production, naturalization, and normalization" (Mendoza et al., 2002, p. 316). Second, a critical approach works against essentialist constructions to legitimate difference within cultural groups (Hecht, Jackson, and Ribeau, 2003; Mendoza et al., 2002). Third, a critical approach allows for identity to be understood as performative and consequential (Calafell, 2007a; Hall, 2002; Inda, 2000; Mendoza et al., 2002). Describing identity critically, Jackson and Garner (1998) note: "Humans are not immalleable fixtures within interaction episodes: instead, we are self- and other-defined composite beings characterized by communicative histories, traditions, behaviors, styles, and values which are sometimes interrupted by unanticipated social forces" (p. 51). Summarizing from a critical standpoint, identity can be understood as emergent, in/visible, contextual, fluid, affirmed, challenged, constituted, and performed (Calafell, 2007b; Hecht et al., 1993; Inda, 2000; Mendoza et al., 2002; Shin and Jackson, 2003).

CRITICAL INTERCULTURAL IDENTITY NEGOTIATION

Returning to my academic introduction to critical understandings of identity, the most valuable lesson that I learned was that I could write about people who look like me in transparent, humanizing, and resistant ways. To be frank, this possibility brought tears to my eyes because if it were true, I could become an academic without having to leave the politically incorrect/taboo/prohibited pieces of me behind. Reflecting on my academic life, school has always been a safe haven for me. From elementary school all the way through my master's program, the "nerd" within me was well nourished but I had never realized that I had not felt an academic sense of "homeplace" (hooks, 1990) even though I was considered to be one of the "smart" kids. Describing the essence of "homeplace," hooks (1990) writes that "one's homeplace was the one site where one could freely confront the issue of humanization, where one could resist . . . where all black people could strive to be subjects, not objects, where we could be affirmed in our minds and hearts" (p. 42). Rather than feeling at home and humanized at school, I was always too brown to be white and never ladylike enough to be a good girl.

In the midst of my educational experiences, the critical paradigm offered me an invitation to develop a new understanding of who I am, my movement through the world, and how I might become a bona fide academic scholar. When Collier lectured using words like "ideology" and "hegemony" that I had to look up, I panicked as any brand new doctoral student would but I determinedly clung to the importance of understanding my identities from a critical standpoint which marked a return to self from other and a turn away from ideological indoctrination toward self-determination. Her classroom was the first space where who I am and my lived experiences made unapologetic sense, which was quite powerful since I had been always been a "fly in the buttermilk" (Davis, Dias-Bowie, Greenberg, Klukken, Pollio, Thomas, and Thompson, 2004, p. 434). This sense of belonging felt nothing short of marvelous; I fell head over heels in academic love. Soon after I realized the richness of the critical paradigm, my heart sunk; I thought that I had been born too late since it had already emerged. Clearly, I did not understand Kuhn (1996) as well as I thought I did.

Shifting from past to present, "critical intercultural scholar" as an academic identity marker pervades every introduction of who I am and easily makes sense to me on the surface. Yet despite the thrill of transformation and the nostalgia of academic puppy love, the underbelly of identifying as a critical scholar has since been revealed as more tumultuous than what I had imagined. Struggling to locate the meaning(s) of the label, it feels important to landscape the paradigm to explore the contours of a critical intercultural scholarly identity.

LANDSCAPING THE CRITICAL INTERCULTURAL PARADIGM

Although critical intercultural scholarship has yet to reach a critical mass, it is more paradigmatically visible now than ever before. Since the publication of the first collection of intercultural communication theories (Gudykunst, 1983), we have seen an outpour of intercultural scholarship mostly allegiant to quantitative and traditionally qualitative approaches. However, Halualani and Nakayama's (2010) recent edited *Handbook of Critical Intercultural Communication* signals the increasing presence of critical works. From my perspective, this visibility births new hopes and struggles for critical scholars at the intersections of agency, power, and praxis. I am hopeful in that although our labor to deconstruct and resist the imposition of power and privilege may not be widely recognized as academically sound by those committed to traditional conventions and epistemological assumptions of quantitative and qualitative approaches (Collier, Hegde, Lee, Nakayama, and Yep, 2001; Halualani, Mendoza, and Drzewiecka, 2009; Orbe, Smith, Groscurth, and Crawley, 2010; Yep, 2003a), the potential of critical intercultural scholarship to progressively articulate the political nuances of identity is increasing. Capturing the essence of critical intercultural work, Halualani and Nakayama (2010) write:

> Many of us dare to go where others steer clear: across and through the junctures and ruptures of historical authority, formidable structures, and power forces that touch our encounters, relationships, and everyday lives; inside the fragmentations and displacements of cultural groups and identities—ours and those of others for whom we care; in and around the contours of our intersecting positionalities in relation to surrounding ideologies and hegemonies of society, and deep within the struggles over power among cultural groups, members, and dominant structures, and forms. (p. 1)

From their description, it is clear that critical scholars are engaged in risky institutional business. They carve out new, and at times unwelcome, intellectual spaces such as the examination of white privilege (Jackson, 1999; Nakayama and Krizek, 1995; Warren, 2001a) and the creation of critical communication pedagogy (Fassett and Warren, 2007). They warn of the dangers of assumption and remind us of how injurious the communicative reproduction of oppression can be (Faulkner, Calafell, and Grimes, 2009; Griffin, 2011; Yep, 2003). They position culture as a site of hegemonic struggle and labor against Eurocentrism (Chuang, 2003; Shome and Hegde, 2002a). They mark the pride and pain of struggling against dominant assumptions of who they are and who they can be (Allen, Orbe, and Olivas, 1999; Calafell, 2007a; Hendrix, 2011). They also pose bold questions like Calafell (2010a), who asks, "When will we all matter?" and push against fantastical notions that we can be "post" identity politics (Squires, Watts, Vavrus, Ono, Feyh, Calafell, and Brouwer, 2010). Taken together, critical scholars place their bodies on the line and wager their time, energy, and livelihood in the struggle for representation, voice, equality, or even just a slight indication that someone who follows in their academic footsteps will not have to experience the same struggle.

Beckoned to offer a more thorough testament to why critical intercultural work matters to the development of my personal/academic (Ono, 1997) self; this body of work helps me locate who I am within and beyond the academy. More pointedly, critical scholars theorize the layered nuances of intersectional identities; necessitate marking the politics of identity differences; create spaces for agency around who someone is and can become; and labor to humanize those who bear the mundane brunt of objectification, ignorance, indifference, silencing, and dismissal. Locating my sense of self and my work within the critical paradigm feels purposeful and marks the first, and thus far only, paradigmatic lifeboat amidst the oceanic vastness of the academy. This is not to imply that my introduction to the quantitive and qualitative paradigms was not academically valuable but rather to mark the significance of feeling beckoned, and more importantly welcomed, both academically and personally as someone who has always felt the tension of being an "outsider within" (Collins, 1986, p. S14). Yet I have learned that the hard part of identifying as a critical scholar or utilizing critical interpretive methods is reflected in playground logic, i.e., when you push, you often get pushed back *hard* which serves as a reminder of the realness of intercultural research that resists traditional publication norms. Offering an example of what I read as playground logic, Orbe recounts his struggles trying to publish race-related research:

> I wallowed in isolation as I read, reread, and tried diligently to address the stinging evaluations of race-related work by people who largely felt as if the work was unproductive ("ungeneralizable"), unscholarly (one reviewer called my work "journalistic"), or incomplete by itself ("why didn't you use whites as a comparative group?"). (Orbe et al., 2010, p. 186)

Like Orbe, numerous communication scholars have documented the vulnerability, risk and pain, amidst the comfort, healing, and reward, brought forth by pushing against dominant norms in our field (Allen et al., 1999; Calafell, 2007a; Faulkner, Calafell, and Grimes, 2009; Hendrix, 2011; Orbe et al., 2010).

ARTICULATING THE "REALNESS" OF MY CRITICAL
INTERCULTURAL SELF

As a social institution in the United States, higher education is founda-tionally rooted in identity-based exclusion and systemic oppression. De-spite public education being initially designed for the common good (Cu-ban and Shipps, 2000), women, people of color, the LGBTIQ (Lesbian, Gay, Bisexual, Transgender, Intersex, and Queer) community, immi-grants, and people with disabilities were, at different and frequently overlapping points in American history, deemed inferior and unworthy of education. Given that exclusion has been historically predicated upon identity differences according to dominant ideologies, I garner a limited sense of personal agency coupled with an overwhelming sense of social responsibility. As a biracial black female[2] scholar, I need to embody my sense of self in a way that respects and cares not only for my own soul but also those of my students and colleagues (hooks, 1994). Recognizing the resolve that humanizing myself and others will require, I aspire to be among the "cultural workers" described by West (1990) as:

> intellectual and political freedom fighters with partisan passion, inter-national perspectives, and, thank God, a sense of humor to combat the ever-present absurdity that forever threatens our democratic and liber-tarian projects and dampens the fire that fuels our will to struggle. (p. 519)

Having consciously been on this critical academic journey for a short time, I must admit that my aspirations have already been flooded with dis/enchantment. The potential housed in the process of being and be-coming a critical intercultural scholar is enchanting. Yet like Delgado (2006), I am disenchanted by the challenges that our mass and boundless-ly optimistic celebrations of cultural progress pose to raising social con-sciousness. Likewise, extending the insight of Washington (2008), as a collective society we seem far more willing to build monuments to ac-knowledge identity politics of the past than we are to build movements to reckon with identity politics of the present. In President Obama's book, *The Audacity of Hope* (2006), he articulates the tensions I feel among cele-bration, commemoration, and consciousness in his reflections on Rosa Park's funeral. He writes:

> We sat in church eulogizing Rosa Parks reminiscing about past victo-ries, entombed in nostalgia. Already, legislation was moving to place a statute of Mrs. Parks under the Capitol Dome. There would be a com-memorative stamp bearing her likeness, and countless streets, schools, and libraries across America would no doubt bear her name. I won-dered what Rosa Parks would make of all this—whether stamps or statutes could summon her spirit, or whether honoring her demanded something more. (pp. 230–31)

Reflecting upon his words, it is the "something more" that identifying as a critical scholar necessitates that has brought me to my knees mentally, emotionally, and physically. It is the "something more" that is incredibly fulfilling and unbelievably draining. The "something more" is what I call critical intercultural soul work which requires that I put all of who I am out there in vulnerable, nerve-racking, and downright terrifying ways; however, what I have learned is that it changes you. Each time I place my body on the line, I never quite get all of myself back which illuminates the significance of understanding our identities as fluid. In addressing the movement of identities that shift across time, space, place, and consciousness, I would be remiss not to address the importance of self-reflexivity in unraveling the politics of understanding self and other.

Self-reflexivity necessitates a close examination of how our own values, ideologies, and social locations labor in the reproduction and contestation of dominant cultural narratives (Alexander, 2006; Johnson, 2006; Madison, 2006). According to Goodall (2000), "To be 'reflexive' means to turn back on our self the lens through which we are interpreting the world" (p. 137). In essence, being self-reflexive requires uprooting our biases, fears, and prejudices while paying close attention to how dominant ideologies inform our understandings of who we and others are. Connecting self-reflexivity to ethics, Madison (2005) offers:

> To examine one's own life and intentions—to question and observe the self—in the process of questioning and interacting with others is an ethical stance, because it requires constant self-evaluation and monitoring relative to our integrity, effectiveness, and political commitment toward the end of helping to make life more worth living. (p. 83)

Drawing from Madison (2005), critical scholars engage with the implications of who they are and the impact of their work while refraining from grandiose assumptions of good intention and social consciousness. Strengthening my understanding of what it means to move through academe reflexively is Pelias (2005), who writes, "They do not believe that they can speak without speaking themselves, without carrying their own vested interests, their own personal histories, their own philosophical and theoretical assumptions forward" (p. 419). Informed by those who have embodied a critical scholarly identity before me, I read my own critical identity performance as one that requires me to responsibly speak to and with (Alcoff, 1991) the experiences of those who are marginalized while simultaneously being accountable to ways that my privilege strengthens the oppressive systems that I strive to work against. Referred to as "thick intersectionalities" by Yep (2010, p. 171), a critical stance toward identity politics necessitates that I, as an American, able-bodied, heterosexual woman of color who was raised in the lower-working class but is now part of the middle class, "position my privileged identities as being of equal importance to my marginalized identities" (Griffin, 2010,

p. 7). Doing so as a critical scholar compels being transparent, self-reflex-ive, and resistant with regard to the everyday, mundane moments in which systemic privilege is produced and reproduced by myself and others.

Given the riskiness of living within critical intercultural spaces, the costly nature of soul work, and the abundance of warnings that I will burn out at best or be vanquished at worst, I have found myself craving a stable source of rejuvenation. What is it that will nourish my commitment to being a critical intercultural scholar and remind me, again and again, that bearing witness to human suffering obligates me to act?[3] How will I renew the energy required to advocate for the importance of intercultural communication? Marking a slippage of faith, when I think about our commitment as intercultural scholars to foster effective communication and meaningful relationships I feel as though a genuine commitment to love is missing. To be transparent, I have never been accused of optimism by anyone who appreciates me (or anyone who does not, for that matter). But I do believe in the possibility of rooting ourselves and our work in love as a wellspring of sustenance and revitalization, both of which I feel are deeply needed by critically oriented scholars since our work and reactions to our work can "hurt to our hearts" (hooks, 2010, p. 250). In the section that follows, I explore the offerings of love to expanding our understanding of self, other, and building coalitions across identity dif-ferences.

LANDSCAPING THE PROMISE OF CRITICAL LOVE

I imagine that the question "Why love?" comes to mind. The answer lies in Lorde's infamous words "the Master's tools will never dismantle the Master's house" (1984, p. 112). Returning to the late night fear that my supply of determination to embody a critical intercultural selfhood will run dry, love seems untapped as a tool, resource, and strategy. Genuine love entrenched in humility and concern for self and others is far differ-ent from hegemonic strategies of domination. Drawing from my own body as a site of knowledge (Moraga and Anzaldúa, 1983; Madison, 1993), the hate that has been hurled across identity differences, by myself and by others, has never been fully confronted by a desire to love through our differences rather than in spite of them. Returning to Lorde (1984) to defend love as a possibility, if critical scholars use only what we have at our disposal rather than being innovative, "only the most narrow perimeters of change are possible and allowable" (p. 111). Currently the tools readily available (e.g., advancing divisive identity politics, hier-archies of need, essentialism, negative difference, divide and conquer mentalities, etc.) to work with identity difference are part and parcel of the Master's house. Positioning love as a means to nourish critical intercultural selfhood and build coalitions among identity differences incites a sense of hope that I have never felt before. Perhaps our common interest in doing so is the need for compassion. In the everyday havoc of uncertainty, insecurity, and fear that phenomena like natural disaster and war or even globalization, as a cultural phenomenon that challenges set understandings of self and other, can bring forth, I have yet to meet anyone unable to benefit from compassion.[4] Shifting into a discussion of what love and compassion have to offer critical identity scholarship and scholars, the next section conceptualizes critical love.

Critical Love

Given that people have been struggling over identity and the power to name, characterize, and define themselves and others for centuries, I am not proposing a "let's all hold hands and bite our tongues for the sake of peace" sense of love, nor is love being positioned as a fountain of endless optimism that dismisses the anguish of oppression. Rather, an ethic of care rooted in critical love supports humanization, dialogue, and strong emotions such as fear, frustration, and anger. This type of love recognizes the pride and pain of humanness at the intersections of complex identities; it bears witness to ignorance, pain, suffering, suspicion, distrust, and conflict; and it allows for ugly—meaning acrimonious, crazy, and cynical—discourse. To more deeply articulate what I mean by the act of loving, I turn to Delgado (1995) who conceptualizes "beyond love" as being systemically excluded from networks of care and concern.[5] Here I extend his insight as a means to articulate not only the marking of negative difference that members of marginalized identity groups typically endure, but also to mark love as a means to resist, include, and inspire.

To critically love across our identity differences in the scholarly sense entails bearing witness to struggle, reaching out to nurture, marking the presence of privilege, and advocating for humanization. Critical love requires diving into the deep end of identity politics in our society which has created a firm hierarchy of whose pain is more worthy of public address.

Having had my critical intercultural self cultivated and cared for, I offer examples of those who have modeled for me what it means to critically love across identity differences in the academy:

> A white female department chair loved me when she was packing up her office and gave her copy of *Spirit, Space, and Survival: African American Women in (White) Academe* (James and Farmer, 1993) to me.

A black male tenured professor loved me when he invited me to call during family time to introduce me to the crux of black masculinity research.

An untenured Chicana female loved me when I showed up on her doorstep having just lost my second adviser during my third doctoral year.

A white male full professor loved me when he read my revised and resubmitted but then rejected manuscript and said "I don't know why an editor would do this, usually an R and R is an indication that a piece will be published. This is good and here are some things you might consider . . . "

They loved me. Also surfacing as an agent of love is Calafell (2007a), who bravely recounts her painful lesson as a woman of color that "Ordinary is not good enough" (p. 428); her words encircle the hollow fear in my heart that only love can alleviate. Allen et al. (1999) also engage love when they voice the complexity of their tears to illuminate a strenuous reality only recognized through love. Encased in love, Yep (2003a) risks the consequences of explicitly marking privilege with a stark reminder of the oppressive damage that heteronormativity does. They too loved me. Each in their own way, but all with a sense of consciousness around what it means to move through educational spaces as "Other." On the receiving end of their generosity, their loving labor bespeaks critical intercultural identity in action, and housed within their efforts is the beautiful yet frightening reality that the validation of identity differences and the humanization of people is what swings in the balance between love and apathy.

Looking to the future, I become hopeful about purposefully threading love throughout our discipline and the ways that we mark, discuss, and write about identity/identities, identity differences, and identity politics. Advocating for love, hooks (2010) writes, "Love heals. We recover ourselves in the act and art of loving" (p. 250). The next section details how love can further theorization of the self, others, and coalitions among identity differences.

Critical Love and Identity Politics

Allowing love to inform my embodiment of "critical intercultural scholar" has made it clear that I must first enact self love to fully engage with students and colleagues. Self love, as a woman of color, requires that I define who I am beyond the bounds of dominant discourse to engage in self-determination (Anzaldúa, 1990; Calafell, 2007a; Collins, 1986; hooks, 1989). Articulating the pleasure of doing so, Calafell (2007a) asserts "I believe that falling in love with the Otherness not only of others *but of ourselves* is a sweet surrender" (p. 438, italics in original). Through love we can dispel the imposition of negative difference and work against the strong tides of self-nihilism that are all too common among those who represent marginalized identity groups. Expressing the significance of love to counter self-nihilism and inspire resistance, West (1993b) writes:

> Nihilism is not overcome by arguments or analyses; it is tamed by love and care. . . . This turning is done through one's own affirmation of one's worth. . . . Self-love and love of others are both modes toward increasing self-valuation and encouraging political resistance in one's community. (p. 19)

For academics, engaging in the act of self love productively positions us to narrate and simultaneously embody by example the significance of loving across identity differences. Yet compassionately humanizing those who identify differently than we do, informed by a desire to love, necessitates acknowledging, validating, and celebrating the other from a position that recognizes the presence of difference but does not divisively capitalize on it.

Although identity struggles are often contextualized by resistance and resentment, the presence of love also heightens our commitment to doing critical work when we examine the connections between identity, communication, and relationships. Located "as a contested terrain of competing interests" (Mendoza et al., 2002, p. 313), struggles over identity at micro and macro levels of society are ubiquitous from a critical standpoint. Therefore, we might consider love as a means to reckon with and respect the struggles and those who feel the need to struggle on behalf of their identities, values, beliefs, etc. As such love can serve as a humanizing means to render the invisible visible, offer compassion when there seems to be none, and extend empathy beyond previous boundaries. Returning to the previous examples of scholars who have modeled love for me, I am not naïve in thinking that they each remember those particular moments or consider their written words as moving as I do. Nor do I know that they read their actions as acts of love. However, I do know that each beckoned me into a compassionate space and validated my humanity which left me ready, willing, and able to communicatively do the same.

Furthermore, in relation to cultural others, love can respond to Yep's (2010) call for "an exploration of the complex particularities of individuals' lives and identities . . . their history and personhood in concrete time and space, and the interplay between individual subjectivity, personal agency, systemic arrangements, and systemic forces" (p. 173) by forging the energy and patience required to explore the "thick intersections" of who we and others are. Perhaps I am naïve, but I firmly believe that if people understood each other's embodied experiences that we would less readily alienate, dehumanize, and maim. To mark myself as realistic (and shy away from blissful optimism), I am not saying that critical scholars can stop cultural genocide and heal the hateful wounds of war with love and love alone. Rather, what if love simply became an option in our repertoire of ways to communicate across identity differences, advocate for our beliefs, and engage in conflict? What if we could teach our students, by example, what critical love across cultural differences is capable of? Or, perhaps the more motivating questions are: At what cost do we continue to ignore the systemic absence of love in our everyday interactions? Might love be part of the solution to generating the coalitions across identity differences that we desperately need in a world that is becoming increasingly more diverse and interdependent?

Throughout world history stretching into the present day, hegemonic force and cultural indifference have yet to spark productive intercultural alliances. Near and far, intercultural conflicts have proven costly with regard to the destruction of identity and loss of life. In the academy, identity conflicts have resulted in fearful silence, toxic competition, and alarming absence with particular regard to marginalized identity groups. Illustrating the capacity of love to build relationships across difference, hooks (2001) notes: "When we choose to love we choose to move against fear—against alienation and separation. The choice to love is a choice to connect—to find ourselves in the other" (p. 93). As an act of intimacy that can compel listening, reflexivity, and humility to bridge differences, critical love houses the potential for progressive growth toward building academic spaces that are more participatory and inclusive. Anzaldúa (1990) beautifully intertwines coalition building with love:

> Alliance work is the attempt to shift positions, change positions, reposition ourselves regarding our individual and collective identities. In alliance we are confronted with the problem of how we share or don't share space, how we can position ourselves with individuals or groups who are different from or at odds with each other, how can we reconcile one's love for diverse groups when members of these groups do not love each other, cannot relate to each other, and don't know how to work together. (p. 219)

Reflecting on Anzaldúa's (1990) insight, there are practical communicative aspects of loving that we can implement as we theorize and attempt to build productive coalitions. First, we must recognize that the ways we speak and treat each other during everyday communicative encounters matters. Second, it is possible to humanize and validate someone without relating to, agreeing with, or accepting their experiences as our own. Third, agreeing to disagree (i.e., agreeing to be different) to move forward in the aim of social consciousness does not have to be apathetic or violent, rather it can be pragmatic and graceful. To be clear, all of the above stem from a commitment to critical love that is not absent of conflict but instead is quite committed to humanizing our identity differences and productively working across paradigms.

CONCLUSION

In closing, I am reminded by Butler (1990a) that identity is performative which to me signals that love must also be continually reconstituted if it is to alter our dealings with identity. Although not every intercultural scholar has lived a life that easily lends itself to give and receive love, there is promise in the possibility of trying something new. Like many, I remain a hopeful and hopeless critical intercultural scholar "in progress." Far from perfect, there are times when I would rather return to playground logic and push back just as hard as I was pushed to hurt someone because they hurt me. I too have to continually work on embodying an ethic of care characterized by patience and a desire to carry myself in a way that is mindful of love. I find daily motivation in my belief that if we can learn to more readily love ourselves and others, then we stand a better chance at forging meaningful coalitions and teaching our students to do the same.

Looking toward the future, the consideration of critical love has the potential to extend our ability to theorize by calling attention to a space in which human interests in compassion might converge. In this space, we can bear witness to the overwhelming complexity of identity politics without constituting a "hierarchy of oppressions" (Lorde, 1983b, p.9) in which systemically marginalized identities are ranked without concern for whose pain is ranked last or simply not first. Likewise, teaching by example how to embody critical love in everyday live offers an opportunity to heighten reflexivity, accountability, and consciousness with regard to privileged identities. Self-love, in particular, offers a rich space to examine the resilience and resistance embraced by members of marginalized identity groups. Finally, via a commitment to praxis, we can theorize how critical love can serve as a defense against "wedge tactics" (Finnerty, 2004, p. 4) that are used to position identity groups against each other.

Another promising venture is for scholars to position critical love as a conduit through which to navigate paradigmatic differences in identity research. Offering wise insight with regard to paradigmatic struggles, Kuhn (1996) reminds us that what is often at stake is far more than the eye can see in that many scholars root their work, and subsequently their scholarly reputation and livelihood, in a specific paradigm. Therefore, what appears to be an academic conflict can also be understood as quite personal as well which easily lends itself to becoming defensive, injurious, and dismissive. If we are mindful of the humanization and validation that critical love calls for, then we can recognize that each paradigmatic understanding (i.e., quantitative, qualitative, and critical) of identity in intercultural communication can be simultaneously valuable and imperfect. Creating a dialogic space for all three approaches to identity to coexist, Martin and Nakayama (1999) metaphorically describe the value of "a dialectic approach that facilitates interparadigmatic dialogue" (p. 1). They write, "Employing these different perspectives is similar to photographing something from different angles. No single angle or snapshot gives us the truth, but taking pictures from various angles gives a more comprehensive view of the subject" (Martin and Nakayama, 2010, p. 73). Drawing upon their insight, I believe that our approaches to identity can coexist if we advocate without romanticizing; work without disparaging the works of others; and bear witness to where scholars paradigmatically locate themselves without insinuating that their location is amiss. I rarely embrace knowing anything with certainty but I do feel confident in asserting that while paradigmatic differences and identity struggles are often incommensurable (or at least seem that way), love is not.

NOTES

1. Tuitt (2008) advocates to utilize "traditionally" opposed to "predominantly" white because in his belief "PWI [predominantly white institution] would not include those higher education institutions whose campus populations have been predominantly white but now have students of color in the numeric majority. I argue that even though institutions like MIT and Berkley have more students of color than Whites on campus, the culture, tradition, and values found in those institutions remain traditionally white. . . . " (pp. 25–26).

2. I choose to identify as a biracial black woman to mark both avowal and ascription in regard to identity performance. Hence, I identify myself as biracial to mark both my African American and white cultural roots; however, my body is often read solely as black.

3. For discussion on how noticing the pain of others necessitates action, please see Holling, Fu, and Bubar (in press).

4. This is not to imply that natural disaster, war, and globalization are the same or experienced similarly but rather to highlight a few examples of macro cultural happenings that most people, across identity differences, are impacted and interconnected by.

5. Delgado (1995) conceptualizes "beyond love" with regard to African Americans in particular, but I extend his insight to marginalized identity groups at the intersections of identity.

FIFTEEN

(Un)covering the Gay Interculturalist[1]

Keith Berry

I struggle to write today. The recent and sudden death of our friend and colleague, John T. Warren, creates a surreal sense of absence and fog. I struggle to write, even though John would encourage us to work through the uncertainty, sadness and anger often related to hardship. He would nudge us to write and perform, following De Salvo (1999), as a "way of healing"; to discover through scholarship an understanding that otherwise feels out of reach. With/for John, I write to excavate possibilities for understanding intercultural practices and identities covered and constituted therein.

This chapter examines the negotiation of a gay interculturalist scholarly identity. With Yoshino (2007), I reflexively explore how gay covering (the making less obtrusive of certain aspects of gay culture and identity) occurs in teaching and the impact this identity negotiation has on LGBTQ culture and cultural performers. This concerning aspect of the interculturalist life, even amid hopeful societal progress, continues to be underscored by covering needs, which, in turn, shape how some LGBTQ scholars live. I close by contemplating other areas in which gay covering might occur, and by suggesting a number of ways the concept of "covering" can strengthen our continuing work as intercultural communication scholars researching identity.

CRAFTING OF INTERCULTURAL SCHOLARSHIP AND SELVES

Johnson and Tuttle (1989) characterize intercultural communication research as a craft and the intercultural communication scholar as crafts-

223

person. "The skills of a craftsperson," they write, "are his or her most valuable possession . . . [and] in its highest form a craftsperson's labors take on the aspects of a calling, becoming an expression of values. The work itself becomes a form of sacrament" (pp. 461–62). Such work entails carefully examining the efficacy of research practices. Through this process, one realizes that intercultural scholarship, as with all cultural inquiry, is always already imperfect. Certainly "the attainment of one plateau is just a preparation for the next higher one" (p. 462).

Crafting intercultural communication scholarship innately implicates scholars' identities. As Johnson and Tuttle (1989) write, "Working on the craft always contains an element of self-discovery, and a recognition that who one is intimately bound up in the work one accomplishes" (p. 462). As someone who is drawn to the ways our research practices constitute scholarly identities, my interest in examining the nuances of this "self-discovery," and the portraits of scholarly selves this work can make available, is significant. For me, the "craft" in question relates specifically to rendering interculturalists through our work in the scholarly world. While my primary focus is on teaching, the work we do as scholars also is "bound up" in other dimensions of our lives, including research programs, university service and faculty searches.

Examining the crafting of an interculturalist identity entails a shift in focus. Foucault (1994) writes:

> [I]n our society, art has become something that is related only to objects and not to individuals or to life. That art is something which is specialized or done by experts who are artists. But couldn't everyone's life become a work of art? Why should the lamp or the house be an art object but not our life? From the idea that the self is not given to us, I think there is only one practical consequence: we have to create ourselves as a work of art. (p. 261)

In this sense, reflecting on how the "art object[s]" intertwined with our work extends beyond the articles, performances, teaching lessons, and strategic plans required of our institutional service work, and onto us, or our identities and the ways those identities come to be. After all, we are not solely scholars who produce research on identity, but also dynamic and vulnerable intercultural selves who are directly impacted by, and who directly impact, our work.

REFLEXIVITY

Exploring this direction entails a call for greater reflexivity. I recently had the honor of co-guest editing a special issue of *Cultural Studies <=> Critical Methodologies* (April, 2011) with Robin P. Clair. The collection focuses on the contested ways in which ethnographic reflexivity is understood and enacted across many traditions of Cultural Studies scholarship. Contributors provide helpful illustrations of reflexivity that assist my work in this chapter.

For instance, we learn from Boylorn (2011) what it means to discursively negotiate race-relations as a new black faculty member in white Alabama; from Adams and Holman Jones (2011) what it looks like from a queer/autoethnographic perspective to construct and convey stories of hardship that are, at once, powerful and important, but also revealing and risky; and from Alexander (2011) what it means to perform possibilities for appreciating and interrogating reflexivity, as it informs and responds to experiences in eulogizing his father. However, as we engage these thoughtful pieces, we also begin to learn about what pursuing this sort of intellectual work means and does for these scholars as implicated beings, persons whose identities shift and reshape as a result of doing the work. We learn more of the life-shaping impact scholarly work has on scholars as cultural beings.

A reflexive orientation provides researchers with a helpful path for studying the ways identities emerge for LGBTQ intercultural scholars. It compels us to ask: How do we individually/culturally come to understand this interpretive moment? What judgment calls are made and values assigned when engaging ourselves as intercultural art, and at whose benefit and expense? Who do we become, and who can we become, through intercultural scholarly living? Reflexivity calls upon us to take complexity seriously, which creates an opportunity to perform as both contested and hopeful selves (Berry, 2008). It implicates us within a challenging and invigorating space of understanding communicators as dynamically constituted cultural beings.

COMMUNICATION, CULTURE, AND IDENTITY

Carey (1989) defines communication as "a symbolic process whereby reality is produced, maintained, repaired, and transformed" (p. 17). In this sense, communication is the dynamic process through which we create, sustain, fix and alter our conception(s) of our worlds—our lenses for understanding interaction itself, culture and identity. The ways we teach and research communication, in turn, increasingly have moved to an explicitly cultural approach.

Culture as a theoretical concept has a rich and debated history. Moon (1996) critically examines the shifts in emphasis with respect to "culture" during its 1970s-1990s evolution. Different than in the 1970s, when it carried more diverse meanings (race, social class, and gender identity), she proposes that culture "predominantly [has been] configured as a variable in positivist research projects" in the 1980s, and since then, typically has come to reference nation/state. Moon contends the field of intercultural communication "has been constructed and how certain definitions have become hegemonic, thereby reading others out" (p. 78). Culture has come to be understood through marked disagreement and debate concerning its definitions and meanings; indeed, it is a "contested zone" (Martin and Nakayama, 2010, p. 90).

This contestation shows itself concerning the LGBTQ context through ongoing questions about whether or not there is a "gay culture" to be studied, a debate that, for some, is situated in a difficulty in connecting LGBTQ experience with a dominant physical place for conducting fieldwork (Adams, 2011; see also Jackman, 2010). Other factors may thwart the acceptance of a gay culture, including scholars' resistance to change, which can be traced to the accepted origins of the intercultural communication field and, more specifically, its original purpose of training international workers (Moon, 1996). The pervasiveness of heteronormativity in the communication discipline (Yep, 2003b) likely also shapes this contestation, prompting some scholars to "read out" some or all aspects of LGBTQ experience from culture, or to not see LGBTQ cultural persons and practices as worthy of being "read" in the first place. Regardless, the absence of substantial intercultural communication research exploring and talking about LGBTQ culture—cultural inquiry that positions sexuality with the same interest and enthusiasm afforded to other dimensions of culture—underscores a great need for additional research exploring what counts as culture in intercultural communication scholarship. As we are poised at this moment of increased and exciting critical intercultural communication research (Halualani and Nakayama, 2011), sexuality needs to be more fully part of these conversations.

My intellectual commitments to ethnography of communication and phenomenology lead me to understand culture as that which is made possible by lived experience. It is a patterned and communal accomplishment of discourse/interaction (Carbaugh, 2005; Philipsen, 1992), always informed by, and which, in turn, informs social constraints (e.g., power). Different than something which we are "born into," or to which we hold membership, culture is a resource we instantiate and use in daily living. As Carroll (1990) writes, "my culture is the logic by which I give order to the world" (p. 3). Thus, I and others study lived experience among LGBTQ communicators as it instantiates LGBTQ culture and cultural persons (see, for example, Berry, 2007; Nicholas, 2004), a commitment that implicates communication and culture as always being intrinsically connected to identity. Simply stated, identity (hereafter: identities) is who we understand ourselves to be. How that understanding comes to be, however, resists simplicity, as it is a consequence of interaction with others and, more specifically, complex identity negotiation (Jackson, 2002b). Identities are not internal phenomena, or aspects inside of "us" that await birth through the expression made possible by interaction; instead, they come to be through communication, through struggle, in/across cultural difference. Identities are the results of historical gains and losses, as negotiated with/for others and across/within diverse contexts. Who we are is the result of shifts, twists and turns occurring in time, as we move joyously and painfully interacting with others.

COVERING SEXUALITY

Yoshino (2007) examines gay covering and the cultural demands that make this distinctive mode of identity negotiation possible and necessary. Creatively drawing together sociology, psychoanalysis and legal studies, and reflections on covering race and sex, he advocates greater human rights for LGBTQ citizens. These freedoms have been eliminated, and more often kept from us, he proposes, as a result of covering.

"Everyone covers," Yoshino (2007) writes. "To cover is to tone down a disfavored identity to fit into the mainstream . . . every reader of this book has covered, whether consciously or not, and sometimes at significant personal cost" (p. viiii). Covering results from continuing and pressing societal demands for assimilation, and the demands for conformity ("straight conformity," more specifically) inherent to the ways in which communicators negotiate difference. Persons' identities are challenged and reshaped through covering practices.

Yoshino distinguishes gay covering from gay conversion (seeking to become straight, to convert) and gay passing (attempting to hide identities from others). Drawing on Goffman, he explains "that passing pertains to *visibility* of a particular trait, while covering pertains to its *obtrusiveness*" (p. 18, italics in original).Yoshino illustrates this complex process by referencing how Franklin Roosevelt typically situated himself behind a table prior to advisers coming in for meetings. "Roosevelt was not passing," he argues, "since everyone knew he used a wheelchair. He was covering, downplaying his disability so people would focus on his more conventionally presidential qualities" (p. 19). The so called "don't say gay bill" that recently passed through Tennessee Senate (HuffingtonPost.com, 2011), which seeks to make illegal any discussions of sexual behavior other than heterosexuality prior to the ninth grade illegal, provides a compelling and disheartening example of gay covering. Also, Glave (2003) offers an additional illustration of the ways many gay folks must carefully negotiate communication, so their LGBTQ identity is less obtrusive with some heterosexual friends; topics referencing same-sex experiences and identities, for instance, are saved for the right time, often which is when young children are not around to hear.[2]

Yoshino provides an instructive and evocative resource for better understanding and responding to cultural practices as they occur in, and inform, intercultural communication. Additionally, by emphasizing gay covering practices, he underscores the importance of communication

practices as instrumental in the negotiation of culture and cultural identities.

Next, I reflect on recent feedback from a student to explore how gay
covering is negotiated in teaching. The feedback prompts a number of
reflections on the ways this identity negotiation occurs and its consequences. I work through past and present experiences to consider how I
handle sexuality in this context, and in hopes that doing so speaks to
others' work in negotiating LGBTQ experiences. I pursue this path
understanding that, while in some ways we might be seeing more scholarship today examining sexuality in intercultural communication research contexts than in years past, sexuality still often gets omitted or
downplayed as a viable and vital topic of inquiry (Collier, Hedge, Lee,
Nakayama, and Yep, 2002). In turn, while more wonderful critical scholarship on communication pedagogy concerning LGBTQ culture is available today than it was in the past (see, for example, Alexander, 2005; Gust
and Warren, 2008), much more is needed (Lovaas, 2010). I pursue this
direction understanding that we are creative and complex cultural beings
who sometimes (often?) negotiate ourselves across difference in complicated and silencing ways.

"TO [*SIC*] MUCH SEXUALITY": CLASSROOM COVERING

Many moments from my fourteen years of teaching resemble the identity
work conveyed by Yoshino (2007). By 1997, when I taught my first class
as a new master's level graduate teaching assistant at Purdue University
Calumet, I had moved on from attempting gay conversion. I accepted
who I understood myself to be as a gay man, had no desires of becoming
straight, and knew of the absurdity of even considering conversion to be
possible or healthy. On the other hand, there were numerous instances in
which I attempted to pass, and often felt I had accomplished that goal.
Indeed, whether I was interacting one-on-one or with the full class, many
moments with students prompted a felt need to avoid being detected as
gay. For instance, I often would engage in a sort of planning work concerning *when* and *how* I would "come out." I felt disclosing my identity in
this way would need to occur at the "right time," and in the "right moment." Passing as straight seemed to enable a manipulation necessary to
properly secure one's footing for/with others. Until that planned moment, I felt my sexuality was to be interpreted as unknown, or presumed
straight. I did so because I was uncertain as to the responses I would
hear, and because teaching was new to me. Being able to negotiate both
meaningful teaching and the defense of myself, should folks respond
negatively, seemed out of reach. I worked to pass because I was afraid.

Indeed, the habits of passing are powerful and lasting. Thus, there
likely are those fleeting moments in the present when old habits resurface

in my teaching. However, I no longer knowingly work to pass, though many persons whom I know and love still do. I understand how opting to do so sometimes does not feel like a choice they have.

Inclusion and appreciation of LGBTQ issues and experiences, in some ways, are more visible and promising today (Savage and Miller, 2011). However, should we take that progress to mean that demands for conversion, passing and covering are no longer a part of LGBTQ cultural lives, including teachers' daily experiences, even for those who are "out and proud," we would be missing issues that are hiding in plain sight. Just as the United States is not "post-racial" in the era of President Barack Obama (Iweala, 2008), we most certainly are not "post-sexual" in the era of Ellen DeGeneres and Adam Lambert. Change, while welcomed, still tends to be slow in coming and, once here, unstable. Tricky negotiations continue.

Since 2004, I have lived in Duluth, Minnesota, and taught at the University of Wisconsin-Superior. The Duluth/Superior area is largely homogenous racially and more diverse ethnically. There is a smaller but present gay community in the Twin Ports region. I am "out" in all classes and across campus. I am out to family and friends and in nearly every essay I have published. In spite of this "outness" and the "security" of holding tenure, interactions still prompt a distinct sort of experience as gay professor. Still today I remain conscious of heterosexual privilege and the ways in which it necessitates complex identity negotiation.

"I think you talk to [*sic*] much about your sexuality in the classroom," writes one student in course evaluations for a recent upper-division theory course. When I first saw this comment on my evaluations, I was sitting at my office desk. My forehead crinkled as it normally does when pressed to engage ideas that feel careless and confusing. In that moment, I contemplate the type of disregard held for another that might instigate this type of feedback. I think of my colleague, a person of color, who during the same semester, was told that he should speak more like "us," calling him to downplay his accent. I am also pressed to understand what the comment means. While it is clear that the person wants to hear less about my gayness, how does one ascertain what "too much" is in terms of who I am? I think about how, when teaching other classes, including intercultural communication, some students' increased rolling of their eyes and doodling in notebooks during moments in which we were examining LGBTQ issues, create conditions that position LGBTQ culture as an issue with which we still must contend. Certainly there are also less constructive responses I have in a moment like this, more defensive ways of responding that feel earned, even if less helpful to the current conversation.

I engage this statement to think more deeply about the thoughts and feelings intertwined with being a professor who identifies as LGBTQ. It is an intercultural experience through which a very specific reality is communicated and has an impact.[3] It communicates a worldview steeped in judgment and cultural assumptions that prioritize one logic and dismiss another. Communicated *at* me in one moment and time, the utterance prompts a range of reflections.

Granted, this comment was an outlier comment in that semester's set of evaluations and, for that matter, all my teaching evaluations. Yet, the moment matters, as I believe it can serve as an illustration of other students' possible perceptions and feelings, those who might agree with such a sentiment, but are not inclined to write it. In turn, even if just one comment, it affects and stays with me, as someone who values students and their feedback. Do more folks, including those with whom I have close and cherished relationships, want me to "talk less about my sexuality" with them, but do not say so because they do not want to hurt my feelings? What would it look like if I were to ask students to display or talk less about their heterosexual lives? Holistically, the evaluation serves as a concrete instantiation of gay covering. It shows a covering demand (a demand that I tone down that aspect of my identity). Talk less gay, talk less about your gayness. In essence, be less of who you are. Don't be yourself.

This reflective moment inclines me to assess how much I include "my sexuality" in the classroom. However, engaging that topic would give into covering demands, pressures that would help some better determine how I *do* perform sexuality in the classroom, just "how gay" I might be, and whether or not that coheres with assumptions of "competence" in teaching and learning. It would offer folks one more tool in assessing how "obtrusive" I am to them. Indeed, there is a subversive anti-covering logic in under-explaining, so I respectfully reject the implicit request to question significantly how much is too much.

"I think you talk to [*sic*] much about your sexuality in the classroom" actually brings into awareness a more constructive understanding of just how much LGBTQ teachers might deliberately or mindlessly cover, or just how *little* we talk about our sexualities. Many LGBTQ teachers still do tone down those aspects of their identities. I see amazing colleagues on my campus and elsewhere, in smaller and larger cities, folks also typically "out," sometimes spend precious energy covering sexuality. For instance, when leading discussion, I find myself instinctively and promptly following up a "gay"-oriented example or topic in class with one that is "straight"-oriented. It is as if students need protection from the LGBTQ idea, or at the very least, they need an example to help balance out their thinking. Surely, we could make the argument that this rhetorical tactic shows how I am being especially in-tune with my audience, a rhetor attending to multiple interests, needs and sensitivities. Maybe it does. I am more inclined, however, to believe that this discursive work in pairing examples also helps cover the "gay one." Not allowing the example to stand on its own prevents it from being deeply engaged in that learning moment and helps steer the class back further into mainstream thinking.

There are additional tactics used that feel covering-like, such as downplaying the differences associated with LGBTQ mattersby assigning to them a sort of everydayness or commonness logic. In this sense, one makes mention of his/her LGBTQ identity, but does so in a very matter of fact way. For instance, I might share with class that I had a disagreement with my boyfriend Thomas about where we wanted to eat for dinner; here the emphasis of the sentence is placed on its main topic, disagreement concerning where to eat. Revealing my same-sex partner is meant to be an ancillary topic that gave a context to the larger topic. I should say this tactic was and still is instrumental in the ways I comfortably out myself to the class. I do this directly and honestly, though typically as part of an example that helps illustrate the larger point we are considering in class discussion. I do so because, in many ways, I believe my participation in LGBTQ culture and my LGBTQ identity is one aspect of many that constitutes my communication and identities. I want students to know that my sexuality is wrapped up with my being attracted to and loving men. I do so feeling they can relate to attraction and love, very human qualities, and so this tactic enables me to set the tone for acceptance and other ways of relating. Admittedly, this tactic also can create the impression of sameness and, consequently, downplay cultural differences and the need to directly engage the topic of difference. Covering in this way, then, can serve as a warm blanket that comforts or numbs teachers and students from needing to grapple with tough topics, and from needing to work at reconciling difference in/across cultural boundaries.

As an intercultural phenomenon dwelling at the intersections of communication, culture, and identity, gay covering practices persist in teaching, as I suspect they do varyingly in other contexts of the interculturalist life. I hear more colleagues talking and writing about LGBTQ cultural issues as an intellectual pursuit grounded in the study of communication and culture, or some other academic area, than I do intercultural communication proper. I observe the progress in my campus's work to create and sustain a organizational culture of "inclusive excellence,"[4] efforts I helped lead for the past three years, and notice, even amidst noticeable and impressive growth, the persisting ways past efforts that have focused solely on racial and ethnic diversity, in effect, covering LGBTQ culture. Also, still today, many friends and colleagues either avoid applying to intercultural communication faculty positions, or face a number of difficult decisions to be made when framing their application materials. Struggles include not knowing how LGBTQ culture and cultural identities will be read by persons in key decision making positions at the desired institution, finding ways to accentuate the relevance of their work to the study of race and ethnicity, and/or playing the guessing

game of the extent to which persons will deem LGBTQ culture as a valuable and needed aspect of department's intercultural communication
course and programs.

With respect to the examples of gay covering in teaching, these moments tend to occur automatically and without much deliberation. They
feel like instincts or impulses, less powerful now, but still influential. If
possible, I typically respond head-on to covering demands, which includes integrating the "I think you talk to [*sic*] much about your sexuality
in the classroom" demand directly into critical investigations in the classroom. However, for a number of reasons, freely and safely negotiating
sexuality in these ways is not possible for others. Some LGBTQ colleagues and allies continue having to persevere through heavy and time-
wasting deliberation on the consequences of being themselves, of uncovering LGBTQ culture and identities, when teaching. These deliberations
are personal, complex and consequential for teachers and students.

Covering entails muting ideas and identities, a closing off of key aspects of persons' lives and selves. It entails "watering down" the essence
and spirit of discourses and identities by holding back what otherwise
feels so natural that it must be communicated. Thus, it involves struggle
to varying degrees, the sort of exchange commonplace to identity negotiation. In these situations, "being yourself" often takes the form of being-
yourself-as-it-is-translated for dominant others. At least in part, it entails
resisting being others' forms of you.

Identity negotiation is rarely a simple phenomenon, and its appearance in gay covering is no exception. Indeed, this process presents us
with a number of intriguing questions. For instance, if someone does not
"out" themselves and/or does not talk about LGBTQ matters in their
teaching, are they covering? Perhaps. After all, even if done inadvertently, leaving out or downplaying LGBTQ culture, in effect, covers it, keeping it from being a topic to be explored. Next, if someone does not out
themselves with/among students, or even generally, are they "less gay?"
Certainly not. However, the lack of outing does, in fact, still keep that
dimension of the LGBTQ communicator's identity downplayed. I do not
attempt here to answer these questions, and rather include them to
underscore how the topics at hand, as with most identity problems in
intercultural communication, are complicated. Insight related to these
questions, along with the story conveyed through this chapter, must be
discerned contingently and in context.

Students wishing for teachers to cover, that is, those who communicate covering demands, engage in an interesting mode of identity negotiation as well. At one level, their demands help maintain or perpetuate a
commitment to the cultural system that helped create the demand in the
first place. These demands also work to reinforce their own cultural identities. However, they also inevitably render students who hold these concerns persons who are more closed than open; in turn, being closed ren-

ders them shut out or walled off from living in more expansive and inclusive ways. It keeps demanders from knowing coverers more genuinely. On the other hand, interestingly, teachers' gay covering practices, in effect, can close off students' abilities to remain open to new ideas, like marginalized sexual identities. By making less obtrusive the very ideas and identities we hope for students to understand and examine, we concomitantly make less obtrusive a needed learning opportunity. Indeed, gay covering is multifaceted and often more intricate and counterproductive than many might at first imagine.

I feel confident reading "I think you talk to [*sic*] much about your sexuality in the classroom" as homophobic speech illustrative of the wider heteronormative ideology that fuels it. I am less confident concerning who wrote the comment, and what might have personally motivated it, in that moment and time. Nevertheless, how would the impression of this message and its rhetor shift if I would disclose that I knew who wrote it, and knew this person to be a closeted gay man struggling with coming out? Could this call to cover myself in teaching be indicative of the student's desire to pass or stay covered, and the ways my persistent uncovering practices threatened his ability to hide or tone down his sexuality?

Seeking insight concerning tough topics of identity in intercultural communication requires a nuanced exploration, which, in turn, calls us to reflect on additional factors, e.g., those macro- and micro-social phenomena that make gay covering possible and/or necessary. I briefly describe a few possibilities next.

For instance, influences of the government and its laws and perspectives encourage gay covering. Still today, the United States lacks a national hate crimes protection law, and yet another sitting president is opposed to marriage equality. Indeed, as of this past year, President Obama announced that his perspective on marriage is "evolving." While Obama achieved the repeal of "Don't Ask Don't Tell," one is pressed to think carefully about how inclined or persuaded citizens are to evaluate and eliminate covering demands or practices when our country's leaders act in ways that implicitly demands covering. These phenomena discourage LGBTQ folks from being able to live the fullest lives possible and, consequently, construct a sort of difference among Americans that tacitly reinforces "I think you talk to [*sic*] much about your sexuality in the classroom."

Physical and psychological harassment among LGBTQ youth remains a significant problem (Kosciw, Greytak, Diaz, and Bartkiewicz, 2010). The Conservative Right continues using anti-LGBTQ discourse as a means of winning over public opinions and elections. When considered and experienced holistically, these damaging actions suggest and perpetuate a negative reality concerning what it means to self-identify as LGTBQ and openly advocate for LGBTQ culture and cultural identities. Although there certainly are counter-narratives that are far more enriching (Savage and Miller, 2011), I would suggest that many students and teachers come to our classrooms with an understanding of the contentious climate surrounding these topics. While there also are persons who come to the classroom charged up and ready to uncover issues, I believe the negative climate thwarts uncovering sexuality and often promotes the downplaying of tough social issues. Not for everyone, but that counterproductive influence on comfort level persists for some. Indeed, this influence serves as a reminder for the importance of continued training with critically-oriented ways to promote inclusive teaching and learning. The stakes are too high to leave these ideas covered.

Additional aspects occurring within intercultural communication concerning LGBTQ culture also must be considered. I hear some folks, often LGBTQ allies, talk about sexuality as a "non-issue." On the surface, I tend to take this statement to be wonderful and loving. When communicated by allies, it typically expresses positive regard. It says, "Because this 'controversial' LGBTQ topic is a non-issue to me, let's not waste time discussing it. I respect, love and embrace you. Let's get on to the work of living and being happy. Let's focus on the positive." Moreover, for some, and especially younger generations of communicators in the United States, sexuality *is* such a non-issue that discussing or problematizing it perceivably creates more problems than it solves. However, beneath the surface of these more encouraging interpretations also dwells a troubling implication. When sexuality is taken to be a non-issue, and should that perspective also not be accompanied by critical questioning and action-taking with respect to the issues that *do* continue to plague us, then the warm regard tends to feel flat. It tends to feel as unhelpful and troubling as when someone narrates themselves as "color blind." A critical consciousness charges us always to look more closely, to look beneath the surface, and to reflect on the potential for an issue where we might take there to be none, especially in situations where bigotry and marginalization have often governed how we interact and who we are.

These conditions offer an expanded context for exploring reasons that encourage gay covering. They also serve as powerful source of motivation for openly and persistently communicating about LGBTQ culture and identities, and for LGBTQ folks, using Yoshino's (2007) term, to "flaunt" their identity. Flaunting is a term often used historically to defile gay persons who were speaking too much or too freely about their sexualities. It has been used against persons who, as the demand would require, instead should be covering. Used differently here, flaunting bravely exposes previously downplayed identities. I contend these larger conditions, and evaluative statements like my student's, compel us to flaunt. They compel us to (re)examine and (re)question the ways we rhetorically include and exclude perspectives and persons, including how we perform ourselves. They compel us to push for a more open way of being with/among difference. Even within the struggle, this work matters and is necessary, now more than ever.

CONCLUSION

This chapter's examination of the crafting of identities for the LGBTQ teacher has offered a portrait of an artistic performance that is, at once, creative and resourceful, and deliberative and contentious. Yet, it also prompts a number of considerations related to other aspects of the gay interculturalist scholarly life world, and to identity research in intercultural communication generally. I engage each piece briefly prior to closing.

Uncovering LGBTQ interculturalists in the spirit that has driven this chapter means also asking other key questions, including: When LGBTQ scholars submit our research or creative work for public display, are we submitting to intercultural communication conference divisions and journals dedicated exclusively to intercultural communication? In turn, are conference program planners and journal editors including sexuality as a dimension of culture in calls for submissions, and are submissions (indeed, those that are well presented) advocated as invaluable contributions to intercultural communication inquiry? As we participate in campus service that aims to advance diversity, inclusion and equity for all campus community members, do we always include sexuality as critical to that important work? When drafting position descriptions for new or vacant intercultural communication faculty positions, does the description "read in" sexuality as culture? In turn, are folks who are applying for intercultural communication positions, those persons who study LGBTQ culture and identities as intercultural phenomena, prioritizing this focus in their submission materials? I suspect that, just as there are more scholars, departments, and institutions exploring this important need and direction, there are just as many that do not. And we should be doing so. We need to more thoroughly investigate answers to these questions, if we are to live out the commitment to diversity that underlies intercultural communication teaching and research in the fullest and most serious ways. If we are to live this commitment with a robust and enthusiastic integrity, much remains to be uncovered.

My hope is that this examination helps spark future identity research by/for/about intercultural communication generally, and I would suggest this can happen in several ways. Although this chapter focuses on LGBTQ culture and identities, the concepts of covering and passing have not been in the past, and need not be in the future, solely tied just to this population. Whether or not one uses Yoshino's (2007) theoretical approach, more work directly engaging these ideas will assist us by providing additional paths for examining the ways intercultural selves are crafted discursively. Also, looking at the hardship embedded in gay covering helps underscore Jackson's (2002b) position that identity negotiation is a site of struggle, for sure, an exchange in which identities are both implicated and altered. This prompts me to have great hope for our work as intercultural communication scholars if we see even more research on identity negotiation, especially that which explores identity for vulnerable populations. Additionally, my philosophical commitments have led me in this chapter to engage identity as more particular than universal, contingent than certain, and complex than simple. Therefore, I necessarily have engaged this project reflexively, which entailed immersing myself into the writing and deliberately seeking alternative vantage points from which to understand any one given phenomenon. Intercultural communication and communicators are too important, uncertain and complex not to engage scholarship in these ways. Future identity researchers in intercultural communication are likely to find that taking reflexivity seriously produces scholarship that, while challenging, also makes available meaningful and compelling accounts of communicators' dance in/across culture.

I end this chapter in a similar way to how I began: remembering John T. Warren. I would trade so much to have John back. Still, I am grateful to have learned from/with John, and take solace in believing his sassy voice shall forever remain available and influential, by our working in ways that honor the commitments that underscore his prolific body of work. Certainly he can and should live on through us. John's scholarship has advocated studying culture, intercultural communication and intercultural communication scholars as inclusive and often messy phenomena. He sought to (re)imagine the possibilities for understanding communication and identity available to us, and those that have been occluded by naïveté and/or neglect. Moreover, John brilliantly advocated reflexive scholarship at the service of something bigger than us. Critical inquiry meant artistically crafting scholarship that sought the good. It meant taking personal risks for the betterment of cultural understanding. Indeed, we should all flaunt these ways of being.

NOTES

1. Many thanks go to Nilanjana Bardhan and Mark Orbe for their helpful feedback through this writing process, and the leadership that made this book possible in the first place. Thanks also to my mother, Linda Berry, a master teacher, for her many important contributions to this chapter.
2. While I do not draw on it for this chapter, Orbe's (2005; 1998) work with cocultural theory provides an instructive and very useful lens for examining underrepresented groups' communication with dominant groups.
3. Scott Gust describes a life-changing statement made by his student Justin, about Scott, during a presentation at semester's end: "If you hadn't said you are gay, I wouldn't have even guessed" (Gust and Warren, 2008, p. 125).

4. Inclusive Excellence is an organizational worldview or philosophy that charges all members to create and sustain institutional cultures of increased diversity, inclusion, and equity. Interested persons can learn more from the Association of American Colleges and University (aacu.org).

SIXTEEN

Praxis-Oriented Autoethnography

Performing Critical Selfhood

Satoshi Toyosaki

I have been teaching intercultural communication for over a decade. I integrate intercultural communication education even when I teach "non"-intercultural communication courses, such as public speaking, small group communication, and/or research methods. As an intercultural communication pedagogue, I believe that intercultural communication is one of the foundational sets of skills through which human beings can enrich their lives and contemplate peace in our globalizing and culturally contested world.

Teaching intercultural communication triggers various emotions for me including joy, happiness, sadness, anger, and more. Teaching intercultural communication is full of challenges, some of which are totally unexpected or beyond my imagination. Many times, I find myself inert because my mind cannot process the depth of complexity upon which intercultural communication comes to be. Further, I believe that intercultural communication research brings forth those emotions and challenges, and consequently those inert moments. From my own experiences in intercultural communication as a pedagogue, researcher, and everyday practitioner, I have learned to reiterate to myself to be on my toes in the culturally political world with seas of emotions and mountains of challenges. Further, I remind myself, "Go back to yourself. Study your 'Self' in this intercultural moment of complexity." I have come to believe that the self is the key and ethical threshold in understanding the complexity of intercultural communication.

As an intercultural communication researcher, in the last several years, I have been after the concept and praxis of critical selfhood performance (Toyosaki, 2007; 2011; Toyosaki and Pensoneau, 2005; Toyosaki, Pensoneau-Conway, Wendt, and Leathers, 2009). Briefly, I understand critical selfhood as self-reflexive, purposeful, and conscious materializations of one's subjectivity, the concept heavily associated with the notion of social agency in cultural studies and critical theory. Critical selfhood performance is the emplotting act, and this emplotting act is always in a dialectical tension between stabilizing and de-stabilizing one's identity. Cavallaro (2001) explains that "subjectivity both underpins our existence as socialized creature and epitomizes our instability" (p. 96). This unstable yet social nature of subjectivity renders its critical potential for change—personal, relational, cultural, and political.

In this chapter, I hope to extend this research agenda on critical selfhood performance. I have two main goals. First, I outline my contemplation on the concept and praxis of critical selfhood as a performative accomplishment. Second, I call for a particular kind of autoethnography, which I refer to as praxis-oriented autoethnography (discussed later) as a methodology of critical selfhood performance both as research and pedagogical praxis and praxis of everyday being. I see praxis-oriented autoethnography as advantageous to identity studies in intercultural communication. In the next section, I start with the current status of cultural identity studies in intercultural communication.

CULTURAL IDENTITY STUDIES IN INTERCULTURAL COMMUNICATION

Many intercultural communication scholars (Collier, 2005; Hecht, Warren, Jung, and Krieger, 2005; Imahori and Cupach, 2005; Jackson, 2002a; Orbe, 1998; Orbe and Spellers, 2005; Ting-Toomey, 2005) study the communicative nature of cultural identities. Reviewing the current literature, I identify two trends, which simultaneously reflect strengths and weaknesses of our intercultural communication discipline: consensual theorization and interdisciplinarity. I do so with hope that this chapter remedies, to some degree, the weaknesses in our identity research.

First, our cultural identity research exhibits its tendency toward or is imbued with its oftentimes implicit reliance on consensual theorization of communication. Consensual theorization presupposes that "a common language serves to promote consensus by communicating shared meanings" (Fiske, 1991, p. 332). This trend embosses in examining how researchers operationalize, define, and conceptualize cultural identity in their research. For example, Imahori and Cupach (2005), in their identity management theory, borrow Collier and Thomas's work and define cultural identity "'as identification with and perceived acceptance into a group that has shared systems of symbols and meanings as well as norms/rules for conduct'" (p. 197). Ting-Toomey (2005), in her identity negotiation theory, defines cultural identity as "the emotional significance we attach to our sense of belonging or affiliation with the larger culture" (p. 214). Further, Collier (2005) explains, "Cultural identifications are shared locations and orientations evidenced in a variety of communication forms" (p. 237). Cultural identity at the level of conceptual definition amalgamates key concepts, such as *acceptance, shared/ing, norms/rules, belonging, affiliation, association,* and *membership,* all of which point to our field's (implicit) reliance on consensual theorization as a predominant cognitive frame for understanding identity.

This trend is also observable in ethnographic research and its methodological assumptions of speech community and shared communicative conduct (see Philipsen, 1975, 1992; Philipsen, Coutu, and Covarrubias, 2005). I think this is our strength in theorizing identity in our field. We, in general, do a good job of consensually theorizing identity in a meaningfully complicated, inter-paradigmatic, interdisciplinary, and dialectical manner.

As a consequence, however, we focus on the identical, same, similar, and repetitive in human communication as empirical sites of credible data. I am not sure if our field does a sufficient job of carefully and meaningfully interrogating the other side of the coin—the different and changing/ed. Y. Y. Kim (2005b) explains a way in which an individual transforms himself or herself by proposing a stress-adaptation-growth dynamic (p. 383). Her theory of change is informed by Dubos's "dialectic between permanence and change," Hall's "identity-separation growth," and Journard's "integration-disintegration-reintegration" (as cited in Y. Y. Kim, 2005b, p. 384). As is evident here, human growth becomes possiblized when we, human beings, understand our identity as an unstable construct and, thus, a conflictual site—the site of both the same and the different. How do we, human beings, change? Isn't this question a very important element of identity studies in intercultural communication?

Second, our cultural identity research has become extremely interdisciplinary (Hecht et al., 2005), ranging from psychology and sociology to anthropology and philosophy, while central attention is placed explicitly on human communication. The central idea here is that "identities are 'played out'" (Imahori and Cupach, 2005, p. 198). Hecht's communication theory of identity (in Hecht et al., 2005) proposes four layers of identity, one of which is the enactment layer. "Identity is enacted in communication through messages. The self is seen as a performance, as expressed" (p. 263). Understanding identity as a performative accomplishment (Butler, 1990a, 1993) renders careful and sophisticated analysis of identity in intercultural communication. However, our identity research in intercultural communication lacks a theoretical foundation in performance studies. I see the interdisciplinary and collaborative approach between inter-

cultural communication and performance studies (particularly, the literature on everyday performativity) to identity research as a theoretically
and methodologically rich amalgamation for advancing our field.

It is my intention to address these two strengths/weaknesses of our
identity research in this chapter. I believe that critical selfhood and autoethnography—particularly, praxis-oriented autoethnography—have the
capacity to address them and meaningfully add to current identity research. Now I turn to autoethnography as it is a base-methodology on
which I plan to build in envisioning praxis-oriented autoethnography.

AUTOETHNOGRAPHY

Pelias (2004) is after a particular kind of scholarship "that fosters connections, opens space for dialogue, [and] heals" (p. 2). Researchers who pursue this type of scholarship promise "to walk, whenever necessary, on
broken glass," "to rejoice, whenever possible, in the stitch," and "to carry,
whenever needed, the weight of the stone" (p. 2). In 2001, in Pelias's
graduate seminar on autoethnography, I was flabbergasted: My life
changed. In the previous year (2000), I wrote a thesis whose title was
"Relationships between uncertainty reduction and interpersonal need
compatibility in initial dyadic interactions." I made a paradigmatic shift
from traditional social scientific studies of interpersonal communication
to autoethnography. Pelias's course shook me hard, and impacted both
my academic and personal identities. It was hard, but I made the foundational paradigmatic move from my thesis advisor's office to Pelias's classroom. I had to. It was, for me, an ethical thing to do.

Pelias's graduate seminar covered topics, ranging from everyday performance to autoethnography. As a PhD student who was trained in
(post)positivistic research in interpersonal communication, I was lost.
Autoethnography, Ellis (2004) explains,

> refers to writing about the personal and its relationship to culture. It is
> an autobiographical genre of writing and research that displays multi-
> ple layers of consciousness. . . . Back and forth autoethnographers gaze:
> First they look through an ethnographic wide angle lens, focusing out-
> ward on social and cultural aspects of their personal experience; then,
> they look inward, exposing a vulnerable self that is moved by and may
> move through, refracts, and resists cultural interpretations. As they
> zoom backward and forward, inward and outward, distinctions be-
> tween the personal and cultural become blurred, sometimes beyond
> distinct recognition. (pp. 37–38)

Autoethnographies are "acts rather than artifacts" (Lockford, 2002, p. 91).
They "do" critical theory with unapologetic axiology, which predicates

that we are in pain, we can ease the pain, and we can change (Miller, 2005, p. 74).

This used to be in my flesh as a code of caring and compassion, like placing my hand over my twisted ankle or reaching my hand out to someone who fell on a playground. Somewhere between the jungle gym and my thesis proposal defense, this ethical thing to do was schooled out as evidence of biases in my research practices. Critical theory as praxis embodies its "commitment based on moral principles of human freedom and well being [and] compassion for the suffering of living beings" (Madison, 2005, p. 5) in our lifeworld into which we are born and for which it begs us to consciously choose to become accountable and responsible. Ellis and Bochner (2006) and Denzin (2006) believe that autoethnography does something for someone in our lifeworld with its "unruly, dangerous, vulnerable, rebellious, and creative" ways (Ellis and Bochner, 2006, p. 433).

I know what hurts me in my life. I have been living with this pain for quite a while. As I sit here in front of my computer screen, I am trying really hard to think of fond memories of my father. I have only two. Thinking of my father, in my mouth, I can still taste bitter cigarette smoke and sweet bourbon. I grew up hating this man. I end up with two—only two—fond memories and piles and piles of the other kinds of memories. The two memories are more like moments. This sucks.

In one memory, I am about three or four years old. It is a sunny day with blue sky, blue ocean, and, of course, a white beach. It's a picture-perfect scene. I am on a family trip, the only one I can remember. Maybe I remember this trip vividly because I repeatedly looked at the pictures. Or, my memory has been constructed through my active imagination triggered by my repetitive viewing of those pictures and by my desire for a particular kind of father. I am sitting on the beach. My sitting spot is strategically selected as I am afraid of the ocean. I sit where the waves barely touch the shore. I am eating a slice of sweet watermelon. I look up, and there he is, smiling, standing in front of me. I feel protected. In the other memory, I am a bit older. My father and I are at one public swimming pool. He carries me on his back. He slowly puts me down into the water. He pushes me away and encourages me to swim. Being afraid, I try to reach him. He slowly backs up. "Swim, swim," he says, and smiles. I feel safe.

In the twenty years I lived with him, these two fond moments were littered with his drinking and smoking and many other things that came with them. This hurts. It is painful to admit, but in my childhood, I spent too much time and energy hating this man.

PERFORMATIVE THEORY OF IDENTITY: FROM REPETITION AS
EPISTEMOLOGY TO REPETITION AS ONTOLOGY

Somewhere between the jungle gym and my thesis proposal defense, I
learned something else. I learned "men" and "women" were legitimated
categories of people, categories made out of similarities and differences.
Sex was one variable in my thesis. I also learned that international students were a category of people. They were "same" in polluting my
thesis data (Toyosaki, 2000; 2007) and "different" from American students, who provided "pure and unpolluted" data for my research. A
problem with identity is that we, human beings, oftentimes trap ourselves in those categories and make them work in an oversimplified manner. In a sense, this is an unsophisticated and rough consensual theorization of identity, oftentimes resulting in unquestioned stereotypes, discrimination, hatred, desire, and attraction. I do that quite often: To some
degree, such categorizations are our linguistic properties.

We are becoming lazy at interpreting social realities, including our
own identities. It's like a math class. Some students memorize a formula
and ask their instructor to teach them how to plug numbers in the formula. We don't have to know how a particular formula comes to be. We just
need to learn how to plug numbers into the formula in solving a problem
while we might not, and, in a lot of cases, we don't have to understand
the complexity and particularity of the problem we have just solved. We
become lazy at living the moment and living in the moment. We become
trapped in the reproductive system of already-lived moments, like the
already-worked-out formulae. Some degree of modernist comfort and
convenience comes with such data-plugging.

This is what Warren (2008) is worried about. In our communication
studies, we rely on reduced, extracted, simplified, bracketable similarities
and differences in theorizing identity. This type of theorization misses
the mark of studying culture and identity. Identity becomes theorized as
a concept of difference without a particular moment, without a particular
context, like mathematic formulae. Warren is concerned about this nature
of understanding identities.

Warren (2001b, 2003b) integrates intercultural communication studies
and performance studies with research on whiteness and racial identity
studies. He borrows Butler's (1990a, 1993) phenomenological theory of
"acts" in gender construction and develops his theoretical and methodological frameworks for analyzing race, particularly whiteness, as a performative accomplishment. Butler (1990a) asserts that "gender . . . is an
identity tenuously constituted in time—an identity instituted through a
stylized repetition of acts" (p. 270). Warren (2001b, 2003b) extends Butler's assertion into whiteness studies and proposes a performative theory
of identity:

> [It] understands the subject to be essentially unstable, never natural and thus constructed through embodied actions. Performativity denies . . . the stability of identity, moving toward a notion of repetition as a way of understanding that those markers used to describe one's identity . . . get constructed through the continual performance of those markers. (Warren, 2001b, p. 95)

Butler's performative theory of identity provides us with an epistemological frame for investigating identity (Warren, 2008). For example, many nights in my childhood, I was awoken by my parents' fights. Many nights, I murmured to myself, "Here it goes again," in my pretend sleep. My monologic murmuring or self-muting and pretend sleep became mundane and normative for a culturally programmed, subordinate Japanese son of my culturally programmed, dominant Japanese father in a Japanese family system. The repetition of my pretend sleep of many nights—cultural identity "simulations" for Baudrillard (1994)—renders narrative coherence of my identity, imbued with and enabling my hatred toward my father—hyperreality or simulacra. Butler's performative theory of identity, in this way, successfully provides an epistemological frame with which I consciously and somewhat systematically come to understand my own identity as Japanese and my father's son through my own repetitive acts. My perceptual activity processes the same, identical, and similar among those acts, repetitively restoring the interpretation, consciously or not.

Acknowledging the importance of Butler's contribution and introducing Deleuze's (1994) political ontology, Warren (2008) extends Butler's work in explaining how interruption, criticism, and change take place in one's identity performance. Warren writes, "The act of repetition always felt very much like the 'doing the same again'" (p. 297). This sentiment goes with mine in thinking of my pretend sleep of many nights. Butler's epistemological approach to identity focuses on consensual theory of normative behaviors or repetitive acts and the hegemonic and reproductive system of those behaviors and acts.

To be honest, this epistemological approach to identity through studying my own repetitive acts gave me some degree of modernist comfort in that I (cognitive and emotional inquiry) could "always" cast my father (his body and acts) as a bad guy and myself (my body and acts) as a victim in the family ritual of pretend sleep. Our mind is trained to use *a priori* conceptions and is accustomed with consensually theorizing repetitive acts by perceptively organizing them as a series. Acts in repetition are ephemeral; one takes place and vanishes, and another emerges. "In this moment, we engage in interpretation, changing the thing different [and] making it appear the 'same'" (Warren, 2008, p. 299).

It is still hard to believe that I can think of only two fond memories with my father. In my early childhood, my negative feeling toward my father was already constructed in the family-cultural discourse into which I was born and with which I was socialized as a member of my family. My negative feeling functioned as a theorizing apparatus for rendering consensus between one interaction and another and among my numerous interactions with my father, including the interactions I had not yet lived. I had already lived those interactions conceptually before I corporeally lived them. In other words, I had learned to imagine my father's red yelling face through the repetition of my pretend sleep. My cognition prohibited his smile even before he smiled or even while he was smiling, turning the moment into skepticism and cynicism. My cognition disabled fond memories with him. It is my analytic preoccupation and obsession toward reductionist and stabilized categories, themes, and types, which prevent me from living in the moment and understanding my identity as it is at the moment of making. The consensual theory of identity as epistemology, thus, leaves temporal complexity and particularity behind.

Now appear the important questions of ontology and agency—who we are or, more importantly to me, who we can and hope to become. These questions are central to critical theory and autoethnography (Ellis, 2004). On this point, Warren (2008) borrows Deleuze's (1994) notion of political ontology as "a repetition of difference—that is, ontology is a transformative and fluid state, characterized by repetitive acts that are always unique, even if they are historically informed repetitions" (Warren, 2008, pp. 296-97). In other words, repetitive identity markers are not, by nature, identical to the ones which have preceded them. My pretend sleep last night, for example, is inherently different from my pretend sleep tonight. So, for Deleuze (1994), each repetitive act is original. "Repetition can always be 'represented' as extreme resemblance or perfect equivalence, but the fact that one can pass by degree from one thing to another does not prevent their being different in kind" (Deleuze, 1994, p. 2). On this point, Warren (2008) explains, "Its originality is [however] only being obscured by the lenses of our perception, a falsehood imposed on us by our cultural [and/or relational] past, imbued with [culture-specific] ideology" (p. 298) or the consensual theory of identity. Thus, Deleuze's political ontology connotes a theoretical shift from consensual to conflictual.

Conflictual theory of identity directs our attention to the complexity and particularity of an act as a site of ontology and agency, framed within cultural criticism. Conflictual theory captures how "the linguistic system is as much a site of conflict as is the social system—the struggle for meanings is part of the social struggle" (Fiske, 1991, p. 332). Conflictual theory of identity situates the struggle for meanings in understanding repetitive acts, by refusing to blindly impose the historically informed categorical perception and paying close attention to the complexity and particularity of each act.

I stand along with Warren when he says, "I feel this move to particularity will . . . dramatically increase our ability to be agents of interruption, critique, and change" (p. 300). Hauser and Whalen (1997) and Touraine (1988) explain that contemporary social movements tend to be mobilized by micro-political social actors. Touraine (1988) writes, "Identity is . . . no longer an appeal to a mode of being but the claim to a capacity for action and for change. It is defined in terms of choice and not in terms of substance, essence, and tradition" (p. 81). This definition of identity traces the shift I am painting here from consensual to conflictual theory of identity. The latter sees an original and ephemeral act as a self-reflexive and political site of interruption, critique, and change. Conflictual theory sees identity as narrative fluidity which frees the present self from the modernist impositions of the past and postmodernizes identity as an entity capable of original, self-reflexive, and political acts.

In advancing Warren's work, I have explained two orientations to performative theories of identity: consensual and conflictual. Consensual theory of identity is a performative way in which we come to understand how our identities emerge from our repetitions of the "same" and "copied" acts. Thus, identity is conceived of or is epistemologically available to us as narrative coherence. The consensual theory as epistemology modernizes identity. The conflictual theory, on the other hand, postmodernizes identity, nullifying ontological stability and validating ontological fluidity. It sees identity as narrative fluidity and valorizes agency because our identity-formative acts are always original, thus different from the ones which have preceded them. The complexity and particularity of an original act construct the difference, possiblizing interruption, critique, and change.

Usually, consensual and conflictual theorizing practices are understood as "oppositional." Extreme and singular practice of these theorizing forces is, however, dangerous. For example, if I employ consensual theorization of identity to the extreme degree, I disable an opportunity to renegotiate and redefine my relationship with my father. However, such utility of the theorization can be found ubiquitously, as discrimination and hatred exist in our culturally political world. If I employ conflictual theorization to the extreme degree, I lose substance in understanding who I am as Japanese and my father's son. Identity becomes a very thin concept, almost meaningless to intercultural communication researchers. I do not particularly see merit in situating them as oppositional. In reality, identity comes to be, exists, and becomes cognitively available to us in the intricate liminal space between these theorizing forces. Consensual and conflictual theories of identity are co-emerging, co-depending, coexisting, and collaborating narrative forces (Bakhtin, 1981; see Toyosaki, 2011) of our identity or selfhood.

Here I suggest the adjective "nuanced." I propose nuanced consensual and conflictual theories of identity as a dialectical way in which we, intercultural communication scholars, can capture identity in our life-world. This dialectic situates identity in a "heuristically rich paradox" of "both/and, yes/but, instead of either/or" (Conquergood, 1985, p. 9). The pressing question here is: How do we capture the complexity and partic-ularity of identity in our studies? As I have already suggested, autoeth-nography is one of a few research methodologies which directly respond to this question. Here I turn to and advance my discussion of the autoeth-nographer self.

PRAXIS-ORIENTED AUTOETHNOGRAPHY

I make an explicit move to praxiology, or autoethnography as praxis-oriented methodology for research and living. This is my return to per-formativity as a unifying philosophical frame for conceptualizing and understanding identity in (inter-intra)cultural contexts. For this discus-sion, I go to Schrag's work (1986, 1997, 2003). In the last few years, his work on praxis-oriented selfhood and intersubjectivity has been influen-tial in recent coauthored work on automethodology (see Pensoneau-Con-way and Toyosaki, 2011a, 2011b).

As a communication scholar, I am attracted to Schrag (1986, 1997) for two reasons; first, he theorizes the self as constituted within communica-tive praxis, and second, he responds to my frustration of the either-or, or modern or postmodern theories of identity. In his *The Self after Postmoder-nity*, Schrag (1997) addresses his dissatisfaction against both modernist and postmodernist configurations of the self. Modernism fantasizes Car-tesian *cogito* or the self/mind as "epistemological bedrock" (Dallmayr, 2002, p. 131); postmodernism debunks the epistemological authority and throws away "'every sense of self'" (p. 131). The postmodern self is too abstract, lacking substance (Dauenhauer, 2002, p. 157). Schrag's work helps us understand the space of the moral paradox, the dialectics or intersection of nuanced consensual and conflictual theories of identity, while anchoring the praxis of selfhood to communicative, concrete ac-tions.

Schrag (1986) translates "praxis" into " 'practice,' . . . 'action,' 'perfor-mance,' or 'accomplishment'" (pp. 18-19). His work calls for a theory of identity anchored in concrete communicative praxis that gives us tools for remaining in the "heuristic paradox" of the present moment, a simul-taneous absence of the "already" (the past) and the "not yet" (future) (Schrag, 1986, p. 146). The subject is an emergent of "a *living* present coming from a past and projecting into a future" (Schrag, 1986, p. 146), oftentimes generating a restoration of the past; in other words, the con-sensual theory of identity. However, this restoration should not be understood as a mere reproduction of the past or already perceived present. This understanding traps the identity as fixed reality—the negative effect of oversimplified consensual theorization of identity. The living present is a hopeful site for autoreferential interruption, critique, and change.

And, this self is "announced . . . in the participatory social practice" (p. 143). Thus, the self is always intersubjective: Intersubjectivity presupposes subjectivity (Giddens, 1991). Thus, our autoreferential interruption, critique, and change are not simply private constructs of our identity. They are already public, working towards a more hopeful future, be that of a father-son relationship, family issues, social inequality, cultural differences, and so on. The living present is indeed a performative accomplishment as we enact our identity in the moment of living and experience the complexity and particularity of the moment of identity performance. It is an ephemeral, yet highly political and politicized moment of our identity.

Here is where praxis-oriented autoethnography emerges. Praxis-oriented autoethnography asks, what do you "do" to meaningfully live in this ephemeral moment in between the already and the not yet? Praxis-oriented autoethnography understands the autoethnographer self as the implicated and intersubjective self, performatively accomplished by the dialectic of nuanced consensual and conflictual theorization of his or her identity/identities. Furthermore, praxis-oriented autoethnography is our search for ways to meaningfully occupy the living present with concrete communicative actions and with ethical considerations of communicative participants in a variety of contexts, such as self-self intrapersonal communication, interpersonal communication, relationship, community, society, etc. Such praxis-oriented being in research should be "openly committed to critiquing the status-quo and building . . . more just [interactions among human beings]" (Lather, 1991, pp. 171-72). Praxis-oriented autoethnography helps us narrate our identity as we make it happen via our communicative praxis with presence of others.

> My praxis-oriented autoehnography helps me employ my critical self-hood performance. Narrative temporality enables the emplotment of the history of the self as a dynamic coming from a past and moving into a future in such a wise [manner] that the past and the future figure as indigenous features of the story of self as it unfolds. And the identity of self in all this consists in the degree to which the self is able to unify its past accomplishments and its future projects. The self that has nothing to remember and nothing for which to hope is a self whose identity stands in peril. (Schrag, 1997, pp. 36–37)

Praxis-oriented autoethnography is a methodology of identity both for research and living for those who have something meaningful to remember and to hope for the future. It is a methodology for doers who critically engage in their doing of their identity.

I don't remember the last time when my father and I really "talked." Our conversations have been very awkward and short. My father and I have been very distant from each other since I was little. Since I can remember, this has been the case. We lived in the same house. He has his own room. He always sat and he still does just inside the doorway, facing the TV. He watches TV a lot. Since I was little, I learned that the room was a place into which I was not supposed to step. Also, he usually does not start a conversation. We exchange awkward short greetings here and there. So, I always stand at and lean against the doorway when I have something to ask and/or get his permission for something. This leaning is the act of repetition which constructs my identity as my father's son. My pretend sleep translates into my leaning quite smoothly. Then, after my act of leaning, I start my line, "Can I talk with you a little bit?" My father always says, "Yes," but he does not turn around or invite me into his room. He keeps watching TV. So, I watch TV over him as I stand behind him and just ask a question. And, I hope that his response is short and to the point so that I can quickly leave the doorway. I don't know how many times we have repeated this "act." Over and over, I have acted without any intention of ameliorating my relationship with my father. Over and over, I have failed in living in each moment of leaning. I have not leaned against the doorway in the past with hope that the interaction which is about to take place is going to be somewhat different. I have leaned against the doorway over and over, fatalistic and mad.

Praxis-oriented autoethnography is not going to make me love my father overnight, but helps me possibilize ways in which I can lean against the doorway a little bit differently each time I lean, because each leaning that I am going to act in the future are all original with its own complexity and particularity. This is, to me, a hopeful and transformative way to understand my relationship with my father. Praxis-oriented auto-ethnography gives me hope that I might have more fond memories of my father in my life.

CONCLUSION: WHAT DOES PRAXIS-ORIENTED AUTOETHNOGRAPHY DO?

Praxis-oriented autoethnography is an autobiographical genre of writing which narrates one's path to the hopeful and transformative way of expe-riencing his or her cultural identity and assists him or her to live in the moment, and to live the moment with present hope and future hopeful-ness. Praxis-oriented autoethnography is a qualitative/critical (auto)-methodology of "doing." In what follows, I discuss what praxis-oriented autoethnography does for us, identity scholars/pedagogues.

Praxis-oriented autoethnography helps capture the intricate narrative dance of nuanced consensual-conflictual theorization of one's identity with an explicit attention paid to concrete, communicative, and repetitive acts of his or her identity performance (in other words, identity markers). In this process, praxis-oriented autoethnographers study, interrogate, and if necessary, dismantle their narrative imposition of perceptual coherence of their identities. They question the unquestioned narrative continuity which cognitively and perceptually fixes their identities in their everyday performance. This autoethnographic interrogation of their identity markers has potential in rendering critical and transformative impetus for it prepares them for living the "living" present, "coming from a past and projecting into a future" (Schrag, 1986, p. 146), a more hopeful future. Praxis-oriented autoethnography is narrative evidence of critical selfhood—self-reflexive, purposeful, and conscious emplotment of one's subjectivity. I believe that praxis-oriented autoethnography strengthens the current status of identity research in intercultural communication by ontologically and epistemologically politicizing the complexity and particularity of the concrete, communicative, identity-making acts in our everyday life. After all, isn't critical selfhood what we are after in teaching intercultural communication?

Bibliography

Adams, T. E. (2011). *Narrating the closet: an autoethnography of same-sex attraction*. Walnut Creek, CA: Left Coast Press.

Adams, T. E., & Holman Jones, S. (2011). Telling stories: reflexivity, 1ueer theory, and autoethnography. *Cultural Studies <=> Critical Methodologies, 11*, 108–16.

Adelman, M. B. (1988). Cross-cultural adjustment: a theoretical perspective on social support. *International Journal of Intercultural Relations, 12*, 183–204.

Adler, N. J. (1975). The transition experience: an alternative view of culture shock. *Journal of Humanistic Psychology, 15*, 13–23.

Adler, N. J. (1981). Re-entry: managing cross-cultural transitions. *Group and Organization Studies, 6*(3), 341–56.

Adler, P. (1977). Beyond cultural identity: reflections on cultural and multicultural man. In R. Brislin (Ed.), *Culture learning: Concepts, applications, and research* (pp. 24–41). Honolulu, HI: University Press of Hawaii.

Ahmed, S., Castaneda, C., Fortier, A., & Sheller, M. (2003). Introduction: uprootings/regroundings: questions of home and migration. In S. Ahmed, C. Castaneda, A. Fortier & M. Sheller (Eds.), *Uprootings/regroundings: Questions of home and migration* (pp. 1–22). New York: Berg Publishing.

Alcoff, L. (1991). The problem of speaking for others. *Cultural Critique, 20*(1), 5–32.

Alexander, B. K. (1999). Moving toward a critical poetic response. *Theatre Topics, 9*, 107–25.

Alexander, B. K. (2004). Performance ethnography: The reenacting and inciting of culture. In N. K. Denzin & Y. S. Lincoln (Eds.), *Handbook of Qualitative Research*, (3rd ed., pp. 411–41). Thousand Oaks, CA: Sage.

Alexander, B. K. (2005). Embracing the teachable moment: The black gay body in the classroom as embodied text. In E. P. Johnson & M. G. Henderson (Eds.), *Black Queer Theory: A Critical Anthology* (pp. 250–65). Durham, NC: Duke University Press.

Alexander, B. K. (2006). *Performing black masculinity: Race, culture, and queer identity*. Lanham, MD: Alta Mira Press.

Alexander, B. K. (2011). Standing in the wake: A critical auto/ethnographic exercise on reflexivity in three movements. *Cultural Studies <=> Critical Methodologies, 11*, 98–107.

Alexander, B. K., & Warren, J. T. (2002). The materiality of bodies: Critical reflections on pedagogy, politics, and positionality. *Communication Quarterly, 50*(3/4), 328–43.

Ali, M., Huezo, J., Miller, B., Mwangi, W., & Prokosch, M. (2011). *State of the dream 2011: austerity for whom?* Boston: United for a Fair Economy.

Allen, B. J. (1998). Black womanhood and feminist standpoints. *Management Communication Quarterly, 11*, 575–86.

Allen, B. J. (2000). Learning the ropes: A black feminist standpoint analysis. In P. Buzannell (Ed.), *Rethinking Organizational and Managerial Communication from Feminist Perspectives* (pp. 177–208). Thousand Oaks, CA: Sage.

Allen, B. J. (2004). *Difference matters: Communicating social identity*. Long Grove, IL: Waveland.

Allen, B. J., Broome, B., Jones, T., Chen, V., & Collier, M. J. (2002). Intercultural alliances: A cyberdialogue among scholar-practitioners. In M. J. Collier (Ed.), *Intercultural alliances: Critical transformation, International and Intercultural Communication Annual XXV* (pp. 279–319). Thousand Oaks, CA: Sage.

Allen, B. J., Orbe, M. P., & Olivas, M. R. (1999). The complexity of our tears: Dis/enchantment and (in) difference in the academy. *Communication Theory, 9*(4), 402–29.

Allen, D. (1997). Social constructions of self: Some Asian, Marxist, and feminist critiques of dominant western views of self. In D. Allen (Ed.), *Culture and Self: Philosophical and Religious Perspectives, East and West* (pp. 3–26). Boulder, CO: Westview Press.

Allman, P. (2009). Paulo Freire's contributions to radical adult education. In A. Darder, M.P. Baltodano & R.D. Torres (Eds.), *The Critical Pedagogy Reader* (2nd ed., pp. 417–30). New York: Routledge.

Althusser, L. (1967). Contradiction and overdetermination: Notes for an investigation. *New Left Review, 41,* 15–35.

Amaya, H. (2007). Latino immigrants in the American discourses of citizenship and nationalism during the Iraqi war. *Critical Discourse Studies, 4*(3), 237–56.

Ang, I. (2000). Identity blues. In P. Gilroy, L., Grossberg & A. McRobbie (Eds.), *Without Guarantees: In honour of Stuart Hall* (pp. 1–13). London: Verso.

Anthias, F. (2001). New hybridities, old concepts: The limits of 'culture.' *Ethnic and Racial Studies, 24*(4), 619–41.

Anzaldúa, G. (1987). *Borderlands/La frontera: The new mestiza.* San Francisco: Spinsters/Aunt Lute.

Anzaldúa, G. (1990). Bridge, drawbridge, sandbar, or island: Lesbians of color Haciendo Alianzas. In L. Albrecht & R. M. Brewer (Eds.), *Bridges of Power: Women's Multicultural Alliances* (pp. 216–31). Philadelphia, PA: New Society Publishers.

Anzaldúa, G. (2009a). (Un)natural bridges, (un)safe spaces. In A. Keating (Ed.), *The Gloria Anzaldúa Reader* (pp. 243–48). Durham, NC: Duke University Press.

Anzaldúa, G. (2009b). Let us be the healing of the wound. In A. Keating (Ed.), *The Gloria Anzaldúa Reader* (pp. 303–17). Durham, NC: Duke University Press.

Aoki, E. (2000). Mexican American ethnicity in Biola, CA: An ethnographic account of hard work, family, and religion. *Howard Journal of Communications, 11,* 207–27.

Appadurai, A. (1996). *Modernity at large: Cultural dimensions of globalization.* Minneapolis, MN: University of Minnesota Press.

Appiah, K. A. (2006). *Cosmopolitanism: Ethics in a world of strangers.* London: Penguin Books.

Apple, M. W. (1993). Constructing the 'other': Rightist reconstructions of common sense. In C. McCarthy & W. Crichlow (Eds.), *Race Identity and Representation in Education* (pp. 24–39). New York: Routledge.

Asante, M. K. (1980). Intercultural communication: An inquiry into research direction. *Communication Yearbook, 4,* 401–10.

Asante, M. K. (2002). Intellectual dislocation: Applying analytic Afrocentricity to narratives of identity. *The Howard Journal of Communications, 13,* 97–110.

Asante, M. K. (2006). The rhetoric of globalisation: The Europeanisation of human ideas. *Journal of Multicultural Discourses, 1,* 152–58.

Asante, M. K. (2007). Communicating Africa: Enabling centricity for intercultural engagement. *China Media Research, 3,* 70–75.

Ashcraft, K. L. (1998). "I wouldn't say I'm a feminist, but . . ." Organizational micropractice and gender identity. *Management Communication Quarterly, 11*(4), 587–97.

Asim, J. (2009). *What Obama means . . . for our culture, our politics, our future.* New York: William Morrow.

Austin, C. N. (1986). *Cross cultural reentry: A book of readings.* Abilene, TX: ACU Press.

Azadovskii. K., & Egerov, B. (2002). From anti-Westernism to anti-semitism: Stalin and the impact of the "anti-cosmopolitan" campaigns on Soviet culture. *Journal of Cold War Studies, 4*(1), 66–80.

Bachelard, G. (1964). *The poetics of space: The classic look at how we experience intimate spaces.* Boston: Beacon Press.

Bakhtin, M. M. (1981). *The dialogic imagination: Four essays* (M. Holquist, Ed., C. Emerson & M. Holoquist, Trans.). Austin, TX: University of Texas Press.

Bakhtin, M. (1986). *Speech genres* (C. Emerson & M. Holquist, Eds.; V. McGee, Trans.). Austin, TX: University of Texas Press.

Bardhan, N. (2011). *Slumdog Millionaire* meets "India Shining": (Trans)national narrations of identity in south Asian diaspora. *Journal of International and Intercultural Communication, 4*(1), 42–61.

Bashir, H. (2009). Theory of co-culture and co-cultural groups: Study of Muslim communications in the USA. *Iranian Journal of Cultural Research, 2*(6), 97–123.

Bate, B., & Bowke, J. (1997). *Communication and the sexes* (2nd ed.). Prospect Heights, IL: Waveland Press.

Baudrillard, J. (1994). *Simulacra and simulation* (S. F. Glaser, Trans.). Ann Arbor, MI: The University of Michigan Press.

Beale, F. (1970/2005). Double jeopardy: To be black and female. In T. Cade Bambara (Ed.), *The Black woman: An anthology* (pp. 109–22). New York: Washington Square Press.

Beck, U. (2006). *The cosmopolitan vision.* Cambridge: Polity Press.

Beck, U., & Sznaider, H. (2006). Unpacking cosmopolitanism for the social sciences: A research agenda. *The British Journal of Sociology, 57*(1), 1–23.

Behar, R. (2005). Foreword. In B. Straight (Ed.), *Women on the verge of home* (pp. ix–xi). Albany, NY: State University of New York Press.

Bennett, J. M. (1998). Transition shock: Putting culture shock in perspective. In M. J. Bennet (Ed.), *Basic concepts in intercultural communication: Selected readings* (pp. 215–44). Yarmouth, ME: Intercultural Press. First published in 1977, in N. C. Jain (Ed.), *International and Intercultural Communication Annual, IV* (pp. 45–52).

Berg, C. R. (2002). *Latino images in film: Stereotypes, subversion, and resistance.* Austin, TX: University of Texas Press.

Berlant, L., Warner, M., Clarke, & E., Denisoff, D. (1994). Forum: On the political implications of using the term "queer," as in "queer politics," "queer studies," and "queer pedagogy." *Radical Teacher, 45,* 52–57.

Berry, J. W. (1992). Psychology of acculturation: Understanding individuals moving between two cultures. In R. W. Brislin (Ed.), *Applied cross cultural psychology* (pp. 232–53). Newbury Park, CA: Sage.

Berry, J. W. (1998). Intercultural relations in plural societies. *Canadian Psychology, 40,* 12–21.

Berry, K. (2007). Embracing the catastrophe: Gay body seeks acceptance. *Qualitative Inquiry, 13,* 259–81.

Berry, J. W., Kim, U., Minde, T., & Mok, D. (1987). Comparative studies of acculturative stress. *International Migration Review, 21,* 491–511.

Berry, K. (2008). Promise in peril: Ellis and Pelias and the subjective dimensions of ethnography. *Review of Communication, 8,* 154–173.

Bhabha, H. (1986). Signs taken for wonders: Questions of ambivalence and authority under a tree outside Delhi, May 1817. In H. L. Gates, Jr. (Ed.), *Race, writing and difference* (pp. 163–84). Chicago: The University of Chicago Press.

Bhabha, H. (1990a). Interview with Homi Bhabha: The third space. In J. Rutherford (Ed.), *Identity: Community, culture, difference* (pp. 207–21). London: Lawrence & Wishart.

Bhabha, H. K. (1990b). *Nation and narration.* New York: Routledge.

Bhabha, H. (1992). The world and the home. *Social Text, 31/32,* 141–53.

Bhabha, H. (1994). *The location of culture.* New York: Routledge.

Bhabha, H. (1996). Culture's in-between. In S. Hall & P. du Gay (Eds.), *Questions of cultural identity* (pp. 53–60). London: Sage.

Black, J. S., Gregersen, H. B., & Merdenhall, M. E. (1992). *Global assignments: Successfully expatriating and repatriating international managers.* San Francisco: Jossey-Bass.

Blackman, L. (2011). Affect, performance, and queer subjectivities. *Cultural Studies , 25* (2), 183–99.

Boler, C., & Zembylas, M. (2003). Discomforting truths: The emotional terrain of understanding difference. In P. P. Trifonas (Ed.), *Pedagogies of difference: Rethinking education for social change* (pp. 110–36). New York: RoutledgeFalmer.

Boylorn, R. M. (2011). Gray or for colored girls who are tired of chasing rainbows: Race and reflexivity. *Cultural Studies <=> Critical Methodologies, 11*, 178–86.

Brabant, S., Palmer, C. E., & Gramling, R. (1990). Returning home: An empirical investigation of cross-cultural re-entry. *International Journal of Intercultural Relations, 14,* 387–404.

Brah, A., & Coombes, A. (2000). *Hybridity and its discontents.* London: Routledge.

Branigan, T. (2011, June 22). Artist Ai Weiwei released on bail by Chinese police. *The Guardian.* Retrieved from: www.guardian.co.uk/artanddesign/2011/jun/22/ai-wei-wei-freed-by-chinese-police

Brislin, R., & Pedersen, P. (1976). *Cross-cultural orientation programs.* New York: Gardner Press.

Broome, B. J. (1991). Building shared meaning: Implications of a relational approach to empathy for teaching intercultural communication. *Communication Education, 40,* 231–49.

Broome, B. J., Carey, C., De la Garza, S. A., Martin, J. N., & Morris, R. (2005). "In the thick of things": A dialogue about an activist turn in intercultural communication. In G.-M. Chen & W. Starosta (Eds.), *Taking stock in intercultural communication, International* and *Intercultural Communication Annual, XXVII* (pp. 145–75). Washington, DC: National Communication Association.

Buber, M. (2004). *I and thou.* New York: Continuum.

Buescher, D., & Ono, K. A. (2009). The content of citizenship. In S. Jacobs (Ed.), *Concerning argument: Selected papers from the fifteenth biennial conference on argumentation* (pp. 78–87). Washington, DC: National Communication Association.

Butalia, U. (2000). *The other side of silence: Voices from the partition of India.* Durham, NC: Duke University Press.

Butler, K. D. (2001). Defining diaspora, refining a discourse. *Diaspora, 10*(2), 189–219.

Butler, J. (1990a). *Gender trouble: Feminism and the subversion of identity.* New York: Routledge.

Butler, J. (1990b). Performative acts and gender construction: An essay in phenomenology and feminist theory. In S. E. Case (Ed.), *Performing feminists: Feminist critical theory and theatre* (pp. 270–82). Baltimore, MD: Johns Hopkins University Press.

Butler, J. (1993). *Bodies that matter: On the discursive limits of "sex."* New York: Routledge.

Butler, J. (1999). *Gender trouble: Feminism and the subversion of identity* (rev. ed.). New York: Routledge.

Calafell, B. M. (2007a). Mentoring and love: An open letter. *Cultural Studies <=> Critical Methodologies, 7*(4), 425–41.

Calafell, B. M. (2007b). *Latina/o communication studies: Theorizing performance.* New York: Peter Lang.

Calafell, B. M. (2008). Performing the responsible sponsor: Everything you never wanted to know about immigration post-9/11. In A. Valdivia (Ed.), *Latina/o communication studies today* (pp. 69–89). New York: Peter Lang.

Calafell, B. M. (2009). "She ain't no diva!": Reflections on in/hospitable guests/hosts, reciprocity, and desire. *Liminalities: A Journal of Performance Studies, 5,* Retrieved from liminalities.net/5-4/diva.pdf

Calafell, B. M. (2010a). When will we all matter? Exploring race, pedagogy, and sustained hope for the academy. In D. L. Fassett & J. T. Warren (Eds.), *The SAGE handbook of communication and instruction* (pp. 343–60). Thousand Oaks, CA: Sage.

Calafell, B. M. (2010b). Notes from an "angry woman of color": Academic policing and disciplining women of color in a post (fill in the blank) era. *Journal of Communication Inquiry, 34,* 240–45.

Calafell, B. M., & Delgado, F. (2004). Reading Latina/o images: Interrogating Americanos. *Critical Studies in Media Communication, 21*(1), 1–24.

Calafell, B. M., & Moreman, S. T. (2009). Envisioning an academic readership: Latina/o performativities per the form of publication. *Text and Performance Quarterly, 29,* 123–30.

Calhoun, C. (2002). Imagining solidarity: Cosmopolitanism, constitutional patriotism, and the public sphere. *Public Culture, 14*(1), 147–71.

Callahan, C. (2010). Going home: Deculturation experiences in cultural reentry. *Journal of Intercultural Communication, 22.* Retrieved from www.immi.se/intercultural/nr22/callahan.htm

Cantú Jr, L. (2009). *The sexuality of migration: Border crossings and Mexican immigrant men.* N. A. Naples & S. Vidal-Ortiz (Eds.). New York: New York University Press.

Carbaugh, D. (1990). Intercultural communication. In D. Carbaugh (Ed.), *Cultural communication and intercultural contact* (pp. 151–76). Hillsdale, NJ: Lawrence Erlbaum.

Carbaugh, D. (2005). *Cultures in conversation.* Mahwah, NJ: Lawrence Erlbaum Associates.

Carey, J. W. (1989). *Communication as culture: Essays on media and society.* Boston: Unwin Hyman.

Carr, D. (1986). *Time, narrative, history.* Bloomington, IN: Indiana University Press.

Carrillo Rowe, A. (2005). Be longing: Toward a feminist politics of relation. NWSA Journal , 17 (2), 15–46.

Carrillo Rowe, A. (2008). *Power lines: On the subject of feminist alliances.* Durham, NC: Duke University Press.

Carrillo Rowe, A. (2009). Moving relations: On the limits of belonging. *Liminalities: A Journal of Performance Studies, 5*(5), 1–10.

Carrillo Rowe, A. (2010a). Entering the inter: Power lines in intercultural communication. In T. K. Nakayama & R. T. Halualani (Eds.), *The handbook of critical intercultural communication* (pp. 216–26). Malden, MA: Wiley-Blackwell.

Carrillo Rowe, A. (2010b). For the love of Obama: Race, nation, and the politics of relation. In H. Harris, K. Moffitt & C. Squires (Eds.), *The Obama effect: Multidisciplinary renderings of the 2008 campaign* (pp. 221–32). Albany, NY: State University of New York Press.

Carroll, R. (1990). *Cultural misunderstandings: The French-American experience* (C. Volk, Trans.). Chicago, IL: University of Chicago Press.

Casmir, F. L. (1997). *Ethics in intercultural and international communication.* Mahwah, NJ: Lawrence Erlbaum.

Cavallaro, D. (2001). *Critical and cultural theory.* London: The Athlone Press.

Chang, Y. Y. (2010). Are you my guest of my child? Mothers' uncertainties in interacting with their returnee children in China. *Chinese Journal of Communication, 3,* 167–84.

Chávez, K. R. (2011). Counterpublic enclaves and understanding the function of rhetoric in social movement coalition building. *Communication Quarterly, 59*(1), 1–18.

Chávez, L. R. (2001). *Covering immigration: Popular images and the politics of the nation.* Berkeley, CA: University of California Press.

Chen, L. (2000). How we know what we know about Americans: How Chinese sojourners account for their experiences. In A. González, M. Houston, & V. Chen (Eds.), *Our voices: Essays in culture, ethnicity and communication* (3rd ed., pp. 220–27). Los Angeles, CA: Roxbury.

Cheney, G., & Ashcraft, K. L. (2007). Considering 'the professional' in communication studies: Implications for theory and research within and beyond the boundaries of organizational communication. *Communication Theory, 17*(2), 146–75.

Cheng, H.-I. (2008). *Culturing interface: Identity, communication, and Chinese transnationalism.* New York: Peter Lang.

Cheseboro, J. (1998). Distinguishing cultural systems: Change as a variable explaining and predicting cross-cultural communication. In D. V. Tanno & A. Gonzáles (Eds.), *Communication and identity across cultures, International and Intercultural Communication Annual* XXI (pp. 177–92). Thousand Oaks, CA: Sage.

Chuang, R. (2003). A postmodern critique of cross-cultural and intercultural communication research: Contesting essentialism, positivist dualism, and Eurocentricity. In W. J. Starosta & G.-M. Chen (Eds.), *Ferment in the intercultural field: Axiology/value/ praxis, International and Intercultural Communication Annual XXVI* (pp. 24–53). Thousand Oaks, CA: Sage.

Cisneros, J. D. (2008). Contaminated communities: The metaphor of "immigrant as pollutant" in media representations of immigration. *Rhetoric & Public Affairs, 11*(4), 569–601.

Cisneros, J. D. (2011). (Re)Bordering the civic imaginary: Rhetoric, hybridity, and citizenship in La Gran Marcha. *Quarterly Journal of Speech, 97*(1), 26–49.

Clifford, J. (1992). Traveling cultures. In L. Grossberg, C. Nelson & P. Treichler (Eds.), *Cultural studies* (pp. 96–116). New York: Routledge.

Clifford, J. (2000). Taking identity politics seriously: "The contradictory, stony ground . . ." In P. Gilroy, L., Grossberg & A. McRobbie (Eds.), *Without guarantees: In honour of Stuart Hall* (pp. 94–112). London: Verso.

Cohen, C. (2005). Punks, bulldaggers, and welfare queens: The radical potential of queer politics? In E. P. Johnson & M. A. Henderson (Eds.), *Black queer studies: A critical anthology* (pp. 21–51). Durham, NC: Duke University Press.

Cohen, M., & Avanzino, S. (2010). We are people first: Framing organizational assimilation experience of the physically disabled using co-cultural theory. *Communication Studies, 61*(3), 272–303.

Collective, C. R. (1983). A black feminist statement. In C. Moraga & G. Anzaldúa (Eds.), *This bridge called my back: Writings by radical women of color* (2nd ed., pp. 210-218). New York: Kitchen Table: Women of Color Press.

Collier, M. J. (1988). A comparison of conversations among and between domestic culture groups: How intra—intercultural competencies vary. *Communication Quarterly, 36*(2), 122–44.

Collier, M. J. (1989). Cultural and intercultural communication competence: Current approaches and directions for future research. *International Journal of Intercultural Relations, 13*, 287–302.

Collier, M. J. (1998). Researching cultural identity: Reconciling interpretive and postcolonial perspectives. In D. Tanno & A. González (Eds.), *Communication and identity across cultures, International and Intercultural Communication Annual XXI* (pp. 122–47). Thousand Oaks, CA: Sage.

Collier, M. J. (Ed.). (2001). *Transforming communication about culture: Critical new directions, International and Intercultural Communication Annual XXIV*. Thousand Oaks, CA: Sage.

Collier, M. J. (2005). Theorizing cultural identifications: Critical updates and continuing evolution. In W. B. Gudykunst (Ed.), *Theorizing about intercultural communication* (pp. 235–56). Thousand Oaks, CA: Sage.

Collier, M. J., Hedge, R. S., Lee, W., Nakayama, T. K., & Yep, G. A. (2002). Dialogue on the edges: Ferment in communication and culture. In M. J. Collier (Ed.), *Transforming communication about culture: Critical new directions, International and Intercultural Communication Annual XXIV* (pp. 219–80). Thousand Oaks, CA: Sage.

Collier, M. J., & Thomas, M. (1988). Cultural identity: An interpretive perspective. In Y. Y. Kim & W. B. Gudykunst (Eds.), *Theories in intercultural communication* (pp. 94–120). Newbury Park, CA: Sage.

Collins, P. H. (1986). Learning from the outsider within: The sociological significance of black feminist thought. *Social Problems, 33*(6), S14–S32.

Confucius Institute Headquarter (n.d.). Retrieved from www.hanban.edu.cn/ .

Conquergood, D. (1985). Performing as a moral act: Ethical dimensions of the ethnography of performance. *Literature in Performance, 5*(2), 1–13.

Conquergood, D. (1998). Beyond the text: Toward a performative cultural politics. In S. Dailey (Ed.), *The future of performance studies: Visions and revisions* (pp. 25–36). Washington, DC: National Communication Association.

Conquergood, D. (1991). Rethinking ethnography: Towards a critical cultural politics. *Communication Monographs, 58,* 179–94.

Cooks, L. (2010). Revisiting the borderlands of critical intercultural communication. In T. K. Nakayama & R. T. Halualani (Eds.), *The handbook of critical intercultural communication* (pp. 112–29). Malden, MA: Wiley-Blackwell.

Corey, F. C. (1998). The personal against the master narrative. In S. Dailey (Ed.), *The future of performance studies: Visions and revisions* (pp. 249–53). Washington, DC: National Communication Association.

Crenshaw, K. (1989). Demarginalizing the intersection of race and sex: A Black feminist critique of antidiscrimination doctrine, feminist theory and antiracist politics. *The University of Chicago Legal Forum,* 139–67.

Crenshaw, K. (1991). Mapping the margins: Intersectionality, identity politics and violence against women of color. *Stanford Law Review, 43,* 1241–1299.

Cross, W. (1991). *Shades of black: Diversity in African-American identity.* Philadelphia, PA: Temple University Press.

Cuban, L., & Shipps, D. (Eds.). (2000). *Reconstructing the common good in education: Coping with intractable American dilemmas.* Stanford, CA: Stanford University Press.

Cummins, J. (2003). Challenging the construction of difference as deficit: Where are identity, intellect, imagination, and power in the new regime of truth. In P. P. Trifonas (Ed.), *Pedagogies of difference: Rethinking education for social change* (pp. 41–60). New York: RoutledgeFalmer.

Cupach, W. R., & Imahori, T. T. (1993). Identity management theory: Communication competence in intercultural episodes and relationships. In R. L. Wiseman & J. Koester (Eds.), *Intercultural Communication Competence, International and Intercultural Communication Annual XVII* (pp. 112–131). Newbury Park, CA: Sage.

Dainian, Z., & Yishan, C. (1990). *Chinese culture and cultural arguments.* Beijing: Renmin University Press of China.

Dallmayr, F. (2002). Transversal liaisons: Calvin Schrag on selfhood. In B. Beck Matuštík & W. L. McBride (Eds.), *Calvin O. Schrag and the task of philosophy after postmodernity* (pp. 129–51). Evanston, IL: Northwestern University Press.

Daniels, R. (2003). Scattered remarks on the ideology of home. *The Minnesota Review, 58* (60), 187–95.

Darder, A. (2009). Teaching as an act of love: Reflections on Paulo Freire and his contributions to our lives and our work. In A. Darder, M. P. Baltodano, & R. D. Torres (Eds.), *The critical pedagogy reader* (2nd ed., pp. 567–78). New York: Routledge.

Darder, A., Baltodano, M. P., & Torres, R. D., (2009). Critical pedagogy: An introduction. In A. Darder, M. P. Baltodano & R. D. Torres (Eds.), *The critical pedagogy reader* (2nd ed., pp. 1–20). New York: Routledge.

Dash, M. (1995). In search of the lost body: Redefining the subject in Caribbean literature. In B. Ashcroft, B. G. Griffiths & H. Tiffin (Eds.), *The post-colonial studies reader* (pp. 202–05). New York: Routledge.

Dauenhauer, B. P. (2002). Schrag and the self. In B. Beck Matuštík & W. L. McBride (Eds.), *Calvin O. Schrag and the task of philosophy after postmodernity* (pp. 152–64). Evanston, IL: Northwestern University Press.

Davila, A. (1986). The seasonality of apprehensions of undocumented Mexican workers. *International Migration Review, 20*(4), 986–91.

Davis, F. J. (1991). *Who is Black: One nation's definition.* University Park, PA: Pennsylvania State University Press.

Davis, M., Dias-Bowie, Y., Greenberg, K., Klukken, G., Pollio, H. R., Thomas, S. P., & Thompson, C. L. (2004). "A Fly in the Buttermilk": Descriptions of university life by successful Black undergraduate students at a predominately white southeastern university. *The Journal of Higher Education, 75*(2), 420–45.

DeChaine, D. R. (2009). Bordering the civic imaginary: Alienization, fence logic, and the Minuteman Civil Defense Corps. *Quarterly Journal of Speech, 95*(1), 43–65 .

Delanty, G. (2006). The cosmopolitan imagination: Critical cosmopolitanism and social theory. *The British Journal of Sociology, 57*(1), 25–47.

Deleuze, G. (1994). *Difference and repetition* (P. Patton, Trans.). New York: Columbia University Press. (Original work published 1968).

Delgado, R. (1995). *The Rodrigo chronicles: Conversations about America and race*. New York: New York University Press.

Delgado, R. (2006). Rodrigo's roundelay: *Hernandez v. Texas* and the interest-convergence dilemma. *Harvard Law Review, 41*, 23–65.

Demo, A. T. (2005). Sovereignty discourse and contemporary immigration politics. *Quarterly Journal of Speech, 91*(3), 291–311.

Dempsey, S. E. (2009). NGOs, communicative labor, and the work of grassroots representation. *Communication & Critical/Cultural Studies, 6*(4), 328–45.

Denzin, N. (2003). *Performance ethnography: Critical pedagogy and the politics of culture*. Thousand Oaks, CA: Sage.

Denzin, N. K. (2006). Analytic autoethnography, or déjà vu all over again. *Journal of Contemporary Ethnography, 35*, 419–28.

Desai, A. (1980). *Clear light of day*. New York: Penguin.

DeSalvo, L. (1999). *Writing as a way of healing: How telling our stories transforms our lives*. Boston: Beacon Press.

Drummond, D. K., & Orbe, M. (2009). "Who are you trying to be?" Identity gaps within intraracial encounters. *Qualitative Research Reports in Communication, 10*(1), 81–87.

Drummond, D. K., & Orbe, M. P. (2010). Cultural contracts: Negotiating a ubiquitous U.S. dominant worldview on race and ethnicity. *Communication Studies, 61*(4), 373–90.

Drzewiecka, J. A., & Halualani, R. T. (2002). The structural-cultural dialectic of diasporic politics. *Communication Theory, 12*, 340–66.

Ellingsworth, H. W. (1983). Adaptive intercultural communication. In W. B. Gudykunst (Ed.), *Intercultural communication theory* (pp. 195–204). Beverly Hills, CA: Sage.

Ellis, C. (2004). *The ethnographic I: A methodological novel about autoethnography*. Walnut Creek, CA: AltaMira.

Ellis, C. S., & Bochner, A. P. (2006). Analyzing analytic autoethnography: An autopsy. *Journal of Contemporary Ethnography, 35*, 429–49.

Ellis, D. G., & Maoz, I. (2009). Dialogue, argument, and cultural communication codes between Israeli-Jews and Palestinians. In L. A. Samovar, R. E. Porter & E. R. McDaniel (Eds.), *Intercultural communication: A reader* (12th ed., pp. 244–50). Boston: Wadsworth Cengage Learning.

Eltahawy, M. (2011, January 15). Tunisia's jasmine revolution. *Washington Post*. Retrieved from www.washingtonpost.com/wp-dyn/content/article/2011/01/14/AR2011011405084.html

Evanoff, R. (2006). Ethics in intercultural dialogue. *International Journal of Intercultural Relations, 30*(4), 421–37.

Fassett, D. L. (2011, April). Eulogy delivered at Service to Celebrate the Life of John Thomas Warren, Carbondale, IL.

Fassett, D. L., & Warren, J. T. (2007). *Critical communication pedagogy*. Thousand Oaks, CA: Sage.

Fassett, D. L., & Warren, J. T. (Eds.). (2010). *The SAGE handbook of communication and instruction*. Thousand Oaks, CA: Sage.

Faulkner, S. L., Calafell, B. M., & Grimes, D. S. (2009). Hello Kitty goes to college: Poems about harassment in the academy. In M. Prendergast, C. Leggo, & P. Sameshima (Eds.), *Poetic inquiry: Vibrant voices in the social sciences* (pp. 187–208). Rotterdam: Sense Publishers.

Finnerty, D. (2004). An open letter to my white lesbian, gay, bisexual, transgender sisters and brothers. Retrieved from www.pflag.org/fileadmin/user_upload/An_Open_Letter_12-04.pdf

Fisher, W. S. (2008). Glimpses of home: Rhetorical and dialogical discourse promoting cosmopolitanism. In K. Robert & R. Arnett (Eds.), *Communication ethics: Between cosmopolitanism and provinciality* (pp. 47–68). New York: Peter Lang.

Fitzgerald, T. K. (1993). *Metaphors of identity: A culture-communication dialogue*. Albany, NY: State University of New York Press.

Flores, L. A. (1996). Creating discursive space through a rhetoric of difference: Chicana feminists craft a homeland. *The Quarterly Journal of Speech, 82*, 142–56.

Flores, L. A. (2000). Constructing national bodies: Public argument in the English-only movement. In T. A. Hollihan (Ed.), *Argument at centurys end: Reflecting on the past and envisioning the future* (pp. 436–45). Annandale, VA: National Communication Association.

Flores, L. A. (2003). Constructing rhetorical borders: Peons, illegal aliens, and competing narratives of immigration. *Critical Studies in Media Communication, 20*(4), 362–87.

Foeman, A. K. (2006). "Yo! What's it like to be Black?": An exercise to help students deepen the content of cross-cultural dialogue. *Communication Teacher, 20*(2), 40–43.

Ford, K. (2009). Critical incidents in the experiences of Japanese returnees. *Language and Intercultural Communication, 9*, 63–75.

Foucault, M. (1994). *Ethics: Subjectivity and truth*. In P. Rabinow (Ed.), *Essential works of Foucault, 1954–1984, Vol. I*. New York: The New Press.

Fox, R. C. (2007). Gay grows up: An interpretive study on aging metaphors and queer identity. *Journal of Homosexuality, 52*, 33–61.

Frazier, S. (2002). *All that apply: Finding wholeness as a multiracial person*. Downers Grove, IL: InterVarsity Press.

Freeman, M. (1998). Mythical time, historical time, and the narrative fabric of the self. *Narrative Inquiry, 8*(1), 27–50.

Freeman, M. (2002). Charting the narrative unconscious: Cultural memory and the challenge of autobiography. *Narrative Inquiry, 12* (1), 193–211.

Freud, S. (2003). *The uncanny*. New York: Penguin.

Frey, L. R., & Carragee, K. M. (Eds.). (2007). *Communication activism: Communication for social change* (Vol. 1). Cresskill, NJ: Hampton Press.

Friedman, J. (1999). Hybridization of roots and the abhorrence of the bush. In M. Featherstone & S. Lash (Eds.), *Spaces of culture: City-nation-world* (pp. 235–55). London: Sage.

Friedman, J., & Randheria, S. (Eds.). (2004). *Worlds on the move: Globalization, migration, and cultural security*. London: I. B. Tauris (in association with the Toda Institute for Global Peace and Policy Research).

Friedman, K. E., & Friedman, J. (2008). *Modernities, class, and the contradictions of globalization*. Lanham, MD: AltaMira.

Freire, P. (1970/2000). *Pedagogy of the oppressed* (thirtieth anniversary ed.). New York: Continuum.

Freire, P. (1974). *Education for critical consciousness*. New York: Continuum.

Freire, P. (1992). *Pedagogy of hope: Reliving pedagogy of the oppressed*. New York: Continuum.

Furia, P. (2005). Global citizenship, anyone? Cosmopolitanism, privilege, and public opinion. *Global Society, 19*, 331–59.

Gajjala, R. (2010). Placing South Asian digital diasporas in Second Life. In T. K. Nakayama & R. T. Halualani (Eds.), *The handbook of critical intercultural communication* (pp. 517–33). Malden, MA: Wiley-Blackwell.

Galinsky, A. D., Hugenberg, K, Groom, C., & Bodenhausen, G. (2003). The reappropriation of stigmatizing labels: Implications for social identity. *Research on Managing Groups and Teams, 5*, 221–56.

Gama, E., & Pedersen, P. (1977). Readjustment problems of Brazilian returnees from graduate studies in the United States. *International Journal of Intercultural Adjustment, 1*, 46–59.

Gavrilos, D. (2010). White males lose presidency for first time: Exposing the power of whiteness through Obama's victory. In H. Harris, K. Moffitt, & C. Squires (Eds.),

The Obama effect: Multidisciplinary renderings of the 2008 campaign (pp. 3–15). Albany, NY: State University of New York Press.

Gaw, K. F. (2000). Reverse culture shock in students returning from overseas. *International Journal of Intercultural Relations, 24*, 83–104.

Geertz, C. (1988). *Works and lives: The anthropologist as author.* Stanford, CA: Stanford University Press.

Gershenson, O. (2005). Postcolonial discourse analysis and intercultural communication: Modeling and connections. In W. Starosta & G-M. Chen (Eds.), *Taking stock in intercultural communication: Where to now?, International and Intercultural Communication Annual XXVIII* (pp. 124–42). Washington, DC: National Communication Association.

Gibson, K. L., Rimmington, G. M., & Landwher-Brown, M. (2008). Developing global awareness and responsible world citizenship with global learning. *Roeper Review, 30*, 11–23.

Giddens, A. (1991). *Modernity and self-identity: Self and society in the late modern age.* Stanford, CA: Stanford University Press.

Giroux, H. A. (2000). Insurgent multiculturalism and the promise of pedagogy. In E. M. Duarte & S. Smith (Eds.), *Foundational perspectives in multicultural education* (pp. 195–212). New York: Longman.

Giroux, H. A., & Shannon, P. (1997). Cultural studies and pedagogy as performative practice: Towards an introduction. In H. A. Giroux & P. Shannon (Eds.), *Education and cultural studies: Toward a performative practice* (pp. 1–9). New York: Routledge.

Glave, T. (2003). On the difficulty of confiding with complete love and trust, in some heterosexual "friends." *The Massachusetts Review, 44*, 583–95.

Godiwala, D. (2007). Postcolonial desire: Mimicry, hegemony, hybridity. In J. Kuortti & J. Nyman (Eds.), *Reconstructing hybridity: Post-colonial studies in transition* (pp. 59–79). Amsterdam: Rodopi, B.V.

Gold, T., Guthrie, D., & Wank, D. (2002). An introduction to the study of *quanxi.* In T. Gold, D. Guthrie & D. Wank (Eds.), *Social connections in China* (pp. 3–20). New York: Cambridge University Press.

Goldberg, D. (1993). *Racist culture: Philosophy and the politics of meaning.* Cambridge, MA: Blackwell.

Goldstein, D. (2011, February 20). The Wisconsin labor fight: An attack on women, too. Retrieved from www.danagoldstein.net/dana_goldstein/2011/02/the-wisconsin-labor-fight-an-attack-on-women-too.html.

González, A. (1989). Participation at WMEX-FM: Interventional rhetoric of Ohio Mexican Americans. *Western Journal of Speech Communication, 53*, 389–410.

González, A. (2010). Reflecting upon "Enlarging conceptual boundaries: A critique of research in intercultural communication." In T.K. Nakayama & R.T. Halualani (Eds.), *The handbook of critical intercultural communication* (pp. 53–58). Malden, MA: Wiley-Blackwell.

Goodall Jr., H. L. (2000). *Writing the new ethnography.* Lanham, MD: Altamira Press.

Griffin, R. (2010). "Yes we can," "Yes we did,"but no we haven't: Marking a moment while remembering reality. *Reflections: Narratives of Professional Helping, 16*(1), 6–4.

Griffin, R. (2011). Placing my brown body on the line: Painful moments and powerful praxis. In M. N. Niles & N. S. Gordon (Eds.), *Still searching for our mothers' gardens: Experiences of new, tenure-track women of color at 'majority' institutions* (pp. 174–91). Lanham, MD: University Press of America.

Gudykunst, W. B. (Ed.). (1983). *Intercultural communication theory: Current perspectives, International and Intercultural Communication Annual VII.* Beverly Hills, CA: Sage.

Gudykunst, W. B., & Hammer, M. (1988). The influence of social identity and intimacy of interethnic groups on uncertainty reduction processes. *Human Communication Research, 14*, 569–601.

Gudykunst, W. B., & Kim, Y. Y. (2003a). *Communicating with strangers: An approach to intercultural communication* (4th ed.). Boston: McGraw-Hill.

Gudykunst, W.B., & Kim, Y. Y. (Eds). (2003b). *Readings on communicating with strangers: An approach to intercultural communication*. Boston: McGraw-Hill.

Gunesch, K. (2004). International education's internationalism complemented by cosmopolitanism: A personal cultural identity model. *IB Research News, 4*, 1–11.

Gust, S. W., & Warren, J. T. (2008). Naming our sexual and sexualized bodies in the classroom: And the important stuff that comes after the colon. *Qualitative Inquiry, 14*, 114–34.

Hall, B. "J." (2004). *Among cultures: The challenges of communication*. Belmont, CA: Wadsworth.

Hall, M. L. (2010). Re-constituting place and space: Culture and communication in the construction of a Jamaican transnational identity. *Howard Journal of Communications, 21*, 119–40.

Hall, M. L., Keane-Dawes, J., & Rodriguez, A. (2004). *Embodying the postcolonial life: stories of immigrant resistance*. Amherst, NY: Humanity Books.

Hall, S. (1990). Cultural identity and diaspora. In J. Rutherford (Ed.), *Identity: Community, culture and difference* (pp. 222–37). London: Lawrence & Wishart.

Hall, S. (1996). Introduction: Who needs identity? In S. Hall & P. du Gay (Eds.), *Questions of cultural identity* (pp. 1–17). London: Sage.

Hall, S. (1997). The local and the global: Globalization and ethnicity. In A. King (Ed.), *Culture, globalization and the world-system* (pp. 19–39). Minneapolis, MN: University of Minnesota Press.

Hall, S. (2002). *Representation: Cultural representations and signifying practices*. London: Sage.

Hall, S., & Werbner, P. (2008). Cosmopolitanism, globalisation and diaspora: Stuart Hall in conversation with Pnina Werbner. In P. Werbner (Ed.), *Anthropology and the new cosmopolitanism: Rooted, feminist, and vernacular perspectives* (pp. 345–60). New York: Berg.

Halualani, R. (2002). Connecting Hawaiians: The politics of authenticity in the Hawaiian diaspora. In M. J. Collier (Ed.), *Intercultural alliances: Critical transformation, International and Intercultural Communication Annual XXV* (pp. 221–48). Thousand Oaks, CA: Sage.

Halualani, R. T. (2008). "Where exactly is the Pacific?": Global migrations, diasporic movements, and intercultural communication. *Journal of International and Intercultural Communication, 1*(1), 3–22.

Halualani, R. T., Mendoza, L., & Drzewiecka, J. A. (2009). "Critical" junctures in intercultural communication studies: A review. *The Review of Communication, 9*(1), 17–35.

Halualani, R. T., & Nakayama, T. K. (2011). Critical intercultural communication studies: At a crossroads. In T. K. Nakayama & R. T. Halualani (Eds.), *The handbook of critical intercultural communication* (pp. 1–16). Malden, MA: Wiley-Blackwell.

Hannerz, U. (1996). *Transnational connections: Culture, people, places*. London: Routledge.

Hansen, D. T., Burdick-Shepherd, S., Cammarano, C., & Obelleiro, G. (2009). Education, values, and valuing in cosmopolitan perspective. *Curriculum Inquiry, 39*, 587–612.

Hansen, K, T. (1992). *African encounters with domesticity*. New Brunswick, NJ: Rutgers University Press.

Hardiman, R. (2003). White racial identity development in the United States. In E. P. Salett & D. R. Koslow (Eds.), *Race, ethnicity and self* (2nd ed., pp. 117–36). Washington, DC: National Multicultural Institute.

Hardt, M., & Negri, A. (2000). *Empire*. Cambridge, MA: Harvard University Press.

Hardt, M., & Negri, A. (2004). *Multitude: War and democracy in the age of empire*. New York: Penguin Press.

Harris, D. R., & Sim, J. J. (2001). *An empirical look at the social construction of race: The case of multiracial adolescents* (Research Report No. 00-452). Ann Arbor, MI: University of Michigan Press, Population Studies Center.

Harris, L. (2003). The cosmopolitan illusion. *Policy Review, 118*, 45–59.

Harvey, M. G. (1989). Repatriation of corporate executives: An empirical study. *Journal of International Business Studies, 20*(1), 131–44.

Hasan, M. (1993). *India's partition: Process, strategy and mobilization.* New Delhi: Oxford University Press.

Hasan, M. (Ed.). (2000). *Inventing boundaries: Gender, politics and the partition of India.* New Delhi: Oxford University Press.

Hasian, M. Jr., & Delgado, F. (1998). Trials and tribulations of racialized critical rhetorical theory: Understanding the rhetorical ambiguities of Proposition 187. *Communication Theory, 8*(3), 245–70.

Hauser, G. A., & Whalen, S. (1997). New rhetoric and new social movements. In B. Kovčić (Ed.), *Emerging theories of human communication* (pp. 115–40). Albany, NY: State University of New York Press.

Hecht, M. L. (1993). A research odyssey: Towards the development of a communication theory of identity. *Communication Monographs, 60,* 76–82.

Hecht, M. L., Collier, M. J., & Ribeau, S. (1993). *African-American communication: Ethnic identity and cultural interpretation.* Newbury Park, CA: Sage.

Hecht, M. L., Jackson II, R. L., & Ribeau, S. A. (2003). *African American communication: Exploring identity and culture* (2nd ed.). Mahwah, NJ: Lawrence Erlbaum Associates.

Hecht, M. L., Warren, J. R., Jung, E., & Krieger, J. L. (2005). The communication theory of identity: Development, theoretical perspective, and future directions. In W. B. Gudykunst (Ed.), *Theorizing about intercultural communication* (pp. 257–78). Thousand Oaks, CA: Sage.

Hegde, R. S. (1997). Hybrid revivals: Defining Asian Indian ethnicity through celebration. In A. Gonzalez, M. Houston & V. Chen (Eds.), *Our voices: Essays in culture, ethnicity, and communication* (2nd ed., pp. 129–35). Los Angeles: Roxbury.

Hegde, R. S. (1998). Swinging the trapeze: The negotiation of identity among Asian Indian immigrant women in the United States. In D. Tanno & A. González (Eds.), *Communication and identity across cultures, International and Intercultural Communication Annual XXI* (pp. 34–55). Thousand Oaks, CA: Sage.

Hegde, R. S. (2002). Translated enactments: The relational configurations of the Asian Indian immigrant experience. In J. N. Martin, T. K. Nakayama & L. A. Flores (Eds.), *Readings in intercultural communication: Experiences and contexts* (2nd ed., pp. 259–66). Boston: McGraw Hill.

Heidegger, M. (1993). *Basic writings.* San Francisco: Harper.

Hendrix, K. G. (2011). The growth stages and maturation of an outsider-within: Developing a critical gaze and earning the right to speak. *Qualitative Inquiry, 17*(4), 315–24.

Hicks, J. (Ed.). (2000). *The literature of California.* Berkley, CA: University of California Press.

Hill Collins, P. (2008). *Black feminist thought: Knowledge, consciousness, and the politics of empowerment.* New York: Routledge.

Holling, M. A. (2006). Forming oppositional social concord to California's Proposition 187 and squelching social discord in the vernacular space of CHICLE. *Communication and Critical/Cultural Studies, 3*(3), 202–22.

Holling, M. A., & Calafell, B. (2007). Identities on stage and staging identities: ChicanoBrujo performances as emancipatory practices. *Text and Performance Quarterly, 27*(1), 58–83.

Holling, M. A. & B. M. Calafell (Eds.) (2011). *Latina/o Discourse in vernacular spaces: Somos de una voz?* Lanham, MD: Lexington Books.

Holling, M. A., Fu, M., & Bubar, R. (in press). Dis/jointed appointments: Solidarity amidst inequity, tokenism and marginalization. In G. Chang, C. G. González, M. Romero, Y. F. Niemann, A. Harris & G. Gutiérrez y Muhs (Eds.), *Presumed incompetent: The intersections of race and class for women in academia.* Logan, UT: Utah State University Press.

Hollinger, D. (2006). *Postethnic America: Beyond multiculturalism.* New York: Basic Books.

hooks, b. (1989). *Talking back: Thinking feminist, thinking black*. Boston: South End Press.

hooks, b. (1990). *Yearning: Race, gender and cultural politics*. Boston: South End Press.

hooks, b. (1994). *Teaching to transgress: Education as the practice of freedom*. New York: Routledge.

hooks, b. (2001). *All about love*. New York: Perennial.

hooks, b. (2010). Living to love. In G. Kirk & M. Okazawa-Rey (Eds.), *Women's lives: Multicultural perspectives* (5th ed., pp. 250–55). Boston: McGraw-Hill.

Hopson, M. C., & Orbe, M. (2007). Playing the game: Recalling dialectical tensions for Black men in oppressive organizational structures. *Howard Journal of Communications, 18*, 69–86.

Horner, W., & Gaillet, L. (Eds.). (2010). *The present state of scholarship in historical and contemporary rhetoric* (3rd ed). Columbia, MO: University of Missouri Press.

Houston, M. (1992). The politics of difference: Race, class, and women's communication. In L. F. Rakow (Ed.), *Women making meaning: New feminist directions in communication* (pp. 45–59). New York: Routledge.

HuffingtonPost.com (2011, April 22). Tennessee "Don't Say Gay" bill advances in state senate. Retrieved from www.huffingtonpost.com/2011/04/22/tennessee-dont-say-gay-bill-advances_n_852616.html.

Hull, G. T., Scott, P. B., & Smith, B. (Eds.). (1982). *All the women are white, all the blacks are men, but some of us are brave: Black women's studies*. New York: Feminist Press.

Hytten, K., & Adkins, A. (2001). Thinking through a pedagogy of whiteness. *Educational Theory, 51*, 433–50.

Imahori, T. T. (2001). Validation of identity management theory in Japan: A comparison of intraethnic and interethnic communication. *Studies in English Language and Literature, Seinan Gakuin University, 42*(2), 25–50.

Imahori, T. T., & Cupach, W. R. (2005). Identity management theory: Facework in intercultural relationships. In W. B. Gudykunst (Ed.), *Theorizing about intercultural communication* (pp. 195–210). Thousand Oaks, CA: Sage.

Inda, J. X. (2000). Performativity, materiality, and the racial body. *Latino Studies Journal, 11*(3), 74–99.

Isa, M. (2000). Phenomenological analysis of the reentry experiences of the wives of Japanese corporate sojourners. *Women and Language, 23*(2), 26–40.

Iweala, U. (2008, January 23). Race still matters: Obama's success doesn't mean that America is "post-racial." *Los Angeles Times*. Retrieved from articles.latimes.com/2008/jan/23/opinion/oe-iweala23.

Jackman, M. C. (2010). The trouble with fieldwork: Queering methodologies. In K. Browne & C. J. Nash (Eds.), *Queer methods and methodologies: Intersecting queer theories and social science research* (pp. 113–28). Burlington, VT: Ashgate.

Jackson II, R. L. (1999). White space, white privilege: Mapping discursive inquiry into the self. *Quarterly Journal of Speech, 85*, 38–54.

Jackson II, R. L. (2002a). Cultural contracts theory: Toward an understanding of identity negotiation. *Communication Quarterly, 50*(3/4), 359–67.

Jackson II, R. L. (2002b). Introduction: Theorizing and analyzing the nexus between cultural and gendered identities and the body. *Communication Quarterly, 50*(3&4), 242–50.

Jackson II, R. L. (2006). *Scripting the black masculine body: Identity, discourse, and racial politics in popular media*. Albany, NY: SUNY Press.

Jackson II, R. L., & Crawley, R. L. (2003). White student confessions about a black male professor: A cultural contracts theory approach to intimate conversations about race and worldview. *Journal of Men's Studies, 12*(1), 25–41.

Jackson II, R. L., & Garner, T. (1998). Tracing the evolution of "race," "ethnicity," and "culture" in communication studies. *Howard Journal of Communications, 9*, 41–55.

Jackson II, R., & Moshin, J. (2010). Identity and difference: Race and the necessity of the discriminating subject. In T. K. Nakayama & R. T. Halualani (Eds.), *The handbook of critical intercultural communication* (pp. 348–63). Malden, MA: Wiley-Blackwell.

Jackson, S. (2004). *Professing performance: Theatre in the academy from philology to performativity*. Cambridge, UK: Cambridge University Press.

Jacobs, J. H. (1992). Identity development in biracial children. In M. P. P. Root (Ed.), *Racially mixed people in America* (pp. 190–206). Newbury Park, CA: Sage.

Jacobson, R. D. (2008). *The new nativism: Proposition 187 and the debate over immigration*. Minneapolis: University of Minnesota Press.

Jagose, A. (1996). *Queer theory: An introduction*. Melbourne: Melbourne University Press.

James, A. D., & Tucker, M. B. (2003). Racial ambiguity and relationship formation in the United States: Theoretical and practical considerations. *Journal of Social and Personal Relationships, 20*(2), 153–69.

James, J., & Farmer, R. (Eds.). (1993). *Spirit, space, and survival: African American women in (white) academe*. New York: Routledge.

Jameson, D. A. (2007). Reconceptualizing cultural identity and its role in intercultural business communication. *Journal of Business Communication, 44*(3), 199–235.

Jameson, F. (1998). Note on globalization as a philosophical issue. In F. Jameson & M. Miyoshi (Eds.), *The cultures of globalization* (pp. 54–77). Durham, NC: Duke University Press.

Jansson, D. P. (1975). Return to society: Problematic features of the re-entry process. *Perspectives in Psychiatric Care, 13*, 130–45.

Jeffries, T. (2002). An autoethnographical exploration of racial 'I'dentity. *Journal of Intergroup Relations, 24*(2), 39–56.

Jen, G. (1991). *Typical American*. Boston: Houghton Mifflin.

Johnson, E. P. (2001). "Quare" studies, or (almost) everything I know about queer studies

I learned from my grandmother. *Text and Performance Quarterly, 21*, 1–25.

Johnson, E. P. (2006). "Quare" studies, or (almost) everything I know about queer studies I learned from my grandmother. In E. P. Johnson & M. G. Henderson (Eds.) *Black queer studies: A critical anthology* (pp. 124–57). Durham, NC: Duke University Press.

Johnson, J. D., & Tuttle, F. (1989). Problems in intercultural research. In M. K. Asante & W. B. Gudykunst (Eds.), *Handbook of international and intercultural communication* (pp. 461–83). Newbury Park, CA: Sage.

Joseph, R. (in press). The conundrum of the Obama bumper sticker: Reading overtly and inferentially racist images of Barack Obama. *Communication Studies, 62*(4).

Jones, S. (2010). The Obama effect on American discourse about racial identity: Dreams from my father (and mother), Barack Obama's search for self. In H. Harris, K. Moffitt & C. Squires (Eds.), *The Obama effect: Multidisciplinary renderings of the 2008 campaign* (pp. 131–52). Albany, NY: State University of New York Press.

Johnson, J. R., & Bhatt, A. J. (2003). Gendered and racialized identities and alliances in the classroom: Formations in/of resistive space. *Communication Education, 52*(3/4), 230–44.

Jones Jr., R. G. (2010). Putting privilege into practice through "intersectional reflexivity": Ruminations, interventions, and possibilities. *Reflections: Narratives for Professional Healing, 10*(1), 122–25.

Jones Jr., R. G., & Calafell, B. M. (in press). Contesting neoliberalism through critical pedagogy, intersectional reflexivity, and personal narrative: Queer tales of academia. *Journal of Homosexuality*.

Jung, E., Hecht, M. L., & Wadsworth, B. C. (2007). The role of identity in international students' psychological well-being: A model of depression level, identity gap, discrimination, and acculturation. *International Journal of Intercultural Relations, 31*, 605–24.

Justus, Z. S. (2009). *Uniting to divide: Coalitional politics and the Minutemen*. Unpublished doctoral dissertation, Arizona State University, Phoenix.

Kanneh, K. (1995). Feminism and the colonial body. In B. Ashcroft, G. Griffiths, & H. Tiffin (Eds.), *The post-colonial studies reader* (pp. 202–205). New York: Routledge.

Kanno, Y. (2000). Bilingualism and identity: The stories of Japanese returnees. *International Journal of Bilingual Education and Bilingualism, 3*(1), 1–17.

Kanno, Y. (2003). *Negotiating bilingual and bicultural identities: Japanese returnees betwixt two worlds.* Mahwah, NJ: Lawrence Erlbaum.

Kaplan, C. (1996). *Questions of travel: Postmodern discourses of displacement.* Durham, NC: Duke University Press.

Kashima, E. S., & Loh, E. (2006). International students' acculturation: Effects of international, conational, and local ties and need for closure. *International Journal of Intercultural Relations, 30*, 471–86.

Kaufmann, E. (2003). The rise of cosmopolitanism in the 20th-century West: A comparative-historical perspective on the United States and European Union. *Global Society, 17*(4), 359–83.

Kaur, R. (2007). *Since 1947: Partition narratives among Punjabi migrants of Delhi.* London: Oxford University Press.

Kellas, J. K. (2005). Family ties: Communicating identity through jointly told family stories. *Communication Monographs, 72* (4), 365–89.

Khan, Y. (2007). *The great Partition: The making of India and Pakistan.* New Haven, CT: Yale University Press.

Kich, G. K. (1992). The development process of asserting a biracial, bicultural identity. In M. P. P. Root (Ed.), *Racially mixed people in America* (pp. 304–17). Newbury Park, CA: Sage.

Kim, M.-S. (2002). *Non-western perspectives on human communication.* Thousand Oaks, CA: Sage.

Kim, Y. Y. (1977). Communication patterns of foreign immigrants in the process of acculturation. *Human Communication Research, 4*(1), 66–77.

Kim, Y. Y. (1997). Adapting to a new culture. In L.A. Samovar & R.E. Porter (Eds.), *Intercultural communication* (8th ed., pp. 405–16). Belmont, CA: Wadsworth Publishing.

Kim, Y. Y. (2001). *Becoming intercultural: An integrative theory of communication and cross-cultural adaptation.* Thousand Oaks, CA: Sage.

Kim, Y. Y. (2002). Cross-cultural adaptation: An integrative theory. In J. N. Martin, T. K. Nakayama, & L. A. Flores (Eds.), *Readings in cultural contexts* (2nd ed., pp. 237–45). Boston: McGraw-Hill.

Kim, Y. Y, (2005a). Association and disassociation: A contextual theory of interethnic communication. In W. B. Gudykunst (Ed.), *Theorizing about intercultural communication* (pp. 322–50). Thousand Oaks, CA: Sage.

Kim, Y. Y. (2005b). Adapting to a new culture: An integrative communication theory. In W. B. Gudykunst (Ed.), *Theorizing about intercultural communication* (pp. 375–400). Thousand Oaks, CA: Sage.

Kim, Y. Y. (2006). From ethnic to interethnic: The case for identity adaptation and transformation. *Journal of Language and Social Psychology, 25*(3), 283–300.

Kim, Y. Y. (2007). Ideology, identity, and intercultural communication: An analysis of differing academic conceptions of cultural identity. *Journal of Intercultural Communication Research, 36*(3), 237–53.

Kim, Y. Y. (2008). Intercultural personhood: Globalization and a way of being. *International Journal of Intercultural Relations, 32*, 359–68.

Kinefuchi, E. (2010a). Finding home in migration: Montagnard refugees and post-migration identity. *Journal of International and Intercultural Communication, 3*, 228–48.

Kinefuchi, E. (2010b). Layers of Nikkei: Japanese diaspora and World War II. In T. K. Nakayama, & R. T. Halualani (Eds.), *The handbook of critical intercultural communication* (pp. 495–516). Malden, MA: Wiley-Blackwell.

Kingston, M. H. (1980). *China men.* New York: Vintage International.

Kingston, M. H. (1989/1976). *The woman warrior.* New York: Vintage International.

Kingston, M. H. (1989/1987). *Tripmaster monkey: His fake book.* New York: Alfred A. Knopf.

Kirby, E. (2007). Organizing to "meet like real Americans": The case of a Hmong nonprofit organization. In B. J. Allen, L. A. Flores, & M. P. Orbe (Eds.), *Communication within/across organizations* (pp. 201–28). Washington, DC: National Communication Association.

Kondo, D. (1997). *About face: Performing race in fashion and theater*. New York: Routledge.

Kondo, D. (1996). The narrative production of "home," community, and political identity in Asian American theater. In S. Lavie & T. Swedenburg (Eds.), *Displacement, diaspora, and geographies of identity* (pp. 97–119). Durham, NC: Duke University Press.

Kraidy, M. (2002). Hybridity in cultural globalization. *Communication Theory, 12*(3), 316–39.

Kraidy, M. (2005). *Hybridity, or the cultural logic of globalization*. Philadelphia, PA: Temple University Press.

Krishna, S. (2009). *Globalization and postcolonialism: Hegemony and resistance in the twenty-first century*. Lanham, MD: Rowman & Littlefield Publishers, Inc.

Koester, J. (1984). Communication and the intercultural reentry: A course proposal. *Communication Education, 33*, 251–56.

Kosciw, J. G., Greytak, E. A., Diaz, E. M., & Bartkiewicz, M. J. (2010). *The 2009 National School Climate Survey: The experiences of lesbian, gay, bisexual and transgender youth in our nation's schools*. New York: GLSEN.

Kuhn, T. S. (1996). *The structure of scientific revolutions* (3rd ed.). Chicago: The University of Chicago Press.

Kuo, E., & Chew, H. E. (2009). Beyond ethnocentrism in communication theory: towards a culture-centric approach. *Asian Journal of Communication, 19*, 422–37.

LaBrack, B. (1993). The missing link: The process of integrating orientation and reentry. In R. M. Paige (Ed.), *Education for the intercultural experience* (pp. 241–80). Yarmouth, ME: Intercultural Press.

Langellier, K. M. (1999). Personal narrative, performance, performativity: Two or three things I know for sure. *Text and Performance Quarterly, 19*, 125–44.

Langellier, K. M., & Peterson, E. E. (2004). *Storytelling in daily life*. Philadelphia, PA: Temple University Press.

Langellier, K. M., & Peterson, E. E. (2006). Family storytelling as communication practice. In L. H. Turner & R. West (Eds.), *The family communication sourcebook* (pp. 109–128). Thousand Oaks, CA: Sage.

Lather, P. (1991). *Getting smart: Feminist research and pedagogy with/in the postmodern*. New York: Routledge.

Lavie, S., & Swedenburg, T. (1996). Introduction: Displacement, diaspora, and geographies of identity. In S. Lavie & T. Swedenburg (Eds.), *Displacement, diaspora, and geographies of identity* (pp. 1–25). Durham, NC: Duke University Press.

Leeds-Hurwitz, W. (1990). Notes in the history of intercultural communication: The foreign service institute and the mandate for intercultural training. *Quarterly Journal of Speech, 76*, 262–81.

Lewis, E. (2006). *Fade: My journeys in multiracial America*. New York: Carroll & Graf Publishers.

Lewis, T., & Cho, D. (2006). Home is where neurosis is: A topography of the spatial unconscious. *Cultural Critique, 74*, 69–91.

Lockford, L. (2002). Breaking habits and cultivating home. In A. P. Bochner & C. Ellis (Eds.), *Ethnographically speaking: Autoethnography, literature, and aesthetics* (pp. 76–86). Walnut Creek, CA: AltaMira.

Loomba, A. (1998). *Colonialism/postcolonialism*. New York: Routledge.

Lopez, D., & Sanchez-Criado, T. (2009). Dwelling the telecare home: Place, location, and habitality. *Space and Culture, 12*(3), 343–58.

Lorde, A. (1983a). The master's tools will never dismantle the master's house. In C. Moraga & G. Anzaldúa (Eds.), *This bridge called my back: Writings by radical women of color* (2nd ed., pp. 98–101). New York: Kitchen Table: Women of Color Press.

Lorde, A. (1983b). There is no hierarchy of oppressions. *Interracial Books for Children Bulletin, 14*(3–4), 9.

Lorde, A. (1984). Age, race, class, and sex: Women redefining difference. In A. Lorde (Ed.), *Sister outsider: Essays and Speeches* (pp. 114–23). Berkeley: The Crossing Press.

Louie, D. W. (1991). *Pangs of Love.* New York: Alfred A. Knopf.

Louisy, P. (2001). Globalisation and comparative education: A Caribbean perspective. *Comparative Education, 37*(4), 425–38.

Lovaas, K. E. (2010). Sexualities and critical communication pedagogy. In D. L. Fassett & J. T. Warren (Eds.), *The SAGE handbook of communication and instruction* (pp. 385–409). Thousand Oaks, CA: Sage.

Lugones, M. (2003). *Pilgrimages/Peregrinajes: Theorizing coalition against multiple oppressions.* Lanham, MD: Rowman & Littlefield, Inc.

Luibhéid, E. (2004). Heternormativity and immigration scholarship: A call for change. *GLQ, 10*(2), 227–35.

Lysgaard, S. (1955). Adjustment in a foreign society: Norwegian Fulbright grantees visiting the United States. *International Social Science Bulletin, 7,* 45–51

Macedo, D. (2000). Introduction. In P. Freire (author), *Pedagogy of the oppressed.* (pp. 11–27). New York: Continuum.

MacLennan, J. (2011). "To build a beautiful dialogue": Capoeira as contradiction. *Journal of International and Intercultural Communication, 4*(2), 146–62.

Madison, D. S. (1993). "That was my occupation": Oral narrative, performance, and black feminist thought. *Text and Performance Quarterly, 13*(3), 213–32.

Madison, D. S. (1998). Performance, personal narratives, and the politics of possibility. In S. Dailey (Ed.), *The future of performance studies: Visions and revisions* (pp. 176–86). Washington, DC: National Communication Association.

Madison, D. S. (2005). *Critical ethnography: Methods, ethics and performance.* Thousand Oaks, CA: Sage.

Madison, D. S. (2006). The dialogic performative in critical ethnography. *Text and Performance Quarterly, 26*(4), 320-324.

Madison, D. S. (2010). *Acts of activism: Human rights as radical performance.* Cambridge: Cambridge University Press.

Makeham, J. (2008). *Lost soul: 'Confucianism' in contemporary Chinese academic discourse.* Cambridge, MA: Harvard University Asia Center.

Mannheim, B., & Tedlock, D. (1995). Introduction. In D. Tedlock & B. Manneheim (Eds.), *The dialogic emergence of culture* (pp. 1–32). Urbana and Chicago, IL: University of Illinois Press.

Manning, R. D., & Butera, A. C. (2000). Global restructuring and U.S.-Mexican economic integration: Rhetoric and reality of Mexican immigration five years after NAFTA. *American Studies, 41*(2/3), 183–209.

Martin, B., & Mohanty, C. (1986). Feminist politics: What's home got to do with it? In T. de Lauretis (Ed.), *Feminist studies/critical studies* (pp. 191–212). Bloomington, IN: Indiana University Press.

Martin, J. N. (1984). The intercultural re-entry: Conceptualization and directions for future research. *International Journal of Intercultural Relations, 8,* 115–34.

Martin, J. N. (1986). Communication in the intercultural reentry: Student sojourners' perceptions of change in reentry relationships. *International Journal of Intercultural Relations, 10,* 1–22.

Martin, J. N., Bradford, L., & Rohrlich, B. (1995). Comparing predeparture expectations and post-sojourn reports: A longitudinal study of U.S. students abroad. *International Journal of Intercultural Relations, 19,* 87–110.

Martin, J. N., & Harrell, T. (1996). Reentry training for intercultural sojourners. In D. Landis & R. S. Bhagat (Eds.), *Handbook of intercultural training,* (2nd ed., pp. 307–26). Thousand Oaks, CA: Sage.

Martin, J. N., & Nakayama, T. K. (1999). Thinking dialectically about culture and communication. *Communication Theory, 9*(1), 1–25.

Martin, J. N., & Nakayama, T. K. (2003). *Intercultural communication in contexts* (3rd ed.). Columbus, OH: McGraw-Hill.

Martin, J. N., & Nakayama, T. K. (2008). Thinking dialectically about culture and communication. In M. K. Asante, Y. Miike, & J. Yin (Eds.), *The global intercultural communication reader* (pp. 73–92). New York: Routledge.

Martin, J. N., & Nakayama, T. K. (2010). *Intercultural communication in contexts* (5th ed.). Boston: McGraw-Hill.

Matsunaga, M., & Torigoe, C. (2008). Looking at the Japan-Residing Korean identities through the eyes of the 'outsiders within:' Application and extension of co-cultural theory. *Western Journal of Communication, 72*(4), 349–73.

May, S. (1999). Critical multiculturalism and cultural difference: Avoiding essentialism. In S. May (Ed.), *Critical multiculturalism: Rethinking multicultural and antiracist education* (pp. 11–41). Philadelphia, PA: Falmer Press.

May, T. (2005). *Gilles Deleuze: An introduction.* Cambridge: Cambridge University Press.

McCarthy, C. (1993). After the canon: Knowledge and ideology representation in the multicultural discourse on curriculum reform. In C. McCarthy & W. Crichlow (Eds.), *Race identity and representation in education* (pp. 289–305). New York: Routledge.

McDonald, K. (2002). From solidarity to fluidarity: Social movements beyond 'collective identity'—the case of globalization conflicts. *Social Movement Studies, 1*(2), 109–28.

McEwan, B., & Sobre-Denton, M. S. (in press). Virtual cosmopolitanism: Constructing third cultures and transmitting social and cultural capital through social media. *Journal of International and Intercultural Communication.*

McIntosh, D. M. (2011). *Performing an embodied feminist aesthetic: A critical performance ethnography of the equestrian sport culture.* Unpublished doctoral dissertation. Denver, CO: University of Denver.

McIntosh, P. (1989, July/August). White privilege: Unpacking the invisible knapsack. *Peace and Freedom Magazine,* 10–12.

McKinnon, S. L. (2009). Citizenship and the performance of credibility: Audiencing gender-based asylum seekers in U.S. immigration courts. *Text and Performance Quarterly, 29*(3), 205–21.

McLaren, P. (1999). *Schooling as ritual performance: Toward a political economy of educational symbols and gestures* (3rd ed.). Lanham, MD: Rowman & Littlefield, Inc.

Mehan, H. (1997). The discourse of the illegal immigration debate: A case study in the politics of representation. *Discourse & Society, 8*(2), 249–70.

Mendoza, S. L. (2002a). *Between the homeland and the diaspora: The politics of theorizing Filipino and Filipino American identities—A second look at the poststructuralism-indigenization debates.* New York: Routledge.

Mendoza, S. L. (2002b). Bridging theory and cultural politics: Revisiting the indigenization-poststructuralism debate in Filipino and Filipino American struggles for identity. In M. J. Collier (Ed.), *Intercultural alliances: Critical transformations, International and Intercultural Communication Annual XXV* (pp. 249–77). Thousand Oaks, CA: Sage.

Mendoza, S. L. (2010). Reflections on 'Bridging paradigms: How not to throw the baby of collective representation with the functionalist bathwater in critical intercultural communication.' In T. K. Nakayama & R. T. Halualani (Eds.), *The handbook of critical intercultural communication* (pp. 98–111). Malden, MA: Wiley-Blackwell.

Mendoza, S. L., Halualani, R. T., & Drzewiecka, J. A. (2002). Moving the discourse on identities in intercultural communication: Structure, culture, and resignifications. *Communication Quarterly, 50*(3&4), 312–27.

Menon, R., & Bhasin, K. (1998). *Borders & boundaries: Women in India's partition.* New Delhi: Kali for Women.

Meyers, M. (2004). African American women and violence: Gender, race, and class in the news. *Critical Studies in Media Communication, 21*(2), 95–118.

Miike, Y. (2007). An Asiacentric reflection on Eurocentric bias in communication theory. *Communication Monographs, 74*, 272–78.

Miike, Y. (2010). Culture as text and culture as theory: Asiacentricity and its *raison d'être* in intercultural communication research. In T. K. Nakayama & R. T. Halualani (Eds.), *The handbook of critical intercultural communication* (pp. 190–215). Malden, MA: Wiley-Blackwell.

Miller, K. (2005). *Communication theories: Perspectives, processes, and contexts* (2nd ed.). Boston: McGraw Hill.

Miyoshi, M. (1993). A borderless world? From colonialism to transnationalism and the decline of the nation-state. *Critical Inquiry, 19*(4), 726–51.

Moffitt, K. R. (2010). Framing a first lady: Media coverage of Michelle Obama's role in the 2008 presidential election. In H. Harris, K. Moffitt, & C. Squires (Eds.), *The Obama effect: Multidisciplinary renderings of the 2008 campaign* (pp. 233–49). Albany, NY: State University of New York Press.

Montagu, A. (1997). *Man's most dangerous myth: The fallacy of race* (6th ed.). Walnut Creek, CA: AltaMira Press.

Moon, D. G. (1996). Concepts of 'culture': Implications for intercultural communication research. *Communication Quarterly, 44*, 70–84.

Moon, D. G. (2001). Interclass travel, cultural adaptation, and 'passing' as a disjunctive inter/cultural practices. In M. J. Collier (Ed.), *Constituting cultural difference through discourse* (pp. 215–40). Thousand Oaks, CA: Sage.

Moon, D. G. (2002). Thinking about 'culture' in intercultural communication. In J. N. Martin, T. K. Nakayama & L. A. Flores (Eds.), *Readings in intercultural communication* (2nd ed., pp. 13–19). Boston: McGraw-Hill.

Moon, D. G. (2010). Critical reflections on cultural and critical intercultural communication. In T. K. Nakayama & R. T. Halualani (Eds.), *The handbook of critical intercultural communication* (pp. 34–52). Malden, MA: Wiley-Blackwell.

Moraga, C., & Anzaldúa, G. (Eds.). (1981). *This bridge called my back: Writings by radical women of color*. Latham, NY: Kitchen Table: Women of Color Press.

Morell, A. (2011, August 14). Pay rate for disabled Wisconsin workers stirs debate. *Green Bay Press-Gazette*. Retrieved from www.greenbaypressgazette.com/article/20110814/GPG0101/108140589/Pay-rate-disabled-Wisconsin-workers-stirs-debate?odyssey=tab|topnews|text|GPG-News

Moreman, S. T. (2009). Rethinking Conquergood: Toward an unstated cultural politics. *Liminalities: A Journal of Performance Studies, 5*(5), 1–11.

Moreman, S. T. (2011). Qualitative interviews of racial fluctuations: The 'how' of Latina/o-White hybrid identity. *Communication Theory, 21*(2), 197–216.

Moreman, S. T., & Calafell, B. M. (2008). Buscando para nuestra latinidad: Utilizing La Llorona for cultural critique. *Journal of International & Intercultural Communication, 1*(4), 309–26.

Moreman, S. T., & McIntosh, D. M. (2010). Brown scriptings and rescriptings: A critical performance ethnography of Latina drag queens. *Communication & Critical/Cultural Studies, 7*(2), 115–35.

Muñoz, J. E. (1999). *Disidentifications*. Minneapolis, MN: University of Minnesota Press.

Muñoz, J. E. (2009). *Cruising utopia: The then and there of queer futurity*. New York: New York University Press.

Myerhoff, B. (1978). *Number our days*. New York: Simon and Schuster.

n.a. (2011, February 12). Budget details: Highlights of Gov. Scott Walker's budget repair bill. *Wisconsin State Journal*. Retrieved from host.madison.com/news/local/govt-and-politics/article_3d93e6aa-363a-11e0-8493-001cc4c002e0.html

Nakayama, T. K. (2004). Dis/orienting identities: Asian Americans, history, and intercultural communication. In A. González, M. Houston & V. Chen (Eds.), *Our voices: Essays in cultural, ethnicity, and communication* (4th ed., pp. 26–31). Los Angeles: Roxbury.

Nakayama, T. K., & Halualani, R. T. (Eds.). (2010a). *The handbook of critical intercultural communication*. Malden, MA: Wiley-Blackwell.

Nakayama, T. K., & Halualani, R.T. (2010b). Conclusion: Envisioning pathway(s) of critical intercultural communication studies. In R. T. Halualani & T. K. Nakayama (Eds.), *The handbook of critical intercultural communication* (pp. 595–600). Malden, MA: Wiley-Blackwell.

Nakayama, T. K., & Krizek, R. (1995). Whiteness: A strategic rhetoric. *Quarterly Journal of Speech, 81*, 291–309.

Nakayama, T. K., & Martin, J. N. (Eds.), (1999). *Whiteness: The communication of social identity*. Thousand Oaks, CA: Sage.

Nance, T. A., & Foeman, A. K. (2002). On being biracial in the United States. In J. N. Martin, T. K. Nakayama, & L. A. Flores (Eds.), *Readings in intercultural communication: Experiences and contexts* (2nd ed., pp. 35–43). Boston: McGraw-Hill.

Nederveen Pieterse, J. (2009). *Globalization and culture: Global mélange*. Lanham, MD: Rowman & Littlefield Publishers, Inc.

Neff, L., & Foval, S. (2011, February 24). In solidarity: Gay workers join anti-Walker protests. *Wisconsin Gazette*. Retrieved from www.wisconsingazette.com/wisconsin-gaze/gay-workers-join-anti-walker-protests.html

Nevins, J. (2002). *Operation gatekeeper: The rise of the 'Illegal Alien' and the making of the U.S.-Mexico boundary*. New York: Routledge.

Nevins, J. (2008). *Dying to live: A story of U.S. immigration in an age of global apartheid*. San Francisco: Open Media/City Lights Books.

Ng, F. M. (1993). *Bone*. New York: Hyperion.

Nicholas, C. L. (2004). Gaydar : Eye-gaze as identity recognition among gay men and lesbians. *Sexuality and Culture: An Interdisciplinary Journal, 8*, 60–86.

Noble, G., Poynting, S., & Tabar, T. (1999). Youth, ethnicity, and the mapping of identity: Essentialism and strategic hybridity among male Arab-speaking youth in south-western Sydney. *Communical/Plural, 7*(1), 29–44.

Nussbaum, M. C. (1997). Kant and stoic cosmopolitanism. *The Journal of Political Philosophy, 5*, 1–25.

Nwanko, R. N., & Onwumechili, C. (1991). Communication and social values in cross-cultural adjustment. *Howard Journal of Communications, 3*, 99–111.

Obama, B. (2006). *The audacity of hope*. New York: Three Rivers Press.

Oberg, K. (1960). Cultural shock: Adjustment to new cultural environments. *Practical Anthropology, 7*, 177–82.

Ong, A. (1999). *Flexible citizenship: The cultural logics of transnationality*. Durham, NC: Duke University Press.

Ono, K. (1997). A letter/essay that I have been longing to write in my personal/academic voice. *Western Journal of Communication, 61*(1), 114–25.

Ono, K. (1998). Problematizing 'nation' in intercultural communication research. In D. Tanno & A. González (Eds.), *Communication and identity across cultures, International and Intercultural Communication Annual XXI* (pp. 193–202). Thousand Oaks, CA: Sage.

Ono, K. A. (2010). Reflections on 'Problematizing "nation" in intercultural communication research." In T. K. Nakayama & R. T. Halualani (Eds.), *The handbook of critical intercultural communication* (pp. 84–97). Malden, MA: Wiley-Blackwell.

Ono, K., & Jiao, J. (2008). China in the US imaginary: Tibet, the Olympics, and the 2008 earthquake. *Communication and Critical/Cultural Studies, 5*, 406–10.

Ono, K. A., & Sloop, J. M. (2002). *Shifting borders: Rhetoric, immigration, and California's Proposition 187*. Philadelphia, PA: Temple University Press.

Onwumechilia, C., Nwosu, P. O., Jackson II, R. L., & James-Huges, J. (2003). In the deep valley with mountains to climb: Exploring identity and multiple reacculturation. *International Journal of Intercultural Relations, 27*, 41–62.

Orbe, M. P. (1998). *Constructing co-cultural theory: An explication of culture, power, and communication*. Thousand Oaks, CA: Sage.

Orbe, M. P. (1999). Communicating about 'race' in interracial families. In T. J. Socha & R. C. Diggs (Eds.), *Communication, race, and family: Exploring communication in black, white, and biracial families* (pp. 167–80). Mahwah, NJ: Lawrence Erlbaum Associates.

Orbe, M. P. (2011). *Communication realities in a 'post-racial' society: What the US public really thinks about President Obama*. Lanham, MD: Lexington Books.

Orbe, M. P., & Allen, B. J. (2008). 'Race matters' in the *Journal of Applied Communication Research*. *Howard Journal of Communications, 19*(3), 201–20.

Orbe, M. P., Bradford, R., & Orbe, V. H. (2011, August). *The [multiple] realities of race in the Obama era: Contemporary negotiations of the 'one-drop rule.'* Paper presented at the biennial meeting of the World Communication Association, Lima, Peru.

Orbe, M. P., & Drummond, D. K. (in press). Competing cultural worldviews in the U.S.: A phenomenological examination of the essential core elements of transnationalism and transculturalism. *The Qualitative Report, 16*(2). Available at: www.nova.edu/ssss/QR/Editorial/contribu.html

Orbe, M. P., & Drummond, D. K. (2009). Negotiations of the complicitous nature of U.S. racial and ethnic categorization: Exploring rhetorical strategies. *Western Journal of Communication, 73*(4), 437–55.

Orbe, M. P., & Harris, T. M. (2008). *Interracial communication: Theory into practice*. Thousand Oaks, CA: Sage.

Orbe, M. P., Smith, D. C., Groscurth, C. R., & Crawley, R. L. (2010). Exhaling so that we can catch our breath and sing: Reflections on issues inherent in publishing race-related communication research. *Southern Communication Journal, 75*(2), 184–94.

Orbe, M. P., & Spellers, R. E. (2005). From the margins to the center: Utilizing co-cultural theory in diverse contexts. In W. B. Gudykunst (Ed.), *Theorizing about intercultural communication* (pp. 173–91). Thousand Oaks, CA: Sage.

Orbe, M. P., & Urban, E. (in press). 'Race matters' in the Obama era. *Communication Studies, 62*(4).

Owens Patton, T. (2004). In the guise of civility: The complicitous maintenance of inferential forms of racism and sexism in higher education. *Women's Studies in Communication, 27*, 60–87.

Papastergiadis, N. (1997). Tracing hybridity in theory. In P. Werbner & T. Modood (Eds.), *Debating cultural hybridity* (pp. 257–81). London: Zed Books.

Pascual, M. (2012). Traversing disparate cultures in a transnational world: A bicultural/hybrid experience. In A. Gonzalez, M. Houston & V. Chen (Eds.), *Our voices: Essays in culture, ethnicity and communication* (5th ed., pp. 297–306). New York: Oxford University Press.

Patterson, O. (1995). The culture of caution. *New Republic, 213* (22), 22–26.

Pelias, R. J. (2000). The critical life. *Communication Education, 49*, 220–28.

Pelias, R. J. (2004). *A methodology of the heart: Evoking academic & daily life*. Walnut Creek, CA: AltaMira Press.

Pelias, R. J. (2005). Performative writing as scholarship: An apology, an argument, an anecdote. *Cultural Studies <=> Critical Methodologies, 5*, 415–24.

Pineda, R. D., & Sowards, S. K. (2007). Flag waving as visual argument: 2006 immigration demonstrations and cultural citizenship. *Argumentation & Advocacy, 43*, 164–74.

Pensoneau-Conway, S. L., & Toyosaki, S. (2011a). Autmethodology: Tracing a home for praxis-oriented ethnography. *International Journal of Qualitative Methods, 10*, 378–99.

Pensoneau-Conway, S. L., & Toyosaki, S. (2011b, April). *An automethodological home for ethnography: Tracing the theoretical roots*. Paper presented at the annual meeting of the Central States Communication Association, Milwaukee, WI.

Pérez, K., & Goltz, D. B. (2010). Treading across Lines in the Sand: Performing bodies in coalitional subjectivity. *Text and Performance Quarterly, 30*(3), 247–68.

Peterson, R. E. (2009). Teaching how to read the world and change it: Critical pedagogy in the intermediate grades. In A. Darder, M.P. Baltodano & R.D. Torres (Eds.), *The critical pedagogy reader* (2nd ed., pp. 305–23). New York: Routledge.

Phalen, P. (1993). *Unmarked: The politics of performance*. New York: Routledge.

Philipsen, G. (1975). Speaking 'like a man' in Teamsterville: Culture patterns of role enactment in an urban neighborhood. *Quarterly Journal of Speech, 61*, 13–22.

Philipsen, G. (1989/1990). Some initial thoughts on the perils of 'critique' in the ethnographic study of communicative practices. *Research on Language and Social Interaction, 23*, 251–60.

Philipsen, G. (1992). *Speaking culturally.* Albany, NY: State University of New York Press.

Philipsen, G. (2002). Places for speaking in Teamsterville. In J. N. Martin, T. K. Nakayama, & L. A. Flores (Eds.), *Readings in intercultural communication* (2nd ed., pp. 192-201). Boston: McGraw-Hill.

Philipsen, G., Coutu, L. M., & Covarrubias, P. (2005). Speech codes theory: Restatement, revisions, and response to criticism. In W. B. Gudykunst (Ed.), *Theorizing about intercultural communication* (pp. 55–68). Thousand Oaks, CA: Sage.

Pineau, E. L. (1994). Teaching is performance: Reconceptualizing a problematic metaphor. *American Educational Research Journal, 31*, 3–25.

Pineau, E. L. (1998). Performance Studies across the curriculum: Problems, possibilities, and projections. In S. J. Dailey (Ed.), *The future of performance studies: Visions and revisions* (pp. 128–35). Annandale, VA: National Communication Association.

Pineau, E. L. (2002). Critical performance ethnography: Fleshing out the politics in liberatory education. In N. Stucky & C. Wimmer (Eds.), *Teaching performance studies* (pp. 41–54). Carbondale, IL: Southern Illinois University Press.

Pollock, D. (Ed.) (1998a). *Exceptional spaces: Essays in performance and history.* Chapel Hill, NC: University of North Carolina Press.

Pollock, D. (1998b). Performative writing. In P. Phelan & J. Lane (Eds.), *The ends of performance* (pp. 73–103). New York: New York University Press.

Pollock, D. (Ed.) (2005). *Remembering: Oral history performance.* New York: Palgrave Macmillan.

Pollock, D. (2008). Moving histories: Performance and oral history. In T. Davis (Ed.), *The Cambridge companion to performance studies* (pp. 120–35). Cambridge, London: Cambridge University Press.

Portes, A. (1977). Labour functions of illegal aliens. *Society, 14*(6), 31–37.

Poston, W. S. C. (1990). The biracial identity development model: A needed addition. *Journal of Counseling and Development, 69*, 152–55.

Prabhu, A. (2007). *Hybridity: Limits, transformations, prospects.* Albany, NY: State University of New York Press.

Pratt, M. L. (1992). *Imperial eyes: Travel writing and transculturation.* London: Routledge.

Pratt, S. (1998). Ritualized uses of humor as a form of identification among American Indians. In D. Tanno & A. González (Eds.), *Communication and identity across cultures, International and Intercultural Communication Annual XXI* (pp. 56–79). Thousand Oaks, CA: Sage.

Rawlins, W. K. (2000). Teaching as a mode of friendship. *Communication Theory, 10*(1), 5–26.

Reimers, F. (2009). Educating for global competency. In J. E. Cohen & M. B. Malin (Eds.), *International perspectives on the goals of universal basic and secondary education* (pp. 422–31). New York: Routledge.

Richardson, B. K., & Taylor, J. (2009). Sexual harassment at the intersection of race and gender: A theoretical model of the sexual harassment experiences of women of color. *Western Journal of Communication, 73*(3), 248–72.

Richardson, T., & Villenas, S. (2000). 'Other' encounters: Dances with whiteness in multicultural education. *Educational Theory, 50*(2), 255–73.

Richmond Ellis, R. (2000). Introduction. In S. Chávez-Silverman & L. Hernández (Eds.), *Reading and writing the ambiente: Queer sexualities in Latino, Latin American, and Spanish cultures* (pp. 3–18). Madison, WI: University of Wisconsin Press.

Ricoeur, P. (1992). *Oneself as another.* Chicago: University of Chicago Press.

Rinderle, S. (2005). The Mexican diaspora: A critical examination of signifiers. *Journal of Communication Inquiry, 29*(4), 294–316.

Roberts, K. G. (2008). Dialogic ethics, cosmopolitanism, and intercultural communication. In K. G. Roberts & R. C. Arnett (Eds.), *Communication ethics: Between cosmopolitanism and provinciality* (pp. 89–104). New York: Peter Lang.

Robotham, D. (1998). Transnationalism in the Caribbean: Formal and informal. *American Ethnologist, 25*(2), 307–21.

Rockquemore, K. A., & Laszloffy, T. (2005). *Raising biracial children.* New York: AltaMira Press.

Rodriguez, A. (2002). Culture to culturing: Re-imagining our understanding of intercultural relations. *Journal of Intercultural Communication, 5.* Retrieved from: www.immi.se/intercultural/nr5/abstract5.htm#rodriguez

Rodriguez, A. (2003/2004). Searching for new models of identity in Spanglish. *Journal of Intergroup Relations, 30*(4), 8-22.

Rodriguez, A., & Chawla, D. (2010). *Intercultural communication: An ecological approach.* Dubuque, IA: Kendall Hunt.

Rogers, J., & Ward, C. (1993). Expectation experience discrepancies and psychological adjustment during cross-cultural reentry. *International Journal of Intercultural Relations, 17*, 185–96.

Rogers, R. (2006). From cultural exchange to transculturation: A review and reconceptualization of cultural appropriation. *Communication Theory, 16*(4), 474–503.

Rohrlich, B. I., & Martin, J. N. (1991). Host country and reentry adjustment of student sojourners. *International Journal of Intercultural Relations, 15*(2), 163–82.

Romero, M. (2002). *Maid in the U.S.A.* (2nd ed.). New York: Routledge.

Root, M. P. P. (1996). A Bill of Rights for racially mixed people. In M. P. P. Root (Ed.), *The multiracial experience: Racial borders as the new frontier* (pp. 3–14). Thousand Oaks, CA: Sage.

Root, M. P. P. (2001). *Love's revolution: Interracial marriage.* Philadelphia, PA: Temple University Press.

Rosaldo, R. (1989). *Culture and truth: The remaking of social analysis.* Boston: Beacon.

Rouse, R. (1995). Thinking through transnationalism: Notes on the cultural politics of class relations in the contemporary United States. *Public Culture, 7*(2), 353–402.

Ruggiero, K. M., Taylor, D. M., & Lambert, W. E. (1996). A model of heritage culture maintenance. *International Journal of Intercultural Relations, 20*, 47–67.

Ruiz, A. (1990). Ethnic identity: Crisis and resolution. *Journal of Multicultural Counseling, 18*, 29–40.

Rushdie, S. (1981). *Midnight's children.* New York: Knopf.

Rowe, W., Bennett, S., & Atkinson, D. (1994). White racial identity development models: A critique and alternative proposal. *Counseling Psychologist, 22*, 129–46.

Rybczynski, W. (1986). *Home: The history of an idea.* New York: Penguin.

Santa Ana, O. (2002). *Brown tide rising: Metaphors of Latinos in contemporary American public discourse.* Austin, TX: University of Texas Press.

Savage, D. & Miller, T. (Eds.) (2011). *It gets better: Coming out, overcoming bullying, and creating a life worth living.* New York: Penguin Group.

Schrag, C. O. (1986). *Communicative praxis and the space of subjectivity.* Bloomington, IN: Indiana University Press.

Schrag, C. O. (1997). *The self after postmodernity.* New Haven, CT: Yale University press.

Schrag, C. O. (2003). *Communicative praxis and the space of intersubjectivity* (rev. ed.). West Lafayette, IN: Purdue University Press.

Sharrad, P. (2007). Strategic hybridity: Some Pacific takes on postcolonial theory. In J. Kuortti & J. Nyman (Eds.), *Reconstructing hybridity: Post-colonial studies in transition* (pp. 99–120). Amsterdam: Rodopi, B.V.

Shin, C., & Jackson II, R. L. (2003). A review of identity research in communication theory. In W. Starosta & G.-M. Chen (Eds.) *Ferment in the intercultural field: Axiology/value/praxis, International and Intercultural Communication Annual XXVI* (pp. 211–40). Thousand Oaks, CA: Sage.

Shome, R. (1998). Caught in the term 'post-colonial': Why the 'post'-colonial still matters. *Critical Studies in Mass Communication, 15*, 203–12.

Shome, R. (1999). Whiteness and the politics of location: Post-colonial reflections. In T. K. Nakayama & J. N. Martin (Eds.), *Whiteness: The communication of social identity* (pp. 107–28). Thousand Oaks, CA: Sage.

Shome, R. (2003). Space matters: The power and practice of space. *Communication Theory, 13,* 39–56.

Shome, R. (2010). Internationalizing critical race communication studies: Transnationality, space, and affect. In T. K. Nakayama & R. T. Halualani (Eds.), *The handbook of critical intercultural communication* (pp. 149–70). Malden, MA: Wiley-Blackwell.

Shome, R., & Hegde, R. S. (2002a). Culture, communication, and the challenge of globalization. *Critical Studies in Media Communication, 19,* 172–89.

Shome, R., & Hegde, R. S. (2002b). Postcolonial approaches to communication: Charting the terrain, engaging the intersections. *Communication Theory, 12*(3), 249–70.

Shuter, R. (1990). The centrality of culture. *Southern Communication Journal, 55,* 237–49.

Sidhwa, B. (1991). *Cracking India.* Minneapolis, MN: Milkweed. (previously published as *Ice-candy-man).*

Simmel, G. (1950). The stranger. In W. Hurt (Trans.), *The sociology of George Simmel* (pp. 402–408). Glencoe, IL: The Free Press.

Simpson, J. S. (2008). 'What do they think of us?': The pedagogical practices of cross-cultural communication, misrecognition, and hope. *Journal of International and Intercultural Communication, 1*(3), 181–201.

Singh, K. (1956). *Train to Pakistan.* New York: Grove Press.

Sleeter, C. E. (1996). *Multicultural education as social activism.* Albany, NY: SUNY press.

Smith, S. (2001). An identity model of reentry communication competence. *World Communication, 30*(3/4), 6–38.

Smith, S. (2002). The cycle of cross-cultural adaptation and reentry. In J. M. Martin, T. K. Nakayama, & L. A. Flores (Eds.), *Readings in intercultural communication: Experiences and contexts* (2nd ed., pp. 246–59). Boston: McGraw-Hill.

Smith, T. W. (1992). Changing racial labels: From 'Colored' to 'Negro' to 'Black' to 'African American.' *Public Opinion Quarterly, 56,* 496–514.

Smith, Z. (2009). Speaking in tongues. *New York Review of Books, 56,* 24.

Sodowsky, G., Kwan, K.-L., & Pannu, R. (1995). Ethnic identity of Asians in the United States. In J. Ponterotto, J. Casas, L. Suzuki, & C. Alexander (Eds.), *Handbook of multicultural counseling* (pp. 123–154). Thousand Oaks, CA: Sage.

Sorrells, K. (2010). Re-imagining intercultural communication in the context of globalization. In T. K. Nakayama & R. T. Halualani (Eds.), *The handbook of critical intercultural communication* (pp. 171–89). Malden, MA: Wiley-Blackwell.

Sparrow, L. M. (2008). Beyond multicultural man: Complexities of identity. In M. K. Asante, Y. Miike & J. Yin, (Eds.), *The global intercultural communication reader* (pp. 239–61). New York: Routledge.

Spencer, R. (2006). *Challenging multiracial identity.* Boulder, CO: Lynne Rienner Publishers.

Spivak, G. C. (1988). Can the subaltern speak? In C. Nelson & L. Grossberg (Eds.), *Marxism and the interpretation of culture* (pp. 271–313). Urbana and Chicago, IL: University of Illinois Press.

Spivak, G. C. (1993). *Outside in the teaching machine.* New York: Routledge.

Spivak, G. C. (2003). Subaltern studies: Deconstructing historiography. In J. Culler (Ed.), *Critical concepts in literary and cultural studies* (pp. 220–244). London: Routledge.

Sprague, J. (1992). Expanding the research agenda for instructional communication: Raising some unasked questions. *Communication Education, 41*(1), 1–25.

Sprague, J. (1993). Retrieving the research agenda for communication education: Asking the pedagogical questions that are 'embarrassments to theory.' *Communication Education, 42*(2), 106–22.

Squires, C., Harris, H., & Moffitt, K. (2010). Introduction. In H. Harris, K. Moffitt, & C. Squires (Eds.), *The Obama effect: Multidisciplinary renderings of the 2008 campaign* (pp. xvii-xx). Albany, NY: State University of New York Press.

Squires, C., Watts, E. K., Vavrus, M. D., Ono, K. A., Feyh, K., Calafell, B. M., Brouwer, D. (2010). What is this 'Post-' in postracial, postfeminist . . . (fill in the blank)? *Journal of Communication Inquiry, 34*(3), 210-53.

Stockman, N. (2000). *Understanding Chinese society*. Malden, MA: Polity Press.

Storti, C. (1997). *The art of coming home*. Yarmouth, ME: Intercultural Press.

Straight, B. (Ed.). (2005). *Women on the verge of home*. Albany, NY: State University of New York Press.

Strathern, A., & Stewart, P. J. (2010). Shifting centres, tense peripheries: Indigenous cosmopolitanisms. In D. Theodossopoulos & E. Kirtsoglou (Eds.), *United in discontent: Local responses to cosmopolitanism and globalization* (pp. 20-44). New York: Berghahn Books.

Stucky, N. (2002). Deep embodiment: The politics of natural performance. In N. Stucky & C. Wimmer (Eds.), *Teaching performance studies* (pp. 131-44). Carbondale, IL: Southern Illinois University Press.

Su, H. (1989). *Savage land: China, or U.S.A., or Chinese-U.S.A. Interpreting Maxine Hong Kingston's "The Woman Warrior: Memoirs of a Girlhood Among Ghosts" from a Chinese perspective*. Unpublished manuscript, University of California at Santa Barbara, Santa Barbara.

Sussman, N. M. (2000). The dynamic nature of cultural identity throughout cultural transitions: Why home is not so sweet. *Personality and Social Psychological Review, 4*, 355–73.

Sussman, N. M. (2001). Repatriation transitions: Psychological preparedness, cultural identity, and attributions among American managers. *International Journal of Intercultural Relations, 25*, 109–23.

Tan, A. (1991). *The Joy Luck Club*. New York: Vintage Books.

Tan, S.-H. (2008). Review on Lost Soul: 'Confucianism' in contemporary Chinese academic discourse. *China Review International, 15*, 576–582.

Tanno, D. V., & Jandt, F. E. (1993/1994). Redefining the 'other' in multicultural research. *Howard Journal of Communications, 5*(1/2), 36–45.

Tajfel, H., & Turner, J. C. (1986). The social identity theory of intergroup behavior. In S. Worchel & W. Austin (Eds.), *The psychology of intergroup relations* (2nd ed., pp. 7–24). Chicago: Nelson-Hall.

Telles, E. E., & Ortiz, V. (2008). *Generations of exclusion: Mexican Americans, assimilation, and race*. New York: Russell Sage Foundation.

Tervalon, M., & Murray-Garcia, J. (1998). Cultural humility versus cultural competence: A critical distinction in defining physician training outcomes in multicultural education. *Journal of Health Care for the Poor and Underserved, 9*(2), 117–25.

Ting-Toomey, S. (1986). Interpersonal ties in intergroup communication. In W. B. Gudykunst (Ed.), *Intergroup communication* (pp. 114–26). Baltimore, MD: Edward Arnold.

Ting-Toomey, S. (1993). Communicative resourcefulness: An identity negotiation perspective. In R. Wiseman & J. Koester (Eds.), *Intercultural communication competence* (pp. 21-111). Newbury Park, CA: Sage.

Ting-Toomey, S. (1999). *Communicating across cultures*. New York: Guilford.

Ting-Toomey, S. (2005). Identity negotiation theory: Crossing cultural boundaries. In W. B. Gudykunst (Ed.), *Theorizing about intercultural communication* (pp. 211–34). Thousand Oaks, CA: Sage.

Ting-Toomey, S. (2009). Identity theories. In S. W. Littlejohn & K. A. Foss (Eds.), *Encyclopedia of communication theory* (pp. 492–96). Thousand Oaks, CA: Sage.

Tomlinson, J. (1999). *Globalization and culture*. Chicago: University of Chicago Press.

Touraine, A. (1988). *Return of the actor: Social theory in postindustrial society* (M. Godzich, Trans.). Minneapolis, MN: University of Minnesota Press.

Toyosaki, S. (2000). *Relationships between uncertainty reduction and interpersonal need compatibility in initial dyadic interactions*. Unpublished master's thesis, Central Missouri State University, Warrensburg.

Toyosaki, S. (2007). Communication sensei's storytelling: Projecting identity into critical pedagogy. *Cultural Studies <=> Critical Methodologies, 7*(1), 48–73.

Toyosaki, S. (2011). Critical complete-member ethnography: Theorizing dialectics of consensus and conflict in intracultural communication. *Journal of International and Intercultural Communication, 4*(1), 62–80.

Toyosaki, S., & Pensoneau, S. L. (2005). Yaezakura—Interpersonal culture analysis. *International Journal of Communication, 15*(1–2), 51–88.

Toyosaki, S., Pensoneau-Conway, S. L., Wendt, N. A., & Leathers, K. (2009). Community autoethnography: Compiling the personal and resituating whiteness. *Cultural Studies <=> Critical Methodologies, 9*(1), 56–83.

Tuitt, F. (2006). Insomnia, paranoia, and my first class: Nighttime confessions of a black professor. In L. Agans, S. Griggs, & L. Merkl (Editorial Board), *Identity and education: The anthology project* (pp. 29–31). Denver, CO: University of Denver, College of Education.

Tuitt, F. (2008). Removing the threat in the air: Teacher transparency and the creation of identity-safe graduate classrooms. *Journal on Excellence in College Teaching, 19*(2), 167–98.

Twitchell-Waas, J. (2004). Preface. In J. S. Wong (Z. Zhang, Trans.), *Fifth Chinese Daughter* (p. 1). Nanjing: Yilin Press.

Urban, E. L., & Orbe, M. (2010). Identity gaps of contemporary U.S. immigrants: Acknowledging divergent communicative experiences. *Communication Studies, 61*(3), 304–20.

Verschueren, J. (2008). Intercultural communication and the challenges of migration. *Language & Intercultural Communication, 8*(1), 21–35.

Vertovec, S., & Cohen, R. (2002). Introduction: Conceiving cosmopolitanism. In S. Vertovec & R. Cohen (Eds.), *Conceiving cosmopolitanism: Theory, context and practice* (pp. 1–22). Oxford: Oxford University Press.

Vignes, D. S. (2008a). 'Hang it out to dry': Performing ethnography, cultural memory, and hurricane Katrina in Chalmette, Louisiana. *Text and Performance Quarterly, 28*(3), 344–50.

Vignes, D. S. (2008b). Hang it out to dry: A performance script. *Text and Performance Quarterly, 28*(3), 351–65.

Visweswaran, K. (1994). *Fictions of feminist ethnography.* Minneapolis, MN: University of Minnesota Press.

Waks, L. J. (2010). Region and culture in cosmopolitan education. *Educational Theory, 59*(5), 589–604.

Walker, R. (2001). *Black, white, and Jewish: Autobiography of a shifting self.* New York: Riverhead Books.

Wang, G., & Liu, Z.-B. (2010). What collective? Collectivism and relationalism from a Chinese perspective. *Chinese Journal of Communication, 3*, 42–63.

Ward, C. (1996). Acculturation. In D. Landis & R. S. Bhagat (Eds.), *Handbook of intercultural training* (2nd ed., pp. 125–147). Thousand Oaks, CA: Sage.

Ward, C., Bochner, S., & Furnham, A. (2001). *The psychology of culture shock* (2nd ed.). East Sussex: Routledge. (Simultaneously published in the United States by Taylor & Francis, Philadelphia, PA.)

Warren, J. T. (1999). The body politic: Performance, pedagogy, and the power of enfleshment. *Text and Performance Quarterly, 19*, 257–66

Warren, J. T. (2001a). Absence for whom? An autoethnography of White subjectivity. *Cultural Studies <=> Critical Methodologies, 1*(1), 36–49.

Warren, J. T. (2001b). Doing whiteness: On the performative dimensions of race in the classroom. *Communication Education, 50*(2), 91–108.

Warren, J. T. (2003a). Performative pedagogy, At-risk students, and the basic course: 14 moments in search of possibility. *Basic Communication Course Annual, 15*, 83–116.

Warren, J. T. (2003b). *Performing purity: Whiteness, pedagogy, and the reconstitution of power.* New York: Peter Lang.

Warren, J. T. (2008). Performing difference: Repetition in context. *Journal of International and Intercultural Communication, 1*(4), 290–308.

Warren, J. T. (2009). Performative and pedagogical interventions: Embodying whiteness as cultural critique. In S. R. Riley & L. Hunter (Eds.), *Mapping landscapes in performance as research: Scholarly acts and creative cartographies* (pp. 179–84). Houndmills, Basingstoke, Hampshire: Palgrave Macmillan.

Warren, J. T. (2010a). Performance is . . . : Performance metaphors as method. *International Review of Qualitative Research, 3*, 217–24.

Warren, J. T. (2010b, April). *Performative pedagogy as a pedagogy of interruption: Difference and hope.* Spotlight presentation at the annual meeting of Central States Communication Association conference, Cincinnati, OH.

Warren, J. T. (2010c). It really isn't about you. In T. K. Nakayama & R. T. Halualani (Eds.), *The handbook of critical intercultural communication* (pp. 446–60). Malden, MA: Wiley-Blackwell.

Warren, J. T. (2011a). Reflexive teaching: Toward critical autoethnographic practices of/in/on pedagogy. *Cultural Studies <=> Critical Methodologies, 11* (2), 139–44.

Warren, J. T. (2011b). Social justice and critical/performative/communicative pedagogy: A storied account of research, teaching, love, identity, desire, and loss. *International Review of Qualitative Research, 4*, 21–33.

Warren, J. T., & Davis, A. M. (2009). On the impossibility of (some) critical pedagogies: Critical positionalities within a binary. *Cultural Studies <=> Critical Methodologies, 9*, 306–20.

Warren, J. T., & Hytten, K. (2004). The faces of whiteness: Pitfalls and the critical democrat. *Communication Education, 53*(4), 321–39.

Warren, J. T., & Zoffel, N. A. (2007). Living in the middle: Performances of bi-men. In K. E. Lovaas & M. M. Jenkins (Eds.), *Sexualities & communication in everyday life* (pp. 233–42). Thousand Oaks, CA: Sage.

Washington, J. (2008, May). *Greater expectations for inclusive excellence: From theme to reality.* Keynote delivered at the 7th Annual Diversity Summit, Denver, CO.

Weick, K. (1995). *Sensemaking in organizations.* Thousand Oaks, CA: Sage.

Weissman, D., & Furnham, A. (1987). The expectations and experiences of a sojourning temporary resident abroad: A preliminary study. *Human Relations, 40*, 313–26.

Werbner, P. (1997). Introduction: The dialectics of cultural hybridity. In P. Werbner & T. Modood (Eds.), *Debating cultural hybridity* (pp. 1–26). London: Zed Books.

Werbner, P. (2008). *Anthropology and the new cosmopolitanism: Rooted, feminist, and vernacular perspectives.* New York: Berg.

West, C. (1990). The new cultural politics of difference. In A. H. Hasley, H. Lauder, P. Brown & A. S. Wells (Eds.), *Education: Culture, economy, society* (pp. 509–19). Oxford: Oxford University Press.

West, C. (1993a). The new cultural politics of difference. In C. McCarthy & W. Crichlow (Eds.), *Race identity and representation in education* (pp. 11–23). New York: Routledge.

West, C. (1993b). *Race matters.* Boston: Beacon Press.

Wijeyesinghe, C. L. (2001). Racial identity in multiracial people: An alternative paradigm. In C.L. Wijeyesinghe & B. W. Jackson (Eds.), *New perspectives on racial identity development* (pp. 138–43). New York: New York University Press.

Williams, M. (2010). *CNN.* Retrieved from politicalticker.blogs.cnn.com/category/the-situation-room/page/2/

Wilson, A. H. (1993). A cross-national perspective on reentry of high school exchange students. *International Journal of Intercultural Relations, 17*, 465–92.

Wise, J. M. (2008). *Cultural globalization: A user's guide.* Malden, MA: Blackwell Publishing.

Witteborn, S. (2004). Of being an Arab woman before and after September 11: The enactment of communal identities in talk. *Howard Journal of Communications, 15*, 83–98.

Wong, J. S. (1950). *Fifth Chinese daughter.* New York: Harper & Brothers.

Wong, K. (2004). Working through identity: Understanding class in the context of race, ethnicity, and gender. In A. González, M. Houston & V. Chen (Eds.), *Our voices: Essays in cultural, ethnicity, and communication* (4th ed., pp. 256–65). Los Angeles: Roxbury.

Wong, R. (1997). Chinese understandings of economic change: From agrarian empire to industrial society. In T. Brook & H. Luong (Eds.), *Culture and economy: The shaping of capitalism in Eastern Asia* (pp. 45–60). Ann Arbor, MI: The University of Michigan Press.

Yep, G. (2002). My three cultures. In J. N. Martin, T. K. Nakayama & L. Flores (Eds.), *Readings in intercultural communication* (2nd ed., pp. 60–66). Boston: McGraw Hill.

Yep, G. (2003a). The violence of heteronormativity in communication studies. *Journal of Homosexuality, 45*(2), 11–59.

Yep, G. A. (2003b). The violence of heteronormativity in communication studies: Notes on injury, healing, and queer world-making. In G. A. Yep, K. E. Lovaas & J. P. Elia (Eds.), *Queer theory and communication: From disciplining queers to queering the discipline(s)* (pp. 11–59). Binghamton, NY: Harrington Park Press.

Yep, G. (2004). Approaches to cultural identity: Personal notes from an autoethnographical journey. In M. Fong & R. Chuang (Eds.), *Communicating ethnic and cultural identity* (pp. 69–81). Lanham, MD: Rowman & Littlefield Publishers, Inc.

Yep, G. (2010). Toward the de-subjugation of racially marked knowledges in communication. *Southern Communication Journal, 75*(2), 171–75.

Yin, J. (2009). Negotiating the centre: Towards an Asiacentric feminist communication theory. *Journal of Multicultural Discourses, 4*, 75–88.

Yin, S. C. (2011, May 10). A revolution's namesake is contraband in China. *The New York Times*. Retrieved from: www.nytimes.com/2011/05/11/world/asia/11jasmine.html

Yoshino, K. (2007). *Covering: The hidden assault on our civil rights*. New York: Random House.

Young, R. J. C. (1995). *Colonial desire: Hybridity in theory, culture and race*. London: Routledge.

Yuqiu, W. (2003). The rise of Chinese American literature in recent 20 years. In A. Cheng (Ed.), *Chinese American literature study* (pp. 51–61). Beijing: Beijing University Press.

Zamindar, V. F. (2007). *The long partition and the making of modern south Asia: Refugees, boundaries, histories*. New York: Columbia University Press.

Zhang, X. (1997). *Chinese modernism in the era of reforms: Cultural fever, avant-garde fiction, and the new Chinese cinema*. Durham, NC: Duke University Press.

Zimmerman, S. (1995). Perceptions of intercultural communication competence and international student adaptation to an American campus. *Communication Education, 44*, 321–35.

Zirbel, K. E. (2005). Concerning the travels and transgressions of a southern Egyptian woman. In B. Straight (Ed.), *Women on the verge of home* (pp. 71–88). Albany, NY: State University of New York Press.

Ziqing, Z. (2003). A Witness to the history of Chinese immigrants in the United States: An interview with Jade Snow Wong in Nanjing, 2002/4/17. *Contemporary Literature: East & West, 5*(1), 190–210.

Index

About the Contributors

Brenda J. Allen is associate dean in the College of Liberal Arts and Sciences and professor in the Department of Communication at the University of Colorado-Denver. Her scholarship concentrates on organizational communication, social identity, and critical pedagogy, and she has numerous publications on those topics. She also presents speeches and conducts workshops on a range of subjects, including diversity and higher education, teamwork, self-empowerment, and presentational speaking.

Nilanjana Bardhan is associate professor in the Department of Speech Communication at Southern Illinois University-Carbondale. Her research interests span intercultural/transnational communication, globalization, postcolonial theory, and the communicative construction of identity in human and mediated environments. She also conducts research in the area of public relations, specifically in global contexts. She has published several articles and book chapters and is the coeditor of *Public Relations in Global Cultural Contexts: Multi-Paradigmatic Perspectives*.

Keith Berry is associate professor in the Department of Communicating Arts at the University of Wisconsin-Superior. He studies ethnographic methods, and cultural and intercultural communication, and is particularly interested in reflexivity and identity negotiation. He has published in journals such as *Cultural Studies <=> Critical Methodologies*, *Qualitative Inquiry*, and the *International Journal of Qualitative Methods*, and books such as *The Handbook of Autoethnography*.

Bernadette Marie Calafell is associate professor of culture and communication in the Department of Communication Studies at the University of Denver. She is author of *Latina/o Communication Studies: Theorizing Performance* and coeditor of *Latina/o Discourse in Vernacular Spaces: Somos de una voz?*

Karma R. Chávez is assistant professor of communication arts at the University of Wisconsin-Madison. Chávez' research emphasizes queer migration, coalition and alliance building, social movement, and the rhetorical practice of marginalized groups using queer feminist of color theories. Along with Eithne Luibhéid, she is the cofounder of the Queer

Migration Research Network. Chávez is currently finishing her first book, *Queer/Migration Politics*.

Devika Chawla is associate professor in the School of Communication Studies at Ohio University. Her intellectual interests include performative and narrative approaches to identity, performance and ethnography, and postcolonial studies. She is the author (with Amardo Rodriguez) of *Intercultural Communication: An Ecological Approach* and *Liminal Traces: Performing, Storying, and Embodying Postcoloniality*.

Hsin-I Cheng is assistant professor of communication at Santa Clara University. Her research explores how multiple identities intersect and are negotiated in relation to border-crossing and neoliberal practices. She is the author of *Culturing Interface: Identity, Communication, and Chinese Transnationalism*.

Rachel Alicia Griffin is assistant professor in the Department of Speech Communication at Southern Illinois University-Carbondale. As a critical intercultural communication scholar, her research interests and publications span critical race theory, black feminist thought, popular culture, gender violence, and pedagogy. She is also a frequent guest on college campuses to present workshops and deliver keynotes that speak to how power, privilege, and intersectionality impact the ability to engage across identity differences.

Maurice L. Hall is associate professor in the Communication Department at Villanova University. He teaches courses in communication in organizations, leadership, interviewing, diversity and multiculturalism, public speaking, and organizational research and consulting. He has won awards for both teaching and research. He is coauthor of *Embodying the Postcolonial Life*, and has published book chapters and scholarly essays in academic journals such as the *Howard Journal of Communications* and *Management Communication Quarterly*.

Richie Neil Hao is assistant professor in the Department of Communication Studies at the University of Denver. His research interests are at the intersections of intercultural, pedagogical and performance studies. He has published in journals such as *Text and Performance Quarterly* and *Review of Communication*.

Kent Ono is professor of Asian American Studies, Media and Cinema Studies, and Communications at University of Illinois-Urbana-Champaign. He researches rhetoric and discourse, media and film, and race, ethnic, and cultural studies. He is the author of *Contemporary Media Culture and the Remnants of a Colonial Past*; coauthor of *Asian Americans and the*

Media (with Vincent Pham) and *Shifting Borders: Rhetoric, Immigration, and California's Proposition 187* (with John Sloop); editor of *Asian American Studies After Critical Mass* and *A Companion to Asian American Studies*; and coeditor of *Critical Rhetorics of Race* (with Michael Lacy) and *Enterprise Zones: Critical Positions on Star Trek* (with Taylor Harrison, Sarah Projansky, and Elyce Helford).

Mark P. Orbe is professor of communication and diversity in the School of Communication at Western Michigan University where he also holds a joint appointment in gender and women's studies. His research and teaching interests focus on explorations of the inextricable relationship between culture and communication across a variety of contexts. He has published widely in the areas of power, co-cultural theory, race, and mass media representations.

Krishna Pattisapu is a doctoral student in the Department of Communication Studies at the University of Denver. She conducts research in the areas of critical communication pedagogy, performance studies, queer theory, and critical intercultural communication. She emphasizes praxis by promoting social change through conversations about marginalized identities.

Sandra L. Pensoneau-Conway is assistant professor in the Department of Speech Communication at Southern Illinois University-Carbondale. Her primary research and teaching interest is in critical communication pedagogy, with secondary interests in automethodology, intercultural communication, and identity construction processes. She has published several articles and book chapters focusing on topics such as qualitative methods, whiteness, pedagogy, and student empowerment.

Miriam Sobré-Denton is assistant professor in the Department of Speech Communication at Southern Illinois University-Carbondale. Her research interests include cosmopolitanism, language and culture, the communication of whiteness and white privilege, auto/ethnographic methods and border/boundary crossings. Her work appears in the *International Journal of Intercultural Relations*, the *Journal of International and Intercultural Communication*, the *Journal of Contemporary Ethnography*, and the *International Journal of Humanities and Social Science*.

Jianhua Sun is associate professor in the School of Foreign Language Education at Jilin University, China, and is a visiting scholar at the Asian American Studies Program at the University of Illinois-Urbana-Champaign. Her research interests include Asian American literature, literary representation of identity construction, and comparison study of cultures. She is currently working on a project on Asian Americans' identity construction between the cultures of home and host land.

Satoshi Toyosaki is assistant professor in the Department of Speech Communication at Southern Illinois University-Carbondale. He teaches international and intercultural communication from interpretive and critical perspectives. His research focuses on critical selfhood as a human communicative and intersubjective accomplishment. He is particularly interested in automethodological approaches which help one to theorize, investigate, realize, and practice his or her critical selfhood. His recent work appears in the *Journal of International and Intercultural Communication*, the *International and Intercultural Communication Annual*, and *Cultural Studies <=> Critical Methodologies*.

John T. Warren was professor in the Department of Speech Communication at Southern Illinois University-Carbondale. A prolific scholar, his work focuses mainly in the areas of communication pedagogy, critical/cultural communication and performance studies. In addition to approximately fifty authored and coauthored journal articles and book chapters, he is the author of *Performing Purity: Whiteness, Pedagogy and the Reconstitution of Power*, coauthor of *Critical Communication Pedagogy*, and coeditor of *Casting Gender: Women and Performance in Intercultural Contexts* and *The SAGE Handbook of Communication and Instruction*.